Computer Networking
first-step

Wendell Odom

Cisco Press
800 East 96th Street
Indianapolis, IN 46240

Computer Networking
first-step

Wendell Odom

Copyright© 2004 Cisco Systems, Inc.

Published by:
Cisco Press
800 East 96th Street
Indianapolis, IN 46240 USA

Printed in the United States of America   3 4 5 6 7 8 9 0

Third Printing   December 2005

Library of Congress Cataloging-in-Publication Number: 2003108109

ISBN: 1-58720-101-1

Warning and Disclaimer

This book is designed to provide information about computer networking. Every effort has been made to make this book as complete and as accurate as possible, but no warranty or fitness is implied.

The information is provided on an "as is" basis. The author, Cisco Press, and Cisco Systems, Inc., shall have neither liability nor responsibility to any person or entity with respect to any loss or damages arising from the information contained in this book or from the use of the discs or programs that may accompany it.

The opinions expressed in this book belong to the author and are not necessarily those of Cisco Systems, Inc.

Publisher
John Wait

Editor-in-Chief
John Kane

Executive Editor
Brett Bartow

Cisco Representative
Anthony Wolfenden

**Cisco Press
Program Manager**
Nannette M. Noble

Production Manager
Patrick Kanouse

Development Editor
Dayna Isley

Project Editor
San Dee Phillips

Copy Editor
Karen A. Gill

Technical Editors
Blair Buchanan, Ron Kovac,
Scott Van de Houten,
Paul Negron

Team Coordinator
Tammi Barnett

Book and Cover Designer
Louisa Adair

Compositor
Mark Shirar

Indexer
Tim Wright

Trademark Acknowledgments

All terms mentioned in this book that are known to be trademarks or service marks have been appropriately capitalized. Cisco Press or Cisco Systems, Inc., cannot attest to the accuracy of this information. Use of a term in this book should not be regarded as affecting the validity of any trademark or service mark.

Corporate and Government Sales

Cisco Press offers excellent discounts on this book when ordered in quantity for bulk purchases or special sales.

For more information please contact: U.S. Corporate and Government Sales 1-800-382-3419 corpsales@pearsontechgroup.com

For sales outside the U.S. please contact: International Sales international@pearsoned.com

Feedback Information

At Cisco Press, our goal is to create in-depth technical books of the highest quality and value. Each book is crafted with care and precision, undergoing rigorous development that involves the unique expertise of members from the professional technical community.

Readers' feedback is a natural continuation of this process. If you have any comments regarding how we could improve the quality of this book, or otherwise alter it to better suit your needs, you can contact us through e-mail at feedback@ciscopress.com. Please make sure to include the book title and ISBN in your message.

We greatly appreciate your assistance.

CISCO SYSTEMS

Corporate Headquarters
Cisco Systems, Inc.
170 West Tasman Drive
San Jose, CA 95134-1706
USA
www.cisco.com
Tel: 408 526-4000
 800 553-NETS (6387)
Fax: 408 526-4100

European Headquarters
Cisco Systems International BV
Haarlerbergpark
Haarlerbergweg 13-19
1101 CH Amsterdam
The Netherlands
www-europe.cisco.com
Tel: 31 0 20 357 1000
Fax: 31 0 20 357 1100

Americas Headquarters
Cisco Systems, Inc.
170 West Tasman Drive
San Jose, CA 95134-1706
USA
www.cisco.com
Tel: 408 526-7660
Fax: 408 527-0883

Asia Pacific Headquarters
Cisco Systems, Inc.
Capital Tower
168 Robinson Road
#22-01 to #29-01
Singapore 068912
www.cisco.com
Tel: +65 6317 7777
Fax: +65 6317 7799

Cisco Systems has more than 200 offices in the following countries and regions. Addresses, phone numbers, and fax numbers are listed on the
Cisco.com Web site at www.cisco.com/go/offices.

Argentina • Australia • Austria • Belgium • Brazil • Bulgaria • Canada • Chile • China PRC • Colombia • Costa Rica • Croatia • Czech Republic • Denmark • Dubai, UAE • Finland • France • Germany • Greece • Hong Kong SAR • Hungary • India • Indonesia • Ireland • Israel • Italy • Japan • Korea • Luxembourg • Malaysia • Mexico • The Netherlands • New Zealand • Norway • Peru • Philippines • Poland • Portugal • Puerto Rico • Romania • Russia • Saudi Arabia • Scotland • Singapore • Slovakia • Slovenia • South Africa • Spain • Sweden • Switzerland • Taiwan • Thailand • Turkey • Ukraine • United Kingdom • United States • Venezuela • Vietnam • Zimbabwe

About the Author

Wendell Odom, CCIE No. 1624, is a senior instructor for Skyline Advanced Technology Services (www.skylinecomputer.com), where he teaches a wide variety of introductory and advanced-level Cisco Systems networking courses. He has been in the networking industry for more than 20 years, working in both presale and postsale technical roles, as well as teaching networking concepts to beginners and CCIE candidates alike. Wendell is the author of numerous best-selling Cisco Press exam study guides, several of which focus on the Cisco Systems introductory-level certification: CCNA. His most recent works include *CCNA INTRO Exam Certification Guide*, *CCNA ICND Exam Certification Guide*, and *Cisco DQOS Exam Certification Guide*.

About the Technical Reviewers

Blair Buchanan's career in telecommunications has spanned nearly 30 years, during which time he has written communication software, participated in ISO standards development, and established a successful consultancy. Blair's involvement with Cisco began in 1991 when he designed his first router-based internetwork for the Canadian Department of National Defense. Shortly after, with the help of Cisco Canada, he became the world's first Learning Partner-based Cisco instructor. That company, Protocoles Standards de Communications (PSC) later merged with the U.S. firm Protocol Interface (PI) to form GeoTrain, which was acquired by Global Knowledge in 1999.

In April 1996, and on his first attempt, Blair earned his CCIE certification and became the 403rd CCIE, No. 1427. Since then, he has designed and audited internetworks for a variety of clients in both the enterprise and service provider sectors. His clients include Nortel Networks, the Government of Canada, Bell Canada, the Government of British Columbia, the Bank of Canada, PSINet, and Mouvement Desjardins.

Dr. Ron Kovac is currently employed with the Center for Information and Communication Sciences at Ball State University in Muncie, Indiana, as a full professor. The Center prepares graduate students in the field of telecommunications. Previous to this, Dr. Kovac was the telecommunication manager for the State of New York and an executive director for a large computing center located on the east coast. Dr. Kovac's previous studies included electrical engineering and education. Dr. Kovac has numerous publications and has done consulting in both the education and telecommunications fields, speaks worldwide on issues related to telecommunications, and holds numerous certifications, including the CCNA, CCAI, and the almost complete CCNP.

Paul Negron is a senior instructor with Skyline Advanced Technology Services, teaching authorized Cisco training courses to a wide range of audiences. Paul teaches the Implementing Cisco QoS course and advanced courses on topics such as BGP, MPLS, high-performance routing, and other CCNP courses.

Scott Van de Houten, CCIE No. 1640, is a distinguished systems engineer for the Technical Operations Group at Cisco Systems. He is currently a technical lead for the Enterprise Routing and Switching Technology Leadership Program. His responsibilities include developing customer requirements for the product teams and customer technical consulting. Scott has been with Cisco for 11 years and has worked as a network engineer for 17 years.

Dedications

For Fay and Raymond, my favorite parents, out of all the parents I've ever met.

Acknowledgments

The process of creating a technical book requires a lot of hard work from a lot of people. I am always amazed at how much the various editing processes improve what I first submit as the text for a book. I'd like to take this opportunity to thank some of the people who have had a big hand in putting this book together.

For this book, I was fortunate to have a great team of technical editors. A handful of technical folks get the opportunity to read over the text and the figures, and make comments. Their primary job is to help make sure that the book is technically accurate, but the good ones also make sure that the topics flow well together and would make sense to the reader. While they all did the core job well, in particular, my buddy Paul Negron, also from Skyline Advanced Technology Services, edited the book, and did a particularly good and gracious job of pointing out when I should change the flow between topics. Scott Van de Houten gets the award for the best tech editor at finding my technical mistakes, while offering lots of good analogies that I added to the text. Blair Buchanan did a nice job keeping the text appropriate for audiences outside the United States. And Dr. Ron Kovac excelled at watching the tone, thinking hard about the audience for the book at each step, and really helping the overall flow of topics.

This book posed a unique challenge compared with previous books because it is intended for people who have no direct experience with networking. Dayna Isley, who worked as the development editor for the book, not only did an excellent job managing the entire book-writing process, but she also did a great job helping me find the right depth for the topics in the book. Dayna provided countless great suggestions on the approach and tone of the book.

Brett Bartow worked with me on this book from initial concept, including working through refining the First-Step Series goals as well as the goals for this book. As always, Brett did a great job dealing with the full life cycle of what it takes to get the book done right.

Typically, I'm directly involved with the development editor, executive editor, and the technical editors. However, lots of people work behind the scenes—at least behind the scenes to me—to help to make the book better. Karen Gill did the copyediting, cleaning up some of the wording and flow with a fresh set of eyes. Patrick Kanouse's production team gets involved in the details of how the book will look on paper, managing the process of getting the book laid out, ready for the printer, and finally into the warehouse. In particular, San Dee Phillips took care of the project-editing tasks, managing the book's progress from completed draft until it was ready for the printer. To the people who made the book come together, thanks very much.

On the personal side, I'd like to acknowledge my lovely wife's contributions to the writing process once again. She's always a steadying force when the writing process gets to me. Thanks again, Doll! Also, no set of acknowledgments of mine would be complete without saying thanks to Jesus Christ, savior, friend, brother, and provider.

x

Contents at a Glance

Contents

Introduction

Often, learning something new can be a chore, particularly with computer technology. In fact, because you've obviously been searching for a book long enough to at least have opened up this one, you've probably looked at a few other books as well. There's no problem finding networking books—there are tons of them—but almost all of them are geared toward people who want to be networking geeks, and the books frequently get deep and technical in a hurry. They're like the old joke where one guy walks through a door with an unseen long drop to the ground below, and his buddy shouts out, "Watch out for that first step. It's a doozy!"

Computer Networking First-Step is an easy first step toward learning about networking, instead of taking a doozy of a step off the networking ledge. With *Computer Networking First-Step*, you don't have to worry about the pain normally associated with getting into something new. This book is designed and written assuming that you come to the game with no experience at all with the topics, but with a lot of interest in them.

This book is intended for anyone who needs to know a little about networking, but it also requires almost no prerequisite knowledge. You might want to know a little about networking, but not a lot, because that's all you need to know for your job. For instance, maybe you're in sales, and you need to be able to talk to networking geeks. Or maybe you work in another information technology (IT) area where you talk to the networking folks occasionally, and you need to be able to have more meaningful conversations. Or maybe you want to learn a lot about networking, but you aren't sure where to start. Simply put, if you're getting started with networking, this book is for you. If you've used a computer before, you've got the right prerequisite knowledge coming into this book.

When you finish reading this book, you will know enough to talk to people about how networks operate. You won't be an expert at any one part of networking, but you will understand the basic concepts behind a wide variety of technologies used in a typical network today. If your goal is to have a conversational level of knowledge, this book will do it for you. If your goal is to become a networking professional, but you don't have much knowledge or experience yet, this book will help you start down that path.

Interested? The next few pages will give you a little more detail about what's between the covers. Then you can dive in to the first chapter and start learning about networking!

There's a Lot Here, but Then Again, There's Not

Computer Networking First-Step covers a lot of topics, so there are many chapters, but each chapter averages 20 pages. And with the book's conversational style, you can grab it when you have 15 spare minutes and complete another chapter. If you're using this book to get started and want to learn networking even deeper, you'll want to take a few more minutes to study the questions and review the terms. In short, you'll find a lot of topics here, but they're pretty much in bite-sized pieces for easy digestion.

The part and chapter titles, as well as the headings inside the chapters, are purposefully nontechie. It seems silly to title things using terms that you might not have heard about before. But you might have heard of a few networking terms, so if you want a little better idea of the main topics in each major part of this book and each chapter, take a look at the following comments about what's hidden inside.

Part I: Networking Basics

Part I covers a broad brush of the basics of networking, with examples referencing tools that many computer users use every day:

- **Chapter 1, "What Is a Network?"** — Defines the basic terms, including defining what different people might mean when they use the term "network."

- **Chapter 2, "A Network's Reason for Existence"** — Covers networks and networking from a user's perspective.

- **Chapter 3, "Building a Network: It All Starts with a Plan"** — Explains the concepts behind an architectural model that vendors use to build networking products and engineers use to implement a particular network.

Part II: Running the Local Department of (Network) Transportation

After Part I's broad coverage, Part II takes a closer look at the basics of small networks, called local-area networks (LANs), using analogies with how the U.S. Department of Transportation (DOT) builds roads:

- **Chapter 4, "How to Build a Local (Network) Roadway"** — Using analogies with how the U.S. DOT builds roads, this chapter shows how to physically construct a LAN using cabling, PCs, and other networking gear.

- **Chapter 5, "Rules of the Road: How to Use the Local (Network) Roadway"** — Just as you need to obey traffic laws, data must follow the traffic laws of the LAN. This chapter tells you how to pass a LAN driving test.

- **Chapter 6, "Reducing Congestion and Driving Faster on the Local (Network) Roadway"** — It's more fun to drive a fast car. This chapter covers how to do the equivalent with LANs.

- **Chapter 7, "Adding Local (Network) Roadways for No Extra Money"** — It's free, and it's better in many cases. "It" is a thing called virtual LANs (VLANs), which allow you to create lots of LANs with no additional hardware.

Part III: Shipping and Logistics: Commerce Using the (Network) Roadways

This part changes the focus to what the end user of a network experiences — the applications. Chapters draw analogies with doing business by shipping goods to market over the roadways:

- **Chapter 8, "Shipping Goods over a (Network) Roadway"** — This chapter focuses on applications that the end user of a network uses — things that you have probably already done yourself, such as use a web browser to look at a website.

- **Chapter 9, "Choosing Shipping Options When Transporting the Goods over the (Network) Roadway"** — Behind the scenes, applications need services from other things in the network, just like most companies use a large shipping company for shipping products. This chapter looks at those basic services.

Part IV: Navigating the Roadways to Find the Right Street Address

The person driving the shipping truck needs to get to the right street address. Part IV covers the equivalent idea in networking, defining how data is delivered across any network, including the Internet:

- **Chapter 10, "Delivering the Goods to the Right Street (IP) Address"** — Internet Protocol (IP) defines logical addresses—the equivalent of a street address. This chapter defines how networking devices together deliver data from one computer to another using IP addresses.

- **Chapter 11, "Knowing Where to Turn at Each Intersection (Router)"** — One of the more important types of networking devices is called a *router*. This chapter covers how routers work, with analogies drawn to how a driver makes decisions about where to turn at each intersection.

- **Chapter 12, "Painting the Road Signs on Your Interstate (Internetwork)"** — If you take a trip, you might rely on road signs to tell you where to turn. Routers can do the networking equivalent of posting road signs, which is explained in this chapter.

- **Chapter 13, "People Like Names, but Computers Like Numbers"** — Let's face it: Computers are better at math than we are. This chapter explains how networks let us use names (such as www.ciscopress.com), and how the computer converts those names to numbers that are more useful to the computer.

Part V: Building an Interstate (Inter-LAN) Highway System

When computers in the network are far apart, the physical connections are called wide-area networks (WANs). This part explains three major branches of WANs, all of which require that you lease someone else's physical network because of the impracticality of having everyone run cables for hundreds of miles:

- **Chapter 14, "Leasing a (Network) Roadway Between Two Points"** — This chapter covers how two routers at two different physical sites can send data using the equivalent of a never-ending telephone call between the two routers.

■ **Chapter 15, "Leasing a (Network) Roadway Between Lots of Places"** — If you have more than two routers at different sites, it's cheaper to use a different type of WAN, called Frame Relay, as explained in this chapter.

■ **Chapter 16, "Driving from Home onto the Globally Interconnected (Internet) Roadway"** — Most everyone knows about the Internet. But what really happens when you connect to the Internet from home? This chapter covers the high points.

Part VI: Securing the Network

This part highlights how to protect your network from both the curious and the malicious people on the Internet:

■ **Chapter 17, "Accepting the Right People and Rejecting the Wrong People"** — You shouldn't just let anyone use a network. This chapter hits the key points of how to make sure only the right people use your network.

■ **Chapter 18, "Keeping a Watchful Eye Over Who Drives into Your (Network) Neighborhood"** — This chapter covers how to set up ground rules for what's allowed into your network from the Internet, and how to watch for crackers who might try to cause harm to your network.

Part VII: Appendixes

■ **Appendix A, "Answers to Chapter Review Questions"** — Each chapter ends with a "Chapter Review Questions" section that contains some open-ended questions. This appendix repeats the questions and lists answers as well.

■ **Appendix B, "Converting IP Addresses Between Decimal and Binary"** — The coverage of IP in Chapter 10 doesn't require you to think about IP addresses in binary. However, for any of you who are interested in learning networking more deeply after reading this book, this appendix can help you with some of the basic math relating to IP addressing.

Glossary

The college professor who first taught me about networking, Dr. Phil Enslow, used to say that 80 percent of networking was understanding the lingo and then understanding how other people used the same lingo. The Glossary will be a valuable tool as you build up your lexicon for having conversations about networking.

Who Ought to Read This Book

This book is meant for anyone who wants a comfortable introduction to a broad variety of networking topics. That's not to say this book doesn't tell you some important technical details, because it does. Primarily, this book is purposefully designed for people who want a solid understanding of the basics of networking, plus a good working knowledge of the terminology that networking professionals use every day.

That said, there are a few specific types of people who come to mind that will especially benefit from this book:

> **People who are beginning their quest to become networking techies.** Anyone who wants to work in the computer networking arena has to start learning somewhere, and this book is an excellent starting point. Whether you are in school and using this book as part of a course, or you are learning on your own, this book can start you on a career in networking.
>
> **IT professionals who are looking to know more about networking.** If you're already in the IT arena but don't know a lot about computer networking, this book can help you as well. You've probably already heard a fair amount of the lingo used by networking types, but now you want to know what they really mean by it all. This book is for you! It covers hundreds of terms with explanations in the context of how you normally build a corporate network.

People who need to talk to the people who build networks, but who have no need to know how to build networks themselves. Lots of people have jobs that require them to have a general idea about how networks work, but without needing to make them work. For instance, businesses that sell networking hardware and software have people who work for them—salesmen, accountants, operations, consultants, customer service reps, and administrators—and all of them can benefit from knowing a little about networking. Also, some companies don't sell hardware and software, but they sell services that rely completely on networking. Insurance companies, banks, shipping companies, and many others rely on their networks for the core business functions. If you want to understand what the network engineers are saying, this book will help!

People who want to pass networking certification exams but who need more background. If you want to get some good résumé material so that you can get a job in networking, you should try to get some networking certifications. Many people need a little more background before diving into the books and courses related to entry-level networking certifications, and this book can help.

Still Hungry? Try Another *First-Step*

Some of you might be thinking something like, "Well, I already know something about networking, and maybe this book can fill in some holes. I really like the approach and comfort of using this book, but what I really want to know a lot about is security, and there are only two chapters on security. What I really need is a *First-Step* book on computer security!"

Well, if you really thought that, the book *Network Security First-Step* is meant for you. Cisco Press introduced the *First-Step Series* in the spring of 2004. You can check http://ciscopress.com/firststep for more information on any new titles. The goal of the *First-Step* books is to provide an easy first step into whatever networking technology is covered by the book. Each *First-Step* book meets you at the beginner stage for the technologies in the book. For instance, *Network Security First-Step* covers some of the basics of a protocol called TCP/IP, but it focuses specifically on network security.

Stuff You'll Find in This Book

This book includes several features to help you digest the materials with minimal heartburn. With the solid foundation gained through this book, you can learn things about new technology more easily, talk networking with others, or be better prepared to begin a career in networking:

- **Chapter objectives**—Every chapter begins with a list of objectives that are addressed in the chapter. The objectives are revisited in the chapter summary.

- **Highlighted keywords and Glossary**—Throughout this book, you will see terms formatted with bold and italics. These terms are particularly significant in networking. So, if you find you aren't familiar with the term or at any point need a refresher, simply look up the term in the Glossary toward the end of the book to find a full definition.

- **Chapter summaries**—Every chapter concludes with a comprehensive chapter summary that reviews chapter objectives, ensuring complete coverage and discussing the chapter's relationship to future content.

- **Chapter review questions**—Every chapter concludes with review questions. These questions test the basic ideas and concepts covered in each chapter. You can find the answers to the questions in Appendix A.

- **Nontechie headings and titles**—The titles and headings used throughout this book avoid the use of technical terms when possible, focusing instead on words that connote something about the underlying concepts.

The illustrations in this book use the following icons for networking devices and connections:

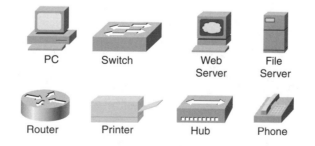

PC	Switch	Web Server	File Server
Router	Printer	Hub	Phone

For More Information...

If you have any comments about this book, you can submit those through the ciscopress.com website. Simply go to the website, select Contact Us, and type in your message.

I hope you enjoy your first step into a deeper knowledge of networking, and I trust that these first steps will be a doozy of a good learning experience!

Networking Basics

Part I provides an introduction to fundamental networking concepts. Chapter 1 introduces you to basic networking terms, Chapter 2 describes the typical activities of network users, and Chapter 3 discusses the building blocks of a network as defined by networking architectural models.

Chapter 1: What Is a Network?

Chapter 2: A Network's Reason for Existence

Chapter 3: Building a Network: It All Starts with a Plan

What You Will Learn

After reading this chapter, you should be able to

✔ Provide a general definition for a *network*

✔ Explain the differences in perceptions about networks based on whether one works on servers, cabling, or networking devices

✔ Generally explain the concept of an enterprise network

✔ Generally explain the concept of the Internet

CHAPTER 1

What Is a Network?

There's an old story about how three blind men all go to the zoo to learn about elephants. They each walk up and touch a different part of the elephant. One touches the trunk and thinks that the elephant is like a snake. Another feels a leg and thinks an elephant is like a tree. Another grabs his tail and thinks an elephant is like a rope. (There are many variations on this story, which you can find by searching the Internet.)

Just like with the elephant and the blind men, many people have their own slanted views of just what a network really is. You and all the other people reading this book come with your own preconceptions about networking. So, depending on your own experiences, you might think of a network in one way, whereas another might think of a network in a different way. This chapter helps you begin to build a more consistent and more complete view of computer networking by explaining a few different views of what a network is and is not.

No, Really, What Is a Network?

I'll start with a nice, purposefully broad definition of *network* and then show some examples:

> *Network* — A combination of hardware, software, and cabling, which together allow multiple computing devices to communicate with each other.

In short, a network gives computers the ability to communicate. However, that definition could apply to a lot of different types of networks. So, some examples can help. Figure 1-1 shows the basic idea of a typical small network used by a company at a single site.

Figure 1-1   Simple Single Site Network

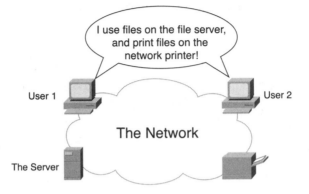

Remembering the definition, a network consists of hardware, cabling, and software. Figure 1-1 does not show some of the hardware, and it shows no cabling; the cloud represents those parts of the network. A *cloud* in a network diagram simply means that there are network components—hardware, software, and cabling—but the details are hidden because they are not important to the current discussion.

Figure 1-1 does show some important parts of the network—in particular, the server and the client end user computers, typically *personal computers* (PCs). In networks, a server provides some form of service to the users in the network. In this case, both users store files on the server, and they print files on the printer that is attached to the network. Many of you probably do that every day you are at work or at school.

This simple network does fit the definition of a network. Even though you cannot see some of the details, this network allows the computers to communicate. But like the three blind men and the elephant, depending on your job, you might have a totally different view from what this network looks like in real life.

What an Elephant—err, a Network—Looks Like

Now would be a good time to take a closer look at what's behind the cloud, shown in Figure 1-2.

Figure 1-2   A Closer Look at the Simple Network

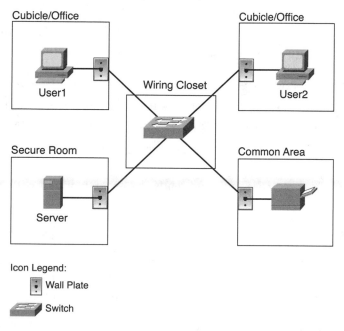

As shown in Figure 1-2, User1's PC has networking software installed. A cable connects that PC to a socket on the wall. That socket has a cable on the (hidden) other side of the wall plate. The cable runs under the floor, in the ceiling, or some other hidden place, with the other end being in a ***wiring closet***. The wiring closet is typically a small room (hence the word *closet*) where all cables from all the computers run.

Inside the wiring closet, all the cables connect to a ***switch***. A switch consists of specialized hardware and software that forwards the network traffic back and forth between the various network devices on the network.

Three Blind Men—The Server Guy, the Cabling Guy, and the Network Guy

Depending on where you work, you might have a lot of different people working on the network. In some companies, one person is responsible for all parts of the network. In other companies, the responsibilities are divided among lots of different people. In some cases, you simply need different skills to perform different tasks. In other cases, one job might reside in a different department for organizational reasons. Union personnel often run the cables.

Because different people often work on a different aspect of a network, they form their own prejudices about what a network really is—and is not. So, like the three blind men and the elephant, each type of worker might develop a tendency to ignore or discount parts of the network. Although most people are not so narrow-minded as the people I'm about to describe, people tend to build their own views based on their own experiences—and that's true when working with networks as well.

For example, imagine the person who is responsible for the server. That person needs some PC hardware skills, but more importantly, he needs strong skills with software. The hard part—and fun part—of supporting the server has to do with software installation, testing, administration, and troubleshooting.

However, the server guy might not know what's on the other end of the networking cable. In fact, he might perceive the world like Figure 1-3.

Figure 1-3   The Server Guy's Perception of the Network "Elephant"

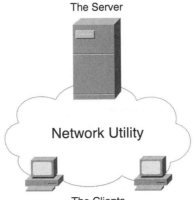

Okay, the size of the server in Figure 1-3 is meant to be a little ridiculous, but that, of course, is the focus of the server guy. He also worries about the client PCs. He views the rest of the network as a network utility. The term ***network utility*** simply refers to the idea of treating the rest of the network just like you think of the telephone, electrical power, water, and so on. You expect it to work, and it usually does; you generally do not think about it unless it's not working.

The cabling guy and the network guy actually create the network utility. The cabling guy, typically called an electrician, might also have a narrow view of the world. His job requires that he run the cables from each cubicle back to the wiring closet. His job requires physical dexterity, knowledge of how to conform to the electrical building standards, and a willingness to get a little dirty when running cables under the floor, in the ceiling, or through some other hole in the wall. To him, the network is the cabling.

The cabling guy makes sure that there's a working cable running from the wiring closet to each place in the building where a computer needs to connect to the network. Figure 1-4 shows the basic perspective of the cabling guy.

Figure 1-4   The Cabling Guy's Perception of the Network "Elephant"

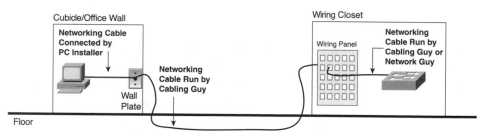

The electrician (cabling guy) typically takes care of running cable from each wall plate to the wiring closet, with the cable being run under the floor or inside the ceiling. The ***wall plate*** simply provides a physical plug into which the electrician can connect a short networking cable from any computer. The ***wiring panel*** gives the electrician a place to physically connect the end of the cables so that the network engineer (or the cabling guy) can easily connect the ends of the cables to the switch. The cabling guy's focus is on installing, testing, and troubleshooting the cabling from each wall plate to the wiring closet.

Finally, the network guy—more often called the network engineer—is responsible for the switch, as well as any other hardware and software used to create a network utility for the computers. The network engineer installs, supports, and troubleshoots the hardware and software on the switch. To do his job, he needs to know where each cable runs and to what port in the switch each cable is connected. However, the network engineer does not always need to know exactly where the cabling travels to get to the wall plate. His view of the world is depicted in Figure 1-5.

Figure 1-5   The Network Guy's Perception of the Network "Elephant"

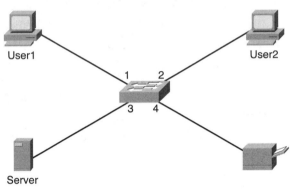

From the networking guy's perspective, there's simply a cable run from the switch to each device; in other words, he ignores all the difficulty the electrician went through to get all the cables run. However, he does know which computer's cable plugs into the various numbered ports on the switch. (A switch typically has lots of places into which you can plug in one of these networking cables; these places where you plug in the cable are called *switch ports*.)

The network guy does want to know where the server sits so that he can confirm that the server can indeed send and receive traffic across the network. The network guy might even care to know what type of services the server is providing. But the network guy typically needs to know a lot less about the servers than the server guy does.

note
The network shown in these past few figures is typically called a *local-area network (LAN)*. A LAN is a network for computers that are nearby or local to each other. The second part of this book covers in much more detail how LANs work.

The interesting thing about all three types of networking workers—and others as well—is that they are all correct to some degree. Without the cabling, the network won't work. Without some networking devices, most networks will not work. If you do both of those things correctly, you have created a network utility, but without working servers, the end users will not have anything useful to do with the network. So, although all three types of workers might have different views of the network, they all need to do their jobs well for the network to be useful.

Different Types of Traditional Computer Networks

So far, you have seen only one simple network with just a few computers. Of course, networks come in many shapes and sizes. So, it is useful to think about a couple of other example networks before diving into the upcoming chapters.

Big Company, Multiple Sites: An Enterprise WAN

Imagine that you work at a company that has multiple physical sites with locations in separate states. As a user of the network, you might realize that the network connects all sites. For instance, you might be able to view information about your benefits program, fill out forms to change something about your retirement plan investments, and so on. You know that the Human Resources department is at headquarters, and you are at a small branch office. So, you can easily assume that your company needs a network—in this case, an enterprise *wide-area network (WAN)*. Figure 1-6 depicts a typical example.

Figure 1-6   A Larger Network: An Enterprise WAN

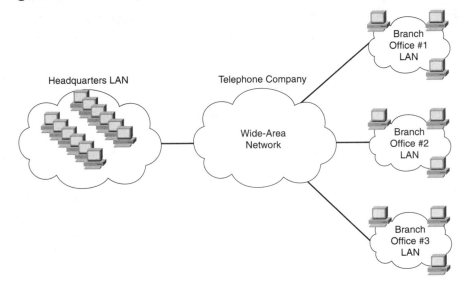

In Figure 1-6, you can see three remote branch offices, each with a couple of PCs and a printer. The headquarters site has more users (hence, more PCs), as well as several servers. Each remote site has a LAN, much like the LAN shown earlier in this chapter. However, now the network includes a cloud labeled WAN. The WAN is simply a part of the network over which the computers at each site can send and receive data from computers connected to the LANs at other remote sites.

Most people call the network shown in Figure 1-6 an *enterprise network* because the network is owned by and created by one company, and a company can be considered to be an *enterprise*. You will also hear of this type of network called an *enterprise WAN* because enterprise networks typically use WANs as part of the overall network.

Just You and Me and the Whole World—The Internet

The *Internet*—and yes, that's a capital "I" in "Internet"—has significantly changed the way people live. It has flattened the earth and allowed the free exchange of ideas worldwide—among billions of people.

The Internet is yet another computer network, but it is unique. The uniqueness comes in that almost all enterprise networks connect to the Internet. Also, individual users can connect to the Internet. To make it all work, companies called *Internet service providers (ISPs)* provide service to companies and individuals to connect them to the Internet. The result? Almost all computers on the planet can communicate with each other. The cultural implications of the Internet far outweigh the coolness of the technology, and the technology is pretty cool! Figure 1-7 shows the basic idea of the Internet.

Figure 1-7   The Internet, with Enterprises and Individuals Connected to It

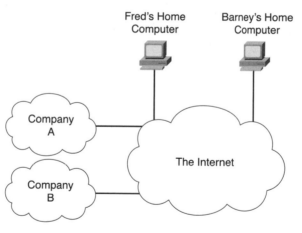

Once again, clouds show that parts of a network exist, but the details are hidden. The idea is simple: If we create a core network called the Internet, and all companies and individuals connect to it, then everyone can communicate with everyone else. The Internet is so pervasive today that you can almost take it for granted!

Chapter Summary

With this chapter, you've taken your first steps toward a clear vision of networking. A computer network might consist of a couple of PCs, some cables, and a little hardware and software, typically called a LAN. Alternatively, a network might comprise hundreds or thousands of computers in a large company, along with multiple and various cables and networking devices and numerous sites, typically called an enterprise network. Or a network might be the whole Internet, which literally includes hundreds of millions of computers, billions of people, most companies in the world, and untold numbers of networking devices and cables.

A network is a combination of hardware, software, and cabling, which together allow multiple computing devices to communicate with each other. Regardless of size, one of the great things about networking is that its basics apply to all these types of networks.

As promised in the Introduction, by the time you are finished with this book, you should have built a wide range of knowledge about networking technology, concepts, and terminology. You should also have a firm and accurate foundation of knowledge from which you can dive into networking to a deeper level.

Chapter Review Questions

You can find the answers to the following questions in Appendix A, "Answers to Chapter Review Questions."

1. In this chapter's definition of a network, what three components are used to create a network?

2. What is the key function provided by a network?

3. Related to the three components of a network, which component does a server support person work with most?

4. Which components of a network does a network engineer work with most?

5. What is an enterprise network?

6. Give a basic definition of the term "Internet."

7. Compare and contrast the terms "enterprise network" and "Internet" in general terms.

8. Describe the concept of a network utility.

What You Will Learn

After reading this chapter, you should be able to

- ✔ List several general categories of network-based applications

- ✔ Compare and contrast applications based on how much knowledge about the network is required of the end user

- ✔ Explain the basic operation of the network-based applications in this chapter

- ✔ Explain the basic structure of the Internet, including the connection of enterprise networks to the Internet

CHAPTER 2

A Network's Reason for Existence

These days, almost everything that a computer user wants to do makes use of a network. Certainly, some computers today do not need to communicate with others. However, most computers do. In fact, many people today have multiple computers in their homes, and even these computers need to communicate with each other.

The computer user, however, does not typically need to know anything about how the network works. In fact, most end users do not know when their computers need the network and when they do not. Most users who use computers at their jobs know that the computers can somehow talk over the network and know that many of their applications quit working when the network is down.

One of the best ways to start learning about networks is to learn about what an end user of the network does. Many of you use networks for work or school already. This chapter covers the basic features that an end user might want to get from his network. Throughout the rest of this book, I'll explain the basics of how a network supports these end user functions.

Using the Network by Accident

Some of the most common network services hide the network from the end user. You can think of these services as causing the end user to use the network by accident because he doesn't realize the network is involved in the tasks he's performing.

To explain these "accidental" network services, I'll use an imaginary employee at a remote office. We'll call this fellow Fred. Fred is the master of his own domain; he has a PC, a printer, and he can do all his work without much interruption from the home office. To perform his normal daily work, Fred opens a document using a word processor, changes some of the text, and prints a copy. He then mails the letter to the customer and saves the changes to the letter. Figure 2-1 shows the basic idea.

Figure 2-1   Fred's Normal Daily Tasks on His Personal Computer

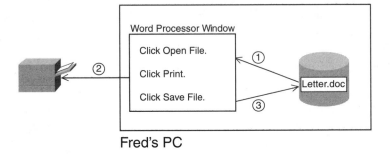

Fred's PC

The steps in the figure are as follows:

1. The word processing program reads the letter from the disk drive.

2. When Fred clicks the Print icon, the PC sends a copy of the letter to the printer.

3. When Fred saves the file, the word processing program writes the file back onto the hard disk.

Step 1 is often called a *file read*, which means that the computer copies the file from a disk drive into computer memory so that the computer can process it. Later, by performing a *file write*, the computer replaces the old file on the disk drive with the newly revised file.

Fred's life is good for a while, but like all things, changes eventually happen. Fred's company grows, and he can't keep up with the work. So, the home office sends a hotshot, named Wilma, to Fred's remote office to work with him and help him get all the work done.

Wilma brings her super-dooper, fast high-end PC with her to the new office and installs a network. She also takes over Fred's old printer and connects it to her own PC. Being a control freak, Wilma also copies all the customer letters from Fred's PC over to her PC. Figure 2-2 shows the general concept, similar to the simple LAN from Chapter 1, "What Is a Network?"

Figure 2-2   A Network with Fred and Wilma

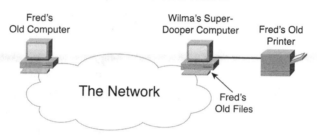

Wilma set everything up, including the network, so she knows how it works. However, Fred has no idea why the new gal would mess things up like this. So, the first morning, after getting his cup of coffee, Fred starts up his word processor, grabs a diskette, and walks over to Wilma's super-dooper new computer and copies a customer letter onto the diskette. He walks back to his desk, updates the letter using his old clonkey computer, and then walks back to Wilma's computer with the diskette. Then Fred copies the file back onto Wilma's computer, replacing the old file, and brings up the word processor on Wilma's computer so that he can print a copy for mailing to the customer. Figure 2-3 shows the idea.

Figure 2-3   Fred's "Sneakernet"

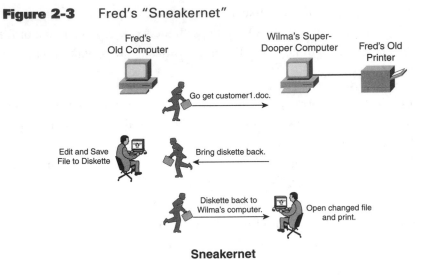

Sneakernet

In this example, Fred does not use the network. He instead uses something called Sneakernet. *Sneakernet* is a sarcastic term that refers to the process of not using a real network, but instead walking back and forth between computers with diskettes or CD-ROMs, moving files manually—and requiring comfortable sneakers!

Fred's Sneakernet method works, but it's way more time consuming than before the home office sent him help in the form of Wilma. Finally, Wilma gets to the office and finds Fred putting on his comfortable sneakers, getting ready for lots of walking around the office.

"Fred, I guess I forgot to tell you how to use the network! You don't even need to know it's there! If you just look on your C drive in the folder called Customers, you will see all the same files you are used to working with. The files are on my PC—a *file server*—but that's hidden from you. Also, when you click on the Print icon from your word processor, you'll see a printer called *sameoldprinter*—clever name, huh? If you print to that printer, it will print on your same old printer, even though it's connected to my PC. My PC is set up as a ***print server,*** so you can print on your same printer. You can do your job the same old way, from your old clonkey computer—but you can still wear your sneakers if you want to!"

For this network to work, Wilma's computer provides file services. ***File services*** include the process by which one computer, typically called a *file server*, keeps files on its disk drive and allows other computers to read to and write to the files by using the network. The term "file server" refers to the computer that provides the service of storing the files on a disk drive and making them available to others for reading and writing—in this case, Wilma's computer. (A ***disk drive*** is a component of a computer on which you can store files permanently.)

Similarly, Wilma's computer provides ***print services***, the process by which a computer allows other computers to print files on a printer that is physically attached to the computer. ***Print server*** refers to the computer that provides printing services.

Fred's computer can still do the three steps that were shown in Figure 2-1, but hidden from Fred is the fact that the read, print, and write operations all happen over the network.

Remember: A network consists of software, hardware, and cabling that allow multiple computers to communicate successfully. Figure 2-4 shows the computers and a ***network cloud***, with the cloud hiding unimportant details of the network. In this case, just like the users, we do not care about the details of most of the network yet, so the network is represented with a cloud.

Figure 2-4   Fred's PC Using the New Network

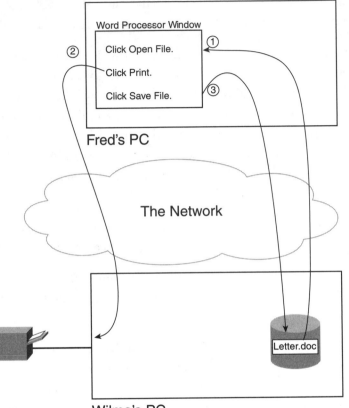

File and print services are two of the most typical network services found in an enterprise network. (An *enterprise network* is a network created for use by a single company or organization.) The users do not actually need or even want one printer on each desk; they simply share the printer located in a central area. They also probably want to use the same files as some of their co-workers. Transparent print and file services allow multiple users to share printers and files. The users can open files, modify them, save them, and print them—doing the same things they did before file and print servers existed.

The next section discusses a few end user applications that presume the existence of a network.

Using the Network on Purpose

For Fred to do his job, he really didn't need to know that the network existed. Sure, intellectually Fred could look at the new cabling Wilma had set up, see the printer cabled to Wilma's computer, and realize that something had to happen to let his computer print on Wilma's printer. But Fred didn't need to act any differently to use the network—he still opened files, saved them, and printed them.

Although some of Fred's job tasks didn't require that he think about being connected to a network, when he goes home and uses the Internet, chances are Fred *will* be aware that he is using a network. The ***Internet*** is the global network to which almost every company and organization in the world is connected.

Unless you've been asleep for the past 10 years, you've probably heard of the Internet. In its most basic form, the Internet is a large number of networks that are connected together, allowing computers in each network to communicate with others. The Internet also includes many individual users that connect to the Internet from their homes. You can make a phone call to most anyone on the planet because all the telephone companies in the world connect to each other; similarly, most computers can communicate with each other over the Internet because most computer networks connect to each other through the Internet.

You can think of the word "Internet" as meaning *interconnected networks*. Many of the networks that comprise the Internet are enterprise networks. To create the basic connectivity between enterprise networks and home Internet users, ***Internet service providers (ISPs)*** provide networking connections among enterprises, individual home users, and other ISPs.

To create the Internet, any single organization simply needs at least one connection to another network. For instance, most enterprise networks connect to at least one ISP. Each ISP connects to at least one other ISP—typically several ISPs—so that there is at least one path from every company to every other company. As a result, everyone who is connected to the Internet can communicate.

The general populace can connect to an ISP of their choosing as well. By doing so, an individual can communicate with the computers in most of the companies of the world, as well as the computers owned by the general populace. Figure 2-5 shows the general idea.

Figure 2-5 Conceptual View of the Internet

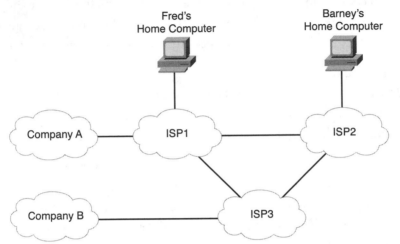

Figure 2-5 shows Company A with a line connecting it to ISP1. The line represents a cable that can allow the enterprise network and ISP1 to communicate. ISP1 has created a network, with the details hidden by a network cloud. ISP1's network allows individual computers, such as Fred's, to connect to it. It also allows corporate networks, such as Company A, to connect. So, Fred could communicate with computers inside Company A, assuming that the security policies at Company A allowed it. But that's another story for Chapters 17, "Accepting the Right People and Rejecting the Wrong People," and 18, "Keeping a Watchful Eye over Who Drives into (Your Network) Neighborhood."

Company A created its enterprise network using hardware, software, and cabling paid for by Company A. ISP1 creates its network as well, using its own funds. ISP1 agrees to allow Company A's traffic to pass through ISP1 and on to other ISPs so that Company A can communicate with the rest of the world. In return for allowing Company A to communicate to the rest of the Internet using ISP1, Company A pays ISP1 an ongoing fee.

Similarly, Figure 2-5 shows Barney connected to ISP2. Barney probably used his phone line, his computer, and a modem to connect to ISP2. A *modem* is a device that allows a computer to communicate with another computer using a plain old telephone line. The vast majority of individual Internet users use a modem and a phone line to connect to the Internet.

After Barney has connected to ISP2, he can communicate with computers in Company A, Company B, and with his buddy, Fred. Like Company A, Barney pays his ISP (ISP2) a fee for allowing him to access the Internet.

The Internet revolution has affected the world as profoundly as almost any invention in history. The ability to communicate across cultures, across national boundaries, relatively quickly, and with (relatively) unfettered freedom of speech has forever changed the way in which people live. News stories routinely emerge more quickly via the Internet than via the world's most powerful news services can find the story.

The ability to communicate between computers in different companies' enterprise networks, as well as with individual users, allowed several popular applications to emerge. This section covers a few of the more popular applications, including web browsing, electronic mail (e-mail), file downloading, and file transferring.

Web Browsing

Almost everyone reading this book has probably used a web browser. A *web browser* allows you to sit at one computer and display information that resides in a web server somewhere on the Internet. The information can be in many forms, including simple text, graphics images, animation, video streams, and audio clips. Even if you've not heard of the term web browser, you might have heard of *Internet Explorer* or *Netscape*, which are the names of two of the more popular web browsers on the market today.

The browser is actually software that resides on the computer used by the end user. The browser requests a web page from a web server, and after the server responds, the web browser displays the information sent to it by a web server.

A *web server* consists of software that resides on the computer that is accessible to the end user via the Internet. After a browser requests a web page from a web server, the server replies by sending the contents of the web page back to the browser.

Many people refer to the actual content—the stuff that shows up on the screen when you are using a browser—as a *web page*. So, if you go to http://www.cisco.com, you will see a web page for Cisco Systems, the largest vendor of networking equipment. If you click other links on that web page, you'll go to other web pages. If you do that, you will be using Cisco's website. The term *website* refers to all the content in the various web pages built by that company.

The basic model revolving around web services is similar to how a new retail business works in real life. Someone has an idea about opening a store to sell something. For instance, perhaps this person wants to sell clothing for children. There's a lot to do before opening the store, including ordering inventory, leasing and preparing the store, hiring employees, advertising, and lots of other things. Finally, the day comes, and the owner opens the store for the first time and hopes someone will show up to buy something.

Web services evolve in the same way. Someone has an idea for a website. Maybe it's a site for this same retail children's clothing store or for some established business, or maybe it's just someone who has something to say. This person then builds a website that consists of multiple web pages. The website resides on a web server that is connected to the Internet. At that point, it's like opening day at the retail store—you hope someone shows up at the website!

The usage of the web—the combination or web servers, web browsers, and websites—has become one of the most prolific applications in the Internet, as well as in enterprise networks. Companies, organizations, and even individuals can create their own websites on the Internet. Anyone can then ask for the content in those web pages and see the results. Figure 2-6 shows an example of a couple of web servers on the Internet, with Fred and Barney browsing their websites.

Figure 2-6   Web Browsers and Web Pages on the Internet

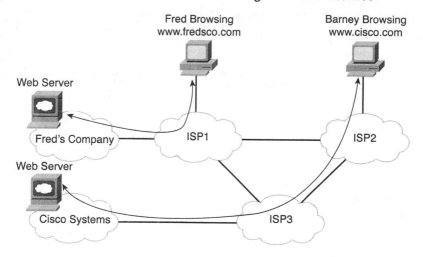

Each company's web server is inside its respective enterprise networks in Figure 2-6. Because each company has a connection to an ISP, Fred and Barney can connect to the web pages and browse the contents. To browse these web pages, Fred and Barney must each bring up the web browser software on their computers and point to the *Universal Resource Locator (URL)* of the website. The URL is a string of characters that uniquely identifies a particular web page. Sometimes, people refer to the URL as a *web address*. For instance, when Barney puts http://www.cisco.com into the right place in his browser, his browser asks for the web page of Cisco Systems. Figure 2-7 shows the Cisco web page.

The web browser, in conjunction with websites, represents one of the most popular network applications today. And because the main purpose of a website is to make information available to other users of the network, it relies on the existence of a network.

Figure 2-7   Example Web Page: http://www.cisco.com

Electronic Mail (E-Mail)

Another popular network application on the Internet is electronic mail, or e-mail. *E-mail* allows the user to create, send, and receive messages electronically. It's essentially the same thing as mail that you would send through the postal service, except that the message is sent electronically over a network, rather than physically sent using planes, trains, and trucks. In fact, the term *snail mail* is often used to refer to traditional paper mail, which takes days to deliver as opposed to seconds.

Of course, the postal service has to overcome a lot more difficulties than e-mail does. For example, the postal service has to physically move tons of letters and packages, so it's reasonable that it takes a few days to deliver letters.

E-mail works on a totally different conceptual model as compared to the web. With web content, if someone has something to say, he creates the content, and at some later time, anyone can look at the contents of the web page. E-mail, however, is sent between one user and another user, or in some cases, to multiple other users. So, the person sending the mail needs to know the e-mail address of the person who needs to receive the e-mail. An *e-mail address* is a text string that represents the address of a person for the purposes of sending and receiving e-mail, much like a mailing address used for snail mail.

With web services, the web server needs to be connected to the Internet before someone can browse the website using a web browser. With e-mail, the sender and the receiver do not have to be connected to the network at the same time. For instance, Fred can connect to the Internet from home and send an e-mail to Barney, even if Barney isn't connected to the Internet at that time. Later, when Barney connects to the Internet, he can check his mail and get the e-mail that Fred sent earlier.

To allow the sender to send an e-mail, even when the recipient is not connected to the Internet, e-mail uses the same general model that the postal service does. If you want to send a letter via snail mail, you put it in a nearby mailbox. The postal service moves the letter to the address of the recipient and puts it in the recipient's mailbox. The recipient does not have to be home when the postal carrier comes by—he just has to look in his mailbox for today's letters when he gets home. Figure 2-8 illustrates how e-mail uses a model similar to that of the postal service.

Figure 2-8 E-Mail in the Internet Using Mail Servers

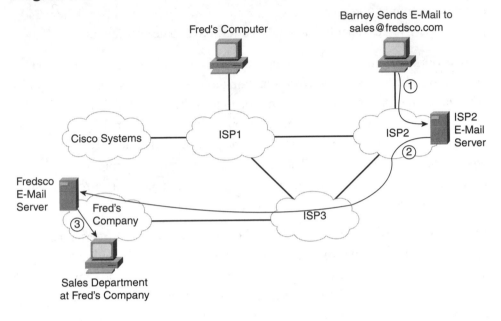

The e-mail passes through three steps before being received by the right person. The following list outlines the three steps, referring to the numbers on the figure. Afterward, I'll give a more detailed explanation of these steps.

1. Barney sends the e-mail to the ISP2 e-mail server.

2. The ISP2 e-mail server sends the e-mail to the fredsco.com e-mail server.

3. The intended recipient checks his e-mail at the fredso.com e-mail server, retrieving the e-mail.

In the first step, Barney has visited the fredsco.com website, where he saw information telling him about some bowling balls for sale. Barney wants to beat Fred the next time they bowl, using a brand new bowling ball built by Fred's own company. So, Barney e-mails the sales department at Fred's Company by sending an e-mail to the address of sales@fredsco.com.

Barney does not actually send the e-mail directly to a computer at Fred's Company. Barney sends the e-mail to his e-mail server, which for an individual Internet user like Barney, typically sits inside the ISP network to which the user is connected. An *e-mail server* is a server that receives, forwards, or holds e-mail, much like the service performed by the postal service. That e-mail server forwards the e-mail to the e-mail server at Fred's Company. By using these two steps, Barney can send the e-mail, even if the e-mail server for Fred's Company is not currently connected to the Internet. ISP2 keeps its e-mail server up and available all the time, just like you would for a web server. The e-mail server at ISP2 simply waits until it can successfully forward the e-mail to Fred's e-mail server.

Finally, when the e-mail sits in the fredsco.com e-mail server, the end user (in this case, a friendly salesman at Fred's Company) can retrieve the e-mail messages at his convenience (Step 3 in Figure 2-8). So, after a morning golf "sales call," the salesman might come in and check his e-mail, finding Barney's e-mail.

The terms *e-mail client* and *client* have specific meanings in networking. Generically, any application program that an end user uses to access some network server is called a client. A web browser, for instance, is a client program. An e-mail client is the client software used for e-mail. Microsoft Outlook is one of the more popular e-mail client programs.

E-mail has become one of the most common networking applications, with a large portion of the population, both young and old, able to send messages to each other for no incremental cost. Even my parents, who grew up in a world where many people did not even have telephones, use e-mail today.

Just like web applications, e-mail works just fine inside a single enterprise network. However, the Internet allows pervasive access to e-mail for literally billions of people, so you can communicate with friends and acquaintances all over the world.

Downloading and Transferring Files

The final end user application covered here is a broad topic area, but with one central theme: moving files into and out of your computer using a network. In most cases, the end user does not have the file, and he wants to get it. However, the user might want to do the opposite; in other words, he might want to move a file on his computer to another computer. Regardless of whether the user wants to retrieve a file or transfer a file to someone else, the action still falls under the category of file transfer. *File transfer* refers to a network application that allows a user to copy files from one computer to another.

The term *download* typically refers to the process of retrieving a file that someone else has and making a copy on your computer. So, downloading would technically be the same thing as file transfer. (Conversely, the term *upload* refers to transferring a file from your computer to another computer—in other words, giving a copy of the file to another computer.) One rather mundane type of file downloading is when you decide to update the software on a networking device. The vendor that sells the device allows you to download new software via the Internet. The vendors are happy to have you download the files; that's a lot cheaper for them than mailing the software to you using the postal service.

A more interesting—and much more controversial—example of downloading is the downloading of music files. I would imagine that a lot of you who are already active on the Internet know what I'm talking about already! It started with a craze called Napster, which eventually reinvented itself after lawsuits from the music industry. Several other tools have also emerged, all with the same goal: to allow people to download copies of music, often without paying for it. Legal and moral issues aside, these services allow you to move files, so they fall into the category of file transfer.

Like web browsing and e-mail, file transfer can be used in an enterprise network or across the Internet. For example, imagine that Fred and Barney need to work on a project, and each needs to update a file called myproject.doc. Fred does not work at the same company as Barney, so Barney's file server is not available to Fred for security reasons. Figure 2-9 outlines the basic process.

Figure 2-9   Copying myproject.doc Between Barney and Fred

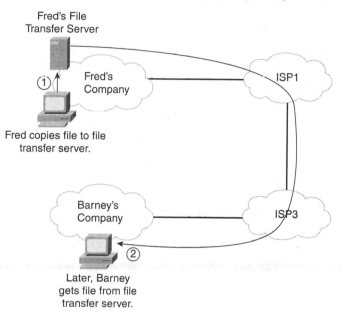

Fred and Barney together do a little dance called the file transfer two-step, as numbered in the figure:

1. Fred places a copy of the file onto a file transfer server, using file transfer client software.

2. Barney gets a copy of the file from the file transfer server, also using file transfer client software.

After this process is complete, both Barney and Fred have a copy of the file. However, if both keep working on their own copies of the file, merging the files back together can be a problem. So, although you can share files using file transfers, you need to be careful regarding who has "control" of the file at any one point in time.

Chapter Summary

Networks exist to provide network services to the users of the network. Although this chapter certainly did not describe all the network applications available in a typical network, it did describe the most popular types of applications. Table 2-1 lists those network applications.

Table 2-1 Network-Based Applications Covered in This Chapter

Service	Description
File services	Files are stored on a computer, called a file server. Other computers, called clients, can read and write to these files, without needing to make a local copy of the file on the client disk drive. This service is typically transparent to the end user.
Print services	Printers are connected to a computer, called a print server. Client computers can send print output to the print server, which in turn prints the files on the printer. This service is typically transparent to the end user.
Web services	The server stores a variety of information, including text, graphics, animation, images, video, and audio. The end user uses a web browser to request the information from the server. The server returns the information, which is displayed by the web browser.
E-mail	An end user creates an e-mail using an e-mail client program and sends the e-mail to a particular person. E-mail servers aid the e-mail delivery process.
File transfer service	Files are also stored on a server. This allows other (client) computers to copy files from the server onto their local disk drives and to replace the contents of files on the file server with files on the client's local disk drives.

File and print services can, and typically do, hide the existence of the network from the end user community. The transparent nature of these applications means that the end user can perform the needed tasks without necessarily knowing whether he is using the network. Conversely, web, e-mail, and file transfer services, by definition, expect that the end user knows that the network exists.

Chapter Review Questions

You can find the answers to the following questions in Appendix A, "Answers to Chapter Review Questions."

1. List the five types of networking application services mentioned in this chapter.

2. Which application services effectively hide the network from the end user?

3. Which application services make use of servers to hold and store data, waiting until another user is available in the network?

4. Which application service allows a server to present multiple text, graphics, video, audio images, and sounds to the client?

5. In general terms, compare and contrast an enterprise network with the Internet.

6. Does the Internet include enterprise networks, home users who connect to the Internet, both, or neither? Explain your answer.

7. Explain the basic difference between a web page and a website.

8. What's a network cloud?

9. Compare and contrast enterprise networks and Internet service provider networks in a few sentences.

10. What three-word term refers to the text that you need to type into a web browser to reach a particular website? What popular jargon might be used instead of that term?

11. Imagine that Fred connects to the Internet using ISP1, and Barney uses ISP2. When Fred sends Barney an e-mail, to what computer does Fred send the e-mail? If the e-mail is not sent directly to Barney's computer, explain why.

What You Will Learn

After reading this chapter, you should be able to

- ✔ Explain the benefits of using standards

- ✔ Summarize the purpose of a networking model

- ✔ List the two most well-known public networking models

- ✔ List and correlate the layers of the TCP/IP and OSI networking models

- ✔ Describe the types of standards created for the TCP/IP model

- ✔ List two major standards bodies upon which TCP/IP relies

CHAPTER 3

Building a Network: It All Starts with a Plan

Let's face it: Without a good plan, most things that involve more than a couple of people are doomed for failure. There are even many popular sayings about how you need to plan, such as "Those who fail to plan, plan to fail."

Networks would not—could not—work today unless all the networking vendors followed the same set of plans, or *standards*. ***Networking standards*** define a set of rules that must be followed by anyone who creates networking products, including cables, hardware, and software. When you follow these standards, the products should work together.

This chapter describes several of the most popular standards and explains some of the benefits of using standards for networking.

Conforming to the Rules

Anyone who has spent time around a teenager—and I figure most people reading this book have at least been teenagers before—knows that those years bring out the rebel inside. Instead of conforming, teenagers sometimes think that rules are meant to be broken! In some cases, breaking the rules might be okay. But often times, as all parents know, the wisdom of having rules and conforming to them become obvious after a little thought—even to a teenager.

Standards are rules that make life a lot easier. For example, look at a power socket on a nearby wall. If you live in the U.S., you probably see an electrical socket with three holes—two that accept flat metal prongs, and one that accepts a round metal prong. The flat metal prongs are parallel to each other. If you go to the store and buy a lamp, you'd expect it to come with a power cord, and you'd expect that one end of the power cord would fit into the wall socket. In fact, you'd be pretty ticked off if the power cord wouldn't fit into the power socket. That's one example of a popular standard. If you go to the store and buy a toaster, a can opener, or a stereo, you would expect the vendor to conform to the standards for how the electrical wall socket works in your country.

Now imagine that you bought a new lamp. You plug it in, and the light bulb instantly "pops," indicating that the light bulb is broken. You put in a new bulb, and it doesn't light up. You decide that the lamp must be broken, so you bring it back to the store and replace it with an identical lamp. When you get it home, the same thing happens to this lamp. Finally, you call customer service and explain your problem. Now imagine this response: "Oh, you bought our special 'We light up your life' model of lamp. It uses the same kind of power cord you are used to using, but it requires less electrical voltage, saving you money. If you read your instructions for the lamp, you will see that it directs you to get an electrician out to your house to rewire and change the voltage coming out of the sockets you want to use for the lamp. Also, note the disclaimer in the instructions: 'If you plug this lamp into a normal wall socket, the extra voltage will fry the lamp, and it will no longer light up your life.' So, go get a new lamp at the store and get your wall socket changed!" If you're like me, you would return to the store to get your money back and buy a lamp made by some other company.

But what does this scenario have to do with networking? A standard tends to define one particular thing, such as the shape of the wall socket and connector used by an electrical socket and electrical power cable. Another standard might dictate how much juice (voltage) flows through the wall socket, whether it is AC or DC, how much current, and the like. Both standards are important and must be followed to prevent exploding lamps. In short, just because you can plug in a lamp does not mean that all the necessary standards have been used. Similarly, networking has standards for physical details so that you can plug in the cables correctly; however, networking devices must support other standards as well for a network to work correctly.

Rules, Schmools for Networking

Even for the simple network with Fred and Wilma in Chapter 2, "A Network's Reason for Existence," several standards were required. To create that network, Fred's PC (the client) and Wilma's PC (the file server) need to be set up to use the built-in networking features of their computer operating systems. Figure 3-1 outlines some of the details.

Figure 3-1   Components of a Simple Network

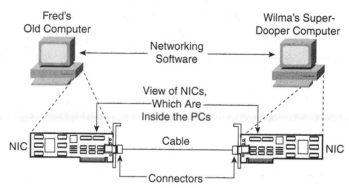

First, the PCs in the network need some form of physical connectivity. *Physical connectivity* refers to the combination of cabling, networking devices, and *network interface cards (NICs)* in the computers, which together provide the physical capability to transmit and receive data across a network. Physical connectivity means that the computers have a physical path over which they can send data to each other—much like having roads so that you can drive your car.

Both PCs have a NIC installed, and each card has a receptacle into which a cable can be connected. (The NICs are shown outside the PCs to emphasize their existence.) A NIC is a computer card that gives a computer the ability to send and receive data across a physical network. The words behind the acronym NIC (network interface card) make sense because a NIC is a computer card that provides an interface between the computer and the network.

Networking standards define several types of connectors. A *connector* is the physical endpoint of the cable, with a certain size and shape. For instance, an electrical power plug on the end of an electrical power cable might have two flat prongs and one round one. With networking cables, the end of the cable is not called a plug; it's called a connector. The connector holds the wires that are inside the cable. Also, the standards for the connector ensure that the connector fits the NIC's interface.

The networking software on Fred and Wilma's computers must understand messages sent back and forth to each other. These messages mean things like "I want to open file customer1.doc," or "Please print the stuff I'm sending you on printer *sameoldprinter*." So, the two computers must implement the same standards for how the networking software on each computer tells the other what it wants to do. It's like Fred and Wilma needing to speak the same language to have a useful conversation. Their computers must speak the same networking language to have a useful conversation on the network.

Examples of Good Rules for Networking

Networks rely on standards—a lot of standards—to be able to do something useful. Before covering more about standards, it's useful to consider a couple of sample networking standards. The next few sections cover the basics of how data is sent between computers, how and why a bunch of bits are sent at the same time, and what to do when the bits experience errors during transmission. But before all that, you need to understand some terms—in particular, bits and bytes.

Traveling a Roadway for a Bit to Get a Byte

Two humans communicate when one person says something and the other person listens. If you ponder that a little more, the two people need to understand the same language. To communicate, the person speaking has to say a bunch of words. The words themselves are sounds that are combined. From one perspective, two people communicate by speaking the same language, but at the other end of the spectrum, you could think of those same people communicating by making a bunch of sounds.

Similarly, computers can communicate with each other using a network, but there are many perspectives. For instance, I'm using Microsoft Word to write the text in this book. When I send the file to my editor at Cisco Press, she uses the same program to open the file and edit the chapter. So, you can think of our computers as speaking the same language. In this case, both of our computers understand files formatted for use with Microsoft Word, which is a word processing program.

It is relatively easy to think of a file that contains the text for this chapter. However, at the same time, the file is really just a bunch of bytes, with each byte containing 8 bits. It's a little like when you put a file folder in a real file cabinet, you might be thinking that you're doing simply that—storing one file in a cabinet. From a different perspective, if the folder contains a bunch of pieces of paper, you are also storing those pieces of paper. Similarly, when a computer stores a file on a disk drive, it is indeed storing one file. However, from a different perspective, the computer is also storing the bits that make up the file.

Computer files consist of a bunch of **binary digits**. Humans normally use decimal numbering—you know, 0, 1, 2, 3... 9, with 10 unique digits. Binary uses only two digits: 0 and 1. That's because computer hardware, at the most basic low level, can store one of two electrical states in its memory, and those represent a binary 0 or 1. And because the phrase *binary digits* takes five whole syllables when speaking (in English, at least), and it's used so often, someone shortened the term to simply **bits**.

To speak to another person, you use a language, but your voice actually makes a lot of small individual sounds. It's the combined sounds that make up words and sentences in your chosen language. Similarly, a computer might have a Word document or any other file that's useful to a computer, but the contents of these files are just a bunch of small individual pieces of information, called bits. It's the combined bits that make up the parts of the file that the computer has in memory. (By the way, the term **byte** refers to a set of 8 bits on most computers.)

When computers communicate, the application needs to send something to an application on another computer. For instance, when you view a web page, it consists of the contents of one or more files. The application needs to transfer the contents of the file to the other computer. To do so, the computer sends a bunch of bits to the other computer because a file is just a bunch of bits. The next section covers an example of how a standard might define how to send bits.

Example Rule for Sending the Bits

When Fred's computer was using Wilma's computer (the file server) in Chapter 2, the network had to take the file from the hard disk at the server, move it across the network, and deliver it to the word processor on Fred's computer. Before the file server could transmit the contents of the file across the network, it had to read the file from the disk. Then it had to transmit the bits over the network.

Any time electricity goes over a wire, you can put a device on the end of the wire that can sense different things about the electricity. One thing that can be sensed is *voltage*. Voltage refers to the amount of electrical power running over the wire. In networking, to send bits, the sender can change the voltage to one level to mean a binary 0, and another to mean a binary 1.

For example, to transmit the bits, the NIC inside Wilma's computer sends some electrical signal over the cable. The device on the other end of the cable—Fred's PC NIC in this case—then interprets the incoming electrical signal. For this to work, both NICs must agree to some standard means of transmission. For instance, imagine that Wilma's NIC sends a +5 volts electrical signal to transmit a binary 0 and +10 volts to send a binary 1. If Fred's NIC expects to receive a +2 volt signal for binary 0 and +4 volts for binary 1, the network will not work because Fred will not understand what Wilma is sending him.

The physical transmission of bits can be a lot more complicated than this example, but the basic idea remains the same. The sending device puts some electricity on the cable, which is interpreted as binary numbers by the device at the other end of the cable. The term *encoding* refers to the general process of taking a binary value and generating the correct electrical signal to be able to transmit the bits across the network. The encoding rules used to transmit data are defined by networking standards.

Sending the Bits a Packet (Package) at a Time

Although you've read about one example of a networking standard for the physical transmission of bits, many other standards are required before two computers can successfully communicate. For example, imagine that Wilma is successfully transmitting the contents of the file, but some of the data gets lost, as shown in Figure 3-2.

Figure 3-2 Data Transmission Using Packets

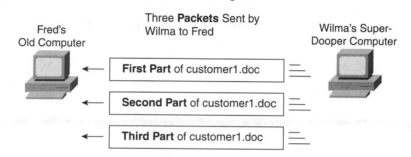

In normal operation, devices in a network send bits in groups, generally called *packets*. For instance, Wilma sends the first part of the file in the first packet, the next part of the file in the next packet, and so on. A ***packet*** is simply a group of bits that are combined for transmission in a network. You can think of a packet as a package—it holds some bits for you while they are being sent across the network.

Why do networks use packets? Well, it's sort of like if you worked at a company that sold widgets, and you needed to ship 1,000,000 widgets to a single customer. Would you put them all in one box? Probably not. You would put some in one box, and then another, until you had put all the widgets in several boxes. You would address the boxes to the same place, and you might even ship them all the same day, but it's easier to deliver the packages if the boxes are a more manageable size.

Similarly, rather than sending the entire contents of a file—possibly billions of bits long, all at once—computers send data in packets, making the delivery of the data a little more manageable. In fact, one of the reasons that networking standards call for the use of packets is for error recovery, which you learn about in the next section.

What to Do When the Bits Get Bashed

Now imagine that the second packet shown in Figure 3-2 had an error. If both NICs think that +5 volts is a binary 0, and +10 volts is a 1, what happens if the voltage is 15 volts? Or 7.5 volts? Certainly, those voltages would confuse the NICs.

How do errors occur? Well, something as simple as someone running a vacuum cleaner near the cable could cause the voltage to change while the electricity is passing over the wire, a phenomenon called *electrical interference*. Formally, electrical interference is the effect of one electrical signal changing because of some other nearby electrical signal. You have all seen or heard electrical interference, such as when your television picture gets a little fuzzy, when you can't hear your AM radio station while you're driving under high-power electrical wires, or when you hear a buzzing noise from your stereo when you are running a blender in your kitchen.

Electrical interference happens. The people who create networking standards can do things to minimize the chance that interference causes transmission errors, but ultimately, electrical interference will cause at least some transmission errors. So, Fred might receive all three packets (refer to Figure 3-2), but one packet might have some bits that just could not be understood. Imagine the first packet had the first paragraph of the customer letter, the second packet had the second paragraph, and so on. Would Fred want to see the letter with the second paragraph missing? Of course not. So, there needs to be a standard for how Fred can realize the second packet had an error, and cause Wilma to send that packet again.

The solution to the transmission error problem typically happens inside software on the two computers with today's networking standards. To recover the errored packet, both Wilma and Fred's computer software must agree to use the same *networking protocol*—a protocol that provides a method to recognize and recover from errors. A *protocol* is like a standard—in fact, in many ways, protocols and standards are the same—but the term protocol typically refers to a process. Figure 3-3 shows a simple protocol that might be used to recover the lost data.

Figure 3-3   A Simple Protocol for Error Recovery

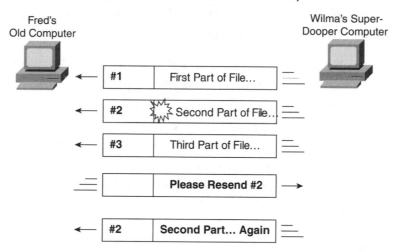

A couple of changes were made to make this new protocol work. (In the figure, the features added to make the protocol work are noted in **bold** letters.) First, this protocol requires that the sender of the packet number the packets. That way, when the receiver (Fred) notices the error, he can send a message back to the sender (Wilma) asking her to send the specific problem packet again—in this case, packet 2. Wilma, of course, replies to Fred's request by resending packet 2.

Error recovery refers to the general process of not only noticing when errors occur in the transmission of a packet, but also requesting for retransmission of the packet until it is received successfully. By using packets instead of sending all the bits in the file at once, Fred and Wilma could recover by resending just part of the file.

The Book(s) of Rules

To make the world work well, we need lots of standards. To make networks work, we need lots of networking standards and networking protocols. Most of the individual standards and protocols are not terribly complicated, and most are somewhat obvious when you think about it. As I like to tell students when I teach, often times, no one part of networking is that complicated; people like you and me make it up, and the people who create networking standards tend to follow the KISS principle (Keep It Simple, Stupid).

The complication occurs when you implement a modern network that conforms to hundreds and thousands of individual standards and protocols. Those Who Came Before Us created a lot of standards, so if you had to sit down and research each networking product to figure out which of the large number of different standards it implemented, you would be thinking hard about another career! (By the way, "Those Who Came Before Us" is just my way of referring to all the people who created the myriad of existing networking standards.) To keep things under control, Those Same People Who Came Before Us created large groupings of networking standards and made edicts like "Hey, if you use products that conform to this larger combined set of standards, they will all work together." You can think of these large groups of rules as a rulebook; as long as everyone follows the rules in the rulebook, everything works well. For instance, a rulebook might include the following:

- A standard for the cables and connectors

- A standard for using a certain voltage to mean 0 or 1

- A protocol to recover from errors

- A protocol for making requests to send and receive files from a file server

As you might guess, no one really uses the term *rulebooks*. I just used the term rulebooks to make a point. So, what do people really call these sets or groups of standards and protocols? Here are some of the terms:

- Networking blueprint

- Networking model

- Architectural model

- Networking architectural model

- Network architecture

Regardless of which term is used, they all mean the same thing: a networking rulebook. Standards and protocols make an individual part or function of the network work well, and *networking models* (I'll use this term the rest of the book, instead of the others) list a set of standards and protocols that, when used together, allow computers to communicate.

Next, I'll describe a few details about a couple of types of networking models: proprietary and public.

Proprietary Network Models Prevent Pervasive Population of Networking Devices

Once upon a time, there were no networks and no computers. Then the first computer was created, but because there was no one else to talk to, there was no need for a network! Finally, the second computer was created, and the need for networking was born.

Networks began to be developed as part of each computer vendor's offerings by the late 1960s, and they became popular by the late 1970s. Each computer vendor created its own networking model, which helped computers from that one vendor communicate easily.

At the advent of networking, the two largest computer vendors in the world were International Business Machines (IBM) and Digital Equipment Corporation (DEC). So, IBM created its own networking model called Systems Network Architecture (SNA), and DEC created its own, cleverly named DECnet.

These vendor-proprietary networking models and others like them were good— they allowed networks to be created and implemented, and they worked—but they weren't perfect. The problem with these proprietary networking models was that they were…proprietary. So, IBM computers could not communicate with DEC computers. Imagine if the same thing had happened with phones; you wouldn't be able to call your buddy if he used a different vendor's phone! Figure 3-4 outlines the problem, and a description of the solution follows.

Figure 3-4   Non-Networking of IBM and DEC Networks in a Single
Company

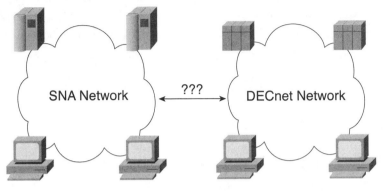

As you can see, if a company wanted to own some IBM computers and some DEC computers, it had to have separate networks. Although that thought might simply be ridiculous today, imagine that you could only buy Dell PCs because a Gateway PC couldn't talk to a Dell. That was the case with proprietary networking models.

Two solutions emerged—one short term, and one long term. The short-term solution, simply put, relates to good, old capitalism: DEC made its computers conform to the IBM SNA model. Why? IBM was roughly 10 times larger at the time in terms of gross revenues. So, DEC created software that converted between DECnet standards and SNA standards. It wasn't pretty, but it worked. Figure 3-5 shows the solution; the next section will get to the long-term solution.

Figure 3-5   DECnet Emulating SNA Using a Gateway

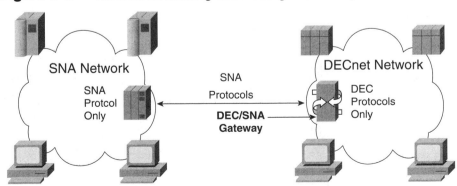

DEC created a DEC-to-SNA gateway, which allowed the DEC and IBM SNA devices to talk. The term *gateway* refers to a wide variety of networking devices that generally convert from one standard to another. As you can see, a DEC computer simply acted like an IBM computer, using the SNA networking model. DEC just wrote some software, running on a device called a gateway, which converted DECnet to SNA, and vice versa.

Public Network Models Provide Pervasively Popular Networks

The second, better, and long-term solution was to get IBM and DEC (and Apple and Novell and Microsoft and Banyan and Xerox and so on) to stop using their proprietary networking models and use a public, open networking model. Today, we enjoy the results of that transformation. We live in a world in which practically every computer uses the same public network model, called *Transmission Control Protocol/Internet Protocol*, or *TCP/IP*. By having all computers use the same networking model, they can all communicate easily.

TCP/IP is just another networking model, but it won out over all the other models. And when I say TCP/IP won, I mean it won big! If you use the Internet, you use TCP/IP. If you send e-mail or text messages from your mobile phone, you use TCP/IP. If you sit at your desk and use a file server, most of the time, you are using TCP/IP. Proprietary models like DECnet and SNA are still used, but far less often than before.

TCP/IP is considered to be a *public networking model* because no one vendor dictates the standards and protocols, with individuals from many companies and organizations participating in the standards definition process. The *Internet Engineering Task Force (IETF)* manages the process of creating TCP/IP standards. The IETF, to quote the IETF website, is "a large, open international community of network designers, operators, vendors, and researchers concerned with the evolution of the Internet architecture and the smooth operation of the Internet. It is open to any interested individual" (http://www.ietf.org). Literally, anyone—including you and me—can participate in the creation of TCP/IP standards and protocols.

How TCP/IP Standards Grow

As mentioned in the preceding section, the IETF manages the creation and approval of TCP/IP standards and protocols. The core TCP/IP protocol definitions are written in documents called Requests for Comments (RFCs). Each *RFC* defines some protocol or standard that is important to the TCP/IP model. The term "RFC" comes from the fact that anyone can comment on the protocol while it is being reviewed before it becomes a standard. In fact, the documents are posted on the Internet so that anyone can look at them and comment before they become an RFC.

If you want to see some of the RFCs that comprise the TCP/IP networking model, all you have to do is use...TCP/IP. That's right—if you use a web browser and connect to http://www.rfc-editor.org, you will be at a website that allows you to look at any and all RFCs. Most people learn about TCP/IP by reading other sources (like this book) before reading RFCs, given the highly technical nature of the RFCs. The point is, anyone can read about the standards, understand them, and implement them.

Some Pretty Popular TCP/IP Protocols

It always helps to think about specific examples when learning something new. TCP/IP is composed of a lot of individual protocols. The name TCP/IP is actually a combination of the two most popular protocols inside the TCP/IP model. The next two sections give you a little background on these two protocols.

Transmission Control Protocol (TCP)

TCP provides several features, which are explained in Chapter 9, "Choosing Shipping Options When Transporting Goods over the (Network) Roadway." But thinking about a few details now can help you with the overall concept of TCP/IP. The most memorable feature of TCP is error recovery, which works like the example back in Figure 3-3. Figure 3-3 showed some imaginary protocol used for error recovery. Figure 3-6 shows the same figure, but with details added for TCP.

Figure 3-6   TCP Error Recovery

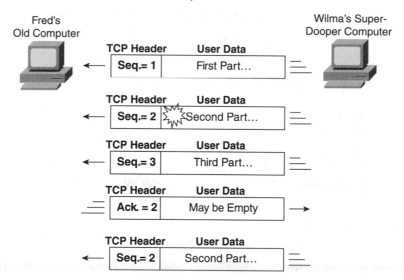

To perform error recovery, TCP uses a TCP header in front of the user data. Notice that Figure 3-6 shows some rectangles, beginning with the words "TCP Header," followed by "User Data." A *header* is a bunch of overhead bits added to the user data so that a protocol can do its job. For instance, to perform error recovery, TCP needs to number the packets. To number the packets, TCP needs a place to put the number, so TCP puts the number, called a *sequence number*, in the TCP header. The TCP header is part of the packet that is sent across the network.

TCP also defines a part of the header to hold the acknowledgment number. TCP uses the *acknowledgment number* field in the header to tell the sender which packets had errors. Notice that Fred sets the acknowledgment number in the packets he sends back to Wilma. The acknowledgment number lists the next packet Fred expects to receive; for example, when Fred shows an acknowledgment value of 2, it means that he got number 1 and expects to get number 2 next. That's how Wilma knows to send packet number 2 again. This process of referring to the next expected packet, rather than listing the last received packet, is called *forward acknowledgment*.

This example scratches the surface of what TCP defines. In addition to checking out Chapter 9 of this book, you can retrieve the TCP RFC free from http://www.ietf.org. Just click the RFC Pages link and search for RFC 793.

Internet Protocol (IP)

The *Internet Protocol (IP)* is another TCP/IP standard protocol. IP defines *logical addressing* and *routing* for the TCP/IP model.

The best analogy for how IP defines addressing and routing relates to the postal service. Before you put a letter in the mailbox, you put an address on the front. Likewise, before a computer can actually send a packet over the physical network, it must put an address in front of the packet. The address structure is defined by IP, as explained in RFC 791.

The need for IP and for IP addresses is not that obvious in the network with just Fred and Wilma. However, Figure 3-7 makes the need for addressing a little more obvious.

Figure 3-7   Routing Based on IP Addresses

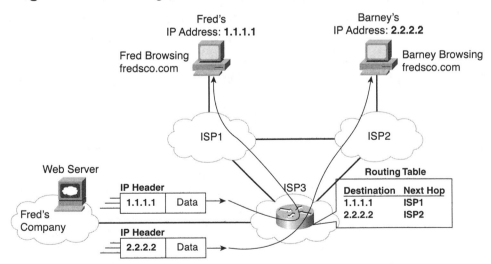

In Figure 3-7, Barney and Fred are both at their homes, and they are excited about looking for the latest in bowling balls from Fred's Company website (www.fredsco.com). So, from their home computers, they each have a browser window open looking at www.fredsco.com.

So that both Fred and Barney can see their web pages, the web server returns packets to both of them. Packets sent to Fred have Fred's IP address in the *IP header*, and packets sent to Barney have his IP address in the header, as shown in the figure. (Headers are extra bytes that are sent with a packet.) A protocol uses those extra bytes to hold information that the protocol needs to do its job, like the IP addresses inside IP headers.

ISP3's network includes a lot of devices and cables, including *routers*. (The router icon looks like a hockey puck with arrowed lines on top in the figure.) When the packets sent by the web server get to ISP3's router, the router looks at the IP address and decides where to forward the packet. Packets sent to Fred go to ISP1, and packets sent to Barney go to ISP2.

To know where to forward the packets, the router uses a table, cleverly called the *routing table*. The routing table works like a road sign by the highway: It tells the traffic which turn to take to reach the right destination.

TCP/IP Standards That Aren't TCP/IP Standards

The IETF numbers new RFCs sequentially. Many of the earlier RFC numbers are no longer used, but you can count on there being several thousand currently active RFCs in the TCP/IP network model.

The people in the IETF tend to be pragmatic. Although many original protocols and standards are needed to make TCP/IP work, other standards bodies might have already defined standards that TCP/IP can easily use. So, the IETF happily reduces its overall workload by referencing other well-known standards created by other standards organizations. This section introduces a couple of the more important standards bodies.

Standards for Physical Networking Nearby

The term *local-area network (LAN)* defines a type of network, or a part of a larger network, in which the devices are relatively close together. Everyone might have a different opinion about what's close together, but for the sake of discussion, consider "close" to mean in the same building or in the same small campus of buildings. Like any other network, a LAN includes the computers, hardware, software, and cabling that allow communications to happen.

The TCP/IP network model does not define the details of LAN standards and protocols. The *Institute of Electrical and Electronic Engineers (IEEE)* defines standards for LANs, so TCP/IP standards simply say "Use IEEE LAN standards if you want to use a LAN."

For a simple LAN, like the one Wilma set up in Chapter 2, TCP/IP protocols and standards are used, as well as IEEE standards. The IEEE standards for LANs define how the bits are physically transmitted across the LAN. TCP/IP defines the standards and protocols used by the two computers that are connected to the LAN.

The IEEE actually does a lot of work for standards in many different technologies, not just networking. The IEEE works to define most modern LAN standards. The IETF, on the other hand, focuses on any protocol or standard that helps make the entire combined set of networking devices work together. You can think of the IEEE as focusing on particular technology areas, with the IETF looking at a broader set of requirements and using many standards defined by other standards organizations, such as the IEEE.

Standards for Physical Networking Far Away

The term *wide-area network (WAN)* defines a type of network, or part of a network, in which the devices are relatively far apart. The distance is relative, but for the sake of discussion, consider a WAN to be a network, or part of a network, for which the cabling must pass outside the property of one company. The distance might only be a few miles, or it might be thousands of miles!

For instance, imagine that Fred's company wants to have a connection between one office in Snellville, Georgia and the home office in Mason, Ohio (about 500 miles away). The problem is that Fred cannot just run a cable between the two offices. So, Fred finds a telephone company that gives him a *leased line*. That leased line helps Fred create a WAN, connecting the two sites, as seen in Figure 3-8.

Figure 3-8   Fred's Alternative to Running a Cable 500 Miles: A WAN Using a Leased Line

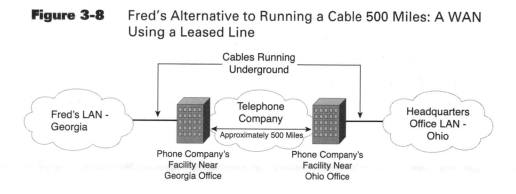

The cloud in Figure 3-8 represents the telephone company network. That means that there is a lot more to the telephone company's network, but the details aren't important right now. As far as Fred is concerned, the leased line gives him the physical ability to send packets from his office, to the home office, and vice versa. The leased line, and the related equipment, is one way you can implement a WAN.

Just like for LANs, the TCP/IP network model does not define all the details of WAN cabling and logic. The *International Telecommunications Union (ITU)* defines standards for WANs, so TCP/IP standards simply say "Use ITU WAN standards if you want to use a WAN." The ITU focuses on standards that impact how the telecommunications companies—the phone companies—of the world operate, and like the IEEE, the ITU focuses on a rather large number of specific technologies. The IETF, which defines the protocols included in TCP/IP, makes good use of the standards created by the ITU.

How to Eat an Elephant, TCP/IP Style

The old question that many of you have probably heard is "How do you eat an elephant?" Well, that's a difficult task, indeed, until you know the simple answer: "One bite at a time."

If you've made it this far into the book, in some respects, you're taking the first bites of eating the network elephant—figuratively speaking, of course. To aid in your learning, the TCP/IP networking model helps you eat—or at least digest—the TCP/IP network model by segmenting the types of protocols and standards into *layers*. Each layer of a networking model represents a general category of protocol. So, you can characterize each protocol as belonging to a particular layer to help keep things organized in your head. Figure 3-9 shows the TCP/IP networking model's layers.

Figure 3-9   Four-Layer TCP/IP Network Model

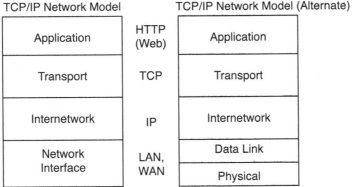

In the figure, you see the four layers of the TCP/IP network model on the left. On the right, you see a five-layer model. The one on the left is correct, but many people use the list of five layers on the right. From a practical perspective, it does not matter whether TCP/IP really has four or five layers; you should just know of these layers so that you can talk about TCP/IP.

Each layer represents a general function that must be accomplished. In later chapters, you will learn more about each layer of the TCP/IP model and the protocols that are part of those layers. You can see the protocols mentioned in this chapter in Figure 3-9, next to their related layer. The figure also includes another protocol—Hypertext Transfer Protocol (HTTP)—which web browsers and web servers use.

All networking models are layered, for basically the same reasons. For instance, none of the logic used by TCP for error recovery relies on knowing anything about the physical transmission of the bits. So, the person writing the TCP/IP software on a computer can ignore the physical details. Similarly, a router, like the one in ISP3's network in Figure 3-7, forwards IP packets based on the IP address, but it does not need to be concerned about error recovery. So, layering helps in product development, and it helps in keeping each protocol simple. The reduced complexity makes for better products and more stable networks.

Well, you are now dangerous with regards to what TCP/IP really is—a set of protocols and standards, some not even defined directly by TCP/IP, that allow you to create networks. You can find countless books on TCP/IP. Before moving on to the next chapter, however, you should know a few things about *Open Systems Interconnect (OSI)*.

How to Eat a T-Rex, OSI Style

The Tyrannosaurus Rex was one of the largest dinosaurs. One website I found re-created a T-rex, at 26 meters long! (See http://www.dinosaurvalley.com/drcdt/wld/.) So, what do dinosaurs have to do with networking? Well, in the same general timeframe that TCP/IP was evolving into a legitimate networking model in the business world, a competing public networking model, called OSI, was being developed by an organization called the *International Organization for Standardization (ISO)*. If TCP/IP is like an elephant, the OSI networking model is more like a T-Rex. In a word, it is huge! It is also complex. In its defense, the ISO wanted to build the end-all networking model—a model that, once implemented by all computers on the planet, would allow pervasive communications among all computers from all vendors in all countries everywhere!

The short version of the history is this: Most computers in the world use the TCP/IP networking model, and almost none use the OSI model. Although the OSI model might have been the bigger networking model and might have had some great features, it was developed much more slowly than TCP/IP. So, TCP/IP took over the marketplace before OSI could be finished. (For you dinosaur fans, yes, I know the T-Rex was faster than elephants, so the analogy fails here.)

Also, you should be aware that ISO still plays an active role in standards development today, working with the IETF, ITU, and other standards bodies. So, although the OSI model lost out to TCP/IP, the organization that created it thrives today.

T-Rex Versus the Elephant

Why bother mentioning the OSI model at all? As it turns out, some of the terminology used by the OSI model ends up being used a lot today. In particular, the names of the layers of the OSI model are used to describe other networking models, TCP/IP included. To talk about networking, you need to know the names of the OSI model's seven layers.

OSI uses a seven-layer model, instead of the four (or five) layers in the TCP/IP model. Figure 3-10 depicts how the layers in the two models match up. For instance, OSI defines that error recovery between end user computers should be implemented by *transport layer* protocols. So, the TCP/IP transport layer, which also defines how end user computers do error recovery with TCP, equates to OSI Layer 4.

Figure 3-10   OSI Model Versus TCP/IP Model (a.k.a. T-Rex Versus the Elephant)

	OSI Model	TCP/IP Model	TCP/IP Protocols
7	Application		
6	Presentation	Application	HTTP, SMTP, POP3
5	Session		
4	Transport	Transport	TCP, UDP
3	Network	Internetwork	IP
2	Data Link	Network Interface	Ethernet, Frame Relay, PPP
1	Physical		

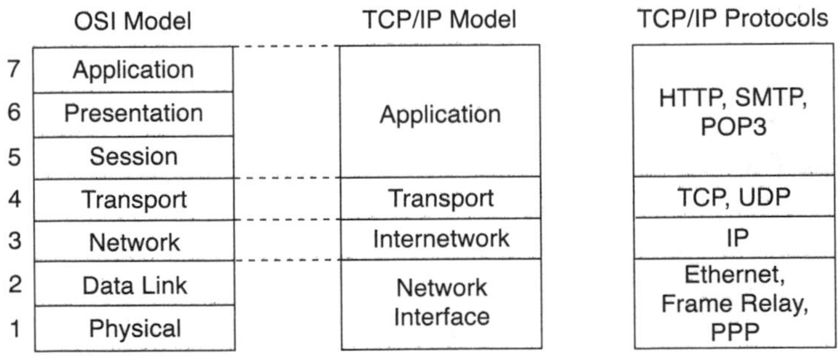

Knowing the OSI model and the names of the layers is useful because most networking jargon refers to protocols and standards relative to the OSI model. For instance, IP sits at the ***internetwork layer*** of TCP/IP. That layer is most closely related to the OSI ***network layer***, or OSI Layer 3. So, using popular networking jargon today, IP would be a ***network layer protocol***. Notice that this term uses OSI's name for the equivalent layer and does not use internetwork—the name of TCP/IP's equivalent layer.

Here are some more examples of phrases you might use today, relating to OSI terminology:

- TCP is a Layer 4 protocol.

- IP is a Layer 3 protocol.

- LANs define both Layer 1 and Layer 2 protocols.

- WANs define both Layer 1 and Layer 2 protocols.

- TCP is a transport layer protocol.

If you are new to networking, you will likely never use a network that implements the OSI model. I've been in networking more than 20 years—I even worked at IBM when they thought that OSI would take over the world of networking—and I've never used a computer with a full implementation of OSI. But, some of the jargon stuck around. So, if you haven't already, you should memorize the layers of the OSI model and how they relate to the TCP/IP model.

If you want some tricks to help you remember the first letters of the names of the seven layers, you might benefit from the following list of mnemonic phrases. The first letters in each word of these phrases match the first letters of the OSI layer names:

— All People Seem To Need Data Processing (Layer 7 to 1)

— Please Do Not Throw Sausage Pizzas Away (Layer 1 to 7)

— Pew! Dead Ninja Turtles Smell Particularly Awful (Layer 1 to 7)

Chapter Summary

For a network to work, someone has to plan. Those plans take the form of standards and protocols, without which any network implementation would fail.

Networking models combine a large set of standards and protocols, with the intent that if network hardware and software use the combined set of standards, the network will work well. Originally, vendors created their own proprietary networking models, with the two most popular being IBM's SNA and DEC's DECnet. Vendor proprietary networking models eventually fell by the wayside, with an open networking model—TCP/IP—becoming the world's most popular networking model.

TCP/IP defines its standards and protocols using RFC documents. In fact, it gets its name from two of the most popular protocols: IP and TCP. TCP/IP also refers to standards from other standards organizations, notably the IEEE, ITU, and ISO for LAN and WAN standards, respectively.

Another public networking model, OSI, did not have real success in the marketplace, and practically speaking, is interesting mostly as a history lesson. However, the layers of the OSI networking model are still important today because most documentation and terminology relating to networking models use the terms inside the OSI model.

Chapter Review Questions

You can find the answers to the following questions in Appendix A, "Answers to Chapter Review Questions."

1. Describe in general terms the benefits of using standards.

2. What were two of the early and popular proprietary networking models?

3. Define the term "networking model," and compare and contrast it with the term "networking standard."

4. List the two public networking models covered in this chapter, including the words represented by their acronyms.

5. List the names of the four layers in the TCP/IP networking model, in order, with the highest layer first.

6. List the names of the seven layers in the OSI networking model, in order, with the highest layer first.

7. List the two standards bodies that define LAN and WAN standards, as referenced by TCP/IP. Which one defines LAN standards?

8. What term refers to where a router stores the information that tells it how to forward packets?

9. Networkers use OSI terminology to describe networking protocols in general. List two OSI terms that might describe the IP protocol.

10. Define the term "packet."

11. This chapter uses the terms "standard" and "protocol," but it suggests one typical difference between a protocol and a standard. What is that difference?

12. What term refers to bits that are added to end user data, for the purpose of allowing a protocol to have a place to keep information important to how the protocol does its function?

Running the Local Department of (Network) Transportation

Part II focuses on roadways—that is, networks—that are small and local. Specifically, it focuses on local-area networks (LANs). Chapter 4 begins this part of the book by explaining the basics of physically creating Ethernet LANs. Chapter 5 follows with coverage of the rules and protocols that computers must follow to use an Ethernet LAN. Chapter 6 explains some improvements to Ethernet LANs, including options for faster LANs. Finally, Chapter 7 completes this part of the book by describing how one collection of LAN hardware can be used to create multiple virtual LANs.

Chapter 4: How to Build a Local (Network) Roadway

Chapter 5: Rules of the Road: How to Use the Local (Network) Roadway

Chapter 6: Reducing Congestion and Driving Faster on the Local (Network) Roadway

Chapter 7: Adding Local (Network) Roadways for No Extra Money

What You Will Learn

After reading this chapter, you should be able to

✔ Explain how computers can communicate binary 1s and 0s using electricity

✔ List the components of popular LAN cables and connectors

✔ Compare and contrast straight-through and cross-over Ethernet cables

✔ Explain the operation of an Ethernet hub

✔ Summarize the benefits of using a structured cabling system

CHAPTER 4

How to Build a Local (Network) Roadway

So far in this book, you have read about how networks allow computers to communicate. Networks include software, some of which sits in the computers, and some of which sits in routers. The network also includes hardware, such as the network interface cards (NICs) in the PCs, mentioned in Chapter 3, "Building a Network: It All Starts with a Plan." Finally, networks include cabling, which provide a physical means to transmit bits across a network.

This chapter is the first one in this book's second major part: "Running the Local Department of (Network) Transportation." In the United States, most cities, all states, and the U.S. federal government have a department of transportation (DOT). Each DOT plans, builds, and fixes problems with roadways. You can learn a lot about networking by comparing networks to roads.

Driving Bits Across the Network Roadway

I just got back from lunch at one of my favorite lunch places: La Frontera Mex-Mex Grill. When it was time for lunch, I got in my car, drove to the restaurant, ordered my usual—numero dos, con pollo, por favor—and drove back home.

When I got home, my wife said, "So you drove over that really cool street outside our house on your way to lunch, huh?" Yeah, right. Who cares what roads I drove on? It's where I drive *to* that's important.

Well, to know networking well, you need to know some of the basics about the networking equivalent of roads. If you find yourself really getting interested in what's in the next few pages, you might just be one of those people who really would like a career working with the technical side of networking. If not, you should at least know the concepts so that you can communicate with the networking geeks of the world and have a firm understanding of networking.

What's a Local-Area Network?

Chapter 3 defined a local-area network (LAN) as a network in which the devices are relatively close together. Of course, a network, once again according to this book, includes computers, software, hardware, and cabling that allow the computers to communicate. Although this definition is accurate, you really do not get a detailed picture of a LAN this way. So, Figure 4-1 shows a LAN, which is one you've seen before in Chapter 3.

Figure 4-1   Components of a Simple LAN

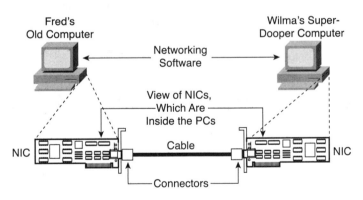

In this case, the LAN consists of some obvious elements. First, you need at least two computers. The computers need to have networking software; otherwise, they will never attempt to communicate. They also need the physical ability to transmit bits from one computer to the other—hence the need for the *cable* and the NICs in each computer. (Figure 4-1 shows the NICs outside the PCs so that you can see them, but they are typically inside the PCs.)

LANs do not get any simpler than this one. Larger LANs can get much more complex, with lots more components like networking hubs and switches, which you will learn more about in the next few chapters.

In this chapter, you learn about how computers can transfer bits across the network roadway. The topics covered here might be the equivalent of what a DOT engineer might talk about over lunch with a stranger: "Hey, you know we're going to be paving Parker-Puckett Parkway pretty soon. Pretty cool, huh?" The reply, "Hey, isn't that near that Mexican place, La Frontera?" And the response from a true DOT engineer: "I don't know—don't care. That's *beside* the road. I just care about the road." Likewise, some network engineers think of the LAN as the cable, possibly the NICs, but they typically don't care a lot about the computers that happen to be connected to the cabling. Likewise, this chapter focuses more on how computers send bits to each other, rather than the applications that run on those computers.

Transmitting Bits Across the Local Network Roadway

Back in Chapter 2, "A Network's Reason for Existence," you saw an example where Fred opened a file that sat on Wilma's disk drive. Later, Fred printed the file on the printer connected to Wilma's computer, and finally, Fred saved the file back on Wilma's disk drive. Figure 4-2 shows the process, in sequence.

Figure 4-2   Basic Flow with Fred Using a File/Print Server

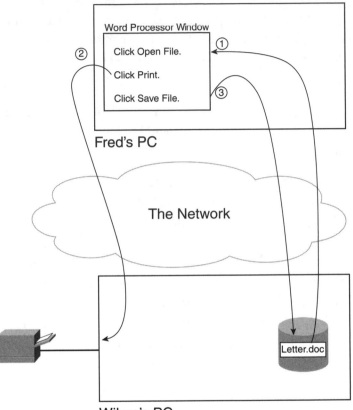

For this process to work, Fred and Wilma must be able to cause a ***bunch of bits*** that sit in memory in one computer to be sent to the other computer. A file is just a bunch of bits. So, imagine that by using a word processing program on a single computer, you can open a file, read the contents, and edit and change the file. Similarly, if you can send the same bits in that file to another computer across the network, you or someone else can edit the file by using the same word processing program on that computer. So, for a network to work, the network needs to be able to get a bunch of bits from one computer to another.

Driving Bits Across a Wire

To send one binary code from one device to another, the sending device puts some electricity on the wire. Electrical signals have many characteristics that a NIC can control and vary. By varying one of these features to two different values, with one value meaning binary 1 and one meaning binary 0, you can transfer data over the wire.

For example, imagine that both PC1 and PC2 have a NIC, and there is a single wire connecting the two cards. The wire is just a skinny, long piece of copper, and copper conducts electricity very well. Now, imagine that the *encoding standard* used by the company that made the NIC defines that a binary 0 is represented by a voltage of ±5 volts, and a binary 1 is represented with ±10 volts. Encoding is the term that refers to a set of rules that defines what a sender should make the electrical signal look like to imply a binary 0 or a binary 1. Figure 4-3 depicts the general idea.

Figure 4-3   Basics of Data Transmission Across a Wire

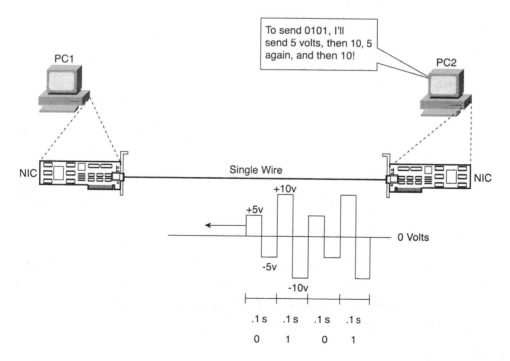

In the figure, PC2 generates some electricity on the wire. In this case, PC2 wants to send the binary value 0101. So, it sends a 5-volt signal, then 10 volts, then 5 volts, and then 10, because the imaginary encoding scheme in this example states that 5 volts means 0, and 10 volts means 1. PC1, on the other end of the wire, senses the incoming electrical signal and interprets the electricity, using that same set of encoding rules to mean 0101, exactly as PC2 intended.

Note that the graph shown in Figure 4-3 shows a discrete, or constant, voltage. Because the X-axis (horizontal axis) represents time, when the voltage changes, it changes immediately to the next value. The use of discrete, constant values, which are then instantly changed to other possible discrete values (as in Figure 4-3), is called *digital transmission*. To transmit binary numbers, or *binary digits*, it is useful to transmit the data using digital transmission.

For the digital transmission of data to work correctly, not only must the sender and receiver agree to what electrical characteristics mean a binary 0 or 1, but they also must agree to the rate at which the bits are transmitted over the wire. In Figure 4-3, the receiver (PC1) must think about the electrical signal at different points in time, on a regular interval. Likewise, the sender (PC2) must use this same regular time interval to decide when it should change the digital electrical signal. For instance, if PC2 varied the voltage to mean either 0 or 1 every .1 seconds, and PC1 sampled the incoming electrical signal every .1 seconds, they could transfer 10 bits in a second. The speed of this network connection would be 10 bits per second.

If the two PCs did not agree on the transmission speed, the devices couldn't transfer the binary information. For instance, imagine that PC2 thought the speed was 10 bits per second, meaning it should encode a new bit every 1/10 of a second. If PC1 thought that it should be receiving a bit 20 times per second, it would sample the incoming electrical signal every 1/20 of a second. PC1 would think it was sending 10 bits each second, and PC2 would think it received 20 bits.

The term *bps* (short for bits per second) often refers to the speed of networking connections. Note that the unit is bits, not bytes. In real life, LANs typically run at much higher speeds, with a slow LAN transmitting at 10 million bits per second (Mbps, also called megabits per second).

Notice that Figure 4-3 represents electricity as a square *waveform*, with positive and negative voltages. You don't really need to worry about the electrical details, but as you progress through learning about networking, you will see other drawings like this one. The networking cards use an alternating current, or AC. The positive voltage means the current is in one direction, and the negative current means the current runs in the opposite direction.

The Need for a Two-Lane (Network) Road

In Figure 4-3, PC2 sends an electrical signal to PC1. As it turns out, if PC1 tried to send some electricity to PC2 at the same time, over the same wire, the electrical signals would overlap, and neither PC1 nor PC2 could understand what was sent.

To solve the problem, PC1 and PC2 need to use two wires—one for PC1 to send bits to PC2, and one for PC2 to send to PC1. Figure 4-4 shows two wires, with PC1 and PC2 sending and receiving at the same time.

Figure 4-4   Concurrent Data Transmission Across Two Different Wires

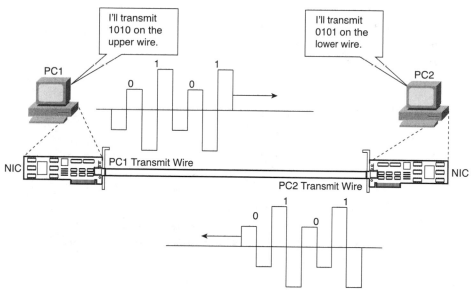

The Equivalent of Asphalt: Cables

You can get in your car and drive around your yard, the sidewalk, in your neighbor's yard, or through the park. Of course, it's better if you drive on the road! The earlier examples in this chapter showed NICs using a single copper wire for data transmission in each direction. But rather than just have a couple of wires somehow stuck into the side of the cards, in real life, we use cabling and connectors to manage the wires, making the job of the electrician much more comfortable and convenient.

The copper wires that networking cards use are encased inside a cable. The cable is made from plastic, with the copper wires inside the cable. Figure 4-5 shows a drawing of the most popular type of cabling used for LANs today.

Figure 4-5   Typical LAN Cable

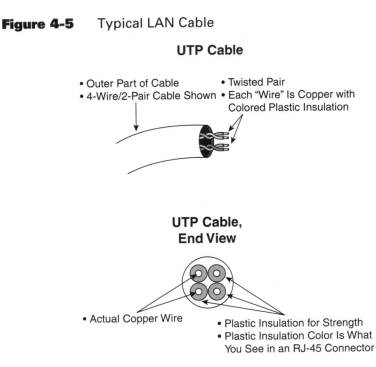

UTP Cable

- Outer Part of Cable
- 4-Wire/2-Pair Cable Shown
- Twisted Pair
- Each "Wire" Is Copper with Colored Plastic Insulation

UTP Cable, End View

- Actual Copper Wire
- Plastic Insulation for Strength
- Plastic Insulation Color Is What You See in an RJ-45 Connector

If you look closely at this figure, you can see each copper wire, as well as the plastic coating on the wire. The copper wire is thin, making it brittle. In fact, the wire could easily break in your hand. To help prevent the wire from breaking, a thin plastic coating is painted onto each wire. Conveniently, each wire uses a different color of plastic coating, so you can look at each end of the cable and figure out which wire is which. As you might guess, and as you will learn more about in the next few pages, it is important that you can identify a particular wire on each end of the cable.

Also note that the wires in Figure 4-5 are twisted together in pairs. Each pair of wires is cleverly called a *twisted pair*. The term refers to a pair of wires twisted around each other to reduce the amount of electrical interface on the wires. In layman's terms, *electromagnetic interference (EMI)* occurs when electrical signals that exist in the air—caused by other wires or other nearby electrically powered devices—change the electrical currents on the wire. If outside EMI changes the signal on the wire, the receiving computer might misinterpret a 0 as a 1 or a 1 as a 0, or it might not have a clue what the sender really sent. Sending the electrical signals over a twisted pair rather than a single wire eliminates a lot of EMI effects. (Besides, the wires are pretty skinny anyway, and copper is cheap, so why not use two?)

Another thing that can be added to the cable to reduce EMI is shielding. Shielding, as the name implies, shields the wires inside the cable from the effects of EMI. However, shielded cabling has more stuff in it, making the cable less bendable and more expensive to produce. Shielded cables are called *shielded twisted pair (STP)*, and you could probably guess that unshielded cables are called *unshielded twisted pair (UTP)*. LAN technology has evolved to the point where less expensive UTP cabling can be used in most environments, with STP cabling being used in environments where significant EMI issues exist. Figure 4-5 showed UTP cabling; Figure 4-6 shows an example of an STP cable.

Figure 4-6   Shielded Twisted Pair (STP) Cabling

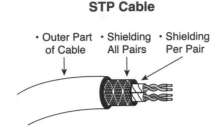

Painting the Lines on the Road: Connectors

Imagine that you see a new road that has just been paved. The road is so new that
the DOT hasn't even painted the lines yet. So, you turn onto the road and enjoy
the ride. After a couple of miles, you look up and see that someone else is on the
road—a huge, speeding truck—and the driver wants to take his half of the road in
the middle of the road. After swerving off the road, you might think to yourself,
"Boy, that reminds me of one of the reasons that you use connectors on the end of
networking cables!"

Okay, that's far fetched, but it does lead into a key point about connectors. If roads
had no lanes, and there were no traffic laws, the roads would be pretty dangerous
so the DOT paints lines on the road to create traffic lanes. Similarly, connectors
line up the wires on the end of a cable into well-defined physical locations inside
the connector. Essentially, each wire in the cable is identified by color, and each
colored wire has a specific reserved place inside the connector that the electrician
attaches to the end of the cable. The connectors put the wires into the right place,
just like the lines on a road guide cars into the right place.

An electrician can take a cable and attach a connector to the end of it. When he
attaches the cable to a connector, each of the wires protrudes into the connector so
that the electricity can flow when connected to a device. The tip of the exposed
wire in the connector is called a pin. A *pin* is nothing more than a physical position
in the end of the connector in which the copper part of the wire sits. You can think
of a pin like you think of a lane on a road. Figure 4-7 shows a photo of a typical
connector, called an ***RJ-45 connector***, along with a drawing of the same connector.

Figure 4-7   Typical Networking Connector (RJ-45)

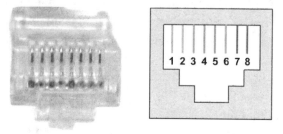

The Telecommunications Industry Association (TIA) and Electrical Industries Alliance (EIA) define standards for cables and connectors. For instance, they define how to use an RJ-45 connector for LANs and options for several types of UTP cabling. (You can learn more about TIA and EIA by going to their websites, at http://www.tiaonline.org and http://www.eia.org.)

If you have never seen an RJ-45 connector, and you use Ethernet LANs at work or school, you could remove the cable from your PC's network card and look at it. In most cases, the cable will be using an RJ-45 connector. (Ethernet is by far the most popular type of LAN today. You'll read more about it in the next several chapters.)

The EIA/TIA defines standards for which wires fit into which pins when you make a cable for use with Ethernet. Two of those standards are shown in Figure 4-8.

Figure 4-8   Pinout Options for RJ-45 Connectors

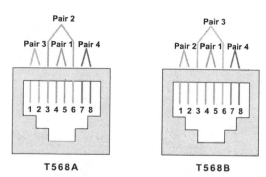

Each of the drawings in the figure represents an RJ-45 connector. The RJ-45 connector allows eight wires to be inserted into it. EIA/TIA standards suggest the numbering schemes for the eight pin locations and the pairs of wires, knowing that a twisted pair is needed for data transmission. The standard also specifies which color of wire goes into pin position 1, 2, and so on.

The RJ-45 connectors have clips on the side that allow you to easily insert the connector into the plug (hole) in the networking card in a computer. At that point, the connector is secure and should stay put. If you push the clip close to the rest of the connector, it releases the connector from the card. So, the clip helps keep the connector secure and allows you to pull the connector out when you are ready.

So, why does all this matter? In the next few pages, it will all come together as you see how NICs try to use the cables and wires.

Driving in the Right Lane (Pair) on the Road

Refer to the simple network of Figure 4-1 early in this chapter. That network consisted of two PCs, each with a networking card, and a cable between them. So far, you've learned the basics about wires, cables, and connectors. However, there's one last important thing about basic LAN data transmission that you need to know, and it relates to which wires are used for actual data transmission by Ethernet LANs.

Ethernet NICs in PCs try to send data over the twisted pair that uses pins 1 and 2 of an RJ-45 connector. These same NICs expect to receive data on the twisted pair that uses pins 3 and 6. However, without the right kind of cabling, two Ethernet NICs cannot communicate. Figure 4-9 depicts the effect when both NICs try to send using the twisted pair that uses pins 1 and 2.

Figure 4-9   Both PCs Using the Same Pair (Lane) to Send Data

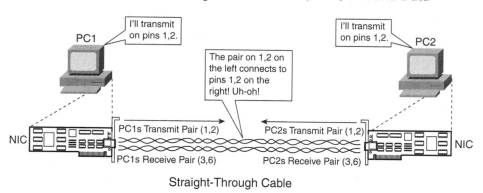

Straight-Through Cable

(Rather than clutter the figure with more cabling, I just drew the two pairs of wires; the wires do indeed sit inside a single cable, with RJ-45 connectors on each end.)

The cable in Figure 4-9 puts one end of a wire in pin 1 of one connector, and the other end into pin 1 of the other connector. Pin 2 on one end of the cable connects to pin 2 on the other side; and so on, for all eight wires. A cable with the wires connected in this manner is called a *straight-through cable*.

Okay, back to the problem illustrated in Figure 4-9. As you can see from the bubbles in the figure, both PC's NICs send on the twisted pair at pins 1 and 2. That electricity goes over the wires and enters the other NIC on pins 1 and 2. But, the NICs aren't receiving data on pins 1 and 2! That's because Ethernet NICs try to send on pins 1 and 2, and they receive data on the pair at pins 3 and 6. In this case, both PCs send, but neither receives data.

The solution is to use a cross-over cable. *Cross-over cables* connect the wire at pin 1 on one end of the cable with pin 3 on the other end; the wire at pin 2 with pin 6 on the other end; the wire at pin 3 with pin 1 at the other side; and the wire at pin 6 with pin 2 at the other side. The result: The PCs can receive the data sent by the other device! Figure 4-10 shows the basic idea.

Figure 4-10   PCs Using Different Pairs (Lanes) to Send Data

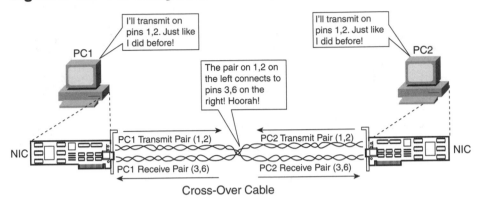

Now you know the basics of how you can allow two PCs to attach to a cable and transfer bits between each other. This chapter focuses on how to build the local network roadway—essentially, the networking components that allow bits to be transferred. Next, you'll read about how to connect several devices on an Ethernet LAN, using a device called a hub.

Sharing the Local Roadway: Ethernet Hubs

An old friend of mine is a native of San Francisco and still lives there. The traffic is horrible there, in part due to the need for lots of people to commute across the San Francisco Bay. There simply aren't enough bridges for the number of cars that need to cross the Bay. His solution: Fill in the Bay with dirt and pave the whole thing. Then there would be plenty of roads to allow people to cross the Bay.

If you tried to connect 10 PCs in a network, using a cross-over cable between NICs (as shown in figure 4-10), you would begin to do the equivalent of paving the San Francisco Bay. You know how two computers can use Ethernet NICs with a cross-over cable to communicate. However, to connect to other PCs, you would need more Ethernet NICs, and your PC probably does not have enough room for all the cards. Also, you would need to run cables between your PC and all the other PCs, or at least get the electrician to run the cables. If you tried to do this for 100 PCs on the same floor of the building, and every PC wanted to connect to every other, you would have 99 cables connected to 99 NICs inside each PC!

The alternative to running a cable to every other PC is to run a cable from each PC to a wiring closet and connect the cables to a networking device, called an Ethernet hub. An *Ethernet hub* provides several functions, but mainly it allows the electrician to cable each device to the hub using only a single NIC and single cable, eliminating the cabling problem. The hub simply listens for incoming electrical signals, and when received, the hub repeats the same electrical signal to every other device that's connected to the hub. Figure 4-11 shows the basic operation.

Figure 4-11   Ethernet Hub Repeats Everything It Hears

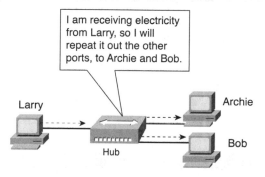

As seen in the figure, Larry sends data to the hub, and the hub repeats what Larry sent out the cables to Archie and Bob. It's that simple!

Figure 4-11 shows cabling, but it does not show which pairs of wires are used. Interestingly, the hub expects straight-though Ethernet cabling between itself and the PCs. Why is that? Well, the people who make hubs, knowing that Ethernet NICs in PCs send on the twisted pair that uses pins 1 and 2 and receive on twisted pair that uses pins 3 and 6, do the opposite. Therefore, a straight-through cable works between a PC NIC and a hub. Figure 4-12 illustrates the concept.

Figure 4-12   Hubs Use Straight-Through Cabling to PCs

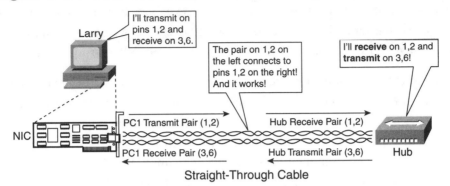

The hub's logic is simple:

1. Receive traffic on pins 1 and 2 on each physical interface.

2. When received, repeat the same electrical signal out all other ports, except the one in which the data was received.

3. When repeating out other ports, repeat the traffic out pins 3 and 6 so that the PCs will be listening.

Dirt Roads Versus the DOT

You can spend a long time working around or in the networking arena and not ever need to worry about how structured cabling works. This section gives you a brief glimpse into the world of structured cabling, just so you know what people are talking about if they bring it up.

You can go to the store and buy premade Ethernet UTP cables with RJ-45 connectors on them. You can even buy a hub—and for not a lot of money, typically less than $20. You could then connect a bunch of computers to the hub using the straight-through Ethernet cables, and voilà, you have a network, or at least the part that allows the computers to send and receive data. Running your own cabling is quick and easy.

In a real network in a real building, you will not typically get away with stringing cables on top of the carpet, over people's cubicles, and so on. Instead, you should allow the electricians to do their job right, which means that the cables will run either under the floor or inside the ceiling. Also, instead of a single cable from a PC to the hub, the equivalent will be created. First, you install a short cable from the PC to a wall plate. The electrician runs another cable from the back of the wall plate to the wiring closet into a patch panel. Finally, either the electrician or the network engineer connects a cable from the patch panel in the wiring closet to the hub. Together, these cables provide two twisted pair between the PC NIC and the hub. Figure 4-13 shows the major components.

Figure 4-13 Major Components of a Structured Wiring Plan

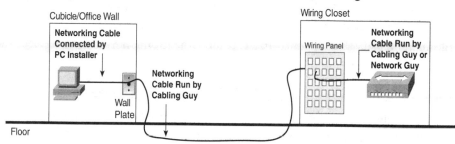

Structured wiring allows the electrician to take care of the difficult part of cabling, with a minimum of cost, effort, and clutter, while still making sure that the cabling works correctly. Even though multiple cables are used, the net result of the cabling simply needs to ensure that the correct twisted pairs end up at the right place in the connectors at the endpoints. And the only cables that the people in the offices can see are the short ones between the PC and the wall plate; the rest of the cables are hidden.

Imagine that if instead of structured wiring, the electrician simply ran a single cable from the computer, under the floor, and straight into the hub in the wiring closet. Later, the person in the cubicle decides that she wants her PC on the left side of her desk, and she might discover that the cable is too short. So what does she do? She calls the electrician and asks for another cable to be run.

Of course, the electrician probably isn't going to want to run a new cable from the cubicle to the wiring closet. If he had used structured wiring, he could have run a cable from the wall plate to the patch panel in the wiring closet. A *patch panel*, sometimes called a *wiring panel*, provides the electrician a place to connect the actual wires in the cable on one side of the panel. On the other side, receptacles, much like the ones in the wall plate in the cubicle, allow the electrician or network engineer to use a short cable to connect those pairs of wires to some other devices, such as the hub shown in Figure 4-13.

Because the patch panel is located in a well-known place, and because the wall plate in the cubicles does not move, the electrician can do the hard part (running the cables under the floor) once. If the PC in the cubicle needs to be moved farther away from the wall, the PC user can get a slightly longer patch cable. A *patch cable* is simply a short LAN cable. Likewise, inside the wiring closet, short patch cables can be used to connect from the patch panel to the networking device, such as the hub shown in Figure 4-13.

You can think of structured wiring as the equivalent of having the DOT build your roads versus just using dirt roads. It takes time, planning, effort, and more cost, but in the end, you have a much better road system. With structured wiring, you end up with much better wiring and far less clutter. Furthermore, you can make changes without a lot of effort.

The benefits of structured cabling can be summarized as follows:

- Helps minimize the need for running new cables because the distance from each wall plate to the wiring panel can be determined easily

- Allows PC installers to run a short patch cable from the wall plate to the PC, without requiring help from the electrician

- Allows network engineers to run a short patch cable from the wiring panel to the networking devices, such as a hub

- Helps keep the wiring closet more organized

Chapter Summary

Computers communicate by transmitting an electrical signal over wires, with differing electrical characteristics meaning binary 0 and binary 1. For effective communication, both transmit and receive paths are needed; with a single path, the electrical signals would overlap, confusing the meaning of both electrical signals. Also, a twisted pair of wires is used for transmission in each direction because a twisted pair reduces the impact of electromagnetic interference on the wires, which in turn reduces transmission errors.

LAN UTP cabling includes up to four twisted pairs of unshielded wires, typically terminated with RJ-45 connectors. Although four pairs are supported, only two pairs are needed for Ethernet LAN communications—one pair for each direction of transmission. Depending on which devices are being connected, you might need a cross-over cable or a straight-through cable, ensuring that the pair used for transmission by one device connects to the pair used for receiving data on the other device.

Ethernet hubs allow multiple devices to connect to it, with the result that all devices receive a copy of whatever each device sends to the hub. By doing so, each device needs a single NIC and a single cable connecting it to the LAN hub, while allowing all devices to communicate with all other devices.

Finally, a structured wiring plan helps prevent unnecessary cabling runs inside the difficult-to-reach parts of the physical location (under the floor or in the ceiling). It also allows other personnel to change cabling later, without involving the electrician.

Chapter Review Questions

You can find the answers to the following questions in Appendix A, "Answers to Chapter Review Questions."

1. Give an example of how a computer might transmit binary 0s and 1s using variations in voltage on a wire.

2. Imagine that two computers are sending and receiving data over a wire. How often would the receiving device need to sample the electrical signal on the wire if the standard called for 20 bps transmission speed?

3. As explained in the chapter, do computers usually transmit data over the same wires they use to receive data? Why or why not?

4. As explained in the chapter, do computers usually transmit data over a single wire, or do they use two wires?

5. How many wires can fit inside the end of an RJ-45 connector?

6. How many wires are needed for a PC to successfully send and receive data to another PC using an Ethernet LAN cable with RJ-45 connectors?

7. Explain why a straight-through LAN cable does not work when connecting two PCs directly, just using the cable.

8. Explain why a cross-over LAN cable *does* work when connecting two PCs directly, just using the cable.

9. Explain why a straight-through LAN cable works when connecting a PC to a hub.

10. What is the main difference between UTP and STP cabling? Which is more popular today?

11. List some of the key benefits of a structured cabling plan.

12. Imagine a hub with ten physical ports, and cables connecting each port to ten different PCs. The hub receives an electrical signal from the PC on port 1. Where does the hub forward the electrical signal?

13. Define the term "pin" in relation to an RJ-45 connector.

What You Will Learn

After reading this chapter, you should be able to

- ✔ Explain the basic rules about when a computer can use an Ethernet LAN

- ✔ List the more important fields inside Ethernet headers and trailers

- ✔ Explain the format of Ethernet LAN addresses

- ✔ Explain how computers use Ethernet addresses as they send and receive data over an Ethernet LAN

- ✔ List the two major branches of Ethernet standards

CHAPTER 5

Rules of the Road: How to Use the Local (Network) Roadway

When the U.S. Department of Transportation (DOT) builds a road, it concerns itself with the physical construction—moving dirt, paving, painting the lines on the road, and so on. However, without traffic laws, too many accidents would happen, and far less traffic would be able to use the road. Everyone needs to know the rules of how to get through an intersection, when to yield to other cars, and how fast you can go. Similarly, with LANs, rules tell you when you can use the LAN, when you should yield by waiting to send data over the LAN, and how fast you can transmit the data. In this chapter, I'll explain the rules of the road for Ethernet LANs.

Preparing for a Trip: How to Make Your Car (Data) "Street Legal"

Before you can drive a car onto a DOT-built, government-owned road, you need to have a registered street-legal car. *Street legal* simply means that the car meets the government's standards for what kinds of cars are allowed on the road. For instance, you can't use a car that goes 230 miles per hour around a racetrack on public roads. Likewise, you can't drive around in a truck with a 40-foot tall trailer behind it because you would almost certainly hit road signs, power lines, and bridges as you tried to pass under them.

Similarly, LANs require that the data sent across the wires in a LAN conform to some rules as well, which you can think of as making the data *street legal*, or *LAN legal*. Like most rules in the networking world, one or more standards define the rules. This book will focus on the world's most popular LAN standard—Ethernet.

Ethernet consists of a set of standards and protocols for LAN communication, as defined by the IEEE. For instance, Ethernet standards define how a network interface card (NIC) should *encode* binary 0s and 1s on a wire by varying the voltage, as discussed in Chapter 4, "How to Build a Local (Network) Roadway." Ethernet standards specify many more details as well, some of which you'll see in this chapter.

LAN-Legal Data: An Ethernet Frame

Before a NIC can send data over a LAN, all the details covered in Chapter 4 must be complete. The LAN must have the proper cabling installed. The NICs must know the electrical encoding scheme used to signal a 0 or a 1. At that point, the computer could ask the NIC to send data, and electrically, the bits could be sent over the LAN.

However, computers can't simply send end user data over the LAN. Before a PC can send the end user data over a LAN, the PC must encapsulate the end user data inside an Ethernet frame. *Encapsulation* refers to the process of taking the data and putting it inside the Ethernet header and trailer.

Encapsulation is similar in concept to putting a letter in an envelope before sending the letter through the postal service. The postal service requires that letters meet certain requirements, and the envelope must have a properly formatted address. The postal service even defines what a properly formatted address looks like. Similarly, Ethernet standards define the headers and trailers so that a NIC can correctly encapsulate the data.

The resulting bunch of bits created by the encapsulation process, including the Ethernet header and trailer, is called an *Ethernet frame*. Figure 5-1 shows an

Ethernet frame, created by encapsulating the data in a header and trailer, for frames sent to Larry from Bob.

Figure 5-1 Ethernet Frame Sent from Bob to Larry

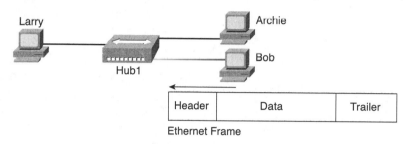

The laws created by government typically do not allow you to ride your bicycle on a superhighway. Likewise, Ethernet does not allow you to send the end user data over the LAN. You must put the data in the proper vehicle—namely, an Ethernet frame. After you put the data into a frame, you can send it across the LAN.

The Ethernet **header** and **trailer** are simply additional bytes of data that are used by the computers, NICs, and networking devices to make the Ethernet work smoothly. For instance, the first 8 bytes in an Ethernet header are called the **preamble**. The preamble contains alternating 1s and 0s so that the NICs receiving the data know that a new frame is being sent across the LAN.

The word **frame** happens to be a particularly important term. Back in Chapter 3, "Building a Network: It All Starts with a Plan," you read about networking standards and how the terms from the OSI model describe networking standards and protocols today. The term "frame" refers to the headers and trailers defined by any Layer 2 standard, as well as the data inside the frame. The term "Ethernet frame" refers to a frame created for use on an Ethernet, conforming to Ethernet protocol specifications.

As you will read in later chapters, protocols that match other OSI layers also have headers, and the networking world uses names besides "frame" to refer to those headers and data.

Throughout this chapter, I will cover more details about what is inside the Ethernet frame header and trailer. To move forward, just think of an Ethernet frame as the car that can actually be sent over the LAN, with the end user data being the equivalent of whomever or whatever is in the car.

Driving Where I Want and When I Want Is Pretty Cool

In real life, it's obvious why you can't just drive anywhere you want, any time you want—you'll have a wreck. Or worse yet, someone else's blatant disregard for the law might cause you to be in a wreck!

Interesting, when you use Ethernet hubs, even if you obey the rules, wrecks (called collisions in Ethernet lingo) occur. A *collision* occurs when two or more frames are sent over a single twisted pair at the same point in time. The result is that none of the frames is intelligible. However, it's better to avoid the collisions if possible. So, Ethernet defines some rules of the road—rules that say when you can use the LAN and when you can't—and what to do if you have a wreck.

Why Wrecks (Collisions) Happen on Ethernet

Even if you obey all the laws of the land, you can still have a wreck. Likewise, even when all devices follow Ethernet rules, wrecks or collisions can happen. To understand why, focus on these two key facts:

- When two or more electrical signals travel over the same pair, both electrical signals are distorted and become a single signal. The receiving device cannot interpret the signal as 0s and 1s.

- A hub repeats received electrical signals out all other physical ports on the hub, except the one in which the signal was received, even if other electrical signals are already being repeated.

Knowing those two facts, consider what happens in Figure 5-2, when both Bob and Archie send an Ethernet frame to Larry at the same time.

Figure 5-2   Collision Between Bob's and Archie's Frames

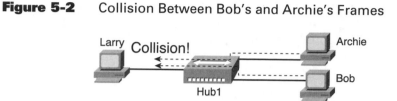

The hub blindly repeats each of the frames sent by Bob and Archie out all other ports, including the one connected to Larry. Although both Bob and Archie wanted to send data to Larry, Larry can't understand either frame because the hub is trying to send both electrical signals over the cable to Larry at the same time.

How to Avoid Most Wrecks

Ethernet standards define a basic algorithm that helps reduce collisions, as well as defining what to do when collisions occur. The algorithm is called the *carrier sense multiple access collision detect (CSMA/CD)* algorithm. Boy, there's a fun trivia question for your next party, huh?

The name CSMA/CD is not as important as the ideas behind it. First, the algorithm starts with this simple concept:

> Listen before sending, and wait until you are not receiving a frame before you try to send your frame.

The concept is pretty simple. Imagine that you are connected to a hub, and you are currently receiving a frame. What would happen if you sent a frame at that time? Well, you would cause a collision. So why not just wait a moment? Well, that's exactly what the algorithm calls for. Figure 5-3 shows the basic logic, with Bob waiting on Larry to finish sending his frame before sending his own frame.

Figure 5-3   Collision Avoidance by Listening Before Sending

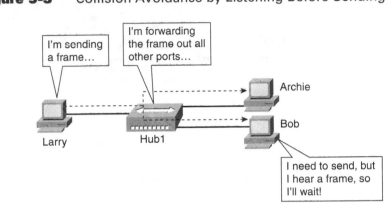

What to Do When a Wreck Happens

Even when you're using CSMA/CD, collisions can still occur. Why? Well, consider this same example, but unbeknownst to Bob, Archie was also waiting for Larry to finish sending his frame before sending a frame. So, Larry's frame has finished, and the LAN is silent. Figure 5-4 shows both Bob's and Archie's logic.

Figure 5-4   An Imminent and Unavoidable Collision

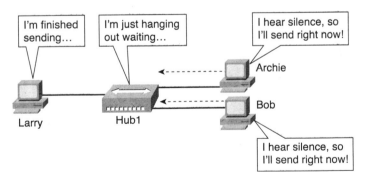

Ethernet standards state that when no one is sending anything, the LAN is silent—in other words, there is no electricity flowing over the wires. Both Bob and Archie

realize that Larry is finished when they stop receiving an electrical signal. So, they both try to send their frames at roughly the same time, because they both realize at roughly the same time that the LAN is silent. And as was shown in Figure 5-2, when Bob and Archie both send at the same time, a collision occurs.

The hub will repeat both frames out to Larry, so Larry will know about the collision. However, the hub won't forward Bob's frame back to Bob or Archie's frame back to Archie, so both Bob and Archie will only be receiving one frame. With the logic discussed so far, Bob and Archie won't know there's a collision! To make sure Bob and Archie know when a collision happens, when a NIC transmits a frame, the NIC also connects what it sends to its own receive pair, right on the card. This bit of hardware is called a *loopback circuit*, and it simply means that the NIC receives its own frame as well.

By using loopback, when Bob sends a frame, he receives the same electrical signal that he sends. When Archie sends a frame at the same time, the hub forwards Archie's frame to Bob—and now Bob knows there is a collision.

So, what do you do when the collision occurs? CSMA/CD suggests the following:

- The senders of the collided frames send a jamming signal to make sure everyone knows a collision has occurred.

- The senders of the collided frames independently pick a random timer value.

- Each sender waits until his own random timer has expired and then tries to send his frames again.

The *jamming signal* is an electrical signal that Ethernet standards specify to let everyone know "Hey, a collision has occurred, so let's clean it up." Next, by having both Bob and Archie wait before trying to send again, but with each of them choosing his own random number for the timer, Bob and Archie should not try to send again at the same time.

So far in this chapter, you have learned that computers send Ethernet frames—which include the Ethernet header, trailer, and end user data—over an Ethernet LAN. You have also learned how CSMA/CD regulates when the LAN is used, much like traffic laws dictate when a road is used. So, enough of this discussion of how to get data across the LAN. Now, let's think about what happens when the frame actually gets to the destination.

Stopping at the Destination: What Happens When Someone Comes to See You

When using an Ethernet with a hub, everyone gets a copy of every frame—that's just a side effect of the fact that the hub repeats incoming frames out all other ports on the hub. You might recall that a hub does this to allow each computer's NIC to have a single cable connecting it to the hub, while still being able to communicate with all other devices on the LAN.

In the second half of this chapter, I'll explain Ethernet from the perspective of the computer receiving the frame, and along the way, I'll talk a little more about what's inside the header and trailer of an Ethernet frame.

Are They Coming to Our House or the Neighbor's House?

In an Ethernet LAN with a hub, a computer receives a lot of Ethernet frames, but only some of them contain data that is meant for that computer. For instance, Larry might need to send data to Bob, but because of the hub's behavior, both Archie and Bob get a copy of the frame.

Now, consider the case when Larry wants to send data to Bob. Both Bob and Archie receive the frame, but Archie should simply ignore the frame, and Bob should examine the data and process it. But how do Archie and Bob know? Well, before Larry sends the frame, he puts Bob's *Ethernet address* into a field in the Ethernet header called the *destination address field*. By putting Bob's Ethernet address in the destination address field of the header, Bob can use the logic shown in Figure 5-5.

Figure 5-5   How Bob Decides the Frame Was Sent to Him

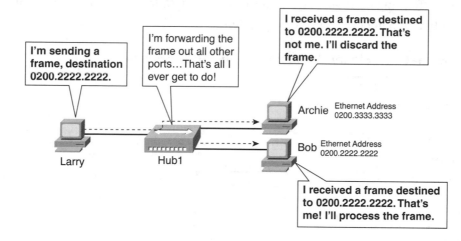

The logic is simple. Each NIC has a unique Ethernet address, which is put onto the NIC by the NIC manufacturer. The sender just puts the correct Ethernet address in the header, so when another NIC receives the frame, it can decide whether to process the frame or ignore it.

The Ethernet header includes both a *source address field* and a destination address field. For instance, Larry included his own Ethernet address in the source address field of the frame in Figure 5-5. Of course, Larry put Bob's Ethernet address into the destination address field.

Ethernet standards specify that addresses be 48 bits long (6 bytes). You can write down Ethernet addresses as binary numbers, but writing down 48 binary 0s and 1s can be a pain in the neck. The creators of Ethernet could have decided to record Ethernet addresses as decimal numbers, but as it turns out, converting between decimal and binary isn't that easy to do. However, there's a better way to represent binary numbers by using fewer digits: *hexadecimal* (*hex*). Hex is an alternative numbering system, similar to decimal and binary. With decimal, you have 10 numerals (0, 1, 2, and so on, through 9). With hexadecimal, the numerals are 0, 1, 2, 3, 4, 5, 6, 7, 8, 9, A, B, C, D, E, F. Essentially, A represents decimal 10, B represents decimal 11, and so on, with F representing decimal 15.

Hex can be used easily to represent binary numbers. In fact, a single hex digit can represent four binary digits. For instance, Table 5-1 shows each combination of a 4-digit binary number and its hex equivalent.

Table 5-1   Binary Numbers and Their Hex Equivalents

Four-Digit Binary Number	Hex Number
0000	0
0001	1
0010	2
0011	3
0100	4
0101	5
0110	6
0111	7
1000	8
1001	9
1010	A
1011	B
1100	C
1101	D
1110	E
1111	F

Although there's a lot more to hex, you don't really have to understand how hex numbering works to appreciate why it is used for Ethernet addresses. Instead of writing down Ethernet addresses as 48-digit binary numbers, you can write them as 12-digit hex numbers because each hex digit represents 4 binary digits. For instance, if the first 4 binary digits of an Ethernet address were 0010, then the first hex digit would be a 2. If the next 4 binary digits were 1010, the next hex digit would be A, and so on.

When you see a hex number, just know that each hex digit represents four binary digits. For example, when you're using gear from Cisco Systems, the device will list Ethernet addresses in the following format:

15CD.3412.5BDA

0200.2222.2222

Note that the numbers have 12 hex digits, so they each represent a 48-bit binary number.

Who Is It, Honey?

If someone drives up your street and stops in the driveway, you're probably curious about whom it is. Likewise, when someone sends you data over a LAN, you might want to know who sent the data.

With Ethernet, the Ethernet header includes a source address field in addition to the destination address field. The *source address* identifies the Ethernet address of the NIC that sent the frame. Figure 5-6 shows an example, listing the addresses for all three PC's NICs, as well as the basic logic used.

Figure 5-6   Ethernet Source and Destination Addresses

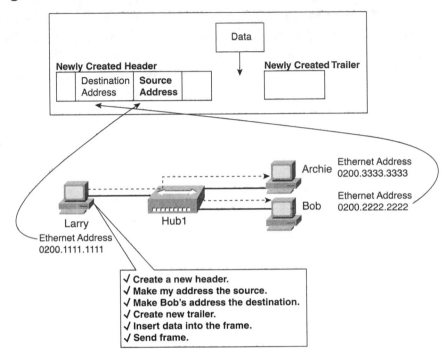

Before sending a frame, Larry adds the Ethernet header and trailer to the data. He puts his own Ethernet address in the source address field of the header and the destination's Ethernet address (Bob again in this case) in the destination address field. After Larry assembles the frame, he can use CSMA/CD logic to determine when he can send the frame.

Also note that Figure 5-6 shows the typical style in which to show a frame, with the header on the left and the trailer on the right. When sending the frame, a NIC sends the bits starting with the header and ending with the trailer, regardless of how it happens to be drawn in a figure.

I Don't Understand a Thing You're Saying

So, someone drives up to your house and parks in your driveway. (Why do we park in driveways, and drive on parkways, anyway?) The person comes up to the door, rings the bell, and you answer it. The stranger smiles and confidently says, "Jwl! Sfk oewp fkas lal. Wwjj. KK45i!!!" Of course, this makes no sense to you, so you ask the visitor to repeat himself, after which he says, "Hi, I'm Archie. If you're Bob, you just won our grand prize of $1 billion." "Oh my! Yes, I am Bob. Please come in."

With Ethernet, a similar process occurs for recognizing that a received frame makes no sense. When the receiving NIC interprets the incoming electrical signal as meaning some string of binary 0s and 1s, the receiver might misinterpret the meaning. That can happen because the electrical signal has changed as it passed over the wire, affected by resistance in the wire, EMI, collisions, and other factors. Simply put, the sender might send a 1 and the receiver might think it was a 0, or vice versa.

To recognize the error, Ethernet uses a field in the Ethernet trailer called the *frame check sequence (FCS)* field. The FCS field holds a 4-byte number that allows the receiver to notice that the frame that it received actually had bit errors in it.

To check for errors, the receiver must rely on the value of the FCS field as set by the sender. The sender runs a mathematical formula, with the input being the contents of the Ethernet frame to be sent, up to the Ethernet trailer. The sender places the results of the formula into the trailer FCS field. Upon receipt of the frame, the receiver applies the same formula to the same part of the Ethernet frame (everything up to the trailer). If the result of the formula as calculated by the receiving NIC is the same as the value in the transmitted FCS, then no errors occurred. If the values do not match, then an error has occurred. Figure 5-7 outlines the process.

Figure 5-7 How the FCS Field Is Used

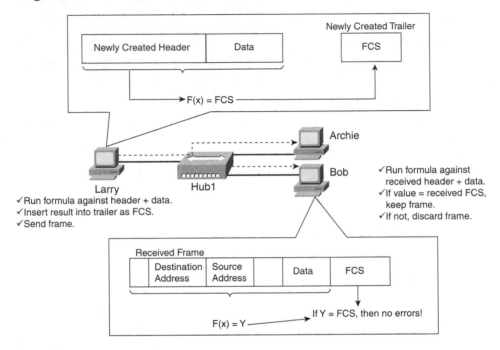

The details of how FCS fields work might be interesting, but the reaction of the receiver of the frame is more important. Ethernet standards specify that the receiver should simply discard frames that have errors. End of story. The receiver does not request that the frame be re-sent, and the sender does not know that the frame was in error. This simple process is called *error detection*.

A related concept, *error recovery*, refers to the process whereby the receiver requests that the sender retransmit the frames that did not pass the FCS check. For example, the Transmission Control Protocol (TCP), as explained in Chapter 3, performs error recovery, but Ethernet does not.

In a way, Ethernet and TCP complement each other. Ethernet defines how to deliver data across the LAN, plus how to perform error detection, with an end result of discarding errored frames. If error recovery is needed, TCP will recognize that some of the data is missing and perform error recovery.

Now you know the basics of how Ethernet works, but you haven't heard much about the standards behind all these concepts. The next section covers some of these standards.

Two Standards for Ethernet

Ethernet was originally created in the 1970s by Robert Metcalfe and some others working for Xerox corporation in Palo Alto, California. They got Intel involved, convincing them to put Ethernet logic on a computer chip, making the mass production of Ethernet cards less expensive. They also got Digital Equipment Corporation (Digital), the second-largest computer maker at the time, to support Ethernet. So, the original standard, as defined by those companies, came to be called ***DIX Ethernet***, using the first letters of those three companies in the name. That standard is also known as ***Ethernet Version 2***; the final version created by these three companies was the second version of their Ethernet protocol specifications.

Later, in the 1980s, the IEEE created committees to standardize evolving LAN standards. Basically, the IEEE took work-in-progress on Ethernet and a couple of other types of LANs, made changes, and approved the new specifications as a standard.

Because the IEEE was standardizing several LAN standards at the same time, it noticed that several functions on each type of LAN were similar. So, to create the standards, the IEEE created a committee to define the Ethernet standards and protocols that were unique to Ethernet. It created another committee to establish standards and protocols that are shared between Ethernet and several other types of LANs. The IEEE named the committee for Ethernet-specific standards the ***802.3 committee***, and it called the committee that defined common LAN features the ***802.2 committee***. The 802.3 standard is also called ***Media Access Control (MAC)***, and the 802.2 standard is also called ***Logical Link Control (LLC)***.

In this chapter, you read about several fields that were either in the Ethernet header or trailer. Figure 5-8 shows the header defined by 802.3 and 802.2, as well as the trailer, as defined by 802.3.

Figure 5-8   IEEE Ethernet Headers and Trailers

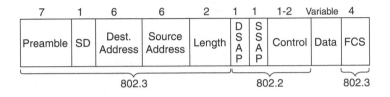

I did not explain all the fields inside the headers in this chapter, but several of the fields should look familiar. First, notice that the header begins with a part labeled as 802.3, followed by a part labeled 802.2. Each committee defined different functions, and for those functions, each committee needed a header in which to put some useful information.

The 802.3 part of the header contains several interesting fields. The source and destination Ethernet address fields are in the 802.3 (MAC) header. Because of that, Ethernet addresses are often called *MAC addresses*. Also, the FCS field is in the 802.3 trailer. At the beginning of the header, the preamble (7 bytes) is shown, with a 1-byte starting delimiter (SD) field. (Remember: The preamble is just a bunch of alternating 1s and 0s, meaning that there's a new frame on the LAN.)

The original DIX Ethernet specifications used an 8-byte preamble field. When the IEEE changed the DIX Ethernet standard, it simply renamed the eighth byte of the preamble to *starting delimiter*, with no change in the value of the field. The first 8 bytes are still a bunch of alternating 1s and 0s.

You don't really need to memorize where things are inside the header or trailer, but it is useful to look at the format of the headers and trailers and see the fields that the protocols use. The rest of the fields in the figure, although useful, simply didn't make the cut for things to put in this book.

Chapter Summary

Building an Ethernet LAN using a hub significantly reduces the cabling effort required, while allowing all devices that are attached to the hub to communicate with all other devices. However, the hub does allow collisions to occur.

The CSMA/CD algorithm defines how to reduce collisions and how to react when collisions occur. A NIC first listens and then sends only when the LAN is silent. If a collision does occur, all NICs that were sending frames wait for a random time and then try to send their frames again.

Ethernet standards define the details of an Ethernet header and trailer that encapsulates the data before being sent over the network. The IEEE defines an 802.3 header, as well as an 802.2 header, with a single trailer defined by the 802.3 committee.

The header defines a source and destination Ethernet address, each 6 bytes in length. When a computer receives an Ethernet frame, it must first look at the destination address of the frame to see if it matches the Ethernet address of its own NIC. If the addresses match, the frame was sent to that device. The receiver can look at the source Ethernet address, which is typically most useful when replying to whatever is inside the data. The receiver must also check the FCS field to ensure that the frame did not experience errors during transmission.

Chapter Review Questions

You can find the answers to the following questions in Appendix A, "Answers to Chapter Review Questions."

1. Complete this sentence: "Before sending end user data over an Ethernet LAN, the sender must _____ the data in an Ethernet _____."

2. Name the three general parts of an Ethernet frame.

3. Imagine that PC1 has built an Ethernet frame, and it is ready to send the frame. What should PC1 do before sending the frame?

4. What does the "CD" in CSMA/CD stand for?

5. Imagine that PC1 and PC2 send a frame at the same time, and the frames collide. Which one sends the jamming signal?

6. Imagine that PC1 and PC2 send a frame at the same time, and the frames collide. How does the CSMA/CD algorithm minimize the chances that PC1 and PC2's frames might collide the next time they attempt to send the frames?

7. How many bytes are in a source Ethernet address? A destination Ethernet address?

8. Imagine that PC1 sends an Ethernet frame to PC2, but that PC3 and PC4 also get a copy, as a side effect of how a hub works. How does PC3 know to ignore the data in the frame?

9. List the IEEE committee that standardized Ethernet-specific details of Ethernet. Use both the numeric name and the three-word text name.

10. List the IEEE committee that standardized Ethernet details that are in common with other types of LANS. Use both the numeric name and the three-word text name.

11. If you were using a networking device from Cisco Systems, and you saw the output of a command that displayed a MAC address, how would it be formatted? Give an example, assuming that all digits in the actual MAC address are 1.

12. What does the acronym FCS stand for?

13. Imagine that PC1 sends a frame to PC2, and PC2 notices that the FCS sent with the frame is different from the value calculated by PC2. What should PC2 do?

14. Explain the difference between error detection and error recovery. Which does Ethernet perform?

What You Will Learn

After reading this chapter, you should be able to

✔ Explain the basic operation of a LAN switch

✔ Describe how LAN switches can eliminate collisions

✔ Explain why LAN switches allow for more throughput in a LAN, as compared to a hub

✔ Describe the conditions under which full duplex operations can be allowed, and describe the advantages of full duplex operation

✔ List the different speeds that Ethernet supports

CHAPTER 6

Reducing Congestion and Driving Faster on the Local (Network) Roadway

So far in this book, I've explained how you can build a small Ethernet with two computers by using a single cable, or build a larger Ethernet by cabling lots of devices to a single Ethernet hub. From what you've read so far, if you have more than two devices, using a hub is the way to go. However, there are some performance issues when using hubs, particularly when you need to send a lot of traffic over the LAN. This chapter explains more about how LANs are created today, using devices called switches. *LAN switches* overcome the performance problems with hubs, allowing much more traffic to pass across the LAN in the same time period.

Another more obvious way to make a LAN support more traffic is to send the traffic more quickly. This chapter ends with some coverage of the versions of Ethernet that simply run faster than the original 10 Mbps Ethernet specifications.

Reducing Congestion by Opening Up More Lanes on Each LAN

When you're using a hub, only one device can transmit data at any one point in time. With a switch, multiple devices can transmit at the same time, increasing the amount of data that can be sent over the LAN. All you have to do is replace the antiquated hub with a LAN switch.

Why is this true? Well, stay tuned—that's what most of the first section of this chapter is about! First, I'll explain why hubs only allow one device to send at a point in time; then I'll explain how a switch overcomes that problem.

Hubs: A One-Lane Road

To appreciate the potential traffic congestion problems when using an Ethernet hub, you need to review a couple of key facts. First, consider the logic used by a hub:

> Hub: When I receive an electrical signal, I repeat it out all ports, except the port in which the signal was received.

That's how a hub operates. Now add to that the logic that NICs use in the PCs that are attached to the hub. Those PCs use carrier sense multiple access collision detect (CSMA/CD) logic, the first part of which is as follows:

> PC: Listen before sending. If you're currently receiving a frame, wait until it is finished before you try to send your frame.

With these two facts combined, any time a device sends a frame, all other devices receive the frame. That means that those other devices choose not to send at the same time. Figure 6-1 illustrates the point.

As seen in the figure, Fred's frame is passing over the cable to the hub, and the hub repeats the frame out all other ports—including the one connected to Betty. Due to CSMA/CD logic—which is useful logic because it prevents collisions— Betty must wait even though she simply wants to send a frame to Wilma. It's like paving a beautiful wide road and only having one lane, so everyone must wait until one car finishes driving past before the next car can use the road.

Figure 6-1   Betty Waiting on Fred's Frame That Was Sent to Barney

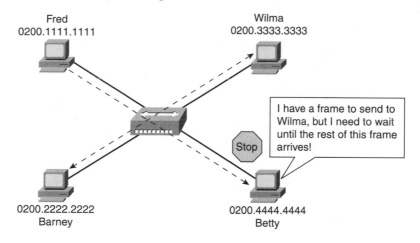

Switches: How to Create Dozens of Lanes on the LAN

LAN switches provide the same cabling advantage that hubs do, while providing significant performance improvements. For example, you can run a single cable from each device to the wiring closet and connect those cables to a switch instead of a hub. You get much better cable management.

To appreciate why switches perform better than hubs, you need to consider the logic that a switch uses and compare it to the logic that a hub uses. A switch allows every device on the LAN to communicate with every other device—the same result as when using a hub—but using different logic, which is summarized as follows:

> When receiving a frame, examine the destination Ethernet address. Forward the frame out the one port—and only that port—through which that address can be reached.

So, in comparison to a hub, a switch does not simply repeat the electrical signal out all other ports. Instead, a switch forwards frames selectively—only forwarding the frame where it really needs to go. Switch logic actually examines the contents of the Ethernet frame and finds the destination Ethernet MAC address to make an intelligent decision. Figure 6-2 illustrates the logic, with Fred sending to Barney.

Figure 6-2   Switch Logic for Fred's Frame Sent to Barney

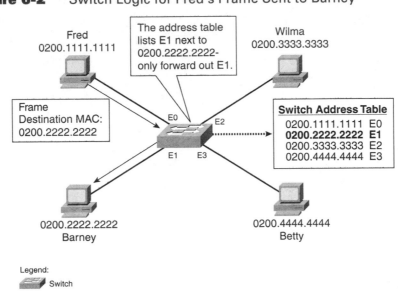

Figure 6-2 shows the same PCs and cables as were in Figure 6-1, but Figure 6-2 shows a switch instead of a hub. In fact, in real life, you can do that same thing: Simply replace a hub with a switch, and use the same cables. The switch still uses a twisted pair for transmission and another for receiving traffic in each cable. It uses the same pinouts in the RJ-45 connector. The switch receives on pins 1 and 2 and transmits on pins 3 and 6, just like a hub—meaning that you need a straight-through cable between the switch and each computer. So, the physical details can remain the same.

The difference between switches and hubs lies in how they choose to forward traffic. To make a *forwarding decision*, a switch uses a table that lists the MAC addresses in the network. As shown in Figure 6-2, the table tells the switch where Barney's MAC address, 0200.2222.2222, sits in the network. So, when the switch receives a frame whose destination is 0200.2222.2222, the switch forwards the frame out port E1—and port E1 only. This table can be called many things; in this book, I'll refer to it as either the *switching table* or the *MAC address table*.

You can think of the MAC address table as a road sign and the switch as an intersection. The switch looks at the road sign and compares it to the destination of the frame (destination MAC address). The road sign gives the directions—which turn, or *switch port*, to take—so the switch can forward the frame appropriately.

LAN switching logic improves LAN performance in part because the frame is not repeated to every computer that is attached to the switch. Notice that unlike Figure 6-1, Betty and Wilma do not receive the frame in Figure 6-2. Betty still uses CSMA/CD logic, which begins with the "Listen first, and wait if you are currently receiving a frame" logic. However, because Betty is not receiving a frame, if she had a frame to send to Wilma, she could indeed send, as shown in Figure 6-3.

Figure 6-3 Fred Sending to Barney, While Betty Sends to Wilma

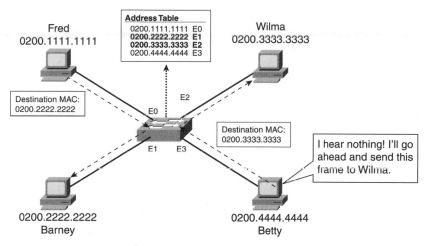

This example shows two devices—Fred and Betty—sending a frame at the same time. With a hub, only one device could send at a time. With two devices sending at the same time, the capacity of the LAN to forward frames doubles!

The original Ethernet specifications define a 10-Mbps transmission rate. In Figure 6-3, two separate transmissions occur, each at 10 Mbps. In one way of thinking, this LAN has 20 Mbps of capacity because it allows two concurrent transmissions at 10 Mbps. Now imagine a switch with 24 ports, with the device on port 1 sending to the device on port 2; the device on port 3 sending to the device on port 4; and so on. All 12 of the odd-numbered ports are sending frames in this case, so this switch supports 12 × 10 Mbps, or 120 Mbps, of capacity.

By using a switch instead of a hub, multiple devices can send at the same time, vastly increasing overall traffic capacity.

The Perfect Roadway: No Wrecks Allowed!

In real life, it would be great if somehow you could drive your car as fast as you like, never have to stop at traffic lights, get where you are going easily, and never have a wreck. It almost sounds like something out of a bad science fiction movie, but with switches, the equivalent does occur—you can create a world without collisions.

With the switch logic you have learned about so far, multiple devices can send, but the example had the guys (Fred and Barney) talking and the gals (Betty and Wilma) talking. What if everyone wanted to talk (send) to Fred at the same time? Figure 6-4 shows the potential problem.

Figure 6-4   Potential Collision When Forwarding Multiple Frames onto the Same Pair

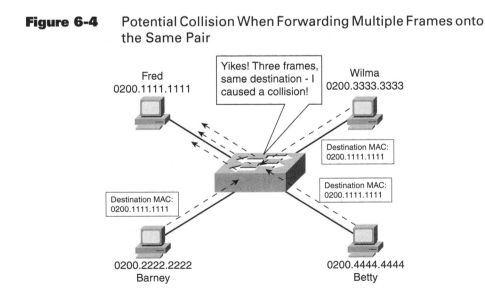

With what you've learned about switches so far, the switch would try to forward all three frames, which would cause a collision. However, to avoid sending all three frames at the same time, the switch uses buffers. *Buffers* consist of memory inside the switch that is used to store frames temporarily. The switch sends one frame, and it keeps the other two frames in buffers. After the switch finishes sending the first frame, it gets one of the frames from the buffers and sends it. Finally, the switch grabs the third frame from the buffer and sends it. By doing so, the switch usually avoids causing a collision. Figure 6-5 illustrates the same logic.

Figure 6-5 Switch Avoids Collisions by Buffering the Frames

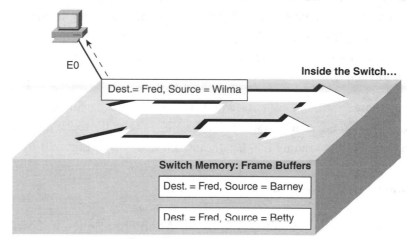

So, the litany of switch logic now reads like this:

- When receiving a frame, examine the destination Ethernet address. Forward the frame out the one port—and only that port—through which that address can be reached.

- If multiple frames need to be sent out the same port, send one frame and buffer the rest, sending them when the port becomes available.

By buffering frames, switches do not create collisions. The original frames make it across the LAN with minimal buffering delay. For instance, if those three frames were each 1250 bytes long, it would only take 3 milliseconds (.003 seconds) for all three to be sent over the cable from the switch to Fred. If collisions had occurred, each frame would have taken longer to reach Fred, and both the collision and the time taken to resend the frames could have prevented other user traffic from crossing the LAN. So, the buffering of frames definitely improves LAN performance.

Using Full Duplex: Making the Streets Two Way

The network interface cards (NICs) in the computers in this chapter still use CSMA/CD logic. In most cases, because the switch forwards frames only out the right destination port, most of the PCs simply weren't receiving frames the majority of the time. With CSMA/CD, if you are not receiving a frame, it's okay for you to go ahead and send. The switch avoids collisions by buffering the frame if the output port is busy.

However, there is still one case for which a computer NIC, using CSMA/CD, believes it should not send. That's when the NIC is actually receiving a frame. Imagine that Fred is sending another frame to Barney, as in Figure 6-6. Barney wants to send a frame. (In this case, Barney wants to send a frame to Fred, but the destination does not really matter in this scenario.)

Figure 6-6   Barney Waiting to Send, When Fred Sends to Barney

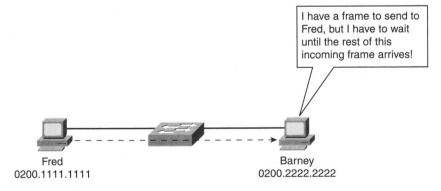

With Barney's CSMA/CD logic enabled, he must wait before sending a frame. However, physically, there is a single cable between Barney and the switch. No collisions can occur on that cable because Barney sends on the pair using pins 1 and 2, and the switch sends to Barney on the pair using pins 3 and 6. And you already know that the switch will buffer any frames, rather than cause a collision, so there is truly no danger of a collision.

In this particular case, Barney chooses not to send the frame to Fred because his CSMA/CD logic tells Barney to wait. But if Barney sent the frame, he wouldn't cause a collision. The solution: Barney's NIC must suspend its CSMA/CD logic. By disabling CSCMA/CD logic, Barney can send and receive at the same instant in time as receiving the frame from Fred. The ability to send and receive at the same time is called *full duplex*. (The CSMA/CD imposed restriction of only sending or only receiving at one point in time is called *half duplex*.) Figure 6-7 shows the result with full duplex enabled on both Barney and Fred.

Figure 6-7   Barney and Fred Sending and Receiving at the Same Time—Full Duplex

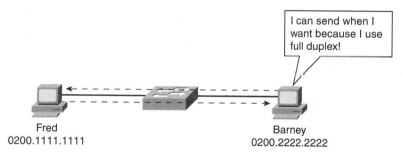

This section started by making an analogy that a hub was like a one-lane road, and that you had to wait until the other car passed before you could use the road. With switches and full duplex enabled, the LAN works like you have a two-lane road between the switch and each device, plus another two-lane road between each port on the switch. The switch plays traffic cop, preventing collisions simply by buffering frames. Figure 6-8 illustrates the basic idea.

Figure 6-8   Full Duplex and Full Switching

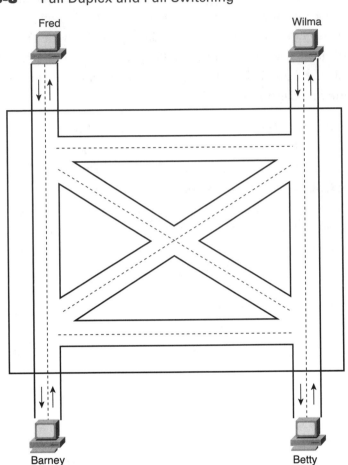

Now that you understand why LAN switches perform better than hubs, you can appreciate why most Ethernet LANs today use switches. However, this chapter hasn't covered everything about how switches work yet. In the next section, you'll read a more thorough description of how switches work.

Switches: The Rest of the Story

In the previous section, the switch had a MAC address table, and it made its decisions about where to forward the frames based on that table. However, you don't yet know how the table got into the switch, or whether the information is accurate. Also, what happens when the switch gets a frame, and the destination MAC address isn't in the MAC address table? Simply put, you haven't seen all the details yet, so in this next section, I'll fill in the holes in the story. First, you'll read about how a switch learns the entries to put in the MAC address table. You'll also read about what a switch does when it doesn't yet have an entry for a particular MAC address. Note: the terms MAC address table and Bridging Table are synonymous

Painting the Road Signs: Learning MAC Addresses

Switches forward frames based on the destination MAC address in the frame. But how does the switch figure out what should be in the MAC address table in the first place? Well, as it turns out, switches dynamically learn MAC addresses and the corresponding ports. This process of learning MAC addresses, according to switch experts, is cleverly called *learning*.

Figure 6-9 shows the familiar old network with Fred and the gang. However, at Step 1, the switch has no entries in the MAC address table. This is typical when the switch first powers up.

Figure 6-9   Learning by Listening—A Great Life Lesson

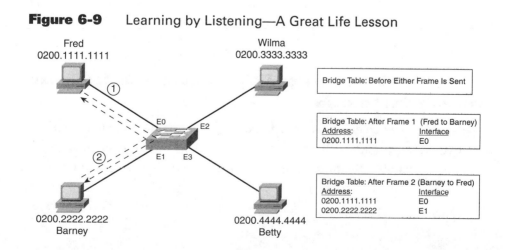

The switch learns the MAC address of the sender of each frame by examining the source MAC address. Whenever a NIC sends an Ethernet frame, the NIC places its own MAC address into the frame as the source MAC address. Figure 6-9 shows two frames: one sent by Fred and one sent by Barney. The following list describes what happens in the switch as a result of each frame:

1. When Fred sends a frame, the frame contains Fred's MAC address (0200.1111.1111) in the source address field of the Ethernet header. The switch knows that the MAC address of whoever sent the frame should be in the source address field. So, the switch believes MAC address 0200.1111.1111 is connected to the port in which the switch received the frame—port E0 in this case. The switch simply adds 0200.1111.1111 to the MAC address table, and it associates port E0 with that MAC address.

2. When Barney sends a frame, the switch learns Barney's MAC address (0200.2222.2222) by looking at the source address of the frame that Barney sent. The switch associates that MAC address with port E1 because that's the port in which the frame was received.

The Forward Versus Filter Decision

Switch pundits refer to the basic logic of how a switch forwards frames as the *forward versus filter decision*. Simply put, when a switch receives a frame, it sends the frame out one port, based on a comparison of the destination MAC address and the MAC address table. That is considered to be a *forwarding decision*. Conversely, by not sending the frame out other ports, the switch has simply filtered the frame from exiting those ports, which is a *filtering decision*.

What to Do When the Road Sign (Address Table) Doesn't List Your Destination

What should a switch do with a frame that is sent before the switch has learned the MAC address table? Well, in short, the switch performs a function called flooding. Essentially, *flooding* means that when the switch receives a frame whose destination address is not in the MAC address table, the switch forwards the frame out all ports except the one in which the frame was received.

note

Docs that switch flooding logic sound familiar? It should. It's the same effect as what a hub does, all the time. So, sometimes people refer to a hub's behavior as flooding as well.

Figure 6-10 shows the same familiar network, this time focusing on the first frame Fred sent to Barney, before the switch knew where Barney's MAC address resided.

Figure 6-10   Switch Logic for Unknown Destinations

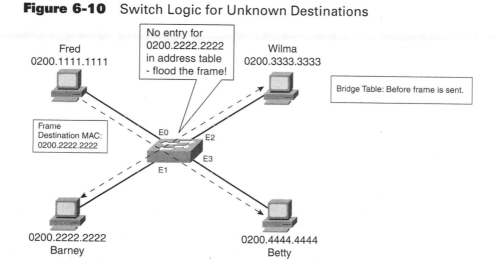

As shown in the figure, the switch floods the frame, so Barney, Wilma, and Betty all get a copy. Barney replies, and at that point, the switch table has an entry for Barney's MAC address. Therefore, any future frames sent to Barney will be forwarded correctly.

How to Go Everywhere at the Same Time

So far, when discussing MAC addresses (in other words, Ethernet addresses), I have always implied that a MAC address represented an individual NIC attached to a LAN. Well, it is true that many MAC addresses represent individual NICs. Addresses that represent an individual NIC are called *unicast MAC addresses*.

Ethernet also defines a special MAC address, called the *broadcast address*. The Ethernet broadcast address is FFFF.FFFF.FFFF. When a computer sends a frame with a destination address of FFFF.FFFF.FFFF, it means that the frame should be forwarded to all devices on the LAN.

So, imagine that a switch receives a frame, a frame whose destination MAC address is the broadcast address. What should it do? The switch simply floods the frame out all ports (except the port in which it was received), as shown in Figure 6-11.

Figure 6-11   Switch Flood Broadcast Frames

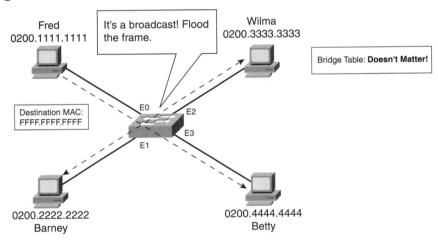

Summary of Switch Logic

Throughout this chapter, you've learned several points about how a switch works. Before you move on to the last section of this chapter, it's worthwhile to review the key points:

- Switches decide where to forward frames by comparing the destination address of the frame to the MAC address table.

- Switches build the entries in the MAC address table by looking at the source MAC address of frames they receive.

- The forward versus filter decision simply means that the switch forwards the frame out only the required ports (forwarding) and does not forward (in other words, it filters) the frame from being sent out other ports.

- The switch floods frames that are sent to unknown unicast addresses; unknown unicast addresses are unicast addresses that the switch has not added to its MAC address table yet.

- The switch floods frames sent to the broadcast address.

- Switches avoid collisions by buffering frames instead of trying to send multiple frames out the same twisted pair at the same time.

I Feel the Need, the Need for Speed

When the IEEE took over Ethernet standards development from Xerox in the early 1980s, Ethernet used a 10-Mbps transmission rate. Whether you were using a hub or a switch, when it came down to the actual transmission of data, the bits crossed the wires at 10 Mbps.

Over the years, the IEEE has created many enhancements to the Ethernet standards. One of the enhancements made over time was an increase in speed. This short section outlines some of the changes to Ethernet over the years, including increases in speed.

A New, Improved, and Faster Ethernet—Let's Call It Fast Ethernet

My mom always used Tide laundry detergent when I was a kid. Every time she bought a new box of detergent, it had a new marketing blurb on it. "New and Improved," it would state. Or "Newer, and Even More Improved" the next time around. Then someone got smart and started looking for Greek and Latin root words that meant really super good, like my personal favorite "Ultra-Cleaning Power," or "Super-Dooper Cleaning Power," and the like.

The first time Ethernet speed was enhanced, the IEEE created a working group and named it 802.3u. (The "u" has no special meaning. The IEEE chooses to name new 802.3 (Ethernet) working groups using letters after the base 802.3 name, and they hadn't used "u" before.) So, the 802.3u working group created a specification for Ethernet to run 10 times faster, at 100 Mbps. So, if Ethernet ran at 10 Mbps, what do you call Ethernet that runs at 100 Mbps? "New and Improved Ethernet"? "Ultra Ethernet"? Well, the IEEE settled on another term—*Fast Ethernet*. So does that mean "normal" Ethernet is slow? Not really. But for today's enterprise networks, Fast Ethernet does help tremendously.

When the IEEE created 802.3u Fast Ethernet, it chose to do something incredibly smart. Yes, I'm overemphasizing this point, but it's hugely important. The IEEE decided that the rest of Fast Ethernet worked the same as plain old Ethernet. So, both Ethernet and Fast Ethernet use the same headers and trailers. The same CSMA/CD logic is used, too. In addition, the same 6-byte MAC addresses are used. The only differences come in how the bits are encoded to cross the wires, including the speed at which they are encoded. In fact, Fast Ethernet fell under a working group of 802.3 because it was only amending the original 802.3 Ethernet, rather than creating a whole new type of LAN.

Why am I so ultra-hyper about this design choice? (There's that "ultra" word again. It's so easy to use!) Well, that one design choice has had a lot of impact on Ethernet's acceptance in the marketplace. If you already knew Ethernet, you could learn Fast Ethernet easily. Also, vendors only needed to make small changes to existing Ethernet products to create Fast Ethernet products, meaning that those products' prices fell quickly, making them popular in the marketplace and making it harder for anyone to choose anything except Ethernet.

Along the way, many new terms were introduced to describe Fast Ethernet. For instance, Fast Ethernet is often simply abbreviated as *FE*. The older 10 Mbps Ethernet, when using twisted pair cabling, was called *10BaseT*, meaning 10 Mbps Ethernet using twisted pair. As a result, FE was called *100BaseT*.

If Fast Ethernet Is Good, Even Faster Is Better: Gigabit Ethernet

Yep, 100 Mbps is fast, but 1000 Mbps—also known as 1 gigabit per second (Gbps)—is even faster. So, the IEEE eventually created even faster Ethernet, using 802.3 working groups 802.3z and 802.3ab. What do you call really super fast Ethernet that runs at 1 Gbps? Well, the IEEE got smart this time, avoiding the pitfalls of the laundry detergent industry, and cleverly called this one *Gigabit Ethernet (GigE)*.

The difference between Gigabit Ethernet and Fast Ethernet is speed. To support the speed, the standards call for better cabling, but everything else is the same—same frame header and trailer, same CSMA/CD (as needed), same MAC addresses, same relatively quick acceptance in the market, same death-knell for all other LAN technologies. Historically speaking, by the time Gigabit Ethernet was becoming accepted in the marketplace, the competition between Ethernet and other LAN technologies was over. Ethernet had won, being faster, better, and cheaper than the competition. That is, in part, why you won't be reading about other types of LANs in this book—they just don't matter much anymore.

By the way, in case you were wondering, the *802.3z* working group defined how to do GigE over optical cable, and the *802.3ab* working group defined how to do GigE over copper cabling. *Optical cabling* uses *glass fibers* instead of copper wire. The devices that are attached to an optical cable send light across the cable, instead of electricity, to encode 0s and 1s. As it turns out, the physics behind optical signals over optical glass-fiber cabling allow for higher speeds, longer distances, fewer errors, and better security, but at a higher cost than copper wiring.

The optical version of GigE(802.3z) came out first, with the copper version (802.3ab) coming out a little later. And because each standard required different types of engineering effort based on whether optical or electrical cabling was used, the IEEE created two working groups to create the standards.

Ultra Super-Fast Fast Ethernet: 10 Gigabit Ethernet

Yep, it's an old story—there's an even faster option now. *10 Gbps Ethernet*, or *10 GigE* for short, defined by the IEEE *802.3ae* working group, does have a few more distinguishing characteristics than normal. For instance, you cannot use hubs for 10 GigE. Also, 802.3ae calls for optical cabling only, with no option for copper wiring as of the time this book went to press. If history is any indication, the thought of 10 GigE using copper wires is more than a twinkle in someone's eye already, though!

As usual, 10 GigE uses the same framing, addresses, and so on as other forms of Ethernet, with the only differences being in the physical encoding details and the requirements on the cabling, which allow the faster speeds.

And yes, there's already talk of 40 Gig Ethernet, but that's still in the working stages.

Summary of Ethernet Speeds

Although you shouldn't feel the need to memorize the IEEE standard names about each type of Ethernet, you should at least know about the different speeds. Table 6-1 lists several of the details in one place for your convenience.

Table 6-1 Ethernet Specifications

Common Name	IEEE Standard	Speed	Type of Cabling
Ethernet	802.3	10 Mbps	Both
Fast Ethernet	802.3u	100 Mbps	Both
Gigabit Ethernet	802.3z	1 Gbps	Optical
Gigabit Ethernet	802.3ab	1 Gbps	Copper
10 Gigabit Ethernet	802.3ae	10 Gbps	Optical

Interestingly, if you walked around asking long-time network engineers things like, "Which IEEE standard defines GigE over optical cabling?," I'd guess at least half the people wouldn't remember. Knowing that standards exist for Ethernet at varying speeds is what's important.

A Switch for All Speeds

LAN switches use logic that relies on information in the Ethernet header. Because all the more advanced forms of Ethernet use the same header, switch forwarding and learning logic do not change based on what speed Ethernet is used. The switch can behave the same way as always, with some ports using Ethernet, some Fast Ethernet, some Gigabit Ethernet, and so on.

Imagine that you want to support a bunch of users on a building floor, some with NICs that only support 10 Mbps 802.3, and some that only support 100 Mbps 802.3u Fast Ethernet. You might buy a switch that has 24 ports—12 10-Mbps ports and 12 100-Mbps ports. Figure 6-12 shows the basic setup, with Fred using a 10-Mbps NIC and Wilma using a 100-Mbps NIC.

Figure 6-12 Supporting Multiple Speeds on a Single Switch

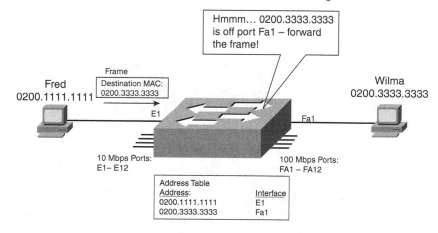

The switch can easily support both speeds in the single switch, mainly because the only difference between Ethernet and Fast Ethernet is in how the bits are transmitted over the cable, and at what speed. Because the headers and trailers are the same, and the addresses are the same, the switch still learns MAC addresses, makes forwarding and filtering decisions, and buffers frames, just like always.

The switch in Figure 6-12 has physical ports that only support 10 Mbps or 100 Mbps; this type of switch does not provide an easy migration path from 10 Mbps to 100 Mbps. For instance, imagine that you have 12 devices migrated to use Fast Ethernet, so you have plugged them all into the 12 Fast Ethernet ports on the switch. Now Fred gets a new 100-Mbps NIC, puts it in his computer, and wants to be moved to a 100-Mbps switch port. Uh oh. No more ports.

To solve problems like this one, the IEEE created a standard, called autonegotiation, that provides an easy migration path from 10 Mbps Ethernet to 100 Mbps Ethernet, or even to 1000 Mbps Ethernet (GigE). Vendors build switches with physical ports that can run at various speeds. *Autonegotiation* allows the switch and NIC on either end of the cable to automatically negotiate to determine the speed. The switch and computer also happen to negotiate whether to use full duplex or half duplex. Figure 6-13 shows the general idea.

Figure 6-13   Autonegotiation with 10/100 Cards

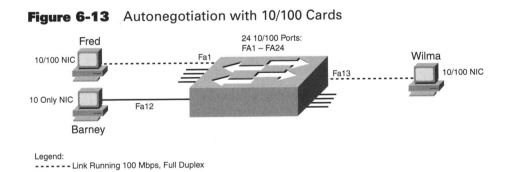

To perform autonegotiation, the switch and the NIC must support multiple speeds, as well as autonegotiation logic. To perform autonegotiation, the switch and NIC send some messages back and forth. These messages simply state things like, "I want to use 100 Mbps," with a response like, "Okay, me, too. Let's do it." Of course, the IEEE specifications aren't so informal, but that's the gist of the mean.

And if the switch and NIC simply can't agree, they fall back to 10 Mbps, half duplex.

Many of the Ethernet NICs in use today are called *10/100 cards*, meaning that they will run at either speed, and they will negotiate with the switch. In Figure 6-13, Fred has a new 10/100 card, and Wilma has her same old 10/100 card. Both have negotiated for 100 Mbps, full duplex. Barney, using an older 10-Mbps only card that does not support autonegotiation, settles for 10 Mbps, half duplex.

Because GigE products keep falling in price, you can now find 10/100/1000 NICs and switch ports, meaning that the NICs and the switches will negotiate the use of Gigabit Ethernet as well.

Chapter Summary

Hubs only allow one device to transmit a frame at a single point in time, whereas LAN switches allow multiple frames to be transmitted at the same time. LAN switches also support the use of full duplex transmission, allowing a single device to send and receive frames over the same cable at the same time. These facts, along with the fact that switches buffer frames to avoid collisions, mean that networks that are built with switches have much more capacity than do similar networks built with hubs.

A switch makes a forwarding and filtering decision for each frame it receives. It compares the destination address of the frame to the MAC address table. If a match is found, the entry in the MAC address table lists the port out which the switch should forward the frame—that's called the forwarding decision. By not sending the frame out the rest of the ports, the switch has filtered frames, which is known as a filtering decision.

Switches build the MAC address table by examining the source MAC address field of incoming frames, placing the MAC address and the incoming port number in an entry in the table. This process is called learning.

The IEEE has created many new and improved versions of Ethernet over the years. Interestingly, many of the details remain the same—the headers and trailers in particular, including the addresses. The one thing that has been vastly improved has been the transmission speed. 100 Mbps Fast Ethernet is installed in almost every network, Gigabit Ethernet is common for servers, and 10 GigE is now available for high-bandwidth applications.

Chapter Review Questions

You can find the answers to the following questions in Appendix A, "Answers to Chapter Review Questions."

1. How many frames can pass through a 24-port hub at one instance in time, with no collisions occurring?

2. How many frames can pass through a 24-port switch at one instance in time, with no collisions occurring, and with full duplex used on all ports?

3. PC1, PC2, and PC3 are all attached to the same switch. Imagine that PC1 and PC2 each send a frame to PC3, at roughly the same instance in time. Will the switch forward both frames? Will a collision occur? Why or why not?

4. PC1, PC2, and PC3 are all attached to the same switch. PC1 and PC2 use full duplex, and PC3 uses half duplex. Can PC1 send a frame to PC2 while PC2 sends a frame to PC3? Why or why not?

5. PC1, PC2, and PC3 are all attached to the same switch, but the switch is powered off. After the switch is powered up, PC1 sends a frame to PC2. How many MAC addresses are in the MAC address table of the switch? Why?

6. Imagine that three PCs (PC1, PC2, and PC3) are connected to a switch. PC2 and PC3 have 10/100 NICs, and PC1 has a 10-Mbps only NIC. Could any PC use 802.3u?

7. Imagine that three PCs (PC1, PC2, and PC3) are connected to a switch. PC2 and PC3 have 10/100 NICs, and PC1 has a 10-Mbps only NIC. What would need to happen before PC2 could transmit at 100 Mbps?

8. If a frame with a destination MAC address of 0200.6666.6666 arrived at a switch, and the switch had the following two entries in its switching table, what would the switch do? Out which ports would the switch forward the frame? Out which ports would the switch not forward the frame?

0200.5555.5555   E5

0200.6666.6666   E6

9. If a frame with a destination MAC address of 0200.7777.7777 arrived at a switch, and the switch had only the following two entries in its switching table, what would the switch do? Out which ports would it forward the frame? Out which ports would it not forward the frame?

0200.5555.5555   E5

0200.6666.6666   E6

10. If a frame with a destination MAC address of FFFF.FFFF.FFFF arrived at a switch, and the switch had only the following two entries in its switching table, what would the switch do? Out which ports would it forward the frame? Out which ports would it not forward the frame?

0200.5555.5555   E5

0200.6666.6666   E6

11. What does the word "flooding" mean in the context of LAN switch operation?

12. What is the most significant difference between Ethernet and Fast Ethernet?

13. How many more bytes did the IEEE add to the address field in the Fast Ethernet header, as compared to Ethernet, when it created the Fast Ethernet standards?

14. How many more bytes did the IEEE add to the address field in the Gigabit Ethernet header, as compared to Ethernet, when it created the Gigabit Ethernet standards?

15. List the differences in the forwarding and learning logic used by a 10 Mbps Ethernet switch and a gigabit Ethernet switch.

What You Will Learn

After reading this chapter, you should be able to

- ✔ Define the terms LAN, VLAN, and broadcast domain

- ✔ Compare and contrast the concept of a physical LAN and a virtual LAN

- ✔ Explain how a single switch operates when multiple VLANs are present

- ✔ List several reasons for wanting to use VLANs

- ✔ Explain the need for VLAN trunking, and list the two options for trunking on Ethernet

CHAPTER 7

Adding Local (Network) Roadways for No Extra Money

At this point in your reading, you already have a pretty detailed view of how LANs work. You can buy some network interface cards (NICs) and install them in some computers, cable each NIC to a switch, and you've created a LAN. As long as the PCs have some networking software on them—and most operating systems today include TCP/IP—you're all set to use the network.

As it turns out, there are many reasons why you would want more than one LAN. Regardless of the reason, you can create another LAN by buying more NICs, more cables, and more switches. However, there's a better way to create more LANs by using *virtual LANs* (*VLANs*).

In this chapter, you will read about physical LANs, with particular attention to some concepts that will help you understand VLANs. Then, you'll read about VLANs and how they are created. Along the way, you'll learn some of the reasons why you might want to use VLANs.

The Physical Reality Precedes the Virtual Reality

Before you can understand virtual LANs, you need to think about physical LANs and how they handle broadcasts. After you have the concepts related to broadcasts firmly in mind, it's much easier to think about VLANs.

Physical LANs: It's All About Broadcasts

Many people have different ideas about what a network really is. For instance, if you ask someone who works on servers, that person might think of a LAN as a server that's attached to an Ethernet. The person who runs the Ethernet cables has a different perspective, thinking of the LAN as a bunch of cables. However, the perspective you need to have to understand VLANs is closer to that of the network engineer, who cares more about hubs and switches.

As you probably recall, hubs and switches behave differently. Hubs repeat all received electrical signals out all ports, except the port in which the signal was received, essentially flooding the frame. Switches do not flood all received frames, but instead use a MAC address table, which tells them how to best forward a frame.

However, hubs and switches process broadcast frames indentically. A *broadcast frame* is an Ethernet frame that has a destination MAC address field set to FFFF.FFFF.FFFF. Broadcast frames are sent for a variety of reasons. (They are particularly useful when a computer doesn't know some piece of information; the computer can send a broadcast to everyone, asking for that tidbit of information.) Regardless of why the broadcast frame is sent, when a switch receives a frame whose destination address is the Ethernet broadcast address, it forwards the frame out all ports except the incoming port. A hub repeats all frames—including broadcasts—out all ports except the incoming port. (In fact, hubs do not even look at the addresses.) So, although the internal processing on switches and hubs is different, essentially a switch acts just like a hub in regards to broadcast frames.

Master of Your Own (Broadcast) Domain

To understand VLANs, you need to understand a few terms, starting with the term *broadcast domain*. A broadcast domain is a group of devices for which a broadcast frame sent by one device is received by all other devices in the same group.

Although the definition is rather formal, you've already read about all the underlying concepts, mainly in Chapter 6, "Reducing Congestion and Driving Faster on the Local (Network) Roadway." Figure 7-1 shows three examples of broadcast domains.

Figure 7-1   Three Broadcast Domains: A Hub, a Switch, and a Hub and Switch

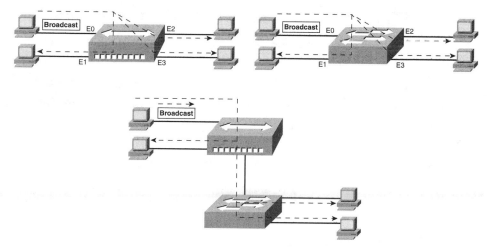

A single hub creates a single broadcast domain, as shown in the upper-left part of the figure. This first broadcast domain consists of the PCs, as well as the cabling and hub. If any of those devices sends a broadcast frame, the hub repeats the electrical signal out all other ports so that everyone receives the signal.

A single switch also creates a single broadcast domain. This broadcast domain includes the devices that are attached to a single switch, along with the cabling and switch. Because the switch forwards all broadcast frames out all ports (besides the incoming port), everyone gets a copy of each broadcast, meeting the definition for broadcast domain.

A hub and a switch, connected together, also create a single broadcast domain. Shown in the bottom of Figure 7-1, if a device on the hub sends a broadcast, the hub repeats it out all ports, including the one that's connected to the switch. When the switch receives the broadcast frame, it forwards the broadcast out all other switch ports, like always. Similarly, when a device that is connected to the switch sends a broadcast, the switch forwards the broadcast on all other ports—including the one that is connected to the hub—and the hub repeats the frame out all other ports.

Multiple Physical LANs Require Multiple Switches

A LAN consists of the devices inside a single broadcast domain. To create multiple physical LANs, you need to use multiple physical switches, because a switch forwards any broadcasts out all ports (except the port on which it was received). For example, imagine that you just took a job as network engineer at a company with the small network shown in Figure 7-2.

Figure 7-2   Small Physical LAN, and You Are in Charge

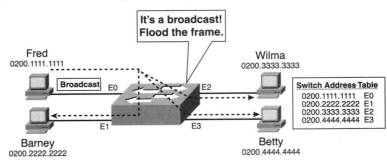

With a single switch, you have a single broadcast domain and a single LAN. However, your new boss told you when you walked in the door, "We've got to get Fred and Barney on a different LAN than Betty and Wilma. They work with super-secret projects, and we can't meet our security requirements if Betty and Wilma are on the same LAN. Now get cracking!"

To put Betty and Wilma in a different LAN than the boys, you have to use two switches. Figure 7-3 shows the alternative design, now with two physical LANs.

Figure 7-3   Two Physical LANs: Broadcasts Do Not Leave the Originating LAN

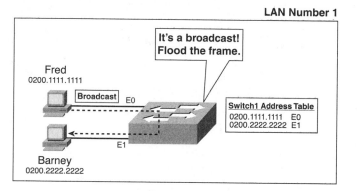

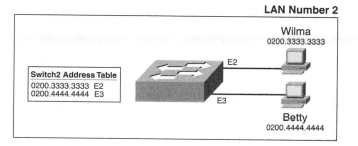

Note that with two switches, each switch has its own address table. When Fred sends a broadcast, switch1 forwards it out all other ports—in this case, only to Barney. Switch2 does not receive a copy of the broadcast—in fact, there is not even a physical cable conneting the two switches in this case.

Because the two switches have created two separate VLANs, both broadcast frames and unicast frames from the top LAN cannot be forwarded to the bottom LAN. For instance, if Fred were to send a frame with a destination address of 0200.3333.3333 (Wilma), switch1 would not have Wilma's address in its address table. Figure 7-4 summarizes the logic.

Figure 7-4 No Forwarding Between the Two Physical LANs

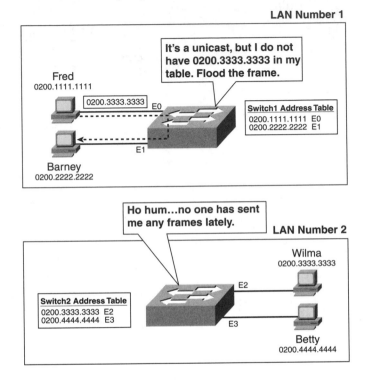

With two separate switches, you can create two physical LANs, each with its own MAC address table. In the next section, you'll read about how VLANs can do essentially the same thing, but using only a single switch. Following are some key points about physical LANs that will help you as you learn about VLANs in the next section:

- Each LAN has an independent MAC address table as compared to the other LANs.

- Broadcasts originating in one LAN are flooded inside that LAN.

- Broadcasts originating in one LAN are not forwarded into the other LANs.

- Unicasts originating in one LAN are not forwarded into the other LANs.

Virtual (LAN) Reality: One Switch, but Multiple LANs

VLANs allow you to create multiple LANs, but without requiring extra switch hardware. This section describes how switches create virtual LANs, followed by a short description of some of the reasons why someone might want to use multiple VLANs.

How to Create a Virtual LAN

To create multiple physical LANs, or broadcast domains, you need multiple LAN switches. However, adding more LAN switches can be expensive. Luckily, LAN switch vendors include a feature in their products that allows you to create multiple broadcast domains in a single switch, essentially allowing you to create multiple LANs, but without the additional hardware. These broadcast domains are called virtual LANs (VLANs). VLANs are defined more formally as follows:

> A broadcast domain, created by a switch, using a subset of the physical ports on the switch.

Earlier in the chapter, you read that a broadcast domain is the group of devices for which a broadcast frame sent by one device is received by all devices in the group. And as you well know now, a physical LAN is the same thing as a broadcast domain.

So, what's the difference between a physical LAN and a VLAN? Very little. The key lies in the fact that the network engineer can configure the switch and tell it to treat some physical ports as if they are in one broadcast domain—one VLAN—and then configure other ports to be in a different broadcast domain—in other words, a different VLAN. When you want multiple LANs, instead of buying a new switch to create a new physical LAN, you could just configure VLANs. Figure 7-5 shows an example, with the same network as in Figure 7-3.

Figure 7-5   Two Virtual LANs: Broadcasts Do Not Leave the
Originating VLAN

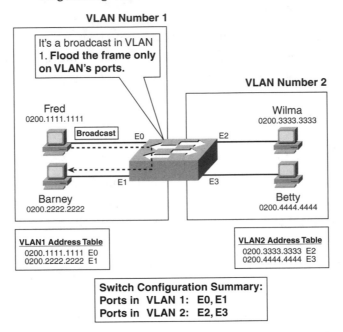

The network engineer configured ports E0 and E1 to be in VLAN 1 and ports E2 and E3 to be in VLAN 2. The switch considers the two VLANs to be separate. In fact, this network behaves just like it would with the two physical switches shown in Figure 7-4. However, you get the advantage of not having to buy another switch!

Notice that the switch keeps a separate address table for each VLAN. So, the switch does learn all four MAC addresses, but the switch does not forward broadcasts or unicasts from one VLAN to the other. Figure 7-6 outlines the process.

Figure 7-6   No Forwarding Between the Two VLANs

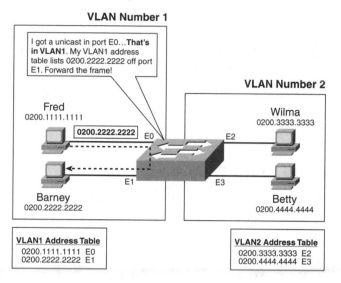

The switch knows that the frame came in port E0 and that E0 has been configured as part of VLAN1. The switch looks only at the VLAN1 address table and finds a match. So, the switch forwards the frame. Even if there had not been a match in the VLAN1 address table, the switch would have flooded the frame, but only out ports in VLAN1. Therefore, neither Wilma nor Betty could get a copy of the frame.

In short, VLANs act just like physical LANs. The only difference is that physical LANs include all physical ports on a switch, whereas VLANs include a subset of the ports on a switch, based on the configuration that the network engineer adds. Actually, you can take the list of facts about physical LANs from earlier in this chapter, change the word "LAN" to "VLAN," and they are all still true:

- Each VLAN has an independent MAC address table as compared to the other VLANs.

- Broadcasts originating in one VLAN are flooded inside that VLAN.

- Broadcasts originating in one VLAN are not forwarded into the other VLANs.

- Unicasts originating in one VLAN are not forwarded into the other VLANs.

That's all there is to VLANs. A VLAN is just a LAN, or broadcast domain, that is created by configuring a switch. By telling the switch to treat some ports as if they are in one LAN, and others as if they are in a second LAN, you can create multiple virtual LANs.

Why You Need More Than One LAN

A VLAN is simply a LAN that is created by configuring a switch, so that a subset of its ports is considered to be in the same broadcast domain. But why would you bother? Couldn't you just leave the switch alone and let it work like always, with one physical LAN? Sure. In fact, often times, particularly in small networks, you do not need to use VLANs. However, in medium to large enterprise networks, VLANs are quite popular. As my daughter would say (over and over again, by the way), "Why?" Well, I'll give you a few of the typical reasons over the next few pages of this chapter. This is not an exhaustive list, but it highlights a few of the popular reasons.

If 100 Devices in a LAN Is Good, 1000 Devices Must Be Better

In some cases, bigger is better, but in other cases, it is not. As a LAN grows, it might become too big. The problem? Well, each PC must spend CPU cycles processing received broadcasts. As the broadcast domain increases in size, every device has more broadcasts to process. As a result, it makes sense not to put too many devices in a single VLAN.

Although there is no exact number to shoot for, most networks today avoid LANs with more than a few hundred devices. If you have 1000 devices and you want no more than 200 per LAN, you could simply create five or more VLANs and put some devices in each VLAN.

OSI Layer 8 Issues

You might be wondering what OSI Layer 8 is. Well, there's more to most network design decisions than just the technical parts; in other words, there's more to life than just the actual, real, technical seven layers of the OSI model. People sometimes use the term *Layer 8* to refer to internal politics at the company, business issues, and so on—all the stuff that is above and beyond the pure technical issues.

Often, Layer 8 issues drive some decisions about when to use VLANs. For example, imagine that the payroll department moves to the same floor as the IT department. The payroll director comes into your cube and says something like this: "Odom, I'm concerned that we will be on the same LAN as the IT group. They might be able to look at sensitive payroll traffic as it passes over the LAN."

First of all, if you're not me, you would be wondering why he called you "Odom," but your reply could be this simple: "Uhhh… how about if we put you on a different LAN? Does that work for you?" He agrees, and not only that, he's so happy that you accommodated him so easily that he promises to put in a good word with your boss. All you have to do is configure the switch to put the right ports into a new VLAN for payroll and enjoy the admiration of your new friend in the payroll department.

OSI Layer 3 Design Goals

One of the more popular reasons to put a group of devices into the same VLAN relates to OSI Layer 3 concepts, and in particular, the Internet Protocol (IP). Unfortunately, you've not read enough about IP to appreciate the details yet. You will learn a lot more about IP in Chapters 10, "Delivering the Goods to the Right Street (IP) Address," and 11, "Knowing Where to Turn at Each Intersection (Router)." While you continue reading, keep in mind that IP uses concepts called networks and subnetworks, or subnets. As it turns out, the devices in the same LAN or VLAN are also in the same TCP/IP network or subnet.

You might have motivations for putting some devices in one IP network or subnet, and some in another. To be in two different IP networks or subnets, those devices must be in two different LANs, so using VLANs could be a convenient way to meet your Layer 3 design goals.

Saving Cash

Regardless of motivation, a network engineer might need to put devices in different LANs. Rather than buying more switching hardware, it is typically way more convenient and cost effective to just configure VLANs. The ultimate motivation for VLANs might simply be that whatever the design choice that makes you want more LANs, VLANs allow you to do it without buying more hardware.

Packing Your VLAN's Frames in a Trunk When Leaving the Switch

So far, most of the examples about switching in this book showed just one switch. However, you can connect multiple switches so that devices on each switch can send frames to each other. Figure 7-7 shows the basic concept, with no VLANs configured.

Figure 7-7   Forwarding Frames Between Two Switches

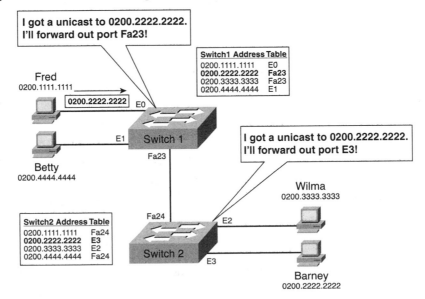

The basic switch logic for each switch does not change when you use multiple switches. In this figure, both switches' address tables have been populated, and each switch knows where to forward the frames. Note that switch1's address table tells it to forward frames sent to Barney out port FastEthernet 23, to switch2. Switch2's table lists port E3 beside Barney's address, so it forwards the frame to Barney out port E3.

In the context of connecting multiple switches, the term *trunk* can be used a couple of different ways. For instance, the Ethernet cable segment between switch1 and switch2 can be called a trunk. In this case, trunk refers to the fact that the segment connects two switches. (The other use of the word "trunk" will be explained in the next section.)

How to Pack Your Trunk for the Trip to the Other Switch

To explain the other use of the term "trunk," Figure 7-8 adds VLANs to the network from Figure 7-7. As shown in previous figures, Fred and Barney are in one VLAN, and Betty and Wilma are in another VLAN. However, now the traffic in both VLANs must cross over the trunk between two switches. When a switch receives a frame over that trunk, it could be confused about which VLAN's MAC address table to use when deciding how to forward the frame. Figure 7-8 shows the sample network and the dilemma that switch2 faces upon receipt of the frame that Fred sent to Barney.

Switch1 now has an address table for each VLAN. Its VLAN1 address table says to forward the frame for Barney (0200.2222.2222) out port Fa23. However, when switch2 receives the frame, it is confused. Is this frame part of VLAN1 or VLAN2? Should switch2 look in both address tables, hoping to find 0200.2222.2222? Should switch2 assume that the frame belongs in a particular VLAN? Because switch2 supports two VLANs, it simply needs more instructions.

Figure 7-8   Switch2's Dilemma: Which VLAN?

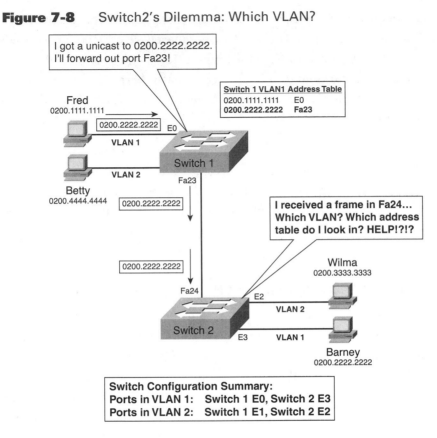

To solve the problem, the switches use something called VLAN trunking. To perform *VLAN trunking*, before sending the frame over the Ethernet cable to the
other switch, switch1 adds another header to the frame. That extra header identifies the frame as part of VLAN1. Switch2 expects frames coming in over port
Fa24 to have that extra header, so it can now process the frame. Figure 7-9 shows
the change in logic.

Figure 7-9   Trunking Header Tells Switch2 What to Do

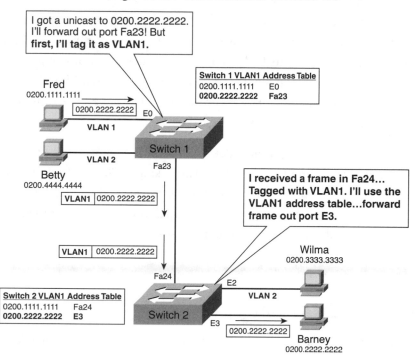

Now, switch2 knows how to process each received frame. When it receives frames in port FastEthernet 24, it expects to see a trunking header, which identifies the VLAN. That tells switch2 which address table to use.

When switch2 needs to send frames out port Fa24 to switch1, switch2 also adds a VLAN trunking header, knowing that switch1 expects to be able to find the header to identify the right VLAN.

So, now to the other use of the term *trunk*, along with some related terms. The term *VLAN trunk*, or sometimes simply *trunk*, refers to a link between two switches over which the additional *trunking header* is added, as in Figure 7-9. The term *VLAN trunking*, or simply *trunking*, refers to the process of adding (when sending) and removing (upon receipt) the extra headers that identify the VLANs.

Tale of Two Trunking Protocols

It was the best of times, it was the worst of times…whoops, wrong tale! Once upon a time, no VLAN trunking existed. Cisco wanted something like trunking in its switches, but no standards body had created a standard protocol for trunking. So, Cisco created its own standard and named it Inter-Switch Link (ISL). *ISL* defines the type of header that should be added to the frame, including the field in which the VLAN can be numbered.

Later, the IEEE 802.1Q committee defined a standard for VLAN trunking called 802.1Q trunking, or simply "dot 1 Q." Unsurprisingly, 802.1Q trunking differs from ISL. As a result, when you connect two switches and you want to trunk, you need to pick between the two options. The switches on each end of the trunk must agree to which protocol to use, or trunking will not work.

Chapter Summary

A physical LAN consists of the end user devices, cables, and networking devices so that if one end user device sends a broadcast frame, all the rest of the devices receive the broadcast frame. In other words, a single physical LAN consists of all the devices in a single broadcast domain and all the associated cabling and networking devices.

Like a physical LAN, a virtual LAN consists of all the end user devices in the same broadcast domain as well. To create a VLAN, the network engineer configures a switch, placing some physical ports in one VLAN, and other physical ports in another. By doing so, the switch creates multiple broadcast domains, and the switch only forwards frames between devices that are in the same VLAN.

You can connect switches, and at the same time, you can put some ports on each switch into the same VLAN. To accommodate a network with VLANs that span multiple switches, the switches use a trunking protocol on the link between switches. The trunking protocol calls for the switches to add a header to each frame before sending a frame across the trunk; the header identifies the VLAN in which that frame resides. The trunking protocol allows the receiving switch to know how to forward the frame. The two trunking protocol options are ISL and 802.1Q.

Chapter Review Questions

You can find the answers to the following questions in Appendix A, "Answers to Chapter Review Questions."

1. Compare and contrast the terms "physical LAN" and "broadcast domain."

2. Define the term "broadcast domain."

3. What happens to a broadcast frame when a hub or a switch receives it?

4. Imagine a standalone switch with no VLANs configured, with 24 physical ports, each connected to a different PC. How many broadcast domains exist?

5. Imagine that a 12-port switch has 11 PCs connected to it, with the twelfth port connected to a hub. The hub has four PCs connected to it as well. The switch does not have VLANs configured. How many broadcast domains exist?

6. Define the term "VLAN."

7. What is the key difference between a physical LAN and a VLAN, according to this chapter?

8. Imagine that three VLANs were created on a single switch. The switch receives a broadcast into a port in VLAN1. Will devices in VLAN2 receive the broadcast?

9. Imagine that three VLANs were created on a single switch. The switch in a port in VLAN1 received a unicast frame sent to MAC address 0200.5555.555. The VLAN1 address table in the switch does not have an entry for that MAC address. What will the switch do with this frame?

10. Imagine that three VLANs were created on a single switch. A unicast frame, sent to MAC address 0200.5555.555, was received by the switch in a port in VLAN1. The VLAN2 MAC address table lists an entry for 0200.5555.5555, referencing port 18. What will the switch do with this frame?

11. List two reasons why a network engineer might want to use VLANs.

12. Imagine one LAN with 100 devices, and another with 1000 devices. Explain the similarities and differences of the impact of broadcasts in each LAN.

13. Compare and contrast physical LANs and virtual LANs.

14. Imagine that two switches are connected with an Ethernet cable. Three VLANs—VLAN1, VLAN2, and VLAN3—are configured on each switch. Name the two trunking protocols that could be used on the segment between switches and explain their basic operation.

15. Imagine that two switches are connected with an Ethernet cable. No VLANs are configured. Describe the meaning of the term "trunk," and tell whether a trunk is needed or used in this small network.

16. Identify the two VLAN trunking protocols and state which is Cisco proprietary.

Shipping and Logistics: Commerce Using the (Network) Roadways

Part III focuses on the data that an end user device ships over a network. Ultimately, the data that flows over the network needs to be the data that is useful to the end user, so the end purpose of a network should be to deliver data on behalf of end user applications. Chapter 8 begins the discussion with a detailed look at web, e-mail, and file transfer applications, including the protocols that those applications use. Chapter 9 focuses on some common services that all applications use.

Chapter 8: Shipping Goods over a (Network) Roadway

Chapter 9: Choosing Shipping Options When Transporting Goods over the (Network) Roadway

What You Will Learn

After reading this chapter, you should be able to

✔ Explain how e-mail uses multiple servers

✔ Describe the two parts of an e-mail address

✔ Name the two most popular e-mail protocols and describe when they are used most often

✔ Explain how FTP clients use an FTP server like a warehouse

✔ Explain what happens before a web browser tries to access a web server

✔ Describe the process and protocols used between a web browser and a web server

CHAPTER 8

Shipping Goods over a (Network) Roadway

The U.S. Department of Transportation (DOT) designs and builds roadways. The roadways are designed to allow cars and trucks of various sizes to drive over the road. However, the DOT doesn't really think much about what's inside the cars and trucks. Similarly, a LAN allows two computers to send data to each other, but the LAN itself—the cables, network interface cards (NICs), switches, and hubs—doesn't care about what data is transported inside the LAN frames.

This chapter covers the details about what users need to send over a network. In particular, this chapter describes the types of data generated by typical network-based applications.

Each application has different requirements for what it needs to ship over the network; that's one of the things that makes each application different. However, many applications have some similar needs in terms of what they send. For instance, many applications not only want to ship the data over the network, but they also want to make sure it gets there. They require a set of common transportation tools to provide important functions, such as error recovery. Those common tools are covered in the other chapter in this section, Chapter 9, "Choosing Shipping Options When Transporting Goods over the (Network) Roadway."

But first, you need to read about the applications covered in this chapter. This chapter focuses on three applications: e-mail, file transfer, and World Wide Web.

Neither Rain, Nor Sleet, Nor Dark of Night: E-Mail

The United States Postal Service (USPS) promises to consistently deliver mail, no matter what's going on with the weather. Although e-mail services make no such promise, they have become equally as important. In fact, I know a lot of people who get nervous when they can't get to their e-mail for just a few minutes!

E-mail works a lot like paper mail with the postal service (otherwise known as *snail mail*). You can write a letter on paper and put it in an envelope. If you put a correct name and address on the front of the envelope and put it in a mailbox, you can reasonably expect the postal service to deliver the mail to the right place. If you put a return address on the envelope, the recipient can reply by putting your address on the front of the envelope.

For those of you who might not have used e-mail before, it allows you to do basically the same thing, but without the paper. E-mail allows you to type some text, identify to whom you want to send the text by putting that person's e-mail address at the top of the e-mail, and send the e-mail. By sending the e-mail, you do the equivalent of giving the e-mail to the postal service. The service delivers the e-mail, and the next time your friend checks his e-mail, he receives the message that you sent.

Each e-mail includes the text you typed, the recipient's e-mail address, and your e-mail address. Because the recipient now knows your e-mail address, he can easily respond to your e-mail. E-mail also enables you to send a message to multiple recipients at once.

Dropping Off and Getting Your (e)Mail

If you live in a house or apartment, a postal worker typically comes by your place every working day. He leaves your mail in your mailbox. He also picks up any outgoing mail that you left either in your mailbox or in a centralized post office box (PO box) that was set up just for outgoing mail. Figure 8-1 shows the general idea.

Figure 8-1   Postal Worker Picking Up and Dropping Off the Mail

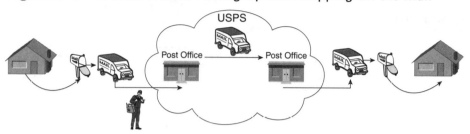

After the postal worker has picked up your mail, he brings it back to the local post office. Eventually, your letter gets to the post office near your friend to whom you are sending the letter. At that point, the local postal worker at the destination puts the letter in the PO box at your friend's place, where he can pick up the letter when he gets home.

Simple and unsurprising, right? Well, e-mail works similarly. If you were to create and send an e-mail to your friend, your PC would not actually send the e-mail to your friend's PC. Instead, you would send the message to your e-mail server, which is the equivalent of dropping off a letter at the local post office. Your e-mail server would send the e-mail to your friend's e-mail server, which is the equivalent of the postal service delivering a paper letter to the post office near your friend. Then, at some point in the future, your friend would check her e-mail and retrieve the e-mail from her local e-mail server, which is the equivalent of retrieving her paper mail from her PO box. Figure 8-2 shows the same basic flow as snail mail, but instead now for e-mail, with Keith sending an e-mail to the sales department at fredsco.com (sales@fredsco.com).

Figure 8-2   Sending E-Mail Using E-Mail Servers

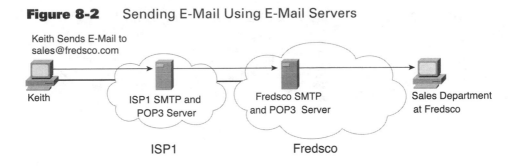

Although not exactly like the postal service, the same general ideas apply. Each company has one (or more) e-mail servers, acting as local post offices. Also, Internet service providers (ISPs) have one (or more) e-mail servers. If you use e-mail from your corporation's enterprise network, you typically use your company's e-mail servers to drop off and pick up e-mail. If you connect to an ISP from home, you would use that ISP's e-mail servers to drop off and pick up e-mail.

Postal Address Versus E-Mail Address

To send snail mail, you need to put the recipient's name and address on the front of the letter. The postal service then delivers the letter to the correct address. Similarly, to send an e-mail, you need to put the recipient's e-mail address on the e-mail. An *e-mail address* identifies the individual user who should receive the e-mail, allowing the e-mail servers to deliver the mail to the right person.

E-mail addresses have two parts: the name of the e-mail user and the name of the e-mail server. The name of the user sits before the @ sign, and the name of the server sits after the @ sign. For example:

tweedledee@fredsco.com

Figure 8-3 shows why a two-part e-mail address is useful. Both Keith and Conner send an e-mail to different people inside Fredsco. The text following the figure explains how the e-mail address helps in delivering the e-mail.

Figure 8-3   How a Two-Part E-Mail Address Is Used

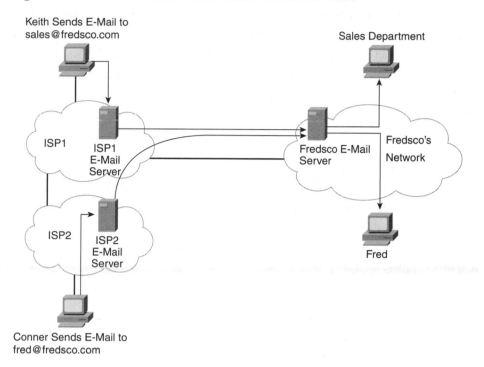

Keith Sends E-Mail to
sales@fredsco.com

Sales Department

ISP1

ISP1
E-Mail
Server

Fredsco E-Mail
Server

Fredsco's
Network

ISP2

ISP2
E-Mail
Server

Fred

Conner Sends E-Mail to
fred@fredsco.com

Note that the e-mail software on Keith's and Conner's PCs do not think about the address at all. The PCs always send their e-mails to their respective local e-mail server. In real life, when you send a paper letter, you probably give the letter to the post office by putting it in the mailbox at the end of your driveway, bringing it to the post office, or dropping it off in a mailbox set up to receive letters. In any case, you probably give your outgoing letters to the post office in pretty much the same way every time you send a letter. With e-mail, the e-mail software on your PC sends the outgoing e-mail to the same e-mail server every time as well, regardless of who the recipient is.

After Keith and Conner's e-mail servers have their respective e-mails, the servers look at the name after the @ sign, but they ignore the name before the @ sign. Their goal is to deliver the e-mail to the e-mail server at Fredsco, and the part after the @ identifies that e-mail server. It's much like how your local post office just looks at the city and state on a letter you give them, or they just look at the zip code, to figure out to which post office to send the letter. The local post office doesn't care about the name of the person on the letter or the street address; it just wants to send the letter to a post office near the recipient.

The ISP1 and ISP2 e-mail servers know how to find the e-mail server for fredsco.com because they ask another type of server called a Domain Name System (DNS) server. The DNS server tells the e-mail servers how to find the other e-mail servers. Chapter 13, "People Like Names, but Computers Like Numbers," covers the details about DNS servers. For now, just know that they can indeed find other e-mail servers easily.

Finally, after the Fredsco e-mail server gets the e-mails, it holds the e-mail, waiting on the users to check the mail. When the person who uses the sales@fredsco.com account checks his e-mail, the Fredsco e-mail server must check the entire e-mail address of all e-mail it is holding for delivery. The e-mails with username *sales* get delivered to that PC. Likewise, when user *fred* checks his e-mail, Fredsco's e-mail server delivers the mail to Fred.

Rules, Schmools: Even More Rules?

Now that you have the general idea of how e-mail works, you should know about a few of the protocols and standards for e-mail. First, Table 8-1 lists the standards. Afterward, I'll explain a little about each.

Table 8-1   TCP/IP E-Mail Standards

Standard	RFC	Description
Internet Message Format	2822	Defines the headers used to encapsulate the e-mail text, including the sender and receiver e-mail addresses
Simple Mail Transport Protocol (SMTP)	2821	Defines protocols for transmitting and receiving e-mails
Post Office Protocol Version 3 (POP3)	1939	Defines protocols for a client to retrieve e-mail from a server

note

TCP/IP includes thousands of different protocols and standards, which are defined in documents called Requests for Comments (RFCs). Table 8-1 lists the common names for three of the protocols, along with their RFC numbers. You can go to the Internet Engineering Task Force (IETF) website at http://www.ietf.org/rfc.html using a web browser if you would like to read more about these or other RFCs.

The protocols shown in Table 8-1 happen to be application layer protocols according to the TCP/IP model. Interestingly, there is an important distinction here between the application itself and the application layer protocol. Figure 8-4 provides a good backdrop to discuss the concept.

A user uses *e-mail client* software to generate, send, receive, and read e-mails. The e-mail client must do work that has nothing to do with communication. It must have a user interface, accept text typed from the keyboard, understand what a user clicks on the screen, store e-mails on the computer hard disk, and so on. None of those tasks requires a network.

Figure 8-4   E-Mail Client Application and Its Use of Application Layer
Protocols

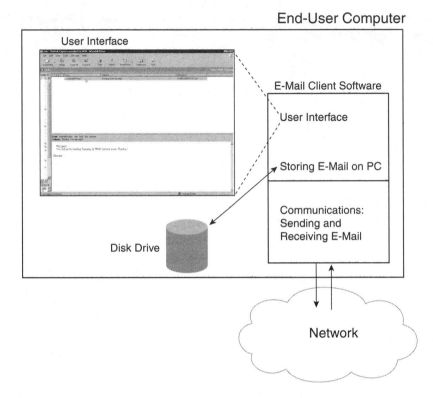

The e-mail client also needs to use the network. To do so, the people who wrote
the e-mail client software had to read, understand, and implement e-mail TCP/IP
protocols in the e-mail client software. So, the e-mail client application is not the
same thing as the application layer protocol; rather, to communicate, the e-mail
client must implement the correct application layer e-mail protocols.

Protocols for Addressing the Envelope Correctly: Internet Message Formats

When an e-mail client sends an e-mail and the e-mail servers forward it, they not only send the text of the e-mail message, but also a header. The header contains several fields, including the recipient's and sender's e-mail addresses, as shown in Figure 8-5.

Figure 8-5   Sampling of the E-Mail Header Defined by RFC 2822

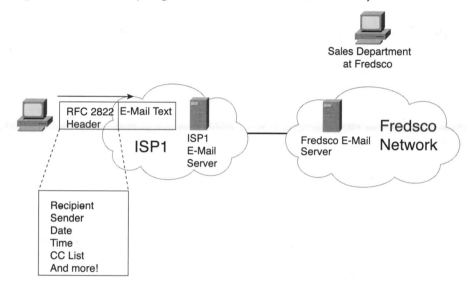

RFC 2822, "Internet Message Formats," defines the, well, uh, format of Internet e-mail messages. Yes, the name is a bit self-defining. RFC 2822 defines the header fields shown in Figure 8-5, and many more, so that all the clients and servers know where to find all the information needed to forward the e-mail correctly.

The KISS Principle and SMTP

The KISS principle refers to a wise adage to *Keep It Simple, Stupid*. Much of what you do every day might be better done if you make it uncomplicated. One of the most popular e-mail protocols also tries to keep things simple: ***Simple Mail Transfer Protocol***, or ***SMTP***.

E-mail clients and servers use SMTP protocols to manage the process of sending and receiving e-mail. As it turns out, instead of just sending an e-mail with the correct RFC 2822 header around it, the e-mail clients and servers need to talk about it first. For instance, a client should identify itself to the server before sending an e-mail. Also, the sender of the e-mail should identify the recipient before sending the e-mail; that way, if the next client/server in the path cannot deliver the e-mail, you do not waste time forwarding the e-mail. Figure 8-6 outlines the process.

Figure 8-6   Simple SMTP Messages: Identifying the Client and the Recipient

Typical SMTP Exchange

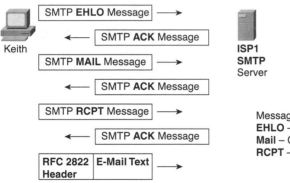

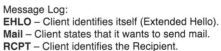

Message Log:
EHLO – Client identifies itself (Extended Hello).
Mail – Client states that it wants to send mail.
RCPT – Client identifies the Recipient.

The SMTP protocol defines messages so that the e-mail clients and servers can manage the e-mail forwarding process. The *Extended Hello (EHLO)* command identifies the client. The *Mail* command tells the server that the client wants to either send or receive e-mail. The *RCPT* (short for recipient) identifies the, well, uh, recipient of the e-mail that is about to be sent. After the server replies with an acknowledgement (ACK) message to each of these first three commands, the e-mail can be transmitted.

Note that when any of the devices actually sends the e-mail, that message conforms to the Internet Message Format (RFC 2822) specifications for the contents of the header and text. The SMTP RFC (RFC 2821) defines the messages that control the process with SMTP, such as EHLO and MAIL.

What to Do When You Need a Little POP in Your Network

The last e-mail protocol I'll cover here is called *Post Office Protocol (POP)*. The current version, *POP3*, also allows you to transfer e-mail, like SMTP. However, POP3 was designed specifically for use between an e-mail client and its e-mail server; it cannot transfer e-mail between servers.

Yes, POP3 essentially lets you do a subset of the functions of SMTP. So, why bother with another protocol when SMTP already allows clients to get their e-mail? Well, POP3 allows for several options for authentication, as well as some other useful features for e-mail clients—features that are not included in SMTP.

One of POP3's better features is authentication. *Authentication* refers to the process of one device identifying itself to another device via a name and a password. The other device then decides whether the first device is allowed access. For instance, if you have an e-mail account through your ISP, at some point you were given an e-mail address and password. When you check your e-mail, if you use POP3 (and you probably do), your e-mail client identifies itself and provides a password. The e-mail server decides if you should be allowed to get the e-mail. Figure 8-7 outlines the process with POP3.

Figure 8-7   Basic Authentication with POP3

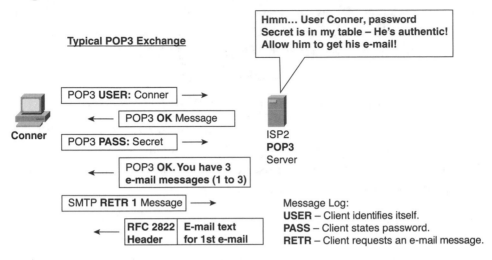

As you can see in the figure, Conner sends both a username and a password to the server. The server checks its list of usernames and passwords and finds a match. So, the server tells the client "OK," meaning that the server is ready to start forwarding e-mails to the client. POP3 also tells the user how many e-mails are waiting for him. To get the e-mails, the client asks for the e-mails, one at a time, as shown in the figure.

SMTP and POP3 Working Together

Often, networks use both SMTP and POP3. Clients use POP3 to get e-mail from their server, but they use SMTP to send e-mail. Servers use SMTP to forward e-mail to other servers. Figure 8-8 depicts the general flow.

Figure 8-8   Typical Usage of SMTP and POP3

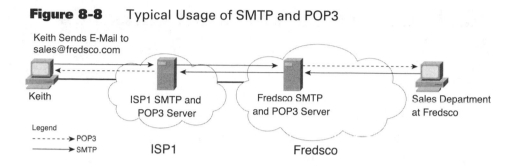

A couple of important facts show up in the figure. POP3 is used only to pull the e-mail from the server. Also, note that the e-mail servers are labeled as ***SMTP server*** and ***POP3 server***. So far, I have simply referred to an e-mail server generically. In practice, to perform SMTP, you need server software that understands SMTP, and that software is cleverly called ***SMTP server software***. So, for all this to work, the servers need to have SMTP server software running. Similarly, to allow a client to retrieve mail, the server hardware must be running ***POP3 server software*** in addition to the SMTP server software. In effect, a single computer needs to run both servers.

The SMTP server and the POP3 server on the same computer store and retrieve e-mails from the same message storage location. For instance, in Figure 8-8, the Fredsco e-mail server received an e-mail using the SMTP server, storing it on the disk drive. Later, when the person using the sales@fredsco.com account checked his e-mail using POP3, the POP3 server, on that same computer, retrieved the e-mail, forwarding it to the client.

Well, at this point, you probably know more than you ever wanted to know about e-mail! Just like with the postal service, as a user, all you need to know is that you send the mail, and it gets there. Now that you are armed with a few more details, you can certainly have a more intelligent conversation about e-mail.

Building a Centralized Warehouse: File Transfer

As you saw in the previous section, e-mail has some obvious comparison points with snail mail. The next application, file transfer, does not compare directly with a noncomputing example, but it does work a little like a warehouse that a company might use to store goods. Imagine that a company has a bunch of stuff, and many people inside the company might need some of the stuff from time to time. Some of the stuff is big, and some of the stuff is small. So, the company leases warehouse space and puts its stuff in the warehouse. Then the company gives everyone a key, and anyone who needs some stuff can go get it when needed. Figure 8-9 shows the general concept.

Figure 8-9   Warehousing Process for Transferring Stuff

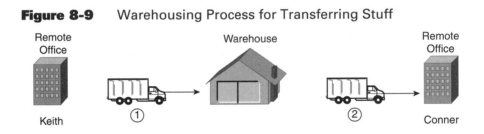

At Step 1, Keith fills the warehouse with widgets that his company has manufactured. Later, at step 2, Conner goes to get a widget so that he can deliver it to a customer.

Now, in addition to putting things in the warehouse and getting them out again, other things have to happen. For instance

- Keith probably put the widgets in the right place in the warehouse so that others could know where to find them.

- Conner has access to the documentation that told him where to find Keith's widgets inside the warehouse.

- Without the ability to find the widgets and keep track of the inventory, the warehouse would soon be useless.

A file transfer application called *File Transfer Protocol (FTP)* works with the same general logic as the warehouse example. You can put things on the FTP server and get them off the FTP server, but you also need documentation as to where things are for FTP to be useful. Figure 8-10 shows the basic process.

Figure 8-10 FTP Process for Transferring Files

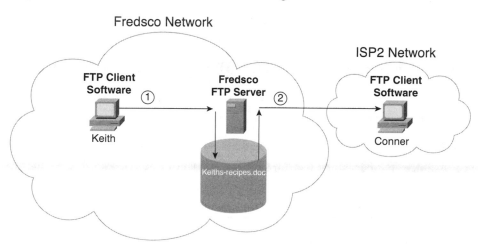

With FTP, everyone puts files on the server, as Keith did at Step 1 in the figure. Later, users can connect to the FTP server and get the files, as Conner did in Step 2. Also, if Conner didn't know the name of the file or in what directory it was stored, he might not find it, so Keith might have had to tell him where it was through some other means.

Also note that Conner connects to the Internet using ISP2, whereas the FTP server sits inside Fredsco's enterprise network. Unlike e-mail protocols, FTP does not call for files to be distributed among various servers. One user simply puts the file on the server so that others can log in to the same server and get copies of the files.

Warehouse Lingo and Procedures

FTP shares many of the same general concepts with applications like e-mail. Here are some of the similarities:

- Like e-mail, FTP uses client software on the end user computer.

- Like e-mail, the FTP client software has both user interface details, as well as code that implements application layer protocols.

- Like e-mail clients, FTP clients need to connect to a server to do anything useful.

- Like e-mail, the client must identify itself to the server before doing anything useful.

- Like e-mail TCP/IP standards, the FTP TCP/IP standard defines messages and headers that FTP uses to do something useful.

- Like e-mail server software, FTP server software runs on a physical server.

Despite the previous similarities, the details between FTP and e-mail are different. For instance, for FTP to be useful, files must exist on the FTP server. So, the first step involves a client connecting to the FTP server for the purpose of putting some files on the server, as in Figure 8-11.

Figure 8-11   Stocking the FTP Warehouse

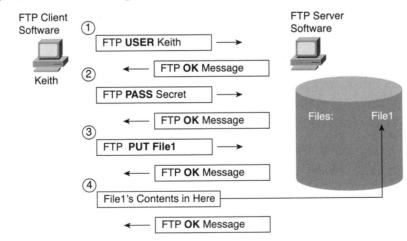

The following list describes what happens with each of the four messages Keith sends in the figure:

1. Keith first sends the server his username, using the FTP USER command. This command allows Keith's FTP client software to supply a username to the FTP server for authentication.

2. Next, Keith's FTP client uses the FTP PASS command to supply a corresponding password to the FTP server. At this point, the FTP server can decide whether Keith is a valid user of the FTP server. When the FTP server replies with an "FTP OK" message, it means that Keith has been authenticated.

3. Next, Keith's FTP client uses the FTP PUT command to tell the server that Keith will send the contents of the file in the upcoming messages, and that the file's name is file1.

4. Finally, Keith sends the actual contents of the file.

This entire process is a waste of time unless a couple of things are true. First, others must have the ability to authenticate to the server so that they can gain access to the files. They must also actually want to get to the files! Figure 8-12 shows Conner connecting to the FTP server and getting the file (called file1) that Keith put on the server.

Figure 8-12 Copying Inventory (Files) from the FTP Warehouse

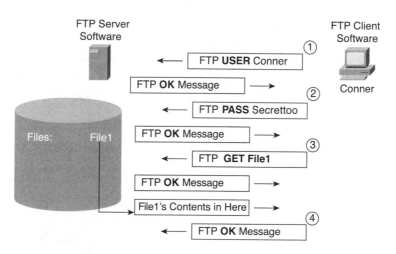

Conner repeats the same basic steps as Keith had in Figure 8-11. However, instead of issuing a PUT command, Conner issues a GET command. In FTP lingo, *PUT* means to copy a file from the client to the server—in other words, to put it on the server. *GET* refers to copying a file from the server to the client—in other words, getting the file from the server.

The following list describes what happens with each of the four messages Conner sends in the figure:

1. Conner first sends the server his username, using the FTP USER command. This command allows Conner's FTP client software to supply a username to the FTP server for authentication.

2. Next, Conner's FTP client uses the FTP PASS command to supply a corresponding password to the FTP server. At this point, the FTP server can decide whether Conner is a valid user of the FTP server. When the FTP server replies with an "FTP OK" message, it means that Conner has been authenticated.

3. Next, Conner's FTP client uses the FTP GET command to tell the server that Conner wants to get a copy of the file called file1.

4. Finally, the FTP server sends the actual contents of the file to Conner.

You should also note that the PUT and the GET commands simply copy the file, but they do not delete the file. For example, when Keith puts the file on the server (Figure 8-11), he actually copies the file, but the file (file1) is still on Keith's PC's disk drive. Similarly, when Conner gets the file in Figure 8-12, Conner copies the file, but the file is still on the FTP server.

Rules, Schmools for FTP

Many standards exist for file transfer. However, the one I've been writing about here, called FTP, has one core RFC that defines the details: RFC 959. The FTP RFC defines the messages that FTP uses to send the username, password, GET, PUT, and many other commands. It also defines the process by which the actual file is transferred, as was shown in Figures 8-11 and 8-12.

Interestingly, FTP uses a different underlying ***TCP connection*** for the control messages, versus the actual file transfer. Huh? Well, it's a small chicken-and-egg problem here: I can't tell you about TCP connections until you read the next chapter, but I want you to know now, when reading about FTP, that FTP uses two TCP connections. So, for now, just know that the process of controlling things—authentication, naming the file to be transferred, and so on—is considered separate from the actual data transfer.

The general idea works like using a shipping company. You might call the shipping company, schedule it to pick up a package, tell it where the package is going, and make sure it has directions to your house. You might even tell the shipping company if the package is an odd size or shape or if it's really heavy. That's the equivalent of a control connection.

The person whom you talked to on the phone probably isn't the person who shows up to pick up your package. The driver of the truck keeps it simple; he puts your package on the truck and delivers it to the destination. Similarly, FTP keeps the processes separated; it sends control information over one connection or channel, and the data transfer happens on another.

In summary, FTP works with clients connecting to a server, for the purpose of putting files on the server, and to get files from the server. The FTP server does not need to talk to other FTP servers; instead, each user who wants to get or put files connects to that one server. The server typically uses authentication, ensuring that each user has the right to get to the files on the server.

Browsing Around the Internet Shopping Mall: The World Wide Web

Back in Chapter 2, "A Network's Reason for Existence," you had a brief look at how the World Wide Web works. In many ways, the web works a lot like the retail model for businesses. In fact, when a retailer decides to offer goods for sale on the web, the retailer can use many of the same business processes that it uses with its bricks and mortar stores to support its Internet sales operations.

In case you do not remember the details from Chapter 2, here are some quick reminders. The end user PC uses software called a *web browser*, or simply a *browser*. When talking about e-mail and FTP, you refer to the software on the end user's PC as an e-mail client or an FTP client, respectively. Along the same line of reasoning, with the web, you could use the term *web client* to refer to the web browser software on an end user PC, but most people use the term "web browser" instead.

The other end of the story depends on someone to create a website, which is located on a web server. With FTP, someone had to put files on the FTP server before it had useful files for other FTP users to retrieve. Similarly, with *web servers*, someone must create some content and put it on the web server before the end user can do anything useful.

The information that sits on a web server, which end users can view with a web browser, is generically called *web content*, or simply *content*. Content consists of individual *web pages*, the collection of which is called a *website*. Figure 8-13 shows many of the concepts and the process.

Figure 8-13   Building and Stocking the New Retail Store, AKA
New Website

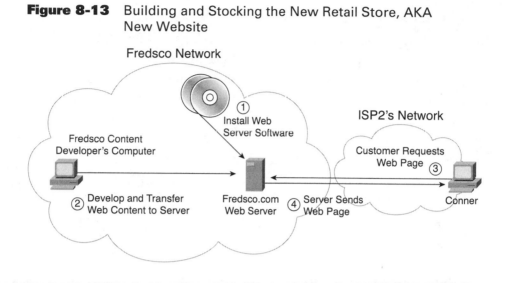

The following list describes what happens with each of the four messages that
Conner sends in the figure:

1. Web server software must be installed on the computer that will be used as
   the web server.

2. Someone creates the content that should be displayed by the http://
   www.fredsco.com website and puts that content onto the web server. The
   content consists of a number of files; the files can be copies from the web
   developer's computer to the web server using any means, including FTP.

3. Now the web server is ready to respond to potential customers. One such
   customer, Conner, opens his web browser and tries to connect to http://
   www.fredsco.com.

4. The web server gets Conner's request and sends the web page back to Conner.

The basic model has many people creating websites and many people with browsers
on their computer viewing these websites. The next sections cover a few details
about the protocols and standards used that web browsers and servers use.

Rules, Schmools for Web Retailing

To start, let's consider how to load a default web page, often called a home page. From the users' perspective, they must identify the website. They can do that in many ways. For now, let's assume that Conner, in Figure 8-14, types http://www.fredsco.com near the top of the browser. Next, the Fredsco home page appears.

Figure 8-14   Connecting to the Fredsco Home Page

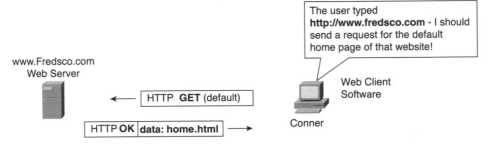

Notice the string of characters that starts with HTTP (http://www.fredsco.com). The whole string is called a **uniform resource locator (URL)**. The URL identifies the protocol in use, as well as the name of the server. For instance, HTTP stands for **Hypertext Transfer Protocol** and is the TCP/IP protocol you use to send the web page content from the web server to the web browser. Next, the stuff after the // lists the name of the server. In Chapter 13, I'll tell you more about names in TCP/IP, but for now, just assume that the name www.fredsco.com identifies the computer where fredsco's web server is running.

The first message that the browser sends includes the HTTP command GET (default). That means that the browser has asked the web server to send the browser that server's **default web page**, also called that server's **home page**. When the web developer created the web pages and moved them to the server, one web page was defined as the default. So, the server then looks in its configuration and finds the name of the file that holds its home page. Using HTTP, the server sends the contents of a file called home.html back to the browser.

The file that the web server sent by Conner's web browser is an .HTML file type, meaning that the file contains text that conforms to a specification called ***Hypertext Markup Language (HTML)***. HTML was the first language used to describe the contents of a web page. When Conner's browser gets the home.html file, the browser understands HTML, so it can then display the right contents in the browser window. Interestingly, when some people got together to create HTTP originally, most of the web content was HTML, and they were creating a protocol with which to transfer the HTML files. That's why the first word in the H17TTP acronym is hypertext.

Interestingly, although TCP/IP standardizes HTTP in RFC 2616, TCP/IP does not define anything about HTML. HTML does tell the browser what to put in the browser window, what color to make it, what size, and so on, but it does not define anything about how to send and receive data; therefore, TCP/IP doesn't care much about HTML!

In summary, the browser uses HTTP to ask for particular web pages, and the server uses HTTP to actually transfer the files. Web pages are simply stored in files on the server's disk drive. By transferring the files to the browser's computer, the browser can read the content inside the files and display the contents for the end user.

Buy One, Get a Bunch for Free

Have you ever tried to load a web page and noticed that some parts show up right away while the rest of the page fills in slowly? In this section, you'll learn what causes that.

In reality, when you load a web page from your browser, you actually get a lot of files, not just one. When the browser gets the first file, as in Figure 8-14, it really has just begun to load what the average user thinks of as the web page. Often, the first ***object*** downloaded by HTTP is an HTML file. (The term "object" refers to individual files that HTTP transfers; each web page consists of one or more objects.)

HTML files include text that goes on the web page, formatting instructions, plus instructions for the browser to download other objects that should also be displayed. For instance, when Conner loaded Fredsco's home page, he got a file called home.html. This file included a lot of the text that goes on the home page and some instructions about where to put various graphical images. However, the HTML file did not include the graphics images; they are in separate files on the web server and are considered to be different objects. So, the real process happens something like this:

1. Conner's browser gets the HTML file using HTTP.

2. Conner's browser reads the file, displaying things on the screen as a result.

3. When Conner's browser reads the file, it might have instructions that require Conner to download other objects. If so, it uses HTTP to get those objects.

4. Conner's browser reads the contents of the new objects, displaying things on the screen as a result.

5. When Conner's browser reads the newly downloaded objects, the objects might have instructions that require Conner to download other objects. And so on....

Eventually, the process ends, all objects are downloaded, and the browser displays something that looks like the web developer intended. Figure 8-15 outlines a simple example.

Conner's browser gets the original home page, reads it, and processes it. The home page HTML file told Conner to get two other objects: a file called logo1.gif and another called ad1.gif. (.GIF files contain graphics images.) The original home.html page included URLs that told the browser that the files were both located in directory /graphics on the server, so the HTTP requests included the directory name when asking for the files. The home.html file also told the browser where to display the two graphics images in the browser window, so after getting the files, the browser put them on the screen.

Figure 8-15   Transferring All the Files That Make Up a Web Page

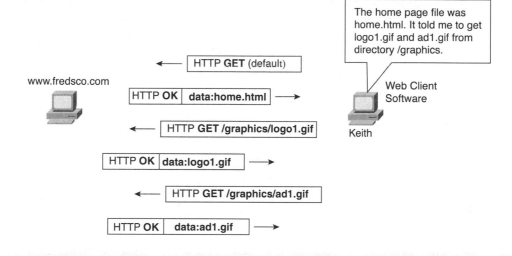

Chapter Summary

This chapter covered a little bit about three popular applications—e-mail, FTP, and the World Wide Web. However, many more applications exist, and there's much more depth to the applications than covered here. Transparent file and print services, database services, remote login, and other options for file transfer and e-mail make the mix of applications and application protocols rich.

Hopefully, after seeing a little detail about some of the applications and their protocols, you have noticed many similarities, like the following:

- The applications include client software that resides in the end user PC, as well as server software that typically resides in a server.

- The client application creates a user interface for the user and communicates with the server using application layer protocols.

- The server application allows the client to make requests for something to be sent through the network, such as sending e-mail, getting a file, or getting a web page.

- In addition to the transfer of data, the application layer protocols include messages that control what is sent through the network.

In particular, e-mail uses an organizational model like the postal service. It uses SMTP and POP3 protocols to deliver e-mail. SMTP is used to send e-mail to servers, and POP3 is used to retrieve mail from its POP3 server. The e-mail transfer includes a header, defined by the Internet Message Formats RFC, as well as the text of the e-mail. The clients and servers know where to forward the e-mail based on the two-part e-mail address.

File transfer—in particular with FTP—uses a model like a warehouse to store goods. Any user who has proper authority can put files on the server. Later, other clients can log in to the FTP server and get copies of the files.

Finally, web browsing uses a model like retail stores. First, a website is built, which includes the server hardware and software and web pages. Later, an end user can browse the web pages of that site, much like when you go to a bricks-and-mortar retail store and browse the items in the store. Browsers use HTTP to retrieve files from the server; oftentimes, the first file of a web page, frequently in HTML format, gives instructions to the browser that it should obtain other files to get everything needed to display the web page correctly.

Chapter Review Questions

You can find the answers to the following questions in Appendix A, "Answers to Chapter Review Questions."

1. Which two TCP/IP protocols transmit e-mails across a network? List the acronyms and what they stand for.

2. Fred and Barney each use a PC. They connect to the Internet using different ISPs. Describe the process by which Fred's e-mail to Barney traverses the Internet, in regard to which e-mail servers are used and how.

3. In a typical network, which e-mail protocol does a client use to retrieve messages from a server?

4. Describe the two parts of a typical e-mail address and tell what each part defines.

5. Under which layer of the TCP/IP networking model do the e-mail protocols described in this chapter fall?

6. What does the acronym FTP stand for, and what is its main purpose?

7. What are the names of the FTP operations to move a file to a server and move a file to a client?

8. Explain the usage of FTP servers for transferring a file from user1, which is connected to ISP1, to user2, which is connected to ISP2. In particular, point out to which servers each client moves the file.

9. Considering the two main FTP commands to move files to and from an FTP server, which commands both move the file and delete the original file from the location it was copied? (For instance, if user1 moves file1.doc to an FTP server, does that delete file1.doc from user1's computer?)

10. What term refers to the process of making sure a user is who he claims to be, before allowing him to use a server?

11. What does the acronym HTTP stand for, and what is its main purpose?

12. From what other standard did HTTP derive the first two letters in its name?

13. What HTTP operation does a browser use to request a particular file from a web server?

14. What does the acronym URL stand for, and how is it used?

What You Will Learn

After reading this chapter, you should be able to

✔ List the main features of TCP

✔ Explain the TCP error recovery process

✔ Describe why a computer needs to use multiple TCP port numbers

✔ Explain the need for well-known TCP port numbers

✔ Explain the process and benefits of segmentation

CHAPTER 9

Choosing Shipping Options When Transporting the Goods over the (Network) Roadway

Tons of businesses around the world use transportation companies to distribute their products. For instance, most small retail stores order goods from wholesalers, but a third company, a shipping company, actually picks up the products at the wholesaler and delivers them to the retailer. Likewise, when you order something over the Internet, typically one of the larger shipping companies, such as FedEx and UPS in the U.S., actually transports the product to your house.

This business model works well. The shipping companies of the world can build large fleets of trucks, planes, boats, donkeys, or whatever is needed to deliver the packages. They can deliver the goods for much less than each company trying to build its own distribution system. So, the companies that need their goods shipped save money, and the shippers make money.

A similar thing happens with application layer protocols and transport layer protocols in networking. The application layer protocols need to send and receive messages to and from another computer. As seen in Chapter 8, "Shipping Goods over a (Network) Roadway," some of those messages are just overhead, and some contain the actual end user data. Lots of application layer protocols need the same basic services to transport their messages across the network to another computer. Similar to companies that use shippers, the application layer protocols do not want to worry about the details of how the data gets between the computers. They just want to give the data to someone else, with the expectation that the data will be delivered to the application layer software at the destination computer.

In this chapter, you'll learn about how transport layer protocols perform several important functions on behalf of the myriad of application layer protocols, including the delivery of application layer messages and data between two computers.

"Hello, I'm at Your Service"

"Hello, this is Fred at Fred's Shipping Company. How can I help you today?" Yep, Fred, the owner, is answering the phones at his small shipping company. He's waiting for the phone to ring so that he can send his one driver, Barney, in his one truck to pick up a package and deliver it across town. To be ready for that first phone call, Fred bought a truck; hired Barney; got an office, phone lines, and Internet website; and did some advertising. Finally, the phone rang, giving Fred his first opportunity to ship the goods and make some money.

Like Fred, transport layer protocols must be prepared for when an application layer protocol needs its services. If you use TCP/IP applications, the application layer protocols use TCP/IP transport layer protocols to send their messages across the network. Whereas the application layer protocols are typically part of the application software, the transport layer protocols are typically part of the *operating system (OS)* of the computer. So, the transport layer software hangs around, waiting on the application program—specifically the part of the application program that implements the application layer protocols—to ask it to do something. Figure 9-1 depicts the general idea.

Figure 9-1   Application Program and Application Layer Asking the
Transport Layer for Help

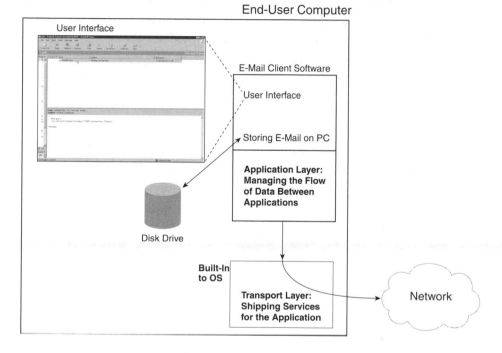

As shown in Figure 8-4 in the previous chapter, the application program includes the user interface and the application layer protocols. In Figure 8-6, you saw some of the SMTP messages that were used to send e-mail. That figure and several others in Chapter 8 showed the messages going back and forth between two PCs. In reality, when an e-mail client like the one in Figure 9-1 sends these types of messages, it asks for a transport layer protocol to help.

Generally speaking, when Those Who Came Before Us created networking models like TCP/IP, they defined a bunch of protocols. As it turns out, the protocols at one layer provide services to the protocols at one layer above. Conversely, protocols at one layer expect services from protocols that are one layer below. In this chapter, you'll read about how the application layer protocols such as SMTP expect the transport layer protocols, such as TCP, to provide the service of transporting the data across the network.

Full-Service Shipping

Just like a company can create its own shipping department, an application layer protocol could avoid using a transport layer protocol, but it almost never happens. Why? Well, the transport layer protocols already exist. They provide great services that many applications need. It takes a lot less time and effort for the application to use a transport layer protocol. In short, it's better, faster, cheaper, and simpler for an application to use a transport layer protocol.

So, what do these transport layer protocols do for the application? This chapter focuses on one of those protocols in particular—*Transmission Control Protocol (TCP)*, which is defined in RFC 793. TCP/IP does have another transport layer protocol—*User Datagram Protocol (UDP)*—but TCP is much more interesting. TCP provides a lot of features, and UDP doesn't. You can think of TCP as providing premium service and UDP as providing cheap service.

This chapter will hit the high points of TCP, such as

- Delivering application data through encapsulation
- Breaking large shipments into manageable sizes using segmentation
- Ensuring delivery through error recovery
- Getting the data to the right individual program, not just the right computer, by using port numbers
- Simplifying the creation of applications by hiding the details of data delivery from the application

You'll learn about each of these features in the next four sections of this chapter.

Shipping Basics: Controlling Shipments Using Shipping Labels

When you decide to ship a package using any well-known shipping company, you fill out a shipping label, attach it to the package, and leave the package where the shipper will find it when he stops by that day. In short, you tell the shipper where to send the package and then choose among several options for delivery. Magically, the package appears at the correct destination.

Although you might think that shipping labels are rather boring, there are a couple of key facts about them that are practically identical to TCP. For instance, shipping labels

- Include the shipper's address on the form

- Include the recipient's address on the form

- Specify other options, such as speed of delivery, insurance, and phone numbers in case there is a problem

- Put each bit of information in the same place, every time

- Ensure that everyone who touches the package at various points in its trip knows exactly what to do with the package

Okay, back to networking. The term "encapsulation" refers to the same general idea for networking as does the shipping label for shipping packages. For example, Figure 9-2 illustrates a more detailed example of a simple HTTP GET request for a home page, with TCP encapsulation shown. Keith's browser requests the home page. However, the browser does not actually send the request over the network; it simply asks the TCP software on Keith's computer to send the data for it. (In this chapter, I am ignoring other network details—such as the physical transmission—but that does happen as well.)

Figure 9-2   Adding Shipping Information to Data by Encapsulating in a TCP Header

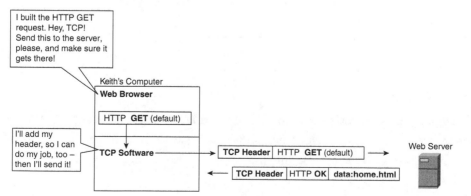

Keith's TCP software, which is typically just a part of the OS, is in charge of delivering the data to the web server. TCP provides several services, so it needs a place to record some information about those services. Therefore, TCP defines a header. As mentioned in Chapter 5, "Rules of the Road: How to Use the Local (Network) Roadway," a header is a bunch of overhead bits that a networking protocol adds to some data. The protocol that adds the header—TCP in this case—uses those bits to record things it needs to know to do its job. Many of the upcoming features covered in this chapter record information in the TCP header to perform some useful function.

The process of adding the TCP header to the application data is called *encapsulation*. Refer to Chapter 5 for a review of encapsulation.

Imagine that Paul drives a truck for the shipping company. He gets to work each morning, and someone has loaded the truck. He gets in, starts driving, and stops to drop off and pick up packages.

Paul doesn't care what's inside the packages. He might care a little about the size of the packages, particularly if a package is too large or heavy to move. Really, he just cares about what's on the shipping label and making sure he delivers the package to the right place.

Similarly, TCP doesn't really care what data it's delivering to another computer. Figure 9-3 shows TCP's perspective on what really happens in Figure 9-2.

Figure 9-3   TCP Treats All the Data as Data

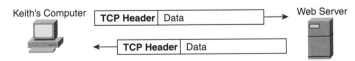

TCP just needs to worry about the TCP header and doing what it says. In this case, as long as TCP gets the first chunk of data to the server and the second chunk back from the server to the browser, its job is finished.

TCP calls the TCP header and the data behind it a ***TCP segment***. Later in this chapter, in the section titled "Big Box, Small Truck—What Do You Do?," it will be clear why the people who made up TCP chose to call it a ***segment***.

One of the largest benefits of a layered networking model relates to how TCP behaves in Figure 9-3. The fact that TCP doesn't have to think about what HTTP is trying to do means that the TCP software does not need to know anything about how HTTP works. So, the person who writes the TCP software can keep it simple. The person who writes HTTP software and any other application protocol that intends to use TCP can keep it simple as well, relying on TCP to deliver the data.

If you're feeling a little uncomfortable about TCP at this point, it's okay. So far, this chapter has described some mechanisms that TCP uses, but it hasn't explained much about why TCP is useful to applications. In the next section, you'll learn about error recovery—one of the most important features of TCP.

Purchasing Insurance for Your (Network) Shipment

When you ship something valuable, you might choose to spend some extra money to buy insurance. Then, if the shipper loses or damages the package, the shipper pays you to replace what you shipped.

With TCP, you get something a little better. With a real physical package, if it gets lost, it's lost. If you lose a bunch of bits, though, you can make more! In fact, Chapter 3, "Building a Network: It All Starts with a Plan," covered the basic idea, which I'll repeat in Figure 9-4 for a quick review.

Figure 9-4   Assuring Data Delivery

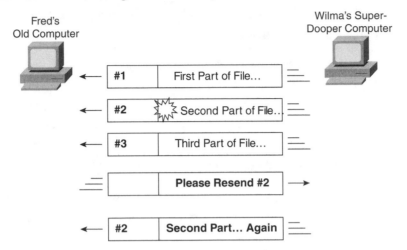

In Figure 9-4, Wilma's computer is sending three TCP segments to Fred. The second segment experienced some errors during transmission, and Fred noticed that errors had occurred. How did he know errors had occurred? Well, you might recall the frame check sequence (FCS) field in Ethernet that tells you whether something transmitted over a LAN had errors. Although this chapter doesn't consider Ethernet much, imagine that an Ethernet is in use, and that Fred does indeed notice that the frame had an error.

The process is simple: The sender (Wilma) numbered the segments so that if one got lost, Fred could not only know that one segment had errors, but he could ask for the missing numbered segment. So, Fred asks Wilma to resend segment 2. In the next two sections, you'll read about how TCP determines which segments were delivered successfully, and then how TCP notices that segments were lost and need to be recovered.

The Mechanics of Delivery Confirmation

TCP uses the same mechanisms to both confirm that data was delivered, as well as to notice when data wasn't delivered—and then to perform error recovery. To do all these things, TCP puts the interesting information in Figure 9-5 into the TCP header. First, look at a full TCP header in Figure 9-5. Then I'll tell you about the parts of the header that are used for error recovery.

Figure 9-5   The Format of the Shipping Label: TCP Headers

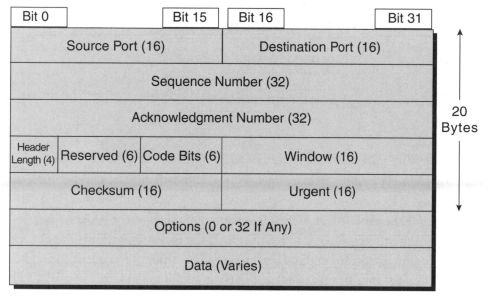

When TCP adds the header, it has several different fields to use. For error recovery, it uses the *sequence number* and *acknowledgment number* fields. The sequence number identifies the segment, and the acknowledgement number is used when an error occurs.

Figure 9-6 shows the sequence and acknowledgement number fields in action, when no errors occur.

Figure 9-6 Delivery Confirmation, No Errors

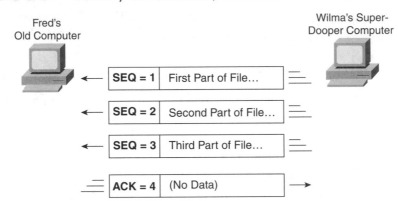

In Figure 9-6, TCP confirms delivery of each segment using the sequence and acknowledgment number fields. However, the acknowledgment number looks a little funny. Wilma numbered the segments 1, 2, and 3, but notice that Fred sent back an ACK field of 4. The ACK field means that this number is the number of the next segment Fred expects to receive. So, Fred is really meaning, "I got everything up to number 4, so send me 4 next." By implication, Fred got 1, 2, and 3, respectively, because he set the acknowledgment field to the next number—4 in this case. The use of the acknowledgment field to imply the next segment that should be received is called *forward acknowledgment*.

By using the sequence number field in the segments it sends and watching the acknowledgment number field in the segment it receives, Wilma's TCP software can know that all three segments were delivered successfully to Fred. Next, you'll see how Wilma deals with the loss of a segment.

Lose All You Want—We'll Make More

So, back to error recovery. Figure 9-7 shows a case in which a segment has errors (segment two), with Fred sending a segment with ACK of 2.

Figure 9-7   TCP Error-Recovery Process

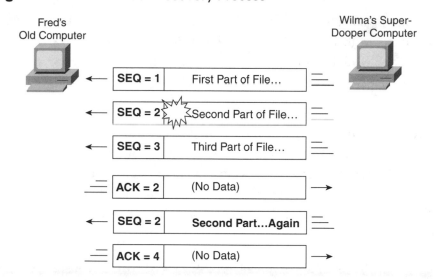

The process is identical to Figure 9-4, but Figure 9-7 shows the TCP header field values. Fred gets segment 1 and 3 successfully, so by implication, he knows that Wilma sent segment 2, but it either didn't make it to Fred, or it had errors in it. So, Fred sends a segment back to Wilma, with ACK set to 2. With forward acknowledgement logic, Wilma knows that Fred expects to get segment 2 next, implying that he got number 1, but not number 2.

In response, Wilma sends segment 2 again. To be able to re-send segment 2, Wilma must have kept a copy of each segment. After a segment has been acknowledged, Wilma can release the memory to be used for other purposes. However, by keeping a copy, Wilma could re-send any lost segments.

Notice that Wilma re-sent segment 2 only, allowing Fred time to send back a segment with ACK of 4. By doing so, Fred acknowledged receipt of the re-sent segment 2, and well as the earlier receipt of segment 3.

Big Box, Small Truck—What Do You Do?

When you ship something, the shipper can easily handle your package, using the normal trucks, with a single driver stopping by to pick up your package. But the shipper does have a limit to the dimensions and weight of the package; otherwise, the package might not fit on the truck, or it might be too heavy for the driver to pick up.

However, sometimes, companies need to send lots of stuff—stuff that, when packaged, far exceeds the shipper's limitations for the size of a package. In some cases, the shipper sends special trucks to pick up the stuff, and maybe uses a forklift to load the truck. Or, the company wanting to ship something works with the shipping company to package the stuff so that the packages can be handled more easily.

In networking, if a large piece of data needs to be sent, it's easy to break up a large number of bits into smaller pieces. As it turns out, Those Who Came Before Us decided to have the transport layer protocol break the data into pieces before transmission. If an application has a large amount of data to send, it gives the whole chunk of data to the transport layer protocol, and the transport layer protocol worries about breaking the data into manageable pieces.

A maximum number of bytes can be put into a TCP segment (including the TCP header). 1480 is the typical maximum, although it can be larger in some instances. The maximum size of a segment is called the *maximum segment size (mss)*.

The application layer protocol does not have a limit to the size of bytes it chooses to send; it just lets the transport layer protocol worry about it. Here's how the application layer protocol thinks about the size of the data that should be sent:

> "I just need to send a big bunch of bytes. Transport layer, please send these bits to the other computer."

The transport layer gets the bytes from the application layer, but it has an mss to worry about. So, the transport layer thinks something like this:

> "I need to send this big bunch of bytes. I'll break them up into pieces, no larger than mss each, before sending it to the other device."

The process of breaking the data into parts is called *segmentation*. The bytes that include the data and the TCP header are called TCP segments because TCP often breaks up, or *segments*, a large chunk of data received from the applications. Figure 9-8 shows an example, where the file that contains the home page has 3000 bytes of data.

Figure 9-8   Segmenting Data Before Sending

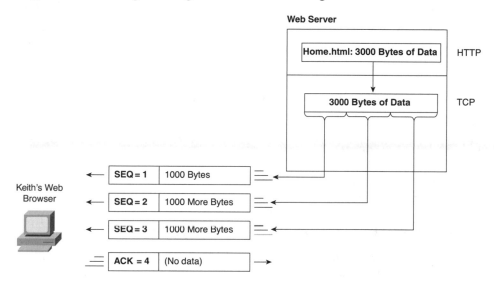

TCP on the web server breaks the 3000 bytes of application data into three segments in this example. HTTP gives all 3000 bytes to TCP. TCP happens to have an mss of 1480, and because each TCP header is 20-bytes in length, only 1460 bytes can be put into the data part of a segment. Because TCP needs three segments in this case, it puts 1/3 or so of the data into each segment, as shown.

Why Three Smaller Segments Is Better Than One Big Segment

Why bother with segmentation? Why didn't the people who made up the TCP protocol just specify a larger mss? To see the need, keep error recovery in mind and consider this example. Imagine that you download a web page, and the web page has a logo of the company in it. The graphics file is called logo.gif, and it is 146 KB(Kilo Bytes) long.

Now imagine that TCP sent all the data in one TCP segment. If you send 146 KB of data in one segment, and it gets there, all is well. However, if a single bit had an error during transmission, then the one and only segment—the one with 146 KB in it—would have to be re-sent. All for one lousy bit error!

By sending logo.gif as 100 segments with 1460 bytes in each segment, you would still send the whole file. However, if a single bit error occurred, only one segment would have had an error, so only one segment would have to be re-sent. Because some transmission errors will occur, limiting segments to some maximum size enhances the overall network performance.

My Little White Lie About Acknowledgments

Okay, let me confess something to you: TCP error recovery and acknowledgements do not work exactly like I showed in Figures 9-7 and 9-8. I purposefully simplified the earlier descriptions to get through some of the detail. Now that you've read most of this chapter about TCP, let me clear something up about TCP error recovery.

note
I could've placed the upcoming details a little earlier in this chapter, but experience from teaching these concepts tells me that it's good to get a little of the concept, and then the rest, so here it goes!

The TCP sequence number and acknowledgement number fields do not number the segments; they identify the first byte in the data portion of the segment. For instance, if a PC sent a segment, and each segment had just 1 byte in it, then sequence numbers and acknowledgements would work just like you read about earlier in this chapter. However, in the example shown in Figure 9-8, all the segments have 1000 bytes in them. So, Figure 9-9 shows the correct sequence and acknowledgement fields.

Figure 9-9   Acknowledging Each Byte

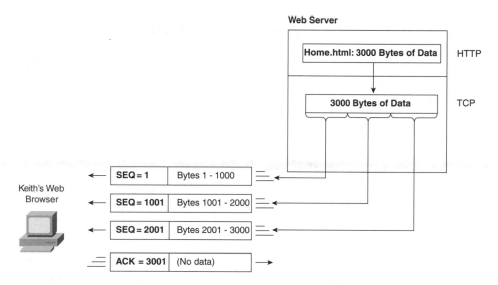

When the server sends the first segment, it starts with a sequence number of 1. However, the sequence number with TCP actually numbers the bytes, not the segments. So, from TCP's perspective, the first byte in the first segment is number 1, and the last byte in the first segment is number 1000. Keith's TCP software sees a sequence number of 1, and sees 1000 total bytes, and decides that the bytes are numbered 1 through 1000.

When TCP at the server builds the second segment, it thinks like this: "The last sequence number was 1, and the segment had 1000 bytes. My next sequence number ought to be 1001 because the last byte in the previous segment was byte number 1000." So, as shown, the server does exactly that. Similarly, the server sends the third segment as sequence number 2001. The last byte of that segment would be number 3000.

Finally, when Keith's TCP software acknowledges the data, it should acknowledge all received data. It received bytes 1–1000, 1001–2000, and 2001–3000 in the three successive TCP segments. Because Keith received all three, without error, Keith's next segment shows an acknowledgement of 3001—the next byte he expects to receive.

Delivering the Package to the Right Person, Not Just the Right Address

When you ship a package, you not only put the address on the shipping label, but you put the name of the person to whom the package is intended. The reason for that is obvious: You want to make sure the right person gets the package you are sending.

Transport layer protocols do the same kind of thing. Imagine, for instance, that Keith has two browsers open: one to look at http://www.fredsco.com, and one to look at http://www.espn.com. Keith also has his e-mail client software up all the time, and he has an FTP client working, downloading some files.

What happens when a new TCP segment arrives at Keith's computer? Well, the segment gets to the right computer, but it might have data for one of the two browsers, the e-mail client, or the FTP client, as shown in Figure 9-10.

Figure 9-10   Keith's Quandary: One Segment, but Four Applications

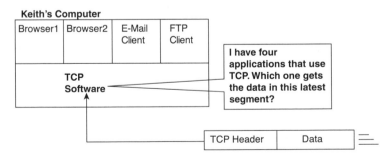

If a package shows up at your office building, whomever happens to be standing around at the time looks at the shipping label, notices the name, and does what needs to be done to get the package to that person. Similarly, there's a field in the TCP header called the *TCP destination port* that tells the receiving computer (Keith's PC in this case) which application program needs to be given the data. For each application program that is currently being used on one computer, the computer assigns that application a unique *TCP port* number. To send data to a specific application on the computer, you send a TCP segment to that computer and plug the correct TCP port number into the destination TCP port number field in the TCP header.

An example certainly helps in this case. Figure 9-11 shows how Keith uses the destination port field. Browser1 uses port number 1030, and browser2 uses port 1031. The e-mail client is using port 1040, and the FTP client is using port 1045. So, when the segment arrives, Keith's TCP software checks the TCP destination port field in the TCP header, which tells the PC to give the data to browser2. As long as each application running on Keith's computer uses a different TCP port number, Keith can receive TCP segments and figure out what to do with the data.

Figure 9-11 Using the Destination Port Field Like a Recipient's Name on a Shipping Label

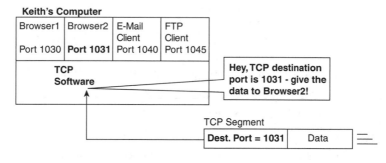

When Keith receives the segment, he looks at the destination port field. In this case, he found destination TCP port 1031, so he gave the data to browser2.

The Chicken, the Egg, and the Destination Port of the First Segment

To allow a computer to have lots of applications that use TCP at the same time, the people who created TCP came up with the idea of a destination port number field. However, there's a small chicken-and-egg problem, and it relates to how things get started with TCP. Imagine that Keith just started his second browser—the one I called browser2 in Figure 9-11. Keith starts clicking on something to bring up browser2, and then he fills in the URL for the web page he wants to get from a web server. Figure 9-12 shows an example of the first segment sent by Keith's PC on behalf of this new browser and the response segment from the web server.

Figure 9-12 Initializing TCP Port Numbers

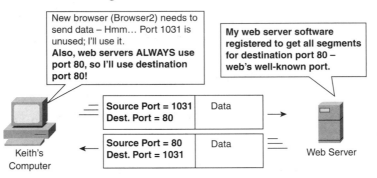

When an application on Keith's PC (browser2 in this case) first asks TCP to send data, TCP software running on Keith finds a TCP port number that he's not currently using and uses it for this new application. As long as no other application that is running on Keith's PC uses this same TCP port number, any future TCP segments that Keith's PC receives can be handled correctly. In Figure 9-12, Keith's PC uses port 1031 for browser2.

Keith's PC hopes that the server will reply to its request for a web page. Keith expects that the segment he receives from the server will have a destination TCP port number field set to 1031. To make sure that happens, Keith's PC sets the *TCP source port* field in the first segment to a value of 1031. The TCP source port file contains the port number used by the application that sent the TCP segment. That way, when the server replies, it knows what to put in the TCP destination port field—1031 in this example.

When a client application first comes up, TCP on that computer dynamically assigns the application a TCP port number. These port numbers are sometimes called *dynamically assigned port* numbers, or *ephemeral port* numbers.

Well, that's only part of the story. When Keith's PC creates the first segment in Figure 9-12, the one sent to the web server, Keith's PC must put something in the TCP destination port field. Why? Well, the computer where the web server software resides might have multiple applications running, so the server's TCP software would want to look at the destination port field in the received TCP segment to figure out to which application to give the data. In this case, Keith's PC put port 80 in the header because port 80 is the well-known port for web servers.

Well-known ports allow the first segment sent between applications on two computers to have a useful destination port in it. Before Keith attempts to connect to the web server, the web server software tells TCP on the web server something like "Hey, if you get something for destination port 80, give it to me." Later, when Keith sends a segment with destination port 80 to that server, the server's TCP software knows to give the data to the web server software. In general, servers use well-known ports, allowing clients to put the correct destination port number in their initial TCP segments.

Starting Off on the Right Foot Using a TCP Connection

So far in this chapter, you have learned about how TCP provides services to application layer protocols. Those services include basic delivery, segmentation, and error recovery. TCP also allows multiple programs to use it at the same time, keeping track of which segments are for which application using port numbers.

To do all these functions, TCP uses several fields in the TCP header. Before useful communication can occur with TCP, both endpoints must agree to the values to use in those fields initially.

TCP uses a process called ***TCP connection establishment*** to initialize several fields in the TCP header. Each time a browser connects to a new website, each time an e-mail client checks for incoming mail, and so on, a new TCP connection is created when the two computers participate in TCP connection establishment. Connection establishment is performed when the two computers send a specific set of three TCP segments to each other. After that, a TCP connection exists between the application programs on each computer, and the TCP header fields have valid initial values that both endpoints agree upon.

The term ***TCP connection*** refers to an agreement whereby one application on one computer agrees to talk with another application on another computer. For example, in Figure 9-12, before Keith's PC could request the web page shown in the figure, a TCP connection had to exist between browser2 and the web server software. To create that TCP connection, three TCP segments flow between the browser and the web server. After that is completed, a TCP connection exists, with agreement on such details as what port numbers the browser and server use, what values to start with in the sequence number field, and other details. Any time you start a new TCP-based application, a new TCP connection is formed before application messages or end user data can be transferred.

Figure 9-13 shows Keith once again, with his two browsers, one e-mail client, and one FTP client. In this case, the servers are also shown. The lines in the figure represent Keith's four TCP connections.

Figure 9-13   Keith's TCP Connections

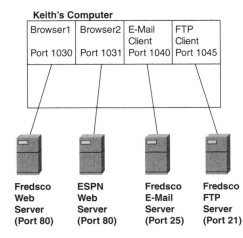

In this figure, Keith has four TCP connections, one from each of his client applications to their respective servers.

Chapter Summary

Almost all application layer protocols have a common set of functions that need to be performed. Rather than have each application protocol implement those functions, the creators of networking models put several of these common functions into the layer below the application layer. In TCP/IP, that layer is the transport layer. In this chapter, you read about the most popular option for TCP/IP transport layer protocols: TCP.

TCP provides several features for applications, including

- Basic delivery through encapsulation

- Breaking large chunks of data into manageable sizes using segmentation

- Ensuring delivery through error recovery

- Getting the data to the right individual program, not just the right computer, by using port numbers

- Simplifying the creation of applications by hiding the details of actual data delivery from the application

Chapter Review Questions

You can find the answers to the following questions in Appendix A, "Answers to Chapter Review Questions."

1. List three of the main features of TCP.

2. Imagine that you visit a website, and as a result, you download a graphics image called logo.gif. The logo is 4000 bytes. How many segment(s) will the server send back to your browser to send you the logo? Assume an mss of 1480 bytes. Explain your answer.

3. Imagine that a web server sent 3 TCP segments to a browser on Keith's PC, each 1000 bytes long, with sequence numbers 4304, 5304, and 6304, respectively. Assuming no errors had occurred, explain how Keith's PC could acknowledge receipt of the data.

4. Imagine that a web server sent 3 TCP segments to a browser on Keith's PC, each 1000 bytes long, with sequence numbers 4304, 5304, and 6304, respectively. Assuming that the third segment had errors in it, explain how the data would be recovered.

5. Define the word *encapsulation*, using TCP encapsulation as an example.

6. Imagine that Keith brings up a browser on his PC and browses a website. He then brings up another browser, browsing a second website. When Keith receives the next TCP segment, how does his PC know to which browser to give the data?

7. How many TCP segments flow between two computers to establish a TCP connection?

8. What is the name of the other TCP/IP transport layer protocol?

9. A TCP header, along with the application data, is called what?

10. Define the term *forward acknowledgment*.

11. Define the term *well-known port*.

Navigating the Roadways to Find the Right Street Address

Part IV gets into more detail about how networks with multiple LANs work. To deliver end user data between different LANs, networking devices called routers are used; these routers forward data based on TCP/IP addresses. Chapter 10 introduces the concepts of TCP/IP addressing and the basics of routing, and Chapter 11 provides more detail on the routing process. Chapter 12 describes the basics of how routers learn how to route packets by using something called a *routing protocol*. Finally, Chapter 13 explains how TCP/IP networks use names and how they are resolved into their corresponding numeric TCP/IP addresses.

Chapter 10: Delivering the Goods to the Right Street (IP) Address

Chapter 11: Knowing Where to Turn at Each Intersection (Router)

Chapter 12: Painting the Road Signs on Your Interstate (Internetwork)

Chapter 13: People Like Names, but Computers Like Numbers

What You Will Learn

After reading this chapter, you should be able to

- ✔ Explain the basic process of routing an IP packet from one computer to another

- ✔ Describe the structure of IP addresses

- ✔ Describe the size of Class A, B, and C IP networks

- ✔ Identify addresses as belonging to a particular Class A, B, or C network

- ✔ Describe the need for IP subnetting

- ✔ Explain how a basic example of IP subnetting works when you're using a Class B network

CHAPTER 10

Delivering the Goods to the Right Street (IP) Address

When people use computers, they like to use names to refer to other computers—especially names that are easy to remember. For instance, it's a lot easier to remember something like http://www.cisco.com, instead of a number like 198.133.219.25. As it turns out, you could plug either the name or the number into your browser's URL field to get Cisco's home page, but the name is much easier to remember.

Computers, however, find it more convenient to identify each computer using a number. Computers, working together with networking devices called *routers*, deliver data from one computer to another. So, although a human might prefer to use names like http://www.cisco.com, computers and routers prefer to forward data to http://www.cisco.com using the server's numeric address, such as 198.133.219.25.

In the previous two chapters, you focused on application protocols and how they use TCP for some common functions. However, to focus on those protocols, those chapters avoided several issues. For instance, when a user types **http://www.cisco.com**, how does she know where the web server is? How does the PC know where to send the data? Assuming Cisco's web server is on a different LAN—which is likely—how do other networking devices, such as routers, know how to deliver the bits to the web server?

The next four chapters finally get around to answering those questions. In this chapter, you learn some important details about the Internet Protocol (IP), including how IP addresses work.

Navigation Basics: Driving to the Right Destination

When you want to drive somewhere near your house, you get in your car, drive on the local roads, and get there. When you need to drive a longer distance, say to another town, you probably start off on those same local roads but then get on a highway. After you drive far enough to get to that town, you get off the highway and use the town's local roads to get to where you want to go.

Now, imagine that you have a visitor staying at your house, and he wants to drive to that next town. You could tell him to drive down the road that runs past your house until he reaches the first intersection, and then follow the road signs. Your friend could simply look at the road sign at that intersection, which tells him where to turn. If he reads the road sign at each intersection, he might make a lot of turns, but he will eventually get where he wants to go, as long as the road signs list the town to which he wants to drive.

In TCP/IP networks, routers act as intersections, with the router making the choice about what direction to forward data packets. In a typical large network, many routers and LAN switches sit between a client PC and a server. When one computer sends data to another computer, the routers make decisions about where to forward the data so that it reaches the correct destination. For example, in Figure 10-1, a user (Hannah) on a LAN in Mason wants to get a web page from a web server (http://www.cisco.com) on a LAN in Cincinnati. At some point, Hannah's PC sends the initial HTTP GET request to the web server. The figure shows that initial request, with the routers deciding where to forward the data so that it reaches the web server.

Figure 10-1 Navigating (Routing) When Going from Mason and Cincinnati

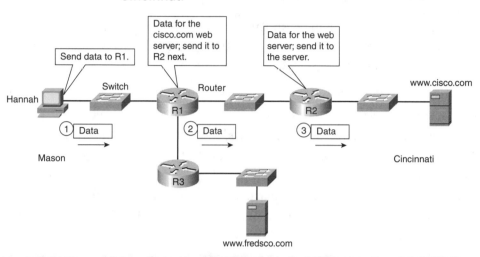

The cylindrical icons in the figure represent *routers*, and the rectangular icons represent Ethernet LAN switches. Routers are networking devices that connect to multiple physical networks, such as the multiple Ethernet networks in the figure. Routers also forward data from one network to the next. When you drive in your car and reach an intersection, the road signs tell you where to turn; in networking, the routers create the equivalent of a road sign, but the router tells the data packets which way to turn. The complete process by which a computer sends the data, passing though all the routers and eventually arriving at the destination, is called *routing*. The following list shows the three main routing steps in Figure 10-1:

1. Hannah sends her data to R1, much like a driver might drive to where he can get on the interstate highway. To send the data to R1, Hannah's PC sends an Ethernet frame to R1's MAC address, much like a driver might use local roads to reach the on-ramp to the highway.

2. R1 knows that to get the data to a computer in Cincinnati, it must forward the data to R2, instead of sending the data to R3 next. This process is much like a driver choosing which direction to go on the interstate highway, based

on the road signs. (Because the physical network between R1 and R2 is an Ethernet, R1 forwards the data to R2 using an Ethernet frame.)

3. R2 sends the data to the destination computer over the LAN much like the driver finishes his trip by getting off the interstate highway and driving over the local roads in Cincinnati.

If you consider these steps a little more closely, three devices need to forward the data at some point: Hannah, R1, and R2, in succession. Each time, to get the data to the next device, the devices need to send the data over an Ethernet LAN—and you already know how that works from reading Chapters 4, "How to Build a Local (Network) Roadway," through 7, "Adding Local (Network) Roadways for No Extra Money." In sequence, Hannah uses Ethernet to send the data to R1; R1 uses the second Ethernet network to send the data to R2; finally, R2 uses the third Ethernet to send the data to the web server.

note

As I mentioned before, the word "network" can be used in a lot of different ways. In one way of thinking, Figure 10-1 shows a single network, but in another way of thinking, it shows four Ethernet networks, which are then separated by three routers. Another related term, called *internetwork*, is sometimes used when you need a more exact term. If you consider each of the four Ethernets in Figure 10-1 as individual networks, you can think of the whole diagram as an internetwork, which is short for "interconnected networks." Keep in mind that people use the term "network" in a lot of different ways.

Although Figure 10-1 shows only LANs, the routers could be connected to a wide-area network (WAN). In fact, one of the main benefits of routers, besides helping forward data through the network, is to connect to many different types of physical networks. In later chapters, particularly in Chapters 14, "Leasing a (Network) Roadway Between Two Points," and Chapter 15, "Leasing a (Network) Roadway Between Lots of Places," you will learn how routers use WANs to transmit data, much like they can use LANs to transmit data. Regardless, the basic process of routing happens the same way, whether you use LANs, WANs, or a combination of the two. In fact, one of the reasons that routers are popular is because they can connect many different types of physical networks with ease.

This first simple example portrays the concepts of routing, which is the overall process by which computers and routers together forward the data to the correct destination. To appreciate more of the details of routing, you need to have a better understanding of IP, IP addresses, and how they affect routing.

IP as the Postmaster General of the Network

The U.S. Postal Service (USPS) uses an address system that consists of a number, street name on which the building is located, town or city, state, and zip code. The USPS intended for each address in the country to be unique in some way. In a given state, all towns must have different names. In each town, each street must have a different name. Finally, on each street, each building must have a different number. This system allows each address in the country to be unique. By having unique addresses, the postal service doesn't get confused about where to send a letter.

The postal service includes information in the address so that sorting the mail is made as easy as possible. A postal worker in Georgia can see a letter addressed to someone in Ohio and make a choice to immediately sort that letter into the bag that's being sent to Ohio. After the letter is in Ohio, the mail sorter can look for the name of the town and send the letter there. At the local post office for that town, the postal sorter can look at the street address. So, the process of sorting is simplified by the information in the address.

IP is the TCP/IP protocol that most closely matches Layer 3 in the OSI networking model. IP defines addressing, as well as routing, including the underlying details of the routing example in Figure 10-1. Like the postal service, IP defines addresses so that they have structure, allowing easy routing—the networking equivalent of mail sorting. IP also states that everyone should have a unique IP address (just like the USPS requires unique postal addresses) to avoid confusion when trying to deliver data to that address. The postal service defines addressing details so that letter carriers can easily and efficiently deliver the mail; similarly, IP defines IP addressing details to facilitate easy and efficient forwarding of IP packets.

Each network interface on a computer needs an IP address. A *network interface* is simply a card inside a computer that has a physical connector for some type of network, such as an Ethernet network interface card (NIC). The NIC takes care of TCP/IP network interface layer details, which are the equivalent of OSI Layers 1 and 2. The TCP/IP internetworking layer, implemented by the IP protocol, defines these logical IP addresses. Most end user computers have a single network interface, meaning that the computer has only one IP address. However, any device that has at least one IP address can send and receive IP packets and is considered to be a *TCP/IP host*, or simply *host*.

Devices that have more than one network interface have more than one IP address. Routers typically have multiple network interfaces, and some servers have multiple interfaces as well.

IP addresses are 32-bit binary numbers, but because humans would find it inconvenient to write down 32-bit numbers, the addresses are written in decimal. The format of IP addresses is often called *canonical* format; sometimes it's called *dotted decimal* format. For example, the next two lines show the binary version of an IP address, followed by the same IP address written as a dotted-decimal number. It's obvious from comparing the two that, given a choice, it's much easier to work with the decimal version:

00001000 00000100 00000010 00000001

8.4.2.1

Each of the decimal numbers in an IP address is called an *octet*. (The term *octet* is just another term for the word *byte*.) So, each decimal octet represents 8 bits of the IP address, and with 4 octets (separated by periods), the whole dotted decimal IP address represents 32 bits.

Appendix B, "Converting IP Addresses Between Decimal and Binary," explains how you can convert back and forth between the binary and decimal versions of an IP address. You really don't need to think about IP addresses in binary to learn what's covered in this chapter. However, if you would like to understand more about converting between binary and decimal formats of IP addresses, feel free to read Appendix B.

Knowing the Address Before Driving to the Destination

Let's get back to the more important conceptual details. When you use a shipping company to send a package to someone, you fill out a shipping label, which includes the street address to which you are sending the package. If you fill out the whole label, you also put your return address on the label, so in case there's a problem, the shipper can return the package to you.

Similarly, IP defines a header that includes a source and destination IP address. So, to send data from one computer to the other, the sender puts the destination computer's IP address into the *destination IP address* field in the IP header. Similarly, the sender puts its own IP address in the *source IP address* field in the header.

Figure 10-2 shows the same network as Figure 10-1, but it now shows Hannah's IP address, as well the web server's. It shows a single IP packet, sent by Hannah, to the server.

Figure 10-2   Using Addresses on the (IP) Shipping Label

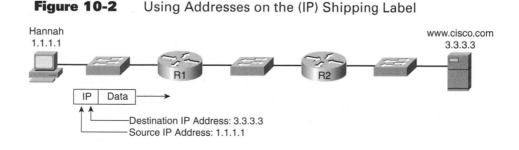

IP defines a 20-byte long header, which includes a 4-byte source IP address and a 4-byte destination IP address. An *IP packet* includes the IP header, along with any data that follows the IP header. Although other parts of the IP header are interesting, the address fields are crucial.

note

You might recall that Ethernet includes a source and destination Ethernet address field in the Ethernet header, and that those addresses are 6 bytes long each. The IP addresses mentioned here are indeed different addresses, and they are used to allow networking devices to send data over a large network that includes other types of physical networks besides Ethernet.

When sending a packet, the destination IP address field in the IP header defines where the packet should be sent. The computers, and the routers between them, understand that the packet should be forwarded based on the destination IP address. The source IP address in the header is also important because after the packet is delivered to the destination computer, it will want to reply. That computer knows the IP address of the computer that sent the original packet by looking at the source IP address. For instance, in Figure 10-2, when the web server gets the packet and needs to respond, it knows to send the response packet to 1.1.1.1.

The term "packet" has a specific meaning in networking. It implies some data that includes the Layer 3 header, plus any encapsulated data. In the TCP/IP networking model, IP is the Layer 3 protocol, so an IP header and the data that follows it are IP packets. The term "segment," which you read about in Chapter 9, "Choosing Shipping Options When Transporting Goods over the (Network) Roadway," refers to data that includes the Layer 4 header (TCP) and any encapsulated data. The difference between a packet and a segment is that a segment does not include the Layer 3 header, but a packet does.

As a reminder, you might also recall from Chapter 5, "Rules of the Road: How to Use the Local (Network) Roadway," that the term "frame" refers to a data link header and its encapsulated data. In that chapter, an Ethernet header and trailer encapsulated some data to send the data over an Ethernet LAN. It's common to use the term "frame" to refer to the data link header, trailer, and data; "packet" to refer to the network layer (IP) header and data; and "segment" to refer to the transport layer (TCP) header and data.

When sending data, the IP software on a computer (Hannah in this example) encapsulates the higher-layer data inside an IP packet. For a more detailed appreciation of that concept, think back to the HTTP coverage in Chapter 8, "Shipping Goods over a (Network) Roadway," and Chapter 9's coverage of TCP. For Hannah to get the web page, she must send an HTTP GET request. To send HTTP messages, she must use TCP. As it turns out, to deliver the TCP segment to the other computer, TCP must use IP. Figure 10-3 shows the process of getting a home page with more detail, including the IP headers and IP packets.

Figure 10-3   IP Packets, Including Details About the Data

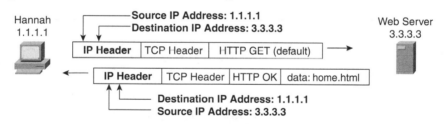

On a single computer, the different layers in the TCP/IP model work together to accomplish the ultimate goal, which is to give the end user the data that he needs. HTTP is concerned about getting a web page to the user. TCP is concerned about segmentation, error recovery, and other things, on behalf of HTTP. So, as you read in Chapter 9, TCP provides service to the application layer—in this case, HTTP.

Similarly, IP (network layer) provides a service to the layer above it, namely TCP (transport layer): the service of end-to-end delivery of packets. TCP wants to send each segment to the other computer, but TCP does not define details about how the segment is delivered. Instead, TCP just asks IP for help. The IP software on Hannah puts an IP header around the segment. That header includes the correct source and destination IP address, which allows the IP protocol to deliver the packet to the web server.

Figure 10-3 shows what is inside the packet; however, just as a shipper does not care about what's in a package, IP does not care about the TCP header, the HTTP header, or the end user data. IP just needs to know the destination address so that it can forward the packet toward the destination. So, from IP's perspective, the IP packet looks like Figure 10-4.

Figure 10-4   IP Packets Ignoring Details About the Data

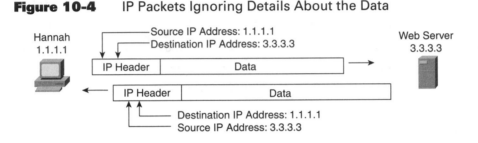

Putting a Name on the Shipping Label

The IP protocol defines how computers forward IP packets from end to end across an internetwork. However, most people tend to use names instead of addresses. Before a computer can send a packet to a particular destination IP address, the user must either supply the IP address of the other computer or a name for the other computer. For instance, Hannah probably typed in something like **http:// www.fredsco.com**; she must somehow correlate the name (such as http:// www.fredsco.com) to the corresponding IP address (such as 3.3.3.3).

The process by which Hannah figures out the IP address of another computer, based on the name, is called *name resolution*. Name resolution is covered in Chapter 13. For now, just to help complete the circle, keep in mind that people do refer to the name of the other computer, and the sending computer figures out the corresponding IP address.

Now that you know some of the basics of IP addressing and IP routing, the rest of this chapter looks into more details about IP addresses. After that, Chapter 11, "Knowing Where to Turn at Each Intersection (Router)," looks more closely at routing. Chapter 12, "Painting the Road Signs on Your Interstate (Internetwork)," examines how routers learn routes, and Chapter 13 covers how a computer resolves the name used by the user into the IP address that name implies.

How to Run a (Network) Postal Service

The postal service provides the public with a wonderful service. You put a letter into the mailbox, and it magically appears at the right address—most of the time, at least. The IP protocol defines a similar service for networks. By sending an IP packet into the network, with a correct destination address, the networking devices should collectively be able to forward the packet to the right destination.

This section takes you a little deeper into IP addressing. To understand these concepts, I'll sprinkle in a few comments about routing. Why? Well, IP addresses work like they do in part to help routing work well. Chapter 11 covers more details about the routing process.

One Location, One Zip Code, One Network Number

So far, you learned what IP addresses look like when written down—4 decimal numbers, between 0 and 255 inclusive, separated by periods. However, you also need to know more about the structure and meaning of these addresses. The structure and meaning of the addresses tells you about how IP addresses are used in an internetwork.

More postal service analogies can help, mainly because the concepts happen to be similar. In addition to the number, street, town, and state, the postal service uses *zip codes* to make it easy to sort the mail. (For anyone not familiar with zip codes in the U.S., a zip code is the U.S. version of what other countries call *postal codes*.) The postal service includes a zip code in everyone's address. It also ensures that everyone in the same general geographical area has the same zip code. For instance, everyone who lives in the same town that I do has the same zip code.

Zip codes allow the postal service to easily sort mail using automated mechanical sorting machines. The sorting machines look for the zip code on the front of the letter and ignore the rest of the address. Early technology for looking at and recognizing hand-written numbers and letters worked a lot better when looking for numbers, so the sorting machines were designed to look for the numeric zip code. Also, by sorting based on zip code, the USPS could overcome issues such as misspelled city names. So, the sorters could sort based on zip code, and the postal workers could deliver the letters for a particular zip code to the post office that handles mail for that zip code.

The only time the whole postal address is needed is when the letter gets to the final post office—the one that handles mail for that zip code. For instance, imagine there's a letter in the post office in Cincinnati, with a delivery address in Mason, Ohio, which is a suburb of Cincinnati, zip code 45040. The sorting machine in Cincinnati just looks at the zip code, which sorts the letter into the bin of letters that will be sent to Mason. When the letter is in the Mason post office, the local postal worker looks at the whole address, including the street name and number, so that the letter is given to the right mail carrier—the one who drives past that address each day. Figure 10-5 depicts this simple example.

Figure 10-5   Postal Sorting Using Zip Codes

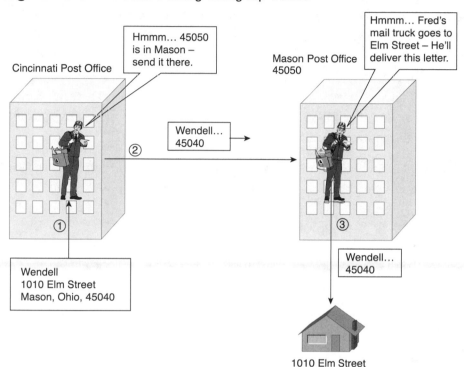

The following list depicts the process shown in the figure:

1. Someone has written a letter and addressed it to me at an address in Mason, Ohio. The person either brings the letter to the post office in Cincinnati or drops it in a mailbox in Cincinnati. Either way, the letter ends up in the post office in Cincy, and a decision needs to be made.

2. Either a postal worker or more likely a mail-sorting machine sorts the letter. The sorter puts the letter shown in the figure into a pile of letters that will be put into a truck and driven to Mason. The letter is sent to the Mason post office.

3. At the Mason post office, the letter is sorted again. However, in this case, the sorter in Mason looks at the whole address, including the street address. The letter is put on the truck that passes by 1010 Elm street in Mason each day. That way, the driver can stop at that address and leave the letter in the mailbox.

IP routing works somewhat like the way the USPS forwards letters. For instance, the IP routing process relies on the fact that all IP addresses on the same physical network—such as all IP addresses on one Ethernet LAN—have a portion of their IP addresses in common. This part of the address that is the same on all IP addresses on that physical network works just like a zip code. Just as zip codes identify a bunch of postal addresses that are in the same general area, all the IP addresses on the same Ethernet are in the same general area, so routing can take advantage of that fact.

Examples definitely help for this idea. Consider Figure 10-6, which shows a simple internetwork with two routers and three IP networks.

Figure 10-6   IP Zip Codes: Network Numbers

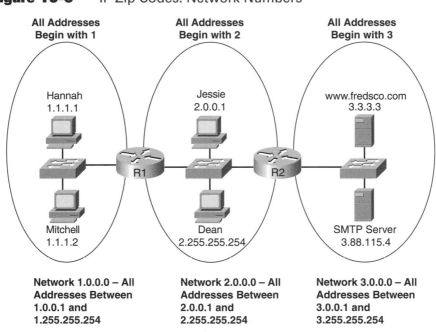

All Addresses Begin with 1

Hannah
1.1.1.1

Mitchell
1.1.1.2

R1

All Addresses Begin with 2

Jessie
2.0.0.1

Dean
2.255.255.254

R2

All Addresses Begin with 3

www.fredsco.com
3.3.3.3

SMTP Server
3.88.115.4

Network 1.0.0.0 – All Addresses Between 1.0.0.1 and 1.255.255.254

Network 2.0.0.0 – All Addresses Between 2.0.0.1 and 2.255.255.254

Network 3.0.0.0 – All Addresses Between 3.0.0.1 and 3.255.255.254

The conventions of IP addressing and IP address grouping make routing easy. In this example, all IP addresses on the Ethernet on the left begin with a first octet of 1. Similarly, all IP addresses that begin with 2 are on the Ethernet in the middle, and all IP addresses that begin with 3 should be on the Ethernet on the right. If you need to put a new computer on the leftmost Ethernet, you just need to give it an IP address that starts with 1, in addition to making sure that no other devices on that LAN are already using that IP address.

These conventions make routing easy. For instance, imagine the logic needed by R1 in Figure 10-6 to forward packets:

- Packets whose destination begins with 1 should be forwarded to the left.

- Packets whose destination begins with 2 should be forwarded to the Ethernet on the right.

- Packets whose destination begins with 3 should be forwarded to the right, sending them to R2 so that R2 can forward the packet.

The routers do not have to know about every IP address in the network; they just need to know about each group of addresses. It's just like the idea that a postal sorting machine in Texas doesn't need to know every street address in Mason, Ohio; it just needs to know that if the zip code is 45040, the letter should be sent to Mason. When Hannah sends a packet to the http://www.fredsco.com web server (IP address 3.3.3.3), Hannah sends the packet to R1. R1 knows that all addresses that start with 3 can be reached by sending the packet to router R2, so R1 just forwards the packet to R2. R2, in turn, knows that all addresses that begin with 3 are on the Ethernet to its right, so it can send the packet directly to the web server on that Ethernet.

IP calls the group of IP addresses that share a common beginning to part of their addresses an *IP network*. Figure 10-6 shows three IP networks.

note
The term "network" is used in a variety of ways and for slightly different meanings. Back in Chapter 1, "What Is a Network?," I defined a network as "a combination of hardware, software, and cabling, which together allow multiple computing devices to communicate with each other." When talking about IP addressing, the terms "network" and "IP network" have a different and more specific meaning, as will be explained in the upcoming pages of this chapter.

To talk about IP networks, you would use phrases such as "network 1" or "IP network 1" when referring to the group of IP addresses that start with a 1. However, when you're writing something down or typing something when you are working with a networking device, you use a special number that represents each network. That special number for each network is called an *IP network number*, or simply *network number*. Each network number represents a network.

Each IP network number has the same first part of the IP address as all the addresses in the network, but it has all 0s for the remaining octets. So, the network number looks like an IP address, but a host cannot use a network number as an IP address in the network. (Remember: A computer that has an IP address is referred to as a "host.") For instance, in the left-side Ethernet in Figure 10-6, all hosts begin their addresses with a single octet of 1. In that case, the network number is 1.0.0.0. Similarly, the other two network numbers in the figure are 2.0.0.0 and 3.0.0.0.

Three Sizes Fit All

How many IP addresses can you have in network 1.0.0.0? As it turns out, you can't use the number 1.0.0.0 because that's the network number. You also can't use 1.255.255.255; that number is reserved for other reasons. However, any other IP address that starts with 1 would be valid. If you counted all the addresses, you would end up with more than 16 million addresses!

IP defines these three sizes of networks as different ***classes of networks***. The three different network classes are called Class A, B, and C. By definition, all addresses in the same Class A, B, or C network have the same numeric value ***network*** portion of the addresses. The rest of the address is called the ***host*** portion of the address. For example, in a Class A network such as network 1.0.0.0, all addresses begin with the number 1 in the first octet. The last 3 octets of these addresses comprise the host part of the address.

When the TCP/IP RFCs first defined the concept of networks, such as networks 1.0.0.0, 2.0.0.0, and 3.0.0.0, those same RFCs defined two other classes of networks. Whereas networks 1.0.0.0, 2.0.0.0, and 3.0.0.0 provide more than 16 million addresses each, another (class B) of network gives us a little more than 65,000 addresses. Still another (class C) gives us 254 addresses per IP network. The people who designed TCP/IP addressing simply decided that the world would need three sizes of networks.

Comparing Class A, B, and C addresses, they each have a different length for the network and host part of the addresses. By doing so, each class of network allows a different number of host addresses. To understand that fully, first consider the formats of the three classes of IP networks, as listed in Table 10-1.

Table 10-1   Sizes of Network and Host Parts of IP Addresses

Any Network of This Class	Number of Network Bytes (Bits)	Number of Host Bytes (Bits)	Number of Addresses per Network*
A	1 (8)	3 (24)	$2^{24} - 2$, or 16,777,214
B	2 (16)	2 (16)	$2^{16} - 2$, or 65,534
C	3 (24)	1 (8)	$2^{8} - 2$, or 254

*Each network has two reserved host addresses.

Class A networks have 1 octet (byte) in the network part of the address, and 3 octets in the host part. Because you can have any values in the host part of the address, you can have 2^{24} different IP addresses that all start with the same number in the first octet. Of those 2^{24} addresses, two are reserved. So, each Class A network has a ton of addresses—more than 16 million.

Each Class B network requires that all addresses in the network use the same first 2 octets. That means the network part of these addresses is 2 octets long, leaving only 2 octets for the host part. Because the host part can have any value in it (except the two reserved values), you can have $2^{16}-2$ host addresses in each Class B network.

Similarly, Class C networks have 3 octets in the network part of the addresses, meaning that every address in one Class C network must have the same value in the first 3 octets. That leaves 1 octet as the host part, implying 2^8-2, or 254, host addresses per Class C network.

Figure 10-7 shows the same network diagram as in Figure 10-6, but this time with three different classes of IP network numbers shown.

Figure 10-7   Small, Medium, and Large IP Networks

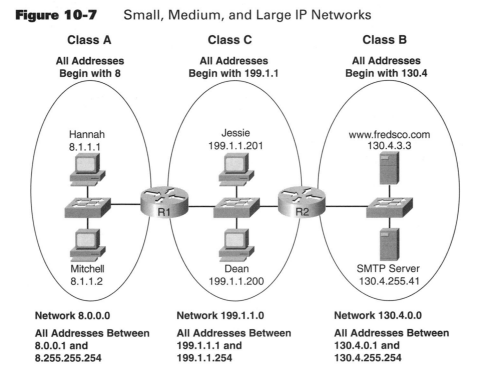

This internetwork still uses three different IP network numbers, as does Figure 10-6. By using one IP network number for each physical network, this internetwork conforms to the rules that allow easy routing. Each network sits on a LAN, with routers separating the networks. However, two of the networks—Class B network 130.4.0.0 and Class C network 199.1.1.0—are much smaller than the Class A networks used in Figure 10-6.

For a closer look, consider network 8.0.0.0 for a moment. It is a Class A network, which means that only 1 byte is used for the network part of the address. As mentioned before, all hosts in network 8.0.0.0 begin with 8. So, 8.0.0.1 is a valid IP address in that network, as is 8.0.0.2, 8.0.0.3, 8.0.0.4, 8.0.0.5, and so on. The actual number of valid host addresses in Class A network 8.0.0.0 is 16,777,214.

Similarly, Class B network 130.4.0.0 has a 2-octet network part, leaving 2 octets for the host part. The valid IP addresses in this network begin with 130.4.0.1 and proceed to 130.4.0.2, 130.4.0.3, 130.4.0.4, and so on—in this case, there are 65,534 addresses in Class B network 130.4.0.0. With Class C network 199.1.1.0, the first valid host address is 199.1.1.1, the second is 199.1.1.2, and so on, with a total of 254 valid host addresses in the network.

The beauty of using one IP network per physical network—such as one IP network per Ethernet LAN—is that routing works well whether you have 10 computers installed or 10,000. In Figure 10-7, R1 and R2 still need only three facts to route packets: where to send packets destined for network 8.0.0.0, where to send packets to network 199.1.1.0, and where to send packets destined for network 130.4.0.0.

Simply put, Class A networks allow for a ton of IP addresses in a single IP network, Class B networks allow for a pretty large number, and Class C networks allow for a smaller number of host IP addresses. The people who made up IP addressing chose three sizes of networks because one size doesn't fit all companies and organizations. Larger companies can use Class A, medium-sized companies can use Class B, and small companies can use Class C.

The Actual Class A, B, and C Network Numbers

The previous example included three networks: Class A network 8.0.0.0, Class B network 130.4.0.0, and Class C network 199.1.1.0. There are other Class A, B, and C networks, however.

The different Class A, B, and C network numbers do not overlap in order to prevent address duplication. If TCP/IP allowed a Class A network 8.0.0.0 and a Class B network 8.1.0.0, IP address 8.1.1.1 would appear to be in both networks, which would cause a lot of confusion. Likewise, if some house on the other side of town had the same mailing address as yours, the postal service would probably get confused.

To avoid such confusion, IP defines a range of Class A, B, and C network numbers. Table 10-2 summarizes the network numbers, the total number of each type, and the number of hosts in each Class A, B, and C network.

Table 10-2   List of All Possible Valid Class A, B, and C Network Numbers*

Class	First Octet Range	Valid Network Numbers	Total Number of Networks of This Class
A	1 to 126	1.0.0.0 to 126.0.0.0	2^7–2, or 126
B	128 to 191	128.1.0.0 to 191.254.0.0	2^{14}–2, or 16,382
C	192 to 223	192.0.1.0 to 223.255.254.0	2^{21}–2, or 2,097,150

*The Valid Network Numbers column shows actual network numbers. There are several reserved cases. For example, network 0.0.0.0 (originally defined for use as a broadcast address) and 127.0.0.0 (still available for use as the loopback address) are reserved. Networks 128.0.0.0, 191.255.0.0, 192.0.0.0, and 223.255.255.0 also are reserved.

You can see that Class A networks can begin with anything from 1 to 126 in the first octet. So, 1.0.0.0, 2.0.0.0, 3.0.0.0, 4.0.0.0, and so on, up to 126.0.0.0, are valid Class A network numbers. Similarly, Class B networks start with anything from 128 through 191. However, because a Class B network has a 2-octet network part, the network numbers are 128.1.0.0, 128.2.0.0, 128.3.0.0, and so on, up through 191.254.0.0. Finally, Class C networks' first octet ranges from 192 through 223, with the first 3 octets comprising the network part of the addresses in those networks.

Subdividing a Network into Subnets

Class A networks contain more than 16,000,000 IP addresses, and Class B networks contain more than 65,000 addresses. Out of context, those might seem like large numbers. When you consider the fact that all hosts in the same IP network cannot be separated from each other by a router, the numbers end up looking huge. These days, LANs with more than a few hundred devices on them are unusual, and single LANs with more than 1000 devices are extremely rare. If you use a Class A or even a Class B network for all the devices on a LAN, many IP addresses will go unused.

Subnetting provides one solution by reducing a lot of the waste. Subnetting refers to a process by which the network engineer in charge of a particular TCP/IP network number, in effect, changes the rules. Next, the chapter shows you an example in which lots of IP addresses are wasted, followed by the same general example, with subnetting being used to reduce waste.

The Problem: Wasting IP Host Addresses

As an example of the possibility of excessive IP address waste, examine Figure 10-8, which uses three Class B networks.

Figure 10-8   Wasting IP Addresses: Room for a Ton, Only Need a Few

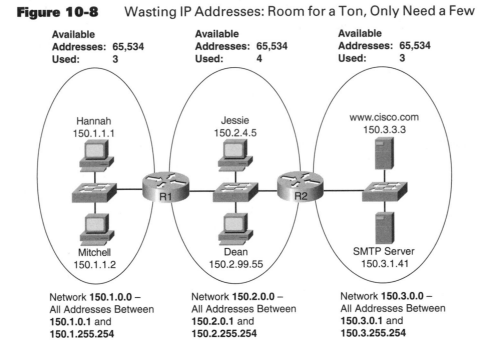

The design in Figure 10-8 requires three networks—in this case, three different Class B networks. Each Class B network has 2^{16}–2 host addresses (65,534) in it—far more than you will ever need for each LAN. Only a few IP addresses have been used so far—one for each computer, plus one each for the router interfaces. (Remember: Each network interface has an IP address. So, in network 150.2.0.0, two addresses are used by the two computers, another is used by R1's right-side Ethernet interface, and a fourth is used by R2's left-side Ethernet interface.)

IP routing processes still work well, based on the fact that all hosts in the same network are in the same place. For instance, all hosts with addresses that start with 150.1 need to be on the Ethernet on the left side of Figure 10-8. However, more than 65,000 IP addresses exist for each of the three networks that are sitting around, unused.

The Solution: Subnetting Saves IP Host Addresses

IP subnetting relaxes the rules a little bit. Without subnetting, the following rules apply:

1. Devices in the same Class A, B, or C network cannot be separated from each other by a router.

2. Devices in different Class A, B, or C networks must be separated from each other by a router.

These two rules might have been somewhat intuitive to you, based on the earlier examples. However, to make sure routing works well, in Figure 10-8, all addresses that start with 150.1 need to be on the left-side Ethernet—that's Rule 1. Hannah and Dean, in networks 150.1.0.0 and 150.2.0.0, must be separated from each other by a router—in this case, R1. That's essentially Rule 2.

Subnetting allows the network engineer to subdivide a Class A, B, or C network into smaller pieces—called subnets—and treat each subnet by the old rules used for networks. So, to subnet a network and reduce IP address waste, the rules are changed a little:

1. Devices in the same subnet cannot be separated from each other by a router.

2. Devices in different subnets must be separated from each other by a router.

This concept is better explained with an example. In Class B network 150.1.0.0, all hosts whose addresses begin with 150.1 are in the same network. An IP network is just a group of hosts with some part of their IP addresses holding the same value. Subnetting allows the network engineer to configure the network devices such that they think that the first 3 octets of the addresses identify the network. In this one example of subnetting, the network engineer can create the following subnets:

- All addresses that begin with 150.1.1
- All addresses that begin with 150.1.2
- All addresses that begin with 150.1.3
- And so on...

Although all the addresses are still in Class B network 150.1.0.0, the networking devices will not think of the network as one big group, but instead, as a lot of smaller groups, called subnets. A *subnet* is just a subdivision of a larger Class A, B, or C network. The term *subnetting* refers to the process whereby the engineer decides to create subnets. Figure 10-9 shows this same network diagram, now with subnetting implemented.

Figure 10-9   Using One Network with Multiple Subnets

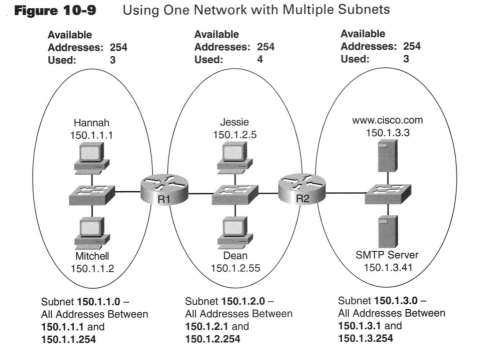

| Available Addresses: 254 | Available Addresses: 254 | Available Addresses: 254 |
| Used: 3 | Used: 4 | Used: 3 |

Hannah
150.1.1.1

Jessie
150.1.2.5

www.cisco.com
150.1.3.3

R1

R2

Mitchell
150.1.1.2

Dean
150.1.2.55

SMTP Server
150.1.3.41

Subnet **150.1.1.0** –
All Addresses Between
150.1.1.1 and
150.1.1.254

Subnet **150.1.2.0** –
All Addresses Between
150.1.2.1 and
150.1.2.254

Subnet **150.1.3.0** –
All Addresses Between
150.1.3.1 and
150.1.3.254

As in Figure 10-8, the design in Figure 10-9 requires three groups of IP addresses. Unlike Figure 10-8, this figure uses three subnets, each of which is a subnet of a single Class B network (network 150.1.0.0). Notice from Figure 10-9 that each subnet is much smaller than the original Class B network, but there are lots of subnets.

IP network numbers represent networks, and similarly, IP *subnet numbers* represent each subnet. The subnet number has the same value in the first part of the number as all the host addresses, and 0s in the last part. For instance, 150.1.1.0 is one of the subnet numbers in Figure 10-9. All addresses in the subnet begin with 150.1.1, so the subnet number includes those numbers as well. Because the fourth octet can be any valid number, the subnet number is simply 0 in the last octet.

Using subnets in the Figure 10-9 network saves IP addresses. This same internetwork of three Ethernet LANs only uses a part of Class B network 150.1.0.0, as opposed to the internetwork in Figure 10-8, which fully uses three Class B networks (150.1.0.0, 150.2.0.0, and 150.3.0.0). Also, if you add another LAN, instead of needing a brand new Class A, B, or C network, you have lots of unused subnets such as 150.1.4.0, 150.1.5.0, and so on.

This example shows just one way to use subnetting. You can subnet in many ways, including subnetting Class A, Class B, and even Class C networks. For now, you understand the basic concepts; just be aware that IP subnetting can get a fair amount more complicated than what's covered here.

Chapter Summary

The IP protocol defines the details of routing and IP addressing. IP routing works similarly to the way that mail sorters work, and IP addresses have structure and meaning that are similar to the way that postal addresses work.

IP addresses are 32-bit numbers that are written in dotted-decimal notation. Each network interface needs an IP address. Any computer that has an IP address is called an IP host.

IP routing relies on the organization of IP addresses into networks or subnets. Without subnetting, all addresses in the same IP network reside on the same physical network. Routers can have a list of all IP networks, with instructions on how that router should forward IP packets to reach those networks. To do so, the router compares the destination IP address in the IP packet header with its list of network numbers.

With subnetting, all addresses in the same IP subnet reside on the same physical network. In effect, each subnet is treated as if it were a different IP network. So, routers can simply have a list of all IP subnets, with instructions on how that router should forward IP packets to reach those subnets. Also, by using subnets, fewer IP addresses are wasted.

IP networks can either be large (Class A), medium (Class B), or small (Class C). In a single Class A network, all addresses start with the same first octet, leaving 3 octets for the host part of the addresses. For Class B networks, all addresses start with the same first 2 octets, leaving 2 octets for the host part of the addresses. Finally, in Class C networks, all addressing starts with the same first 3 octets, leaving 1 octet for the host part of the addresses.

Chapter Review Questions

You can find the answers to the following questions in Appendix A, "Answers to Chapter Review Questions."

1. Imagine that a router receives a packet over an Ethernet. What does the router look at inside the IP packet to decide what to do with the packet?

2. PC1 sits on an Ethernet, with a web server on another Ethernet. A router, R1, is connected to both Ethernets. How does PC1 get its HTTP request to the web server?

3. PC1 sits on an Ethernet network, along with R1, and R1 and R2 are connected to a second Ethernet. Finally, R2 is connected to a third Ethernet, along with a web server. PC1's IP address is 5.5.5.5, and the server's is 6.6.6.6. What IP address is in the destination IP address field of a packet sent from PC1 to the web server?

4. PC1 sits on an Ethernet network, along with router R1. Routers R1 and R2 are connected to a second Ethernet. Finally, R2 is connected to a third Ethernet, along with a web server. PC1's IP address is 5.5.5.5, and the server's is 6.6.6.6. When the web server sends a packet back to PC1, what IP address is in the source IP address field of the packet?

5. For Class B networks, what is the range of numbers allowed for the first octet?

6. For Class C networks, what is the range of numbers allowed for the first octet?

7. How many IP addresses exist in Class A network 7.0.0.0?

8. How many IP addresses exist in Class B network 166.5.0.0?

9. How many IP addresses exist in Class C network 192.55.0.0?

10. Describe the structure of a Class A IP address.

11. Describe the structure of a Class C IP address.

12. What is an *octet*?

13. Define the term *IP network*. List a sample network, along with the first and last valid IP addresses.

14. All hosts on a particular LAN segment use IP addresses that begin with 150.1.1. What network number describes the network in which these addresses reside?

15. All hosts on a particular LAN segment use IP addresses that begin with 150.1.1. Subnetting was used, treating the first 3 octets as the subnet. What subnet number is used to represent the subnet?

16. What is the main motivation for using IP subnetting?

17. Describe how subnetting is accomplished, particularly how it changes or relaxes some rules about how IP addresses are structured.

18. Imagine that Class B network 128.1.0.0 is subnetted by treating the first 3 octets as if they were the network number. A network diagram requires four subnets. Describe how you might go about deciding what the addresses should look like in each subnet.

19. What two main functions does the IP protocol define?

What You Will Learn

After reading this chapter, you should be able to

- ✔ Explain the process of routing an IP packet from one computer to another

- ✔ Describe the purpose of a default gateway

- ✔ Explain how to encapsulate IP packets inside an Ethernet frame for delivery

- ✔ Describe the contents of a router's IP routing table

- ✔ Define the logic that a router uses when it makes a forwarding decision

CHAPTER 11

Knowing Where to Turn at Each Intersection (Router)

In Chapter 10, "Delivering the Goods to the Right Street (IP) Address," you learned about IP addresses and the basics of IP routing. You can understand addressing better if you understand routing. This chapter takes the routing concepts a little deeper, now that you understand the basics of IP addressing.

In many ways, IP routing works like driving somewhere in your car. You leave the house, and generally leave your neighborhood to get to the main road. After you get to the first intersection, you make a decision of whether to turn left, right, or keep going straight. Every time you get to another intersection, you make a choice of where to turn, until you eventually get to your destination.

With IP routing, a PC sends an IP packet to some nearby router. That router chooses the interface that the router uses to forward the packet. The packet travels across the physical network, for instance, over a LAN switch, to the next router. Eventually, the packet arrives at the last router, which routes the packet to the destination address.

The routing process is actually pretty simple, and you've already seen the basics in Chapter 10. This chapter covers more details of the routing process that pull some important concepts together.

A Short Trip from Your House (PC) to the Local Store (Server)

I sometimes sit back and think about how big and populous the world has gotten. Sometimes I'll drive down a large highway in rush hour, see all the cars, and wonder how many cars drive on that road each day. Okay, maybe I've got a little too much time on my hands if I have time to ponder such things, but let's face it: The U.S. Department of Transportation (DOT) has to worry about building roads that accommodate a lot of cars.

When the DOT builds highways in a major city, it typically has to be ready to build lots of lanes, expecting possibly hundreds of thousands of cars to drive over the road each day. Likewise, routers forward a lot of IP packets on the average day. Some of the more expensive, faster routers claim to be able to forward hundreds of millions of packets per second. Even the least expensive routers from Cisco can forward tens of thousands of IP packets per second. Like a busy intersection handles a lot of cars passing through it, a router needs to handle a lot of individual packets passing through it.

Now, think like the people who made up IP and IP routing for a moment. If you need to define protocols and standards about how to do something, and that thing has to happen thousands or millions of times per second, you had better follow the KISS (Keep it simple, stupid) principle! If you made routing overly complicated, you would need really expensive router hardware to forward all those packets. By keeping the amount of work per packet to a bare minimum, the vendors could create routers that could meet the need to forward lots of packets, while keeping the cost of the routers a little lower.

This part of the book takes a look at the life of a packet as it goes from one computer (Hannah) to a web server (http://www.example.com). The process that each computer and router performs is indeed pretty simple, which allows the router to move on to the next packet that's waiting to be forwarded.

Overview of the End-to-End Routing Process

Let's review the basic process of routing as covered in Chapter 10. Figure 11-1 is similar to several figures from Chapter 10, but this one has a little less clutter so that you can focus on how to get a packet from Hannah to the www.example.com web server.

Figure 11-1   Internetwork with Two Routers and Three IP Networks

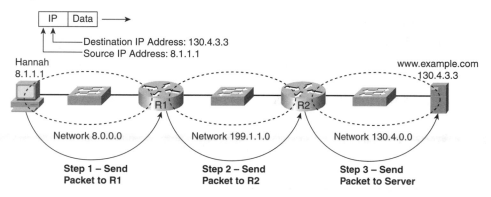

This internetwork uses three different IP network numbers, with one IP network number for each physical network. Simply put, this internetwork does not use subnetting.

note
To keep things straight in this chapter, I will use the word "internetwork" to refer to the entire network shown in a figure, and the word "network" to refer to an individual physical network, such as the three separate Ethernet networks shown in Figure 11-1. Remember: You can use the word "network" in many different ways; to describe routing, using "internetwork" and "network" as described here will make the text a little more readable.

For Hannah to send a packet to the web server, a few separate steps happen:

1. Hannah sends the packet to R1. (Of course, the packet passes through the LAN switch on the left to get to R1, but you're focusing on the router logic for IP routing right now.)

2. R1 makes a forwarding decision to send the packet to R2.

3. R2 decides to forward the packet directly to the web server.

Figure 11-1 shows each of these three steps; the next three sections of this chapter take a closer look at each.

Step 1: Leaving Your Neighborhood the Same Way, Every Time

For most people who have a car, when you leave your house or apartment, you can only drive one direction. Eventually, you'll get to some intersection, where you can make a choice of where to turn. If you know where you're going, you can go ahead and turn. If not, you can look for road signs at each intersection, with the road signs telling you which way to turn.

In Figure 11-1, Hannah is in the same basic situation. After Hannah's PC's IP software has built the IP packet that needs to be sent to the server, it needs to know where to send the packet first. As it turns out, because R1 is the only router attached to Hannah's IP network (network 8.0.0.0), she needs to send the packet to R1.

To send the packet to R1, Hannah needs to know R1's IP address—specifically, the IP address of the router interface that's connected to the same Ethernet as Hannah. In TCP/IP terminology, R1 would be Hannah's *default router*, or *default gateway*. A PC's default router is simply the router to which that PC sends packets when the destination is in another network or subnet. As you can see in Figure 11-2, Hannah knows her default router is R1.

Figure 11-2   By Default, Leave Your Network Via the Default Router

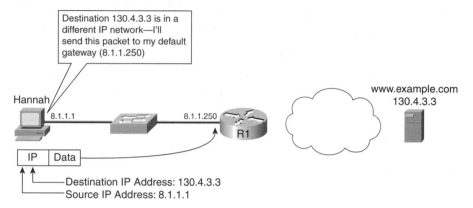

Hannah is in IP network 8.0.0.0, and R1 is the only router that's connected to that IP network. Because Hannah knows that routers know how to route packets, it makes sense that Hannah should forward the packet to R1. However, there are several little details that are important to note in Figure 11-2. First, Hannah's PC knows its default router by the IP address, not by the name. Routers typically have one IP address per physical interface; Hannah needs to know R1's IP address on R1's *Ethernet1 interface* in this case, because R1's Ethernet1 interface is connected to the same Ethernet LAN that Hannah is. (Because routers have lots of interfaces of many different types, routers label the physical interfaces with a name and a number, such as Ethernet1.)

note

Although the term "default router" makes sense, most people use the term "default gateway" to mean the same thing. Before the term "router" became popular, people called the same kind of device a "gateway." Oddly enough, although almost everyone uses the term "router" when speaking of a hardware device that performs routing, many people still use the term "default gateway," whereas others use "default router."

The last details to point out have to do with how the packet gets from Hannah to R1. Notice in Figure 11-2 that Hannah's IP address (8.1.1.1) is listed as the source and www.example.com's IP address (130.4.3.3) is listed as the destination. So, how does Hannah get the packet to R1? Well, there are a few things to cover to get the full story, including encapsulation and a protocol called *Address Resolution Protocol (ARP)*, which you will learn about in the next sections.

Getting into Your Car to Drive to Lunch

When it's time to take a lunch break and your office building isn't close to any restaurants, you might have to get in your car and drive. If you're meeting some friends or business associates for lunch, and you talk before meeting them there, you probably don't bother to mention how you'll be driving to the restaurant. They typically aren't that interested in how you get there.

Likewise, before an IP packet can do the equivalent of driving over the roads, it needs to do the equivalent of getting into a car. Before an IP packet can cross an Ethernet, it has to be encapsulated inside an Ethernet frame. When performing the encapsulation, Hannah happens to overcome two different problems:

- She can't send an IP packet over an Ethernet, but she can send an Ethernet frame over an Ethernet.

- The destination IP address field in the IP header holds the true destination's address—130.4.3.3 in this case. There's no place for a "default gateway IP address" in the header; therefore, Hannah must have another means to ensure that R1 receives the packet.

The solution to the first problem, as you've probably guessed, is encapsulation. Remember: Each layer in the TCP/IP acrchitecural model provides services to the layer above it. Ethernet sits at the network interface layer of TCP/IP, right below the internetwork layer. To get the packet from Hannah to R1, IP uses Ethernet. Hannah encapsulates the IP packet in an Ethernet frame for transmission over the LAN. Figure 11-3 shows the details.

Figure 11-3   Encapsulating an IP Packet in an Ethernet Frame

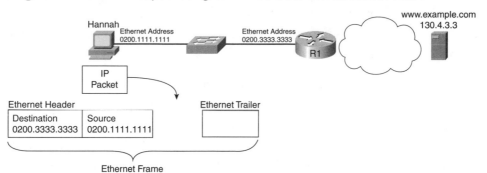

A quick review of Ethernet encapsulation might be helpful. Other layers' protocols add only a header when they encapsulate data. However, data link layer protocols—Ethernet included—add both a header and a trailer, with the IP packet being placed between the header and trailer. The Ethernet header contains several fields, including both the source and destination Ethernet address fields. The trailer contains the *frame check sequence (FCS)* field, which determines whether errors occurred during physical transmission; if errors did occur, the receiver discards the frame.

In Figure 11-3, Hannah's PC takes the following steps to encapsulate and send the IP packet into an Ethernet frame:

1. Create a new Ethernet header.

2. Set the source Ethernet address to Hannah's Ethernet address.

3. Set the destination Ethernet address to R1's address.

4. Create a new trailer.

5. Insert an IP packet into the frame.

6. Send the frame.

By encapsulating the IP packet in an Ethernet frame, Hannah has created something that can be transmitted across the Ethernet LAN. Now Hannah just has to solve the other problem of making sure that the frame gets to R1 and making sure that R1 processes the frame when it is received.

While you're thinking about encapsulation, it's a good idea to review encapsulation at the other layers. All layers of the TCP/IP model use encapsulation, but now you've seen how it works at each layer. For instance, the HTTP protocol defines headers, and when a web browser or web server sends data, HTTP encapsulates the data inside an HTTP header. It's useful to see all the headers in at least one example, as shown in Figure 11-4. This figure shows the Ethernet, IP, TCP, and HTTP headers, along with the end user data (a web page) in the response from the web server.

Figure 11-4   Encapsulating an IP Packet in an Ethernet Frame

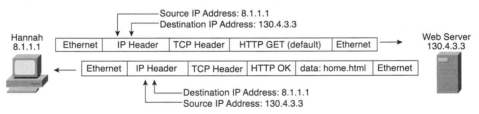

For the rest of this chapter, you'll read about routing and ignore anything after the IP header. However, keep in mind that the whole goal is to deliver application data, as shown in Figure 11-4.

The other dilemma that Hannah faces is that she wants to deliver the packet to R1. Not only does the packet need to get to R1, but R1 needs to think that it should process the packet. As you can see in Figure 11-4, Hannah put her own Ethernet address in the frame as the source address, and she put R1's address as the destination. The fact that Hannah included R1's Ethernet address as the destination is the key to solving her second dilemma. As shown in Figure 11-5, when you send a frame whose destination address is 0200.3333.3333, the frame should be delivered to R1.

Figure 11-5   Using the Ethernet Frame to Deliver the Packet to the Default Router

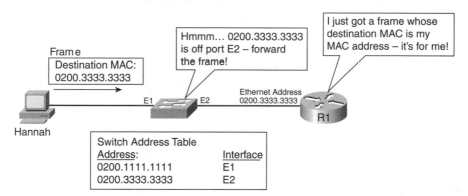

In this figure, the Ethernet switch happens to have already learned its entries for Hannah's (0200.1111.1111) and R1's (0200.3333.3333) Ethernet MAC addresses. With a destination address of 0200.3333.3333, the switch simply looks at the frame and decides to send the frame out its E2 interface. The frame, which, of course, has the IP packet in it, is delivered to R1. Finally, the packet has made it to the default router. The router will know to process the incoming frame because the destination Ethernet address is its own address.

Learning How to Go to the Default Post Office (Router)

The first time Hannah tries to build the Ethernet header, she will need more information. To finish building the Ethernet header, Hannah needs to put R1's Ethernet address in the header as the destination address. The problem is that Hannah knows the default gateway IP address—in this case 8.1.1.250—but she doesn't know R1's Ethernet address on that same interface.

A host can learn its default gateway IP address in two ways. In some cases, the default gateway IP address is simply typed into the right place in the PC's configuration. In other cases, the host learns the default gateway IP address dynamically, using the Dynamic Host Configuration Protocol (DHCP). IP hosts use DHCP to automatically discover their own IP address, as well as the IP address of their default router. To keep the coverage focused on the basics, this chapter doesn't cover the details of how DHCP works. Regardless of how Hannah knows her default gateway IP address, she must know it.

In contrast, a host does not know—at least ahead of time—the MAC address used to reach the default router (0200.3333.3333 in this example). To learn the MAC address information, Hannah uses ARP. *ARP* is a TCP/IP protocol that can specifically help solve the problem of knowing an IP address and needing to know the corresponding LAN MAC address. To see how ARP works, examine Figure 11-6, which shows what Hannah and R1 know before Hannah uses ARP.

Figure 11-6 What Hannah and R1 Know Before Using ARP

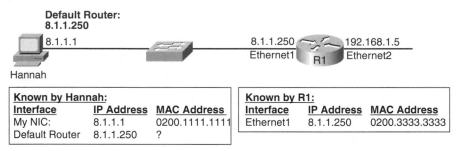

For Hannah to learn what R1's Ethernet MAC address is, she just needs to ask R1. Hannah does so by sending an ARP broadcast. An *ARP broadcast* is a message that simply says, "Hey, if this is your IP address, tell me your Ethernet MAC address." It's called a broadcast because the destination MAC address of the ARP broadcast is the Ethernet broadcast address of FFFF.FFFF.FFFF. Because switches forward LAN broadcasts to all devices in the network, everyone on the LAN gets the ARP broadcast.

Each IP host on the LAN examines the ARP broadcast, but only R1 has IP address 8.1.1.250 configured, so it is the only one that should reply. Figure 11-7 shows the basic process.

Figure 11-7   Hannah Sending an ARP Broadcast, Looking for 8.1.1.250's Ethernet Address

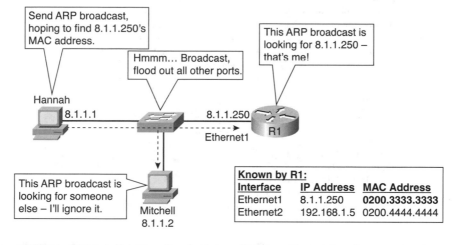

In Figure 11-7, all other IP hosts on the LAN receive the ARP broadcast because the switch floods the frame out all physical interfaces except the port connected to Hannah. Because everyone in network 8.0.0.0 should be somewhere on this Ethernet, if IP address 8.1.1.250 exists, then that device should get the ARP request.

The ARP broadcast lists the IP address for which it is searching for the corresponding MAC address. Therefore, Mitchell ignores the request, and R1 decides to reply.

R1 replies with an ARP message called an ***ARP reply***. Note that the ARP reply does not use a broadcast destination Ethernet address; instead, the destination address of the sender of the ARP broadcast is used. In this case, the destination is Hannah's Ethernet address (0200.1111.1111). As a result, the LAN switch does not flood the frame holding the ARP reply out all ports; instead, it forwards the frame only to Hannah. Figure 11-8 shows the ARP reply.

Figure 11-8   ARP Reply from R1 to Hannah

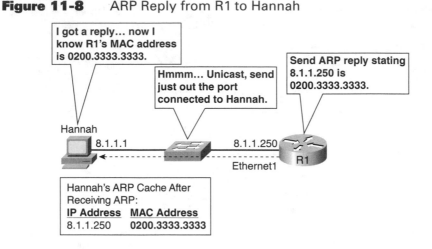

Inside the data portion of the packet, the ARP reply contains the original IP address (8.1.1.250) and the corresponding MAC address (0200.3333.3333). Finally, Hannah knows the Ethernet MAC address that corresponds to the default gateway IP address.

Hannah puts the information in a place called the *ARP cache*, so that the next time she needs to send a packet to the default gateway, she does not need to send another ARP broadcast. An ARP cache is nothing more than a place in memory in an IP host where IP addresses and their corresponding MAC addresses are recorded.

Summary of Step 1

Although it took about 10 pages of this chapter, the first step in this simple routing example boils down to a pretty basic process, as follows:

1. Create the IP packet by encapsulating transport layer data after an IP header.

2. Check the ARP cache to see if the MAC address of the default gateway is known. If it's not, use ARP to learn that MAC address.

3. Encapsulate the packet inside an Ethernet frame.

4. Send the Ethernet frame.

Although this short routing algorithm doesn't match every possibility, it certainly matches the logic Hannah uses to try to send a packet to the web server at 130.4.3.3. Toward the end of this chapter, you'll learn a few exceptions to how an IP host might behave, but for now, Hannah's part of this example is complete. The next section discusses what R1 does with the packet.

Step 2: Choosing Which Road to Take at the First Intersection

When you drive from your house in your car, you typically leave your neighborhood going the same general direction until you get to an intersection. Of course, you know how to get where you are going, so you don't need to look at the road signs to choose which way to turn. However, someone who's been visiting you might not know the local roads. When the visitor get to the intersection, he can look at the road signs to decide where to drive.

Comparing networks to roadways, routers are like an intersection; however, the router makes the choice of where to send a packet, rather than a driver choosing where to turn. When a packet arrives at a router, the router looks at the equivalent of a road sign—something called a *routing table* in networking. The router looks at where the packet wants to go (the destination IP address) as well as at the routing table. By comparing the two, the router can choose where to send the packet next.

The same internetwork is used for the examples throughout this chapter. At this point in the example, an Ethernet frame is arriving on R1's left-side (Ethernet1) interface. The frame contains the IP packet, sent by Hannah (8.1.1.1), with the destination address being the www.example.com web server (130.4.3.3). Figure 11-9 depicts this point in the process.

Figure 11-9 The Beginning of R1's Routing Logic

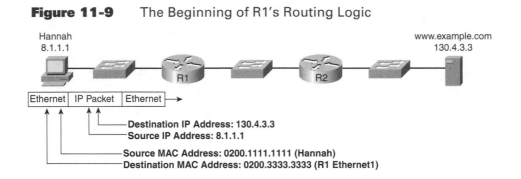

At this point in the process of routing the packet to the web server, the frame is just entering R1. R1 needs to forward the packet to R2 next. The process that R1 uses to forward the packet can be broken down into three steps:

1. Decapsulation

2. Decide where to forward the packet next

3. Encapsulation

The next sections cover each topic in sequence.

The Useful but Short Life of an Ethernet Frame

After receiving the frame that Hannah sent, the first steps in R1's logic can be summarized as follows:

- Check the incoming frame's FCS. If there are errors, discard the frame.

- If no errors were found, remove the Ethernet header and trailer, leaving the original IP packet.

The FCS field in the Ethernet trailer is the field that lets an Ethernet NIC find out if the frame experienced errors. If the frame is error free, R1 removes the Ethernet header and trailer. In Figure 11-9, after R1 checks the FCS and finds out the frame has not had errors, R1 removes the Ethernet header and trailer. R1 is left with an IP packet, whose source IP address is 8.1.1.1 (Hannah), and whose destination is 130.4.3.3 (web server).

Deciding Where to Go Next

Routers perform routing by looking at the destination IP address of the IP packet. The term *routing* refers to the process by which a router examines a recently received packet, looks at the destination IP address, and makes a decision about where to forward the packet next.

For routing to work well, the router needs to know how to reach the various IP networks and subnets in the internetwork. Routers choose where to forward packets by looking at a routing table.

The key to understanding the process of routing revolves around the *IP routing table*. The IP routing table includes a list of IP network or subnet numbers, along with instructions on how this router should forward packets in order to deliver the packets to that network or subnet. Whew, that's a long definition, but the concept is simple, particularly with an example. Figure 11-10 shows R1's routing table.

Figure 11-10 Routing Decisions Based on the Routing Table

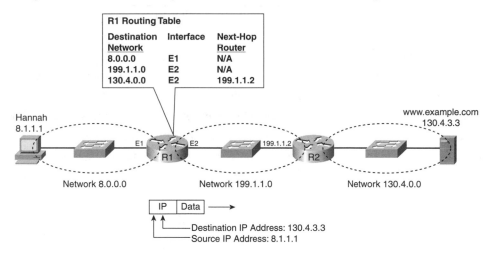

R1 Routing Table

Destination Network	Interface	Next-Hop Router
8.0.0.0	E1	N/A
199.1.1.0	E2	N/A
130.4.0.0	E2	199.1.1.2

Hannah
8.1.1.1

www.example.com
130.4.3.3

E1   E2   199.1.1.2
R1   R2

Network 8.0.0.0   Network 199.1.1.0   Network 130.4.0.0

| IP | Data | → |

Destination IP Address: 130.4.3.3
Source IP Address: 8.1.1.1

Before the packet arrives at R1, R1 will have built the routing table with the expectation that it will need to know this information one day. In the internetwork used for the example in this chapter, there are three IP networks, so R1's routing table lists three IP networks. Each line in the routing table lists the IP network, along with the routing instructions for this router. These instructions tell R1 how to forward packets so that they will reach each network.

When R1 receives the Ethernet frame from Hannah, it first checks for errors. If there are no errors, R1 discards the Ethernet header and trailer and is left with the original IP packet. That IP packet is listed underneath R1 in Figure 11-10. From that point, the process of routing works as follows:

1. Match the destination IP address in the packet to the list of entries in the routing table.

2. After a match is found, send the packet out the outgoing interface, to the next-hop router, as listed in that entry of the routing table.

For instance, notice the routing table entry for network 130.4.0.0. You know from Chapter 10 that network 130.4.0.0 includes all IP addresses between 130.4.0.1 through 130.4.255.254, inclusive. Of course, the web server's IP address, 130.4.3.3, is in that range, so the packet matches that entry in the routing table.

The last two columns of the routing table tell R1 what to do with packets so that they are delivered successfully to the right destinations. From Figure 11-10, it's pretty obvious that R1 should forward the packet out its Ethernet2 interface, so that R2 gets the packet next. In this case, notice that the routing table entry for network 130.4.0.0 lists Ethernet2 as the outgoing interface. It also references R2's IP address as the next-hop router. The ***next-hop router*** is simply the next router that needs to receive the packet so that the packet will be delivered correctly. The ***outgoing interface*** is the interface on this router out which the packet should be forwarded next.

In short, a router receives a packet, matches its routing table, and decides to forward that packet based on the instructions in the routing table. That process is typically called "routing," and it is sometimes called a *forwarding decision*. However, R1 is not yet finished. Now let's move on to R1's last step for this packet.

Yet Another Ethernet Data Link Frame

You can almost feel the excitement in the air. R1 has received the frame, discarded the Ethernet header and trailer, and made a routing decision. However, R1 has an IP packet sitting in memory, and R1 knows it can't simply send an IP packet out its Ethernet2 interface. The solution is simple, and hopefully a little familiar: R1 needs to encapsulate the packet in another Ethernet frame.

Until R1 transmits the bits out its Ethernet2 interface, R1's logic is just like Hannah's logic was earlier. R1's logic goes something like this, in this example:

- Before sending the packet out Ethernet2, it needs to be encapsulated inside an Ethernet frame.

- The source MAC address of this new Ethernet header is the MAC address of my Ethernet2 interface.

- The destination MAC address of this new Ethernet header is the MAC address of R2.

- Before forwarding the first packet to R2, an ARP broadcast is required to find R2's MAC address. R1 records that information in its ARP cache for any additional packets.

Imagine that R1 doesn't know R2's MAC address. Figure 11-11 shows the ARP broadcast, the ARP reply, and finally, the new Ethernet frame, which delivers the packet from R1 to R2.

Figure 11-11   R1's ARP Broadcast, R2's Reply, and Finally Packet Forwarding

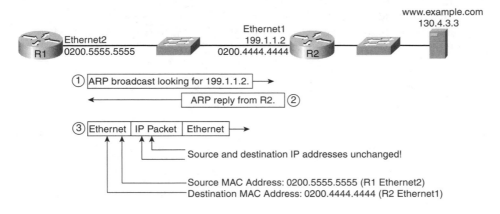

The process shown in the figure is as follows:

1. R1 sends an ARP broadcast looking for 199.1.1.2's MAC address. The switch floods the broadcast frame, so R2 and all other devices on that LAN get the ARP broadcast.

2. R2 replies telling R1 that its MAC address is 0200.4444.4444.

3. R1 finishes creating the Ethernet header and trailer, with R2's MAC address of 0200.4444.4444 as the destination, and forwards the frame.

By the way, R1 keeps an ARP cache as well, so it knows that 199.1.1.2's MAC address is 0200.4444.4444. The next time R1 needs to forward a packet to R2, R1 will not have to ARP.

Also, notice that this new Ethernet frame is not the same frame that Hannah created and sent; the new Ethernet frame has a new source and destination addresses. However, the IP packet inside the frame is mostly unchanged. Because the IP packet is the entity that makes it through the network without being changed, many people say that routers and routing forward packets end to end through a network. That's because the word "packet" refers to the IP header and data and does not include the data link header and trailer.

Summary of Step 2

The routing logic that R1 uses can be summarized as follows:

1. Receive incoming Ethernet frames that are addressed to my own MAC addresses.

2. If not in error, extract the encapsulated IP packets and discard the old data link headers and trailers.

3. Match the destination IP address of each packet with the list of destinations in the routing table.

4. After matched, notice the outgoing interface and next-hop router listed by that entry in the routing table. Use that information to encapsulate and forward the resulting frames out the outgoing interface.

Step 3: Choosing Which Road to Take at the Final Intersection

In the sample internetwork for this chapter, only two routers exist. Now that the packet, encapsulated in an Ethernet frame, is crossing the Ethernet between R1 and R2, only one more router needs to process the packet—namely, R2.

If many more routers existed between Hannah and the web server, they would use logic similar to R1 in the previous section. However, after you get to the final router, the logic changes slightly. To finish this example and to end the discussion of routing, this section covers the same three steps as those for R1 but instead focuses on the differences.

The Still Useful, but Still Short Life of an Ethernet Frame

Earlier, R1 began its logic when it received an Ethernet frame that was addressed to itself. Likewise, R2 begins its logic the same way. In this case, R2 receives the frame that R1 sent to R2's Ethernet address, with the frame containing the original packet Hannah sent to the web server. This first step in R2's logic matches R1's:

1. Check the incoming frame's FCS. If errors exist, discard the frame.

2. If no errors were found, discard the Ethernet header and trailer, leaving the original IP packet.

In the sample internetwork, after R2 receives a frame, it is left with the same IP packet, whose source IP address is 8.1.1.1 (Hannah), and whose destination is 130.4.3.3 (web server).

The Routing Table at R2: Same Destination, Different Forwarding Instructions

Like R1 before it, R2 next looks at the destination address of the packet, and it compares the address to the routing table. Like R1, R2 should match an entry in the table, and that entry tells R2 what to do with the packet. However, R2's routing table differs from R1's because R2's routing table includes instructions about how R2 should forward IP packets. It's like taking a trip where you turn left at one intersection and right at another. The turn you make depends on where you are. Likewise, the instructions about which interface out which to forward a packet depends on where the router is in the internetwork. Figure 11-12 shows R1's and R2's routing tables to illustrate how R2 behaves differently from R1.

Figure 11-12   R2's Routing Table—Same Destinations, Different Instructions

R1 Routing Table

Destination Network	Interface	Next-Hop Router
8.0.0.0	E1	N/A
199.1.1.0	E2	N/A
130.4.0.0	E2	199.1.1.2

R2 Routing Table

Destination Network	Interface	Next-Hop Router
8.0.0.0	E1	199.1.1.1
199.1.1.0	E1	N/A
130.4.0.0	E2	N/A

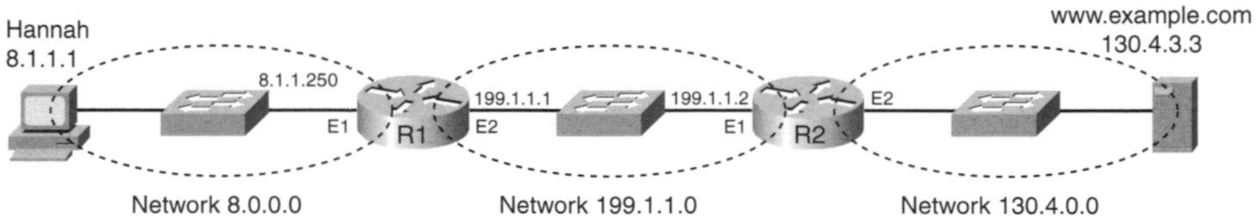

Like R1, to route the packet, R2 needs to compare the destination IP address of the packet to the list of destinations in the routing table. Also like R1, R2 matches its entry for network 130.4.0.0 because the destination, 130.4.3.3, is part of that network.

The difference between how R1 and R2 behave relates to the fact that unlike R1, R2's matched routing table entry does not list a next-hop router. From Figure 11-12, you can see that R2 does not need to send the packet to another router, but it should instead send the packet directly to the web server. R2 knows that there's not another router because no next-hop router is listed in the matched routing table entry. R2 simply needs to send the packet directly to the web server at IP address 130.4.3.3.

Yet Another Short-Lived Ethernet Frame

Just like Hannah and R1 before it, R2 needs to send an IP packet across an Ethernet. It knows the source and destination IP addresses in the packet because those haven't changed during this whole process. R2 knows its own Ethernet address on the outgoing interface. All R2 needs to know is the MAC address that corresponds to the web server so it can finish building the Ethernet frame and send the frame to the web server.

To find the web server's Ethernet MAC address, R2 uses the same ARP protocol messages as did Hannah and R1. R2 sends an ARP broadcast, looking for the Ethernet address of host 130.4.3.3 (web server). After the web server replies with an ARP reply, R2 can finish building the Ethernet frame and forward it.

After R2 transmits the frame, the LAN switch forwards it so that the web server receives the frame. Finally, the web server has the frame and extracts the packet. The routing of the packet is complete!

Other Rules of the Road

Although a single example might help you understand routing, one example can't cover every nuance of how routing works. Before wrapping up this chapter, you should be aware of a few additional short topics about routing. These last few topics do not change the rules of routing, but they do clarify what happens in a couple of different instances.

Routing with Subnets

In the example used throughout this chapter, three different IP networks were used, with no subnetting. As it turns out, even with subnetting in use, routing works basically the same way. For example, look at Figure 11-13, which has the same internetwork with two routers, but now with subnets of Class B network 150.1.0.0 in use.

Figure 11-13   R2's Routing Table—Same Destinations, Different Instructions

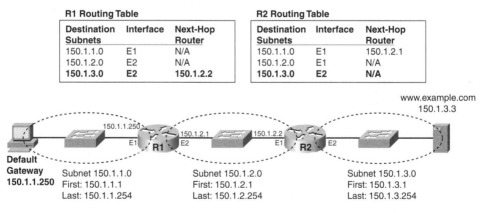

In this new internetwork, a single Class B IP network, 150.1.0.0, is used. This IP network is subdivided into three subnets—namely, 150.1.1.0, 150.1.2.0, and 150.1.3.0. In this case, subnetting has been set up to work like it did in Chapter 10, with all hosts in the same IP subnet having the same value in the first 3 octets of their IP addresses. (Notice that the IP addresses of the host computers, as well as the routers, have changed, as compared to the earlier examples in this chapter.)

Now take a closer look at the routing tables. In the earlier example, the list of destinations was a list of Class A, B, and C network numbers. In this case, the list shows the IP subnet numbers. To route packets correctly, the router needs a routing table that lists all the possible groups of IP addresses. As you read in Chapter 10, a subnet is just a subset of a larger class A, B, or C network—in other words, just a smaller group of addresses.

Hannah, R1, and R2 use the same basic logic as before. When Hannah sends a packet to the web server, the destination address is 150.1.3.3. Hannah's default gateway still points to R1's Ethernet1 IP address. Hannah's logic works like it did without subnetting, with Hannah sending an ARP broadcast for IP address 150.1.1.250, R1 replying, and Hannah sending a frame to R1 with the IP packet inside the Ethernet frame.

R1's logic is also the same as before. R1 receives the frame, and if it is error free, it extracts the IP packet. The destination address is 150.1.3.3 in this case, so R1 looks at its IP routing table and finds an entry for 150.1.3.0. R1 knows that this subnet includes addresses 150.1.3.1 through 150.1.3.254, so the packet's destination address matches this entry. Just like before, the routing table entry tells R1 to forward the packet out its Ethernet2 interface, to R2 next. The only difference this time is that R2's IP address is different (150.1.2.2).

Finally, when R2 receives the frame, it does the usual error check and extracts the IP packet. R2 then compares the destination IP address to its own routing table and finds an entry for 150.1.3.0. In this case, there's no next-hop router listed, so R2 can forward the packet directly to the web server, just like before.

In short, whether or not an internetwork uses subnetting, the basic routing logic remains the same.

How to Drive When You Aren't Leaving the Neighborhood (Subnet)

The examples in this chapter always started with Hannah sending the packet to her default router. But what if Hannah needs to send a packet to someone who's on the same subnet? It would be better, of course, for Hannah to send the packet directly to the destination. Figure 11-14 depicts the topology and the solution.

Figure 11-14   Decision Process with Local Subnet Destinations

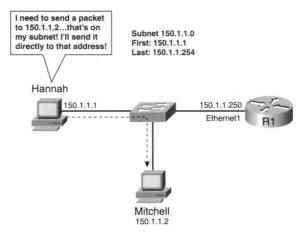

Hosts do not always send packets to their default gateway. Instead, they start by asking a simple question: "Is the destination address of this packet in the same subnet that I am in?" If so, the host needs to send the packet directly, as shown in Figure 11-14. If the packet's destination is in a different subnet, the host simply needs to send the packet to its default router. So, each host computer knows the range of valid IP addresses in its own subnet, so all the computer has to do is compare the destination IP address of the packet to that list of valid addresses.

By the way, in either case, the host might need to use ARP to learn the MAC address either of the other host computer or the default gateway.

Chapter Summary

Routing starts with a host computer that has a packet to send. The host computer starts by deciding whether the packet destination is on a different subnet. If the destination is on a different subnet, the host sends the packet to the default gateway. If the destination is on the same subnet, the host sends the packet directly to that host, ignoring the default gateway.

Before the host can send a packet over an Ethernet NIC, it must know the destination MAC address of the device. The host looks in its ARP cache, which is a list of IP addresses on the same subnet, along with the corresponding Ethernet MAC addresses. If there are no entries, the host uses ARP to broadcast a request for the information, expecting to get a reply that includes the missing information.

A router receives Ethernet frames addressed to it, and if the frame is free from errors, the router de-encapsulates the IP packet from inside the frame. The router compares the destination IP address of the packet to the routing table entries. The entry that the router matches tells the router where to send the packet next. Those forwarding instructions include the router interface out which to forward the packet, called the outgoing interface, along with a next-hop router, if appropriate. This basic logic works whether or not subnetting is in use.

Chapter Review Questions

You can find the answers to the following questions in Appendix A, "Answers to Chapter Review Questions."

1. PC1 sits on an Ethernet and uses IP address 130.1.1.1. PC1 needs to send a packet to an FTP server whose IP address is 19.1.1.1. To what IP address should PC1 forward the IP packet next?

2. Imagine that PC1, with IP address 130.1.1.1, needs to send a packet. PC1 decides to send the packet to its default router, at IP address 130.1.1.2. PC1 has never sent a packet to that router. Two messages must flow over the network before PC1 can forward the packet. Identify the acronym for the protocol that defines those two messages, and state what the letters in the acronym stand for.

3. Imagine that PC1, with IP address 130.1.1.1, needs to send a packet to its
   default router at IP address 130.1.1.2. Both PC1 and the router are attached
   to the same Ethernet switch, along with PCs Larry, Moe, and Curly. PC1
   doesn't know the router's Ethernet MAC address. Name the message that
   PC1 sends to try to find out the router's MAC address, and identify which of
   the devices on the LAN will receive the message.

4. PC1, with IP address 130.1.1.1, needs to send a packet to Curly, at IP
   address 130.1.1.3. PC1's default router is the router whose IP address is
   130.1.1.2. Both PCs and the router are attached to a single Ethernet switch
   and are in the same subnet. Describe the role of the default router for routing
   this packet from PC1 to Curly.

5. PC1 (130.1.1.1) is attached to an Ethernet switch. It needs to send a packet to a
   web server (19.1.1.1). The IP packet is sitting in memory in PC1. Describe
   the process of encapsulation that is required before PC1 can transmit the
   bits.

6. Refer to Figure 11-15 for this question. In the sample network, PC1 is sending
   a packet to PC2. Describe whose IP and MAC addresses would be contained
   in the Ethernet frame that passes between PC1 and R1.

Figure 11-15   Internetwork Referenced in Some of the Questions in
                    Chapter 11

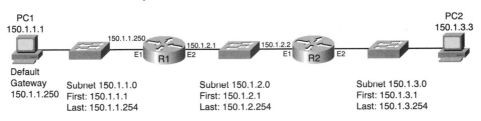

7. Refer to Figure 11-15 for this question. In the sample network, PC1 is sending
   a packet to PC2. Describe whose IP and MAC addresses would be contained
   in the Ethernet frame that passes between R2 and PC2.

8. Refer to Figure 11-15 for this question. In the sample network, PC1 is sending a packet to PC2. Describe the contents of the routing table entry on R1 that would be needed for R1 to forward the packet correctly.

9. Refer to Figure 11-15 for this question. In the sample network, PC1 is sending a packet to PC2. Describe the contents of the routing table entry on R2 that would be needed for R2 to forward the packet correctly.

10. Define the term "routing."

11. Define the term "default gateway."

12. Describe the differences between routing when you are not using subnetting and when you are using subnetting.

13. Describe the logic that a host computer uses when deciding whether it needs to send a packet to its default gateway or directly to the destination host.

14. Referring to Figure 11-15, between the time that PC1 sends the packet and PC2 receives it, many things might have changed. Explain what is the same and what is different about the transmitted data. Compare what PC1 sends versus what PC2 receives.

15. This chapter suggests that you will find three items in a single routing table entry. What are they, and which one(s) are useful for knowing where to send the packet next?

16. Of the three parts of a routing table entry from the previous question, which one of these parts might not always be needed? Using R2 from Figure 11-15 as a reference, describe one routing table entry where that field would not be needed in the routing table entry.

What You Will Learn

After reading this chapter, you should be able to

- ✔ Explain how a router learns to put routes in its routing table for networks or subnets that are connected directly to the router

- ✔ Describe how a network engineer can configure a router to use static routes so that it adds routes to its routing table

- ✔ Explain the basic idea of how multiple routers can use a routing protocol to exchange routing information with each other

- ✔ List several IP routing protocols

CHAPTER 12

Painting the Road Signs on Your Interstate (Internetwork)

If you take a trip in your car and you don't use a map, you can still get where you're going by just reading the road signs. Routing, as covered in Chapter 11, "Knowing Where to Turn at Each Intersection (Router)," works a lot like taking a trip and relying on road signs. Think of the IP packets as cars, each intersection as a router, and the routers' routing tables as the road signs. Just like a driver might rely on good information found on the road signs, IP packets rely on the routers' routing tables having good information in them. When a router receives a packet, it must match the destination IP address of the packet to the routing table to figure out where to send the packet next. Similar to cases in which you might see a road sign when driving and turn off onto another road, a router directs the packet down the next network roadway to get to its destination. (Note that the router forwards the packet and makes the decision of where to send the packet, which is a slight departure from the analogy with driving, in which the driver of the car decides where to turn.)

In short, IP packets rely on the routers having good, complete routing information in their routing tables. This brief chapter covers the most basic concepts of how a router creates and fills its routing table.

Routing to Nearby Places

Imagine a sleepy little town with a couple of fellows sitting around at the only gas station. Because I grew up in a town like that, I'll call the town Snellville, after my hometown. These guys are just talking, waiting around for the next customer.

A stranger drives up, rolls down his window, and asks, "Excuse me. Can you tell me how to get to Snellville?" I'm sure a dozen funny or sarcastic answers would probably leap to mind, but the fellows at the gas station would eventually tell the stranger that he had just missed the sign that told him he was already in Snellville. No need to drive any further!

Interestingly, routers first fill their routing tables based on a similar concept. Each router knows which of its physical interfaces are up and working. It knows the IP addresses used on each interface. Each router also knows what IP networks or subnets exist on the physical networks that are connected to those interfaces. The router can add a route to the subnet that exists on the physical networks to which it is attached.

Before a router can add routes to these subnets, it must have an IP address assigned to each network interface. When you buy a brand new router, it doesn't know which IP addresses you want it to use. A network engineer needs to somehow tell the router which IP addresses to use; to do so, the engineer configures the router.

Configuring a router means that the engineer connects to the router and types in some information about what the router should do. For instance, in Figure 12-1, R1 needs to know its IP addresses for interfaces Ethernet1 and Ethernet2. When the engineer configures the IP address for each interface, he also (coincidentally) tells the router which subnets or networks are attached to those two interfaces. Figure 12-1 shows the basic concepts.

Figure 12-1   Configuring a Router with Its IP Addresses and Attached Subnets

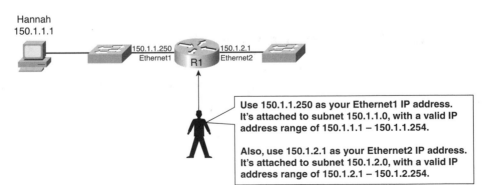

Before all the routing in Chapter 11 could work, the routers needed to know what their interfaces' IP addresses were. In this figure, you see that the engineer told R1 that its IP addresses were 150.1.1.250 (Ethernet1) and 150.1.2.1 (Ethernet2). Based on what the engineer told the router, the router can deduce the subnet numbers connected to those two interfaces and the range of valid IP addresses. (Although this book doesn't cover the details, for those of you who have some router configuration experience, the engineer configures an IP address and subnet mask for each interface. The router uses those two numbers to figure out the range of valid IP addresses in each subnet.)

After R1's two interfaces are up and working, R1 knows a few important facts:

- The subnet numbers of the subnets that are connected to these two interfaces.

- The outgoing interface it should use to forward packets to those subnets.

- It does not need to send packets to another router so that it can reach these subnets.

As a result, R1 simply adds a route for each directly connected subnet to its routing table. A ***directly connected subnet*** is a subnet that is, well, connected directly to a router. Back in Chapter 10, "Delivering the Goods to the Right Street (IP) Address," you learned how all the IP hosts in the same IP subnet were attached to the same physical network. In Figure 12-1, R1's Ethernet1 interface is attached to the same physical Ethernet as Hannah; therefore, R1's Ethernet1 interface is connected directly to the same subnet as Hannah. By adding a route for that subnet to its routing table, R1 can then forward packets to Hannah and other hosts in that subnet.

Likewise, R2 can add two routes to its routing table after the network engineer has configured R2 and the two interfaces are working. Figure 12-2 shows the routing tables on R1 and R2, this time with the newly added directly connected routes shown.

Figure 12-2 You're Already There: Directly Connected Routes in R1's and R2's Routing Tables

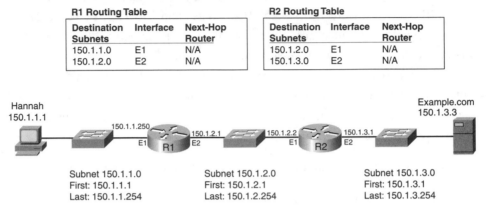

Routers always add routes for directly connected subnets and networks, as long as the interface is both configured and working. Although it is important that the routers include the directly connected subnets in their routing tables, if that's all R1 and R2 know about, then they do not know enough routes in their routing table. For instance, if Hannah tries to send a packet to the web server (150.1.3.3), then R1 will not have a route that matches the packet's destination address, and R1 will simply discard the packet.

Painting Road Signs and Other Long-Lasting Directions

It takes a long time to build a highway and even longer to build a new town or city. But whenever a new road is finally finished, some old road signs might need to be updated because there might be a better way to drive to some nearby town. Thankfully, because it takes a long time to build a road, the road signs do not have to be repainted very often.

With routers, the network engineer can do the equivalent of painting the road signs. To do so, the engineer can configure a ***static IP route***, which is configuration for a router that tells the router to add a particular entry to its routing table. For instance, in Figure 12-2, R1 didn't have a route to subnet 150.1.3.0, meaning it couldn't forward a packet that was destined for IP address 150.1.3.3. In Figure 12-3, the engineer solved the problem by configuring a static route on R1 for subnet 150.1.3.0, with outgoing interface Ethernet2, and next-hop router of 150.1.2.2.

Figure 12-3 Painting a Routing Table with a Static Route

R1 Routing Table

Destination Subnets	Interface	Next-Hop Router
150.1.1.0	E1	N/A
150.1.2.0	E2	N/A
150.1.3.0	**E2**	**150.1.2.2**

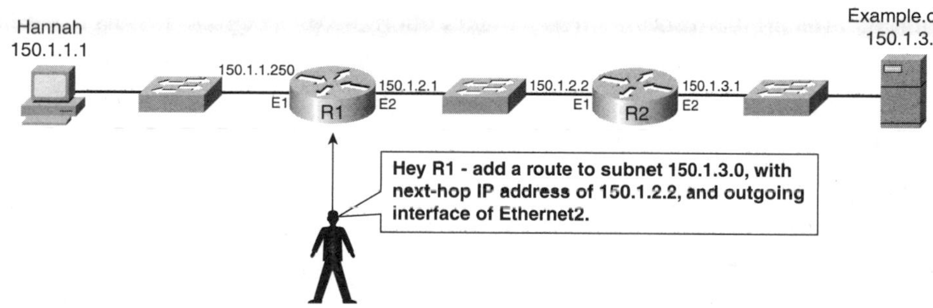

Before adding the static route, R1 did not know how to forward packets whose destinations were in subnet 150.1.3.0. Now R1 knows to forward those packets to R2 next.

Static routes work, but they can be a pain in the neck to maintain. Network topologies tend to change a lot more frequently than roads do, and static routes make it difficult to use all the possible routes to the same part of the network when you have multiple possible physical paths. As a result, most companies do not use static routes throughout their networks; instead, they use routing protocols, as described in the next section.

Dynamically Learning and Changing Routing Tables

In most cities, there are multiple ways to drive to some other part of town. During rush hour, you might listen to the radio for traffic updates or watch for electronic signs by the road that show the latest information about road congestion. For instance, a reporter might be flying over roadways in a helicopter or observing traffic through cameras installed beside the major roadways. The reporter passes the information on to a radio announcer or to someone who types in a warning to appear on an electronic sign by the road. Then you might pass the sign or hear on the radio that the road you're on is closed 8 miles ahead due to an accident, and you decide to try an alternate road.

A similar (but not identical) concept happens in networking. The most typical way a router learns all the rest of the routes in an internetwork, beyond just its directly connected routes, is by using a routing protocol. ***Routing protocols*** define messages by which routers can exchange route information with other routers. A router can tell other routers about the routes that it knows, and that same router can listen for messages from neighboring routers about the routes that they know. If all the routers participate, all routers should have routes for all subnets or networks in an IP internetwork.

In Figure 12-2, R1 and R2 knew about their directly connected subnets, but no others. The example shown in Figure 12-4 begins like Figure 12-2, but in this case, R1 uses a routing protocol to tell R2 about its routes.

Figure 12-4   R2 Learning Routes from R1

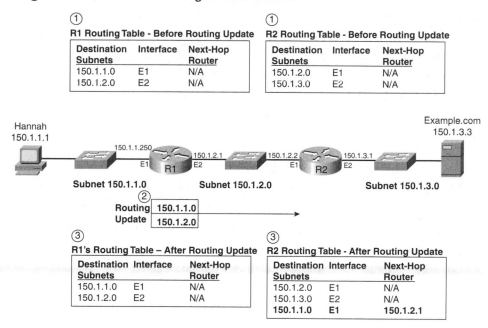

① **R1 Routing Table - Before Routing Update**

Destination Subnets	Interface	Next-Hop Router
150.1.1.0	E1	N/A
150.1.2.0	E2	N/A

① **R2 Routing Table - Before Routing Update**

Destination Subnets	Interface	Next-Hop Router
150.1.2.0	E1	N/A
150.1.3.0	E2	N/A

② Routing Update

150.1.1.0
150.1.2.0

③ **R1's Routing Table – After Routing Update**

Destination Subnets	Interface	Next-Hop Router
150.1.1.0	E1	N/A
150.1.2.0	E2	N/A

③ **R2 Routing Table - After Routing Update**

Destination Subnets	Interface	Next-Hop Router
150.1.2.0	E1	N/A
150.1.3.0	E2	N/A
150.1.1.0	E1	150.1.2.1

Figure 12-4 shows several steps that occur over time, as follows:

1. Each router knows only its respective, directly connected routes, as shown by the routing tables at the top of the figure.

2. R1 sends a routing update to R2. The term ***routing update*** refers to a routing protocol message that contains information about IP networks and subnets. Notice that R1's routing update simply lists the subnets that R1 has in its routing table.

3. Each router still has a routing table, with R2's now larger because it learned some routes. R2 decided to add a route to subnet 150.1.1.0 — the subnet where Hannah resides. R2 didn't have a route to subnet 150.1.1.0 before, but after R2 learned about that subnet from the routing update that R1 sent, it now knows about this additional subnet.

Also notice the outgoing interface and next-hop router of this new route. R2 uses its own Ethernet1 interface as the outgoing interface. From Figure 12-4, it seems that R2 would use its interface E1 to forward packets to subnet 150.1.1.0, but R2 chooses to put that interface into the route because that's the interface in which it received the routing update. R2 also puts R1's IP address of 150.1.2.1 as the next-hop router because that's the IP address of the router that sent the routing update. From Figure 12-4, you can see that this route's next-hop router IP address should be R1's IP address 150.1.2.1.

Notice that although R2 learned a route based on getting the routing update from R1, R1 has not learned any routes yet. Routers learn routes with routing protocols when they receive routing updates from other routers; routers send routing updates so that other routers can learn from them. For R1 to learn routes, another router needs to tell it about other routes with a routing update. Figure 12-5 shows R2 advertising its routes, with R1 learning a route to subnet 150.1.3.0.

Figure 12-5   R1 Learning by Listening for Routing Updates

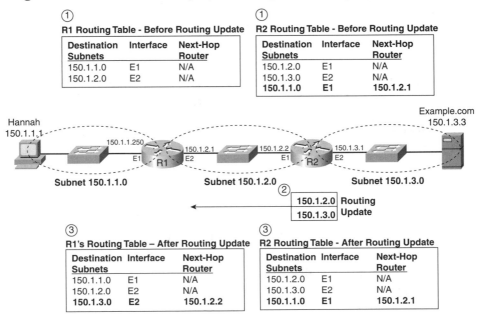

① **R1 Routing Table - Before Routing Update**

Destination Subnets	Interface	Next-Hop Router
150.1.1.0	E1	N/A
150.1.2.0	E2	N/A

① **R2 Routing Table - Before Routing Update**

Destination Subnets	Interface	Next-Hop Router
150.1.2.0	E1	N/A
150.1.3.0	E2	N/A
150.1.1.0	**E1**	**150.1.2.1**

③ **R1's Routing Table – After Routing Update**

Destination Subnets	Interface	Next-Hop Router
150.1.1.0	E1	N/A
150.1.2.0	E2	N/A
150.1.3.0	**E2**	**150.1.2.2**

③ **R2 Routing Table - After Routing Update**

Destination Subnets	Interface	Next-Hop Router
150.1.2.0	E1	N/A
150.1.3.0	E2	N/A
150.1.1.0	**E1**	**150.1.2.1**

Figure 12-5 shows several steps that occur over time, with R1 learning routes from R2, as follows:

1. Each router knows only its respective, directly connected routes, as shown by the routing tables at the top of the figure.

2. R2 sends a routing update to R1.

3. R1's routing table now holds a route to subnet 150.1.3.0. Also, notice that R1's outgoing interface for that route is Ethernet2, which is the interface in which the routing update was received. The next-hop router is 150.1.2.2, which is R2's IP address.

Now both R1 and R2 have routes to all three subnets in the figure, with both routers learning the rest of the routes by receiving and processing incoming routing updates.

Picking the Best Road (Route)

I travel a lot to teach classes. Occasionally, I ask for directions about how to go somewhere when class is over, and invariably, I get three different answers from three different students. Everyone has a favorite shortcut or back road that will get you there a little quicker.

Routing protocols not only help routers learn routes, but they also help routers learn the best routes to a destination when there is more than one way to get there. Routers learn about all the possible routes and then have to decide which is best. For instance, in Figure 12-6, the internetwork has been expanded with three routers. R1 can still reach the subnet where the web server resides (150.1.3.0) through R2, but it can also reach that same subnet through R3.

Figure 12-6   Multiple Ways to Get to the Same Place

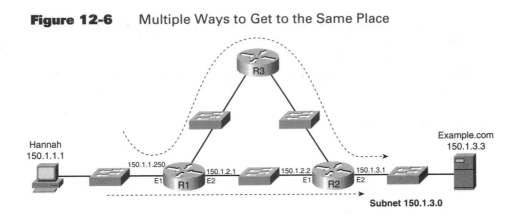

You can see by looking at the figure that R1 could send packets to subnet 150.1.3.0 through R2 or through R3. However, it seems like the direct route through R2 makes more sense. Routing protocols solve this problem by using an objective tool called a metric. A *metric* is a number that's associated with each route in a routing update. That number represents how good or how bad that route is. When a router receives multiple routing updates, it might learn of multiple ways to reach a network or subnet. By looking at the metrics associated with each route in each update, the router can pick the best route.

First, you need to see how R1 can learn about two routes to subnet 150.1.3.0. (Refer to Figure 12-7.) Then, it will be easier to see how the metric works.

Figure 12-7 shows the following steps:

1. R2 advertises the same routing information directly to R1.

2. R2 advertises those same routes to R3, including subnet 150.1.3.0.

3. R3 turns around and advertises to R1 about those same subnets.

4. R1, after learning of both ways to reach subnet 150.1.3.0, has chosen the route through R2 and adds that route to the routing table.

Figure 12-7   Choices, Choices: Using the Metric to Pick the Best Route

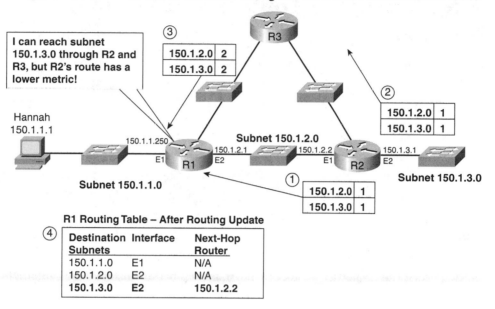

The key point to consider is why R1 chooses the route through R2 instead of the route through R3. Notice that the routing updates in Figure 12-7 also include a metric for each route or subnet listed in the update. With metrics, smaller is better. As shown in Figure 12-7, R3 advertises a larger metric (metric 2) than R2 does (metric 1), so R1 decides to use the route through R2. Step 4 shows the resulting routing table entry.

Routing protocols allow routers to use the best route if it's available, but they use less desirable routes if the best route is unavailable. Imagine that someone turns off the power on the Ethernet switch between R1 and R2. That route would then fail and be unavailable. The routing protocol on R1 would notice that the formerly best route had failed and remove the route from the routing table. At the same time, R1's routing protocol would notice that another route exists—the one through R3—and add that route to the routing table.

This one example demonstrates a couple of important points about routing protocols. First, they learn all the possible paths, or routes, to reach each subnet. Second, they pick the best route currently available for each subnet, reacting to changes in the network.

Introducing the Long List of Routing Protocols

Over the years, many different routing protocols have been developed. To exchange routing information as in the examples in this chapter, the routers would use a single routing protocol. Each router would use the same routing protocol.

However, you have a choice as to which routing protocol to use. The details of why you would choose one routing protocol over another is beyond the scope of this book. However, to have a conversational knowledge of networking, you should at least know the names of the IP routing protocols and a few basic facts about each. For instance, some routing protocols are defined as public Internet standards in RFCs, whereas others are proprietary from Cisco Systems, which has a significant percentage of the router product market. Also, one routing protocol in particular, Border Gateway Protocol (BGP), is intended for use between Internet service providers (ISPs) and their customers, whereas most others are more appropriate for use inside a single company or organization. A routing protocol that is designed for use inside a company is called an *Interior Routing Protocol*, and one that is designed for use between different companies is called an *Exterior Routing Protocol*. Table 12-1 lists the protocols, along with some of these comparison points.

Table 12-1   IP Routing Protocols

Routing Protocol	Public or Proprietary?	Interior or Exterior?
Routing Information Protocol (RIP)	Public	Interior
Interior Gateway Routing Protocol (IGRP)	Proprietary	Interior
Open Shortest Path First (OSPF)	Public	Interior
Enhanced IGRP (EIGRP)	Proprietary	Interior
Border Gateway Protocol (BGP)	Public	Exterior

Most companies choose a single interior routing protocol for use on all the company routers. Of the routing protocols listed, OSPF and EIGRP are the more popular protocols for use inside a single enterprise.

Chapter Summary

Routers use a routing table to figure out where to send packets. If a packet arrives at a router, and that router does not have a matching entry in its routing table, the router discards the packet. For routing to work well, the collective routers in an internetwork need to have routes to all the IP networks and IP subnets in the internetwork.

Routers first learn about any directly connected routes. If a router interface is working and has an IP address configured, the router can add a route for the connected subnet to the routing table. Network engineers can also statically configure a route, telling the router the routing table entry that it should add to its routing table.

The most common way that a router learns routes is by running a routing protocol. Routers exchange information about the routes they know about by sending routing update messages. Other routers receive those messages and learn the routes. If all routers advertise their routes, eventually all routers will know about all the IP networks and subnets.

Many IP routing protocols are available. RIP and IGRP are older interior routing protocols, meant for use inside a single company. EIGRP and OSPF are the most popular interior routing protocols today, with OSPF being a public standard, and EIGRP being Cisco proprietary. BGP is the main option for an exterior routing protocol.

Chapter Review Questions

You can find the answers to the following questions in Appendix A, "Answers to Chapter Review Questions."

1. Router R4 has two working Ethernet interfaces, and each interface has been configured with an IP address. What is the least number of routes that R4 should have in its routing table, and why?

2. Router R4 has a working Ethernet1 interface whose IP address is 10.10.10.10. The subnet number of the subnet attached to that interface is 10.10.10.0, with all hosts that share the first 3 octets of 10.10.10 in the same subnet. List the routing table entry that R4 will place in its routing table for this route, including the destination, outgoing interface, and next-hop router fields.

3. Referring to Figure 12-8, list the three parts of the IP route that could be statically added to R1's configuration so that it could forward packets to the web server. Include the destination, outgoing interface, and next-hop router as appropriate.

Figure 12-8   Figure Referenced in Chapter 12 Review Questions

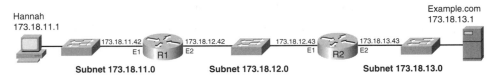

4. Referring to Figure 12-8, list the three parts of the IP route that R1 would learn from R2 using a routing protocol. Include the destination, outgoing interface, and next-hop router as appropriate.

5. Referring to Figure 12-8, list the three parts of the IP route that R2 would learn from R1 in the figure. Include the destination, outgoing interface, and next-hop router as appropriate.

6. What is the primary purpose for using a routing protocol?

7. What is a routing update?

8. What two routing protocols are the most popular ones used today inside a single company?

9. What routing protocol is most often used to exchange routing information between an ISP and its customers (exterior routing protocol)?

What You Will Learn

After reading this chapter, you should be able to

- ✔ Describe how a TCP/IP host can keep a local list of names and IP addresses

- ✔ Explain the process by which a TCP/IP host can learn the IP address that corresponds to a host name

- ✔ List the terms related to the name resolution process in TCP/IP networks

CHAPTER 13

People Like Names, but Computers Like Numbers

I was driving in the car with my wife the other day, and I needed to call my good friend, Gary. I didn't tell my wife "Hey, I need to call 555-555-1234," but I said something like, "I need to call Gary." (Nope, that's not Gary's real phone number. He might get a few extra calls if I had put his real number in here.) When I actually called Gary, I didn't punch his name into a keypad; rather, I typed in the number. I want to talk to Gary, but the phone company just cares about the phone number I want to connect to.

Similarly, users typically refer to names, but computers use numbers—specifically IP addresses—to deliver data across the network. Routers route packets based on the destination IP address; there's not a place in the IP header for the name of the destination host computer. So, before a user can succeed at connecting to a server using a name, his computer has to figure out which IP address to plug into the IP packet header as the destination IP address.

This chapter covers the basics of how a PC performs name resolution. *Name resolution* refers to the process of a computer taking a name, typically supplied by the user of the computer, and figuring out the corresponding IP address.

Looking Up the Name and Number in the Phone Book (Host Table)

If you need to call someone and you know the person's name but not the phone number, you can just look up the information in the phone book. It's simple, easy, and convenient. However, it only works if the phone book that you have happens to have that person's name and number in it.

TCP/IP hosts can have the equivalent of a phone book sitting in a file. The *local host file* contains a list of TCP/IP host computer names and their corresponding IP addresses. That host computer just needs to look at the local host file for the name and read the address next to it. Figure 13-1 shows the basic process.

Figure 13-1   Using a PC's Local Host File

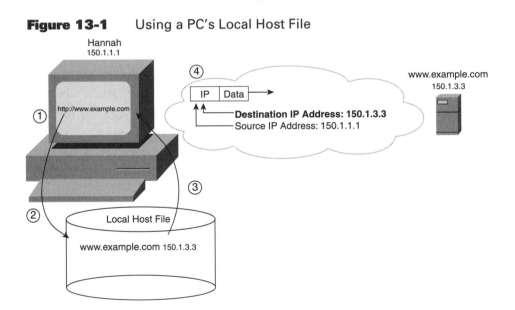

Figure 13-1 shows four steps, as follows:

1. Hannah opens a browser and types in **http://www.example.com**.

2. Before Hannah's PC can send an IP packet to the example.com web server at 150.1.3.3, she must look in her host file. The host file lists www.example.com, along with IP address 150.1.3.3. All the higher-layer

work—such as HTTP GETs, TCP connection establishment, and the like—flows in IP packets, and when Hannah sends those IP packets, they go to IP address 150.1.3.3.

3. Hannah retrieves the IP address from the local host file.

4. Hannah's PC then sends packets to the web server using destination IP address 150.1.3.3.

Even though using the local host file might be easy to understand, it has some drawbacks, just like when you use the phone book. Your phone book simply doesn't list the names and numbers of everyone on the planet. Such a book would probably fill your entire house, and finding the name would be a big hassle.

Similarly, a local host table does not solve all TCP/IP naming problems. People frequently add new server names in a single enterprise network, and many new server names are added to the Internet every day. In addition, the user of each PC is ultimately responsible for updating his own host file. Keeping the local host file updated and accurate is pretty impractical; even if the local host file could be kept updated, the file would probably get really large and unwieldy. As a result, most host computers do not use a local host file; instead, they use something called the *Domain Name System (DNS)*, which you'll learn about in the next section.

Asking Someone Else to Look Up the Phone Number (IP Address) for You

Instead of using your local phone book, you can always call the phone company and ask for help. Phone companies call this service *directory assistance*, and almost everyone else in the U.S. calls the service *information*. You just call directory assistance (dialing 411 in the U.S.), tell the operator the name of the person or business that you want to call, and the operator tells you the number.

The TCP/IP protocol called DNS behaves something like a phone company's directory assistance service. *DNS* defines protocols for the purpose of discovering which names correspond to which IP address. DNS also defines the structure and format of TCP/IP *host names*. Similar to the way that you can dial 411 in the U.S. and get help finding a phone number, a TCP/IP host can send a message to a DNS server to get help finding an IP address.

DNS defines how to figure out names and IP addresses for the entire Internet, as well as inside a single site at a single company. In the next sections, you'll first walk through the simpler processes used inside a single company; then you'll learn about DNS in the Internet and the conventions for what names look like.

Asking for Name Resolution Help Inside the Company

When you use directory assistance in the U.S., you pick up the phone and dial 411. To use DNS inside a single company, each TCP/IP host asks for help from a computer that is running a service called a *DNS server*. For the process to work, two key facts must be true:

- The host computer must know the IP address of the DNS server, similar to how everyone in the U.S. knows to call 411 to reach the phone company's directory assistance service.

- The DNS server must know the names and corresponding IP addresses, similar to how the phone company has a long list of names and phone numbers.

The *DNS server* is a computer that is running DNS server software. The DNS server has a list of all the TCP/IP host names in the network, along with their corresponding IP addresses. You can think of the list as the same general concept as a local host table, but instead of needing a copy on every host computer, there's one copy on the DNS server. Keeping one copy of the list of names and IP addresses current is much easier than having everyone in the company try to do the same! As you'll learn more about in the section titled "Asking for Name Resolution Help Outside the Company," a DNS server doesn't need to know all the names and IP addresses in the Internet, but just a small portion of them.

To support DNS, each TCP/IP host needs to know the IP address of the DNS server. It's similar to the idea that everyone in the U.S. knows to dial 411 to get telephone directory assistance. In this case, the DNS server's IP address is 150.1.3.4, and Hannah needs to know that address before she can send packets to the server.

Hannah's PC has two ways of knowing the DNS server's IP address. First, the address might be statically configured at Hannah's PC. Alternatively, Hannah might dynamically learn that address using the DHCP protocol, as mentioned in Chapter 10, "Delivering the Goods to the Right Street (IP) Address." Regardless of how Hannah knows that her DNS is at 150.1.3.4, she must know that fact ahead of time.

The main concept is simple, as shown in Figure 13-2. This time, Hannah is inside the fictitious example.com corporation's enterprise network.

Figure 13-2   Resolving Names and Addresses: The Basic DNS Process

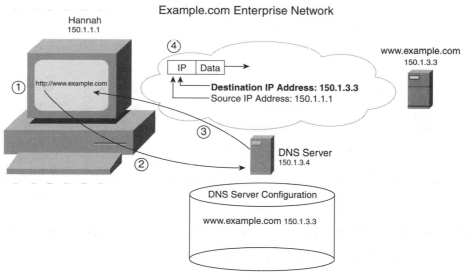

Figure 13-2 shows four steps, which can be explained as follows:

1. Hannah wants to connect to web server http://www.example.com, so she opens a browser, types in the name, and presses **Enter**.

2. Hannah's PC sends a DNS resolution request to her DNS server. A ***DNS resolution request*** is simply a DNS message that lists the host name (www.example.com), and the fact that the requesting host would like to know the IP address that corresponds to that name.

3. The DNS sends a DNS reply back to Hannah. The DNS reply has information in it, such as the IP address of 150.1.3.3.

4. Hannah can now send a packet to the web server. In fact, from this point onward, Hannah works just like she did back in Figure 13-1, when she used a local host file.

For DNS to work well inside a company, someone must be responsible for supporting it. That work includes updating and changing the list of names and IP addresses. When new names are added, old ones are no longer used, and when TCP/IP hosts change their IP addresses, that person has to keep the DNS server updated.

note

Although the examples in this book use web browsers, any TCP/IP application that uses names can, and probably does, use DNS. For instance, if you send an e-mail to barney@example.com, the "example.com" part identifies the host name of the SMTP server that is used for example.com.

Asking for Name Resolution Help Outside the Company

Your local telephone company has a list of all its customers and their local phone numbers. But there are a lot of people in the world who are not customers of your local telephone company, so those people won't be on your local phone company's list of names. However, these days, you can typically dial 411 in the U.S. and get help finding a phone number of someone anywhere in the country. But if you use one local phone company, say Bell South, and the person you are calling is a customer of Verizon, how can the Bell South directory assistance person help you find the phone number? As it turns out, the phone companies share information about the names and phone numbers so that they can each provide better customer service to their own local customers. In effect, the master list of names and phone numbers is distributed among lots of phone companies.

A similar kind of thing happens with DNS, although there are some underlying differences. Multiple DNS servers work together, with each DNS holding different sets of names and IP addresses. Figure 13-3 points out the need for DNS servers to cooperate to support name resolution for any name. In this case, Hannah is still in the example.com enterprise network, but now she wants to reach the http://www.fredsco.com website, which is located in the Fredsco enterprise network.

Figure 13-3   DNS Request Is Made, but DNS Server Doesn't Know the Name

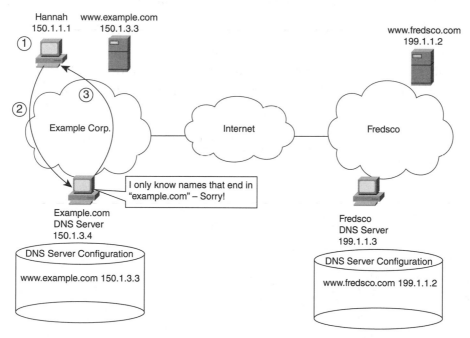

The key to understanding the problem and its solution is to know that a DNS server only knows about some of the names and addresses. For instance, the example.com company's DNS server (150.1.3.4) only knows about names that end with "example.com." The three steps numbered in Figure 13-3 show how Hannah does not learn the IP address of www.fredsco.com from her name server:

1. Hannah plugs **http://www.fredsco.com** into her browser.

2. Hannah's PC sends a name resolution request to the same DNS server at example.com.

3. Because the example.com DNS server only knows about names that end in "example.com," the DNS server returns a response that says that it can't resolve the name.

Hannah's PC does not learn the IP address of www.fredsco.com, so she can't reach the www.fredsco.com website. She'll probably see a message in her browser window that implies that the site cannot be found.

The DNS in the Fredsco enterprise network knows the name www.fredsco.com and its IP address. However, Hannah, like all well-behaved TCP/IP hosts, asks the only DNS server she knows about for name resolution help. To solve the problem, the DNS servers must work together, as shown in Figure 13-4.

Figure 13-4   How DNSs Work Together

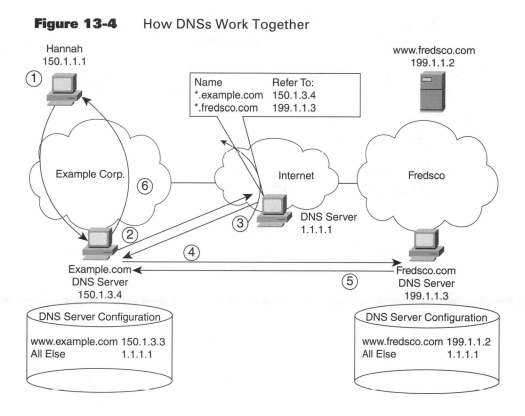

Here's the process shown in Figure 13-4:

1. Hannah opens a browser, types in **www.fredsco.com** (just like in the previous example), and sends a DNS resolution request to her DNS.

2. example.com's DNS doesn't know the name http://www.fredsco.com. However, the DNS now has some configuration that tells it that if it doesn't know the name, it should ask the DNS server at IP address 1.1.1.1.

3. The DNS server at 1.1.1.1 has a table that lists the IP addresses of a bunch of name servers. DNS server 1.1.1.1 knows that for all names that end in "example.com," DNS 150.1.3.4 can resolve the names. It also knows that for all names that end in "fredsco.com," DNS 199.1.1.3 can resolve the names. Finally, DNS server 1.1.1.1 knows about a lot of other name servers and the names they know about, so this name server can direct each request to the right name server. This DNS sends a message back to the example.com DNS, referring it to the DNS at 199.1.1.3.

4. The example.com DNS repeats the name resolution request, now sending the request to the DNS server at Fredsco (199.1.1.3).

5. The Fredsco DNS gets the request, and it knows the name and IP address. It sends a reply to the requesting host—namely, example.com's DNS server.

6. Finally, the example.com DNS server replies to Hannah, telling her that www.fredsco.com resolves to IP address 199.1.1.2.

Ultimately, Hannah learns the IP address of the www.fredsco.com web server. Before this process could work, special DNS servers, called ***root DNS servers***, are installed somewhere in the Internet. Root DNS servers do not really perform name resolution; rather, they know the IP addresses of several other DNS servers. (In Figure 13-4, the DNS server at IP address 1.1.1.1 served as a root DNS server.) Each company's DNS server can refer to one or more root servers, so when it doesn't know a name, a DNS server can ask a root DNS server for help. The root DNS refers the original DNS server to the right DNS server, as in Figure 13-4.

After Hannah knows the IP address of the server, everything else can happen as was described in earlier chapters because the name resolution process is complete. For instance, Hannah can send packets to the web server, and those packets can hold TCP segments. Those TCP segments, in turn, hold HTTP messages, as well as the contents of a web page.

How Names Should Be Formatted

For the DNS processes to work well, DNS defines some rules for how hosts are named. This section covers the structure and meaning of TCP/IP host names, plus some terminology related to name resolution.

First, the names must follow a format that helps the DNS servers decide which DNS should handle DNS requests for a particular name. You have probably noticed that the names used in this chapter, such as www.example.com and www.fredsco.com, have some sort of organization and structure. The last part of the name actually helps identify the DNS that can resolve the name.

TCP/IP hosts are organized into groups of hosts called ***domains***. A domain consists of all hosts whose names end with the same text. For instance, the names www.example.com, ftp.example.com, and smtp.example.com would all be host names inside the example.com domain. The part in common among all the names—example.com in this case—is called the **domain name**.

One or more DNS servers are considered to be the ***authoritative DNS*** server for a particular domain. That means that any names that end in that domain name should be resolved by that DNS server, and that DNS server has the ultimate authority for which names have which IP addresses—at least for names in that domain. For instance, in Figure 13-4, the DNS server at address 150.1.3.4 was the authoritative DNS for domain example.com.

The structure of the DNS system works well. Inside a single company, the DNS administrator can change and add all the names he wants to. As long as the root DNS server knows the list of all the DNS servers and the domain names that they support, anyone on the Internet can ask for name resolution, have the request referred to the right DNS server, and learn the correct IP address.

Chapter Summary

The Domain Name System (DNS) defines the terminology, naming conventions, and protocols required to allow users to use host names. When a user refers to a host name, the host, called a DNS resolver, sends a DNS request to a DNS server. The server ultimately returns a response that tells the resolver the IP address that corresponds to that name.

Each company or organization should have a DNS server that is the authoritative DNS server for that domain. That DNS server can resolve names inside that domain. When that DNS server gets DNS requests for names in other domains, it asks for help from a root DNS server, which helps it locate the authoritative DNS server for the domain in which that name resides.

Although impractical today, a host could use a local host table, which is simply a list of host names and their IP addresses.

Chapter Review Questions

You can find the answers to the following questions in Appendix A, "Answers to Chapter Review Questions."

1. What is the one alternative for name resolution that doesn't use DNS?

2. What does DNS stand for?

3. Imagine that Lenny uses a PC inside the fredsco.com domain. Lenny opens a browser and tries to browse http://www.fredsco.com. His PC is configured to use DNS. How many DNS requests will Lenny's PC likely send before he gets a response to a request for host name www.fredsco.com?

4. Imagine that Lenny uses a PC inside the fredsco.com domain. Lenny opens a browser and tries to browse http://www.example.com. His PC is configured to use DNS. How many DNS requests will Lenny's PC likely send before he gets a response to a request for host name www.example.com?

5. Imagine that Lenny uses a PC inside the fredsco.com domain. Lenny opens a browser and tries to browse http://www.example.com. Imagine that his PC gets a DNS response that www.example.com's IP address is 192.0.33.166. When Lenny's PC sends a packet to that web server, does the PC include the destination IP address of 192.0.33.166 in the IP packet header, or the destination name of www.example.com in the IP packet header, or both?

6. State whether you agree with the following statement and why: "Each TCP/IP host refers to its DNS server using a well-known IP address 0.4.1.1."

7. Given a name like www.example.com, identify the likely domain name, and using that example, define the term "domain name."

8. When a client inside one company tries to browse a web server in another company, using a name, describe in general terms how the authoritative name server for the web server name is found.

9. State whether you agree with the following statement and why: "When a user who is configured to use DNS opens a web browser and types in http://www.example.com, the next IP packet that he sends is to the web server."

Building an Interstate (Inter-LAN) Highway System

Part V covers three categories of WANs. Chapter 14 describes a type of WAN that is best suited for use between two business sites. Chapter 15 covers Frame Relay, which is useful for connecting more than two business sites. Finally, Chapter 16 discusses a couple of WAN technologies that let you connect to the Internet from your home.

Chapter 14: Leasing a (Network) Roadway Between Two Points

Chapter 15: Leasing a (Network) Roadway Between Lots of Places

Chapter 16: Driving from Home onto the Globally Interconnected (Internet) Roadway

What You Will Learn

After reading this chapter, you should be able to

✔ List several similarities and differences between using an Ethernet cross-over cable or a WAN link between two routers

✔ List two reasons why using a telephone company for WAN services makes sense

✔ Explain the meaning behind basic telephone company jargon used with WAN links

✔ Explain IP routing over point-to-point WAN links

✔ Describe the HDLC and PPP encapsulation processes

CHAPTER 14

Leasing a (Network) Roadway Between Two Points

Throughout this book, you've seen many analogies to driving, roads, and the like, both in the text and in the titles. This part of the book makes a few analogies with roads, but the upcoming chapters will also make other analogies with things you already know—at least if you've read the chapters in sequence! In the next few chapters, you'll compare new networking topics to other networking topics, particularly Ethernet. Novel concept, huh?

Wide-area networks (WANs) refer to physical network connections that typically run between sites that are far apart. Local-area networks (LANs) are also physical networks, but they typically connect devices that are relatively close together.

As it turns out, WANs and LANs have another difference—a difference that matters a lot to basic understanding of how each is built. With LANs, you are in control. You can buy cable, run it, connect it to the switches, plug in things where you want them in the switch, and it works. With WANs, you can't just run a cable. Even if the WAN link is a mile long, you typically can't run a cable over the streets to your other building. It's typically illegal, even if you could run the cable under the street where hopefully no one would mess with it.

In short, to build WANs, you must lease a physical network from someone who can run a cable between the buildings that you want to connect. This chapter focuses on WANs that work well between a pair of sites.

Leasing the Cable When You Can't Run the Cable

If two routers in two cities need to forward packets to each other, they need some sort of *physical medium* over which to send the packets. Back in Chapter 4, "How to Build a Local (Network) Roadway," you learned that you could just run an Ethernet cross-over cable between two devices, and the two devices could communicate with Ethernet. That works well, but we aren't allowed to run Ethernet cables through other people's property.

This section introduces the general idea of a WAN link, which conceptually is equivalent to an Ethernet cross-over cable. Figure 14-1 depicts the general idea.

Figure 14-1   WAN Link—It Quacks Like an Ethernet Cross-Over Cable

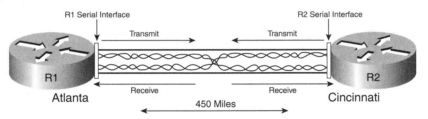

If you remember much about the physical details of Ethernet, Figure 14-1 should look familiar. When R1 sends out an electrical signal over the cable, R2 needs to receive that same signal on the wires that it expects to receive data. Likewise, R1 needs to receive what R2 transmits. Because the physical interfaces on the routers use the same pins to transmit, the cable connects the twisted pair used for transmitting by R1 over to R2's receive pins, and vice versa. In effect, the cable in the figure looks like an Ethernet cross-over cable. All that the two routers need is a cable between them, with transmit and receive pairs of wires, so that they can send and receive anytime they want.

The temptation might be to simply use Ethernet. However, two problems stop you from using Ethernet in this case:

- You aren't legally allowed to run a cable between Atlanta and Cincinnati (the sites in the figure).

- Those who can run the cable—namely, the telephone companies (telcos)—don't lease or sell 450-mile Ethernet cross-over cables.

As you might imagine, there is a solution that acts like using an Ethernet cross-over cable between two routers; the details are just a little different. The next section describes the details.

note
Many telephone companies are beginning to offer WAN services based on Ethernet. However, the vast majority of existing WAN connections work like what is described in this chapter and Chapters 15, "Leasing a (Network) Roadway Between Lots of Places," and 16, "Driving from Home onto the Globally Interconnected (Internet) Roadway."

You Can't Lease the Cross-Over Cable, So Lease Something Almost Just Like It

We've established the fact that you can't buy or lease an actual Ethernet cross-over cable from the telco. But what if the telco would lease to you something like the following?

- Use a service between two routers that acts like a cable with four wires (two pairs) in it.

- When a router sends on one pair, that pair is crossed to the other pair before it gets to the other end cable. That way, when one router sends on one pair, the other router receives on the other pair.

■ Because the service requires that you physically encode data a little differently than on Ethernet, your routers have to use a different type of interface, called a *serial interface*.

■ The end result will be that two routers can send and receive data to and from each other.

Well, the end result is that the routers can forward packets to each other, and that's exactly what the telco offers. The telco essentially can lease you a 4-wire cable, or *4-wire circuit*, between two points. Although it's not exactly Ethernet, it sure acts a lot like an Ethernet cross-over cable.

The telcos have been well prepared to offer 4-wire circuits to their customers for decades. They have already run cables between almost every town and city. They have offices, called *central offices (COs)*, almost everywhere as well. In addition, telcos have the *right-of-way*, which is the legal right to dig up roads and put cabling in the ground and overhead, all for the common good of the populace. In effect, the telco can run the cable for you to create this 4-wire circuit.

It's Not Really a 450-Mile Cable, but It Works Like One

You like the idea of this new WAN link from Atlanta to Cincinnati, so you meet with the telco salesman. You sign the papers, and then his more technical colleague, typically called a *sales engineer (SE)*, happens by. You ask him what the salesman really meant when he said, "It's just like we're running a 450-mile cable for you." The SE says simply, "We didn't run no stinkin' cable, but what we did do acts just like we did run a cable for you—at least that's the technical description."

If the telco actually had to run a cable for 450 miles, you wouldn't be able to afford to pay the installation charges. So, the telco does some other things inside its network, all of which is hidden from the customers. In the end, the service really does act like a 4-wire cable.

To build this service, the telco needs to install a 4-wire cable between your office building and theirs, as shown in Figure 14-2.

Figure 14-2 Establishing a Physical Path from the Customer to the Telco

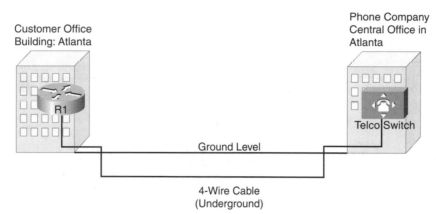

One end of the cable is inside a CO, which is where the telco keeps the equipment used to create the telephone network. Generically speaking, the switches in the CO are called ***telco switches***, ***phone switches***, or ***WAN switches***. There are lots of other names for specific types of equipment that the telco uses in the CO. The cable is plugged into a physical interface in a telco switch in the CO, with the other end of the cable connecting to the router at the customer site.

The cable runs from the CO, typically underground, and then comes up into the customer building. Installing the cable requires the right-of-way to go under the street, block traffic, and dig up a street or yard to run the cable. Thinking ahead, the telco often runs extra wires between the CO and large buildings, office complexes, and other business centers, just so it doesn't have to interrupt traffic and dig up the earth all the time.

To complete the path between Atlanta and Cincinnati, you'll need two more things. First, you need a similar cable run from the office building in Cincinnati where the other router sits and the telco CO in Cincinnati. The other requirement is that the telco needs to somehow get the electrical signals between the Atlanta CO and the Cincinnati CO. To do so, the telco does something like what is shown in Figure 14-3.

Figure 14-3   A Leased Line, A Leased Circuit, A Point-to-Point Link, and A WAN Link

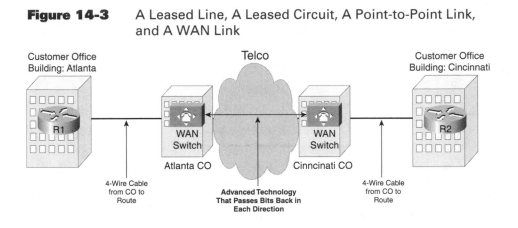

Before you needed this new WAN link, the telco had thought about supporting lots of customers in Atlanta and Cincinnati. In anticipation of future business, they installed gear and additional cabling. That equipment and cabling together can take the bits sent by R1 over the cable to the Atlanta CO, deliver them across the telco network, and send the bits to R2 in Cincinnati. Of course, the telco does the same with bits coming into the Cincinnati CO, delivering those to the Atlanta CO and then out to R1.

Regardless of what happens between the COs, as far as the routers are concerned, when they send data on that cable, the other router gets it. The details of how the telco does things inside its network are important if you work for the telco, but the goal of this chapter is simply to briefly highlight how the two routers could communicate.

The Many Personalities of a WAN Link

I've been using the terms *WAN link* and *4-wire circuit* to describe the service that acts like a 4-wire cable between routers. However, several other terms mean the same thing. Hey, why use one name when you can let people pick their favorite?

Table 14-1 summarizes the names, along with some of the reasons why the terms are used.

Table 14-1 Different Names for WAN Link

Term	Rationale
Leased circuit	In telco lingo, when you pick up the phone and make a voice call, the telco sets up a temporary circuit. When a customer pays money to have a permanently up circuit between two sites, the telco considers the circuit to be leased.
Leased line	The term "leased" is used for the same reasons as for *leased circuit*. The term "line" refers to the fact that the service is supposed to always be working, so it's like a cable, or a line, between the two sites.
Point-to-point link	The term "point-to-point" refers to the fact that exactly two end points exist on the circuit. The term "link" refers to the way the two end points are linked together so that they can communicate.
WAN link	The term "link" is used for the same reasons as in point-to-point link. The term "WAN" just refers to the link being used for wide-area networking at a relatively long distance.
Serial link	The term "serial" refers to the fact that the routers use serial interfaces on each end of the link.
4-wire circuit	The "4-wire" part refers to the number of wires in the cable between each CO and each site; a telco often uses the term "circuit" to refer to a communication path between two customer devices.
Serial link	A WAN link connects to serial interfaces on routers, hence the name "serial link."

Differences Between a Cross-Over Cable and a Leased Circuit

If you install an Ethernet cross-over cable between two routers and plug the cable into some type of Ethernet interface on the routers, the two routers can forward

Ethernet frames to each other. If you install a WAN link between two routers, the telco does create something similar to a cross-over cable, but a few details are different. In case you're wondering, there are lots of legitimate reasons for doing things differently for leased circuits, most of which have to do with supporting the service over a large and varied telco network.

I Feel the Need, the Need for Speed

Ethernet can support transmission speeds of 10 Mbps, 100 Mbps, 1000 Mbps (1 gigabit/second), and even 10 Gbps with the most recent version of Ethernet. As you read in Chapter 6, "Reducing Congestion and Driving Faster on the Local (Network) Roadway," the speeds can often be automatically negotiated, so a PC that is connected to a switch can negotiate to use 100 Mbps, as long as both the PC and the switch support that speed.

With WAN links, many different *transmission speeds* are supported. There are various WAN transmission speeds, but a lot of WAN links today use speeds that are multiples of 64 Kbps. (When the telcos built their first digital networks 50 years ago, they needed 64 Kbps to support a single voice call; that's why WAN links are multiples of 64 Kbps today.) The telco can offer multiples of 64 Kbps, up through the equivalent of 24 times 64 Kbps, which is about 1.5 Mbps. In telco jargon, the service in which you get to send 1.5 Mbps of data is called a *T1 circuit* or *T1 line*.

For example, imagine that you think you need 128 Kbps for the serial link between Atlanta and Cincinnati. When you order the leased line from the telco and sign the contracts, the contracts state the speed of the link. If you try to go faster or slower, the link won't work, so you have to configure the router (or CSU/DSU—more on that in the next section) to run at the right speed.

You should be aware of two other terms that refer to the speed at which bits are sent over a WAN link: clockrate and bandwidth. *Clockrate* refers to the actual timing of how often a bit is sent; for instance, a bit is sent every 1/64,000 of a second on a 64-Kbps link. *Bandwidth* is another term that refers to the transmission speed of the link.

The telco offers speeds faster than 1.5 Mbps as well. You can order links in multiples of 1.544 Mbps, which is the exact speed of a T1. You can also order even higher speeds that generally come in multiples of 51.84 Mbps. Suffice it to say, you have tons of options, for a large variety of requirements, and all at different prices as well. Following are the key points you should remember about the speed of WAN links:

- Many different speeds are possible, some of which aren't mentioned here.

- You specify the speed when you order the leased line.

- You need to configure the routers (or CSU/DSU) to use the right speed.

The Need to Control the Speed

Some types of Ethernet NICs and router interfaces can run at various Ethernet-supported speeds. For those NICs and interfaces, you can either configure the PC or router to use one speed, or the device can autonegotiate the speed.

Serial links can run at different speeds, but the speed must be preconfigured. A component of a serial interface called the *CSU/DSU* (channel service unit/data service unit) controls the speed. The CSU/DSU functions, which include several other things besides setting the speed, can be done with an external device or as a function of the serial interface card on the router. If you use a CSU/DSU that sits outside the router, you must configure the speed on that external device; if the CSU/DSU is built into the router, you must configure the speed of the WAN link on the router.

When you order a router, you can order a serial interface either with or without the CSU/DSU on the serial interface. If you order a serial interface with a CSU/DSU, it's called an *internal CSU/DSU*, and if you order a router's serial interface without a CSU/DSU, you have to use an *external CSU/DSU*. Figure 14-4 shows an example of both an internal and an external CSU/DSU.

Figure 14-4   Cabling with Internal and External CSU/DSUs

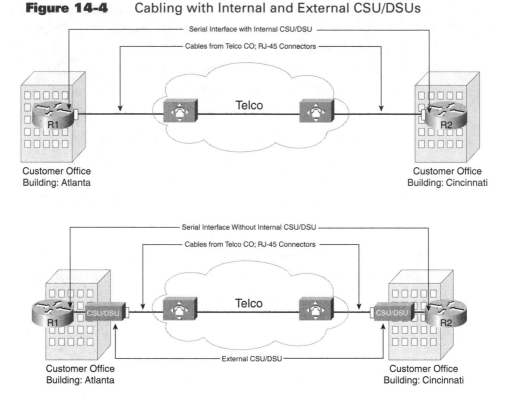

When you're using internal CSU/DSUs, the cable from the telco plugs into the serial interface of the router. With external CSU/DSUs, the cable plugs into the CSU/DSU. An external CSU/DSU connects to the router using another short cable, typically less than 50 feet long. These short cables have numerous options for their connectors, so this book won't get into details about these cables. However, when you order the router and the CSU/DSU, the product documentation will suggest cables, which you'll typically buy from the router vendor when you order the router.

Double Your Speed at No Cost

By the way, you can send at full speed in both directions on a WAN link—a feature called *full duplex*. As a result, you could argue that you get twice as much bandwidth. Talk about a closing line for the telco salesman when his customer can't decide if he wants to order a new leased line: "How about if we double your speed for free, just because I like you? Sign here, please."

The trick is that with two pairs of wires in a 4-wire circuit, one pair is used for transmitting data in each direction, so there's no contention. Each router can send at the full speed of the link at the same time.

A WAN Link Installation Plan

So far in this chapter, you have learned some of the details about leased lines (or WAN links, or leased circuit...choose your favorite term). The goal is to allow two routers to send and receive data between two sites, particularly when you do not have the right-of-way or capability to run a cable yourself. The steps you take to create the leased line are as follows:

1. Contract with the phone company to provide a leased line between two street addresses, even specifically into a certain floor and closet, and at a certain speed.

2. Install a router at each site, near where the telco will run its cable.

3. Install an external CSU/DSU near the routers at each site, if you didn't buy routers with internal CSU/DSUs.

4. Configure the CSU/DSUs (internal or external) with the correct speed.

5. After the phone company runs the cables, install the cables into the CSU/DSU (external) or serial interface of the router (internal CSU/DSU) at each site.

Now the routers are ready to send and receive data, at least at OSI Layer 1. Before the routers can send useful end user traffic, however, they need to know a few more things relating to OSI Layers 2 and 3, which the next section covers to round out the chapter.

Routers and WANs: A Match Made in Heaven

Routers and WAN links have the same general goals, so they are often used together. Routers are designed to forward IP packets between different subnets, whether those subnets are near to each other or far apart. WAN links are designed to forward bits to remote sites. It's only natural that routers would use WAN links when they need to forward IP packets to a subnet at a remote site.

End user devices at a company's office site typically use an Ethernet NIC; they never directly connect to a WAN link. To send traffic to an IP host at another site, end user devices send the data to a router. The router forwards the IP packet to another router at the other site, which then forwards the packet to the other IP host. Sound familiar? Yep, that's IP routing.

The best way to understand how WAN links are used is to review routing. Figure 14-5 shows a network diagram that includes some familiar details from the coverage of IP routing in Chapter 11, "Knowing Where to Turn at Each Intersection (Router)," as well as the same WAN link discussed in the first part of this chapter.

Figure 14-5   Same Subnets, Similar Routing Table, Over the WAN Link

R1 Routing Table				R2 Routing Table		
Destination Subnets	**Interface**	**Next-Hop Router**		**Destination Network**	**Interface**	**Next-Hop Router**
150.1.1.0	E1	N/A		150.1.1.0	S1	150.1.2.1
150.1.2.0	S0	N/A		150.1.2.0	S1	N/A
150.1.3.0	S0	150.1.2.2		150.1.3.0	E2	N/A

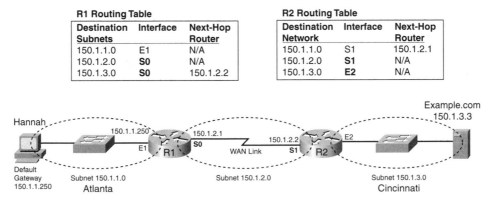

Figure 14-5 shows two LANs (Atlanta and Cincinnati), a WAN link between the two routers, and the routing tables of each router. People typically use a *lightning*

bolt type of line to represent a WAN link, as shown in the figure. Note also that R1 is using its serial0 interface, abbreviated s0 in the figure, and R2 is using its serial1 interface, abbreviated s1.

Now take a closer look at the routing tables in Figure 14-5. Comparing this inter-network to the one in Chapter 11, Figure 11-13, the only physical difference is that there is now a WAN link between the routers instead of an Ethernet. The routing tables differ in what outgoing interfaces they list. For example, R1's route to 150.1.3.0 lists an outgoing interface of S0, with a next-hop IP address of 150.1.2.2.

Now that we have an established internetwork to talk about, the next sections explain three topics related to the WAN data link layer and IP routing. In order, you'll read about WAN data link framing, WAN data link addressing, and the two most popular WAN data link protocols: HDLC and PPP.

You Can't Just Send Data; You Have to Send a Frame

You can't just send end user data, such as the contents of a web page, over an Ethernet. The thing that is actually sent over the Ethernet is an Ethernet frame. Inside the frame, after the other various headers, is the true end user data. In this section, you learn how to build a frame that is appropriate for a WAN serial link between two routers.

In Figure 14-5, when Hannah sends a packet to the www.example.com web server at IP address 150.1.3.3, she sends the IP packet to her default gateway—namely, R1. When R1 receives the Ethernet frame, it checks to see whether errors occurred. If errors did not occur, R1 extracts the IP packet and begins the process of making a routing decision.

Figure 14-6 picks up the routing process at this point. R1 has the packet with destination address 150.1.3.3. That destination address matches the route for subnet 150.1.3.0, which lists outgoing interface Serial0 and next-hop IP address 150.1.2.2, which is R2's IP address.

Figure 14-6   Forwarding an IP Packet over a WAN Link

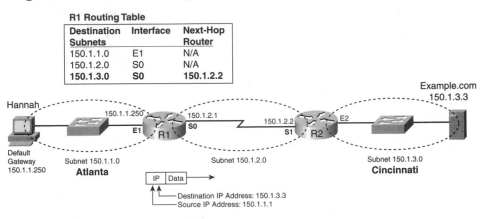

R1 has the same dilemma and the same solution that it had when it used Ethernet to connect to R2 back in Chapter 11. R1 needs to encapsulate the IP packet inside a data link layer frame.

Routers often support many options for data link layer protocols for point-to-point WAN links. The two most popular are *high-level data link control (HDLC)* and *Point-to-Point Protocol (PPP)*. Regardless of which of these two is used, R1 does the same general thing: It encapsulates the packet into a frame—either an HDLC or PPP frame, depending on which of the two protocols the router is using. Figure 14-7 shows the encapsulated packet, using HDLC.

Figure 14-7   Encapsulation in HDLC

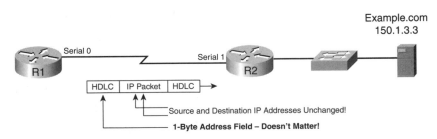

WAN data link protocols such as HDLC and PPP perform certain tasks just like Ethernet. HDLC and PPP encapsulate the packet in a header and trailer. They also have a frame check sequence (FCS) field in the trailer, which allows the receiver of the frame—R2 in this case—to know if the frame experienced errors.

Addressing on WAN Serial Links

One major difference between Ethernet and HDLC or PPP lies in the address field inside the HDLC and PPP header. There's only one address field, and it's 1 byte long. However, if you sit back and think about it, why do you need an address at all? When R1 sends anything on this point-to-point WAN link, the only device that could possibly get the data is R2. So, although the address field exists, it doesn't really matter. Moreover, most people don't think about the existence of an HDLC or PPP address field in the header.

A convenient side effect of the boring address field for HDLC and PPP is that there is no need for Address Resolution Protocol (ARP) or anything like it on the serial link. You might recall from Chapter 11 that when R1 forwarded an IP packet to R2 over a LAN, R1 had to use ARP to learn R2's data link (Ethernet) MAC address. With point-to-point WAN data link protocols, R1 doesn't need to find R2's HDLC address because the frame will be delivered to R2 over the link anyway. It's the only place the frame could go!

The Choice of Two Data Link Protocols

As mentioned earlier in this section, the two point-to-point WAN data link protocols used most often are HDLC and PPP. Both protocols work well but, of course, there are differences; otherwise, you wouldn't need both of them. The most important things to remember about these two protocols are their similarities:

- You use HDLC and PPP on point-to-point WAN links.

- You don't need to worry about data link layer addresses.

- There's an FCS field so that the receiver can discard frames that have errors.

The differences between the two protocols are mainly an outgrowth of when they were created, with HDLC being defined by the ITU in the 1970s, and PPP being defined in RFC 1661 during the 1990s. As a simple result of being designed later, PPP has several advanced features, some of which have to do with security, as covered in Chapter 17, "Accepting the Right People and Rejecting the Wrong People." Cisco uses a nonstandard version of HDLC, mainly to add features to the relatively old HDLC. Because Cisco's HDLC implementation is proprietary, both routers on each end of the link must be Cisco routers if you use HDLC. However, Cisco conforms to the standard for PPP, so when you use PPP, you could have a Cisco router on one end of a link, and another vendor's router on the other end of the link.

Chapter Summary

Routers typically route traffic between different subnets. To forward traffic between subnets that aren't in the same location, the router uses connectivity that a telephone company (telco) provides. One way the telco can provide that basic connectivity is through WAN links, also called leased lines, leased circuits, and point-to-point links.

With a WAN link, two routers can send and receive traffic to and from each other. To create the physical transmission medium, the telco installs a cable between each site and a local central office (CO). The telco then somehow passes the bits over the internal telco network. The end result is that the routers believe that they have a 4-wire cable between each other, over which they can send and receive at any time.

At each customer site, a router is installed, along with either an internal or external CSU/DSU. The CSU/DSU is configured with the speed of the link, with the lower-speed options from the telco being multiples of 64 Kbps.

To pass traffic over the WAN link, a data link protocol needs to be used; HDLC and PPP are the two most popular options today. Interestingly, because any data sent out a point-to-point WAN link goes to the device on the other end of the link—and only to that device—these data link protocols don't have a lot of work to do. They mainly provide the ability to encapsulate a packet and to check for errors. PPP does provide additional features as compared to HDLC.

Chapter Review Questions

You can find the answers to the following questions in Appendix A, "Answers to Chapter Review Questions."

1. How many twisted pairs of wires are typically used in a leased line between two routers?

2. Imagine that you wanted to create a WAN link between two routers (Router A and Router B) in cities that are 1000 miles apart. How long are the cables that the telco needs to run?

3. What is a WAN link?

4. What are some of the other names for a WAN link?

5. Explain whether point-to-point WAN links need something like the Ethernet CSMA/CD algorithm.

6. What kind of physical interface does a router use to connect to a WAN link?

7. Imagine that a WAN link has been installed between routers A and B. The physical cable from the telco was plugged directly into the serial interfaces on the routers. What feature must be included in the serial interface cards on these routers to allow the cable to be connected directly to the routers?

8. What is the main function of the CSU/DSU, as covered in this chapter?

9. What is the base transmission speed typically used for WAN links that run at relatively lower speeds (up to 1.5 Mbps)?

10. What are the two most popular data link protocols used on WAN links?

11. What does HDLC do to alert a router that is receiving a frame that an error has occurred?

12. Of the two more popular WAN link data link protocols, which was developed later and has more features?

13. Explain whether IP ARP is needed on WAN links. Why or why not?

What You Will Learn

After reading this chapter, you should be able to

- ✔ Compare and contrast point-to-point WAN link's physical layer with Frame Relay physical topologies

- ✔ Compare and contrast HDLC and PPP with Frame Relay

- ✔ Explain the basic forwarding process in Frame Relay using DLCIs

- ✔ Explain the concept behind the term *virtual circuit*

- ✔ List several reasons why Frame Relay is a widely used WAN technology

CHAPTER 15

Leasing a (Network) Roadway Between Lots of Places

The U.S. Department of Transportation (DOT) could plan to build a road directly between your house and every other place to which you might want to drive. It could do the same for everyone else as well. That would be ridiculous, of course, because the DOT would end up paving practically the entire country! Instead, the DOT built one road to your house, which is in turn connected to other roads, ultimately allowing you to drive anywhere you want to drive.

Chapter 14, "Leasing a (Network) Roadway Between Two Points," covered the basics of how a serial link could be used between two routers, which can be compared to paving a road directly between. This chapter covers a WAN technology called *Frame Relay*. Frame Relay uses one physical WAN link connected to each site, while allowing each site to send data to each other site. That's a lot like the DOT paving one road to your house, and you driving anywhere you want, always leaving your house by driving over that one road.

When you want to build a network to connect multiple remote sites, you could just order a lot of serial links. However, Frame Relay requires less work and less new hardware, making Frame Relay a much more cost-effective solution compared to leased lines.

In many ways, Frame Relay acts like a network built with an Ethernet switch. With an Ethernet switch, more than two devices can be cabled to the switch. To send an Ethernet frame to any of the other devices, the sender just needs to put the right destination Ethernet address in the frame. As you'll read in this chapter, a Frame Relay network acts like a big WAN switch, with routers connecting to it. To send data to another router, the sending router just needs to send a frame with the right address in it.

Making the Telco Look Like One Big Whopping Switch

By the end of this first section of this chapter, you'll know the basics of Frame Relay and how it behaves like a LAN switch in many ways. Before a LAN switch can switch frames between PCs or routers, the devices have to be physically connected to the switch. I'll start by explaining the equivalent in Frame Relay. The next section explains how the telephone company (telco) creates a Frame Relay service that switches frames to the routers that are connected to the Frame Relay network. The details of Frame Relay do differ from Ethernet switching, but many of the same general concepts apply.

Cabling a Router to the Big Frame Relay Switch

To make Frame Relay work, each router needs a physical cable between itself and a device called a *Frame Relay switch*. The telco uses Frame Relay switches in its local central offices (COs) that together switch the data to the correct sites. Like a PC attaches to a LAN switch with an Ethernet cable, a router needs a physical connection to a Frame Relay switch to use Frame Relay.

When a router physically connects to a Frame Relay switch, it is connecting to a *Frame Relay service*. The company that sells Frame Relay services is called a *Frame Relay service provider*. Often, a Frame Relay service provider is also a telco, but in most cases, that company works with other telcos to create the Frame Relay network. The service that the provider is selling is the ability for a router to send a Frame Relay frame and have it be delivered to another router that is also connected to the same Frame Relay network.

To create the physical connection between a router and the Frame Relay service provider, the provider needs to run a cable from all your sites to their local COs. Sound familiar? It should. Frame Relay is a set of protocol specifications, all matching the functions of OSI Layer 2. For Layer 1 functions—things like the cabling and how the bits are actually transmitted over the wire—Frame Relay uses the same standards that serial links do, as shown in Figure 15-1.

Figure 15-1   Physical Parts of Frame Relay

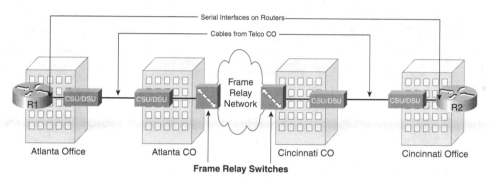

To physically connect to a Frame Relay switch, the provider runs the physical equivalent of a leased line between the router and a nearby Frame Relay switch. The telco needs to be able to send and receive data to and from each router, and leased lines do that. Because Frame Relay doesn't define standards for Layer 1 features, such as basic physical transmission and cabling, Frame Relay relies on the same standards that point-to-point WAN links do for the physical cabling and electrical details. Frame Relay standards refer to this physical serial link between a router and a Frame Relay switch as a Frame Relay *access link*.

Although the cabling and CSU/DSUs are the same as with a leased line, the telco does something different in the CO: It connects the cable to a *Frame Relay switch*. A Frame Relay switch is any equipment that understands Frame Relay and can forward traffic based on Frame Relay protocols. The provider's collective set of Frame Relay switches, along with the other equipment between them, form that provider's *Frame Relay network*.

Basic Logic Used by the Big Whopping Frame Relay Switch

To understand LAN switching, you first had to understand something about the set of protocols and standards that together form what we call Ethernet. Likewise, to see how Frame Relay works, you need to know a little about Frame Relay protocols.

The original Frame Relay protocols were defined by a vendor consortium called the *Frame Relay Forum*. A *vendor consortium* is a group of vendors that get together and agree to make their products work a particular way, while they wait on standards bodies to formalize a standard. The Frame Relay Forum is one such consortium. Later, the ITU formalized Frame Relay, as did the American National Standards Institute (ANSI).

Like its LAN cousin Ethernet, some of Frame Relay's most important features are addressing, framing, and switching. Figure 15-2 gives me a good backdrop from which to talk about the basics of all three.

Figure 15-2   Frame Relay Switching Using Frame Relay Addresses

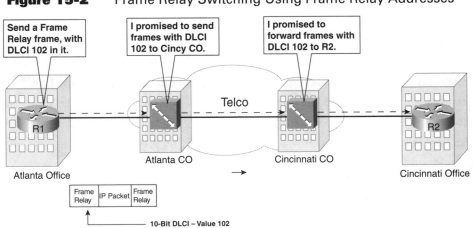

When a telco sells you a Frame Relay service, in essence the telco promises to forward Frame Relay frames sent by one router to one of many other routers. Before a router can send a packet, it must add the correct data link header and trailer to the packet. In Figure 15-2, R1 starts by putting an IP packet into a Frame Relay frame, between a Frame Relay header and trailer.

When building the frame, R1 must put the correct address in the header. Each Frame Relay header holds an address field called a *data-link connection identifier (DLCI)*. The DLCI is a 10-bit number, usually written as a decimal number between 0 and 1023. R1 puts a particular DLCI into the Frame Relay header, expecting that the frame will be forwarded by the Frame Relay network to the other router—R2 in this case.

Finally, the provider's Frame Relay network forwards the frame to the other router. To accomplish the task, each Frame Relay switch forwards the frame, based on the DLCI, through the network, until it gets to the router on the other side. It's similar in concept to how a PC might send an Ethernet frame, with a destination MAC address, and the LAN switch forwards the frame to the right destination.

Although the general ideas behind Frame Relay switching and Ethernet switching are similar, the processes do differ a lot when you look at the details. For instance, Frame Relay has a single address field, which is only 10 bits long, as opposed to Ethernet, which has a source and destination address field, each 48 bits (6 bytes) long. And Frame Relay switches must be configured to know where to forward frames with particular DLCIs in their headers, instead of automatically learning addresses and their locations like Ethernet LAN switches do.

When comparing this Frame Relay example with a serial link between two routers, the details are different, but the end result is the same. When R1 wants to forward a packet to R2, regardless of whether you use a leased line and PPP, or Frame Relay, when R2 gets the frame, it soon discards the data link header and trailer and leaves them with the packet. The routers are happy because they can forward packets.

If Two Sites Are Good, Three (or More) Must Be Better

Although you might have found the past few pages fascinating, the real advantage that Frame Relay holds over leased lines isn't obvious until you see an example with at least three Frame Relay sites. With Frame Relay, a router can use its single physical access link to forward traffic to multiple remote routers. If you're hanging with me on the analogy with Ethernet switches, that's an easy concept because the same thing happens with Ethernet. With Ethernet, a PC sends frames with varying destinations, over the one Ethernet cable that connects it to the LAN switch, and the LAN switch forwards the frames based on the destination MAC address. With Frame Relay, the same thing happens, except the Frame Relay switch forwards the frames based on the DLCI. Figure 15-3 shows the basic concept.

Figure 15-3   Frame Relay Switching to Multiple Remote Sites

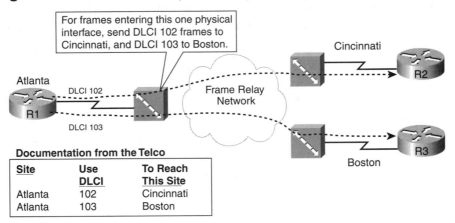

In Figure 15-3, R1 uses its single physical access link to send data to both R2 and R3. When you order the Frame Relay service, you tell the telco that you want to be able to send data from the Atlanta router (R1) to both Cincinnati (R2) and Boston (R3). To make it work, the telco gives you some documentation that tells you how it will program the Frame Relay switch. A shorthand version of that documentation is shown in the lower-left section of the figure. According to the provider, if R1 sends a frame with DLCI 102, the Frame Relay network forwards the frame to R2 (Cincinnati); if the provider puts 103 in the header, the Frame Relay network forwards the frame to R3 (Boston).

It's Virtually Like a Leased Circuit, So Let's Call It a Virtual Circuit

In Frame Relay lingo, the ability for R1 to send data to R2 over the Frame Relay network is called a ***virtual circuit (VC)***. A VC is like a leased circuit, in that exactly two devices can send and receive data using it. It's called *virtual* to contrast it with a physical leased circuit. And because a VC is typically predefined to always be there, VCs are often called ***permanent virtual circuits (PVCs)***.

When you're drawing network diagrams, it is useful to show PVCs separately from the physical cabling, as shown in Figure 15-4. (Frankly, there's no real standard for how to draw a PVC, so I tend to draw a single PVC with an odd-style of line—really three parallel lines—as shown in the figure.)

Figure 15-4   Frame Relay PVC Concepts

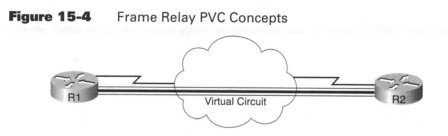

Typically, the service provider preconfigures all the required details of a PVC. For instance, in Figure 15-3, the switches knew to forward frames with DLCI 102 to Cincinnati, and frames with DLCI 103 to Boston.

One reason that drawing the PVCs is important is that when you order Frame Relay service, you do not have to have a PVC between each pair of routers. For instance, Figure 15-3 shows three sites, and frames going from one site (R1) to the other two sites (R2 and R3). That network does not have to have a PVC between R2 and R3. The choice of which sites need to have a PVC depends on where the network engineers think that traffic needs to flow in the network. When routers use Frame Relay, and there is a PVC between each pair of routers, the PVCs are in a *full mesh*, as shown in Figure 15-5; when not all routers have a PVC, it's called a *partial mesh*, as was shown in Figure 15-3.

Figure 15-5   Frame Relay Full Mesh

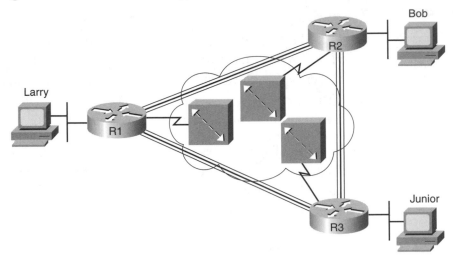

Faster, Cheaper, Better—You Can't Go Wrong with Frame Relay

These days, sites that use Frame Relay hugely outnumber sites that use leased lines. The reasons for Frame Relay's popularity vary, but it boils down to some basics: For less cash up front and less per month, you can send more data. Hmmm…that seems like a no brainer to me, and most people agree. But it is useful to consider why Frame Relay is faster, cheaper, and better than using leased lines. That will give me a good reason to talk about a few other important things relating to the technology.

You Can Still Use Serial Links, but It Will Cost You Up Front

Point-to-point WANs tend to require more hardware than does the equivalent network built with Frame Relay. To see why, consider what the telco does to create three leased circuits, as shown in Figure 15-6.

Figure 15-6   Three Leased Lines to Connect Three Routers

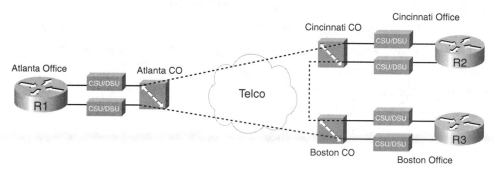

It takes twice as much hardware and twice as many cables to accomplish the network in Figure 15-6, as compared to using Frame Relay. In the figure, R1 requires two serial interfaces and two separate CSU/DSUs. Also, the telco has to install two cables between the local CO and the office building in Atlanta where R1 resides. Likewise, R2 needs two CSU/DSUs, and it needs two cables run to the telco; the same goes for R3. With the three-site Frame Relay network in Figure 15-5, you only needed one cable from each router to the telco, one serial interface, and one CSU/DSU at each router. Even in this small network, you already need more hardware and more cables.

Now think about what happens when the company grows to 10 sites or 100 sites. For each point-to-point line, R1 will need a separate physical serial interface and a separate CSU/DSU, and the telco will need to run another 4-wire cable from the Atlanta CO to Fredsco's Atlanta headquarters. That requires a lot of extra money for router and CSU/DSU hardware on Fredsco's part, and the telco has to run many more cables. Running those cables costs money, and, of course, Fredsco gets to pay for that.

In short, using leased lines will end up requiring more hardware and costing more cash up front than using Frame Relay.

Get Your Free Bandwidth Here! Free Bits!

So, you can save a little (or a lot) of money based on how much hardware you need to buy when using Frame Relay. Now imagine that Fred, the president of Fredsco, has a network with two sites and a single WAN link with a speed of 128 Kbps. The Frame Relay company's salesman gets a bonus if he signs up a new customer today, so he stops by to see Fred. "You know, we can install Frame Relay instead of your 128 Kbps point-to-point WAN link. For the same price, we can guarantee that you can send at least 128 Kbps between those two sites using Frame Relay. But most of the time, you'll be able to send double that—256 Kbps—for no extra cash! And after you sign, I'll buy lunch."

Although the salesman's promise sounds suspicious, Frame Relay really would provide equal or higher speeds at the same price, just as he claims. Frame Relay protocols actually define the technical details behind the salesman's claims. To see how that works, look at Figure 15-7, which shows three routers using Frame Relay.

Figure 15-7   Typical Frame Relay Network with Three Sites

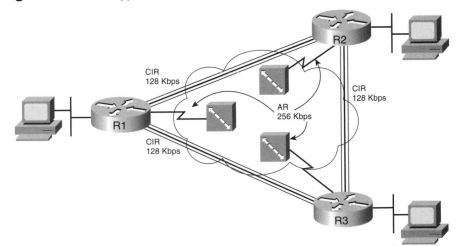

The Frame Relay provider has two speed settings that let the salesman make the claims he made to Fred. First, to guarantee the least amount of bandwidth between the two sites, the provider would set the *committed information rate (CIR)* for the PVC. Remember: A PVC is the closest thing in Frame Relay networks to a leased circuit, so the Frame Relay provider commits to a minimum amount of traffic on that PVC. Inside the Frame Relay network, hidden from us, is a large network that can forward the frames. The sophisticated equipment watches the volume of traffic for each PVC. Those devices know to do everything possible to ensure that for that PVC, over time, the PVC gets to send at least the CIR's worth of bits.

Because the CIR is the speed of a logical or virtual thing, it does not define the physical transmission rate (clock rate) at which the bits are transmitted. CIR is more of a legal contract, with the equipment carrying out the contract, as configured by the Frame Relay provider. When a router actually sends the bits, it sends them at the physical transmission speed (clock rate) of the access link. That speed is referred to as the *access rate*. In the example in Figure 15-7, the access rate of each access link has been set to 256 Kbps.

Now, let me pull together a few conclusions from these facts about speed:

- Routers always physically send data at the physical transmission speed of the access links, called the *access rate*.

- The Frame Relay provider knows that if the access rate is larger than the CIR of a PVC, the router can send more bits than the CIR on that single PVC.

- The Frame Relay provider commits that its network will support *at least* CIR's worth of bits per second.

- When a router sends more than the CIR worth of bits on a PVC (and it will), if the provider's internal network isn't currently overloaded, it will send the traffic anyway, giving the customer more than he paid for!

That last point in the list is what makes the salesman's suspicious claims actually become true. In reality, many Frame Relay providers engineer their Frame Relay networks so that the network almost never gets too busy to forward the excess traffic. In spite of my tongue-in-cheek pretend sales pitches, it really is great for the Frame Relay provider when the salesman can say something like the following to close a deal, and have it be true: "Hey Fred, since you're my buddy now, let me tell you, we never throw away traffic you send over the CIR for a PVC. You'll really get that 256 Kbps, and you'll just be paying for 128. Just don't tell my boss that I let you in on our secret." Wink wink, nudge nudge, sale made, and it's time for the golf course.

It might seem that no one would use leased lines any more now that Frame Relay is available. As it turns out, in some remote rural sites, there might not be a Frame Relay service available. Some companies simply don't bother changing an existing leased line to Frame Relay. Also, a Frame Relay network might delay packets a small fraction of a second, causing slightly more delay as compared to a leased line. However, you can do things on the routers to minimize the impact of that slight sub-second delay.

Seriously, from a business perspective, Frame Relay is easy to choose over leased circuits. It's like free money—it's cheaper, and you get at least as much bandwidth (and typically more) than you would with WAN links. Knowing that, it's no surprise that Frame Relay is popular.

Routers and WANs: Still a Match Made in Heaven

In Chapter 14, you learned some of the details of PPP and HDLC in the context of routers and routing, because these days, most of the devices on the ends of leased lines are routers. Similarly, most of the devices on the ends of Frame Relay PVCs are routers, so it helps to discuss routing briefly with Frame Relay in the picture. To hit the highlights, look at Figure 15-8, with IP addresses shown, three sites, and Frame Relay used for WAN connectivity.

Figure 15-8   Routing over PVCs

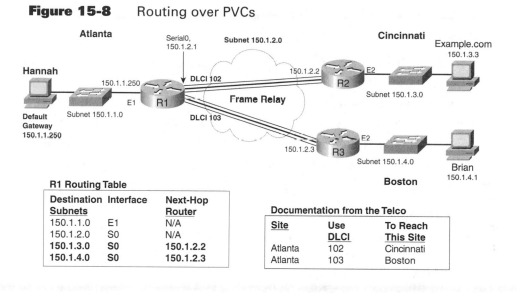

R1 Routing Table		
Destination Subnets	Interface	Next-Hop Router
150.1.1.0	E1	N/A
150.1.2.0	S0	N/A
150.1.3.0	**S0**	**150.1.2.2**
150.1.4.0	**S0**	**150.1.2.3**

Documentation from the Telco

Site	Use DLCI	To Reach This Site
Atlanta	102	Cincinnati
Atlanta	103	Boston

This internetwork uses three routers at three sites. Each has an access link to a local CO, and there's no PVC between R2 and R3, making the network a partial mesh of PVCs. The Frame Relay provider supplied some information to this company when it installed the Frame Relay service, as shown in the legend on the bottom right in the figure. The telco told the customer to configure R1 so that it uses DLCI 102 to send frames to R2, and DLCI 103 to send frames to R3.

For this internetwork to work correctly, each of the three routers needs an IP address for its serial interfaces. Notice that the IP addresses shown next to the routers' serial interfaces are in the same subnet—subnet 150.1.2.0. If you study Frame Relay in more depth than is covered here, you'll learn that there are many options for IP addressing over Frame Relay networks; this is just one option. In this case, just like subnet 150.1.2.0 was used when there was Ethernet between R1 and R2 (Chapter 11, "Knowing Where to Turn at Each Intersection [Router]), and just like subnet 150.1.2.0 was used on the WAN link between R1 and R2 (Chapter 14), this example uses that same subnet between R1 and R2.

Now that you have an established internetwork to refer to, the next sections review Frame Relay encapsulation and DLCIs and then close with a discussion of Frame Relay Inverse Address Resolution Protocol (ARP).

You Can't Just Send Data—You Have to Send a Frame Relay Frame

In this example, Hannah will be opening a browser to connect to the www.example.com website. After using DNS to discover that www.example.com's IP address is 150.1.3.3, Hannah sends a packet to 150.1.3.3. Because 150.1.3.3 is in a different subnet, Hannah's PC sends the packet to her default gateway—namely, R1. When R1 receives the Ethernet frame, it checks to see if errors occurred. If no errors occurred, R1 extracts the IP packet and begins the process of making a routing decision.

Figure 15-9 picks up the routing process at this point. R1 has the packet with destination address 150.1.3.3. That destination address matches the route for subnet 150.1.3.0, which lists outgoing interface Serial0, and next-hop IP address 150.1.2.2, which is R2's IP address on its serial0 interface.

Figure 15-9   Forwarding an IP Packet over a Frame Relay PVC

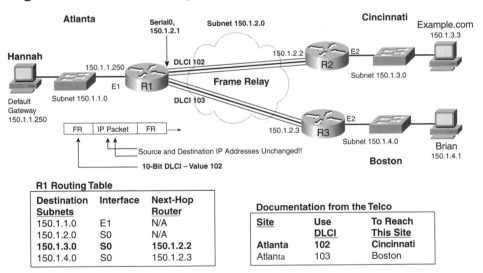

R1 needs to send the packet to R2, physically using its serial0 interface, and logically using the PVC with DLCI 102. First, R1 has to perform Frame Relay encapsulation like the other data link protocols covered in this book by putting the IP packet

between a Frame Relay header and trailer. As usual, the trailer has a *frame check sequence (FCS)* field that allows the receiver of the frame—R2 in this case—to know if the frame experienced errors. And, as was mentioned before, the Frame Relay header holds the 10-bit-long DLCI field that identifies the PVC. By putting the right DLCI into the Frame Relay header (102 in this case), the Frame Relay switches inside the telco can forward the frame correctly to R2.

Addressing Is Much More Interesting on Frame Relay Than on Serial Links

The last big concept I'll cover for Frame Relay relates to a dilemma that should be familiar because it happens with Ethernet as well. When R1 needs to build the Frame Relay header, it must put something in the DLCI field—102 in this most recent example.

You know that R1 should use DLCI 102 because that's what the telco told you would work. The router, however, doesn't have a copy of the documentation from the Frame Relay provider, so it needs more help. To see why, take a close look at the routing table entry for subnet 150.1.3.0 in Figure 15-8. Note that it lists next-hop router of 150.1.2.2, which is R2's IP address, and outgoing interface S0. It does not list which DLCI to use to get to 150.1.2.2. R1 knows the outgoing interface and the next-hop IP address, but it doesn't know which DLCI to use.

If there were an Ethernet between R1 and R2, and R1 was faced with this same dilemma, R1 would use IP ARP. R1 would send an IP ARP broadcast that listed the next-hop IP address (150.1.2.2), expecting that R2 would hear the broadcast and send an ARP reply. The reply would include R2's Ethernet MAC address.

Frame Relay solves the same problem, but in a different way. As soon as the PVC starts working, R2 announces its IP address to R1, using the VC between the two routers. R1 also announces its IP address to R2, using that same VC. By doing so, both routers learn the other router's IP address that is used on that VC. The message used to announce the IP address and DLCI is called an ***Inverse ARP*** message. An Inverse ARP is like an ARP, in that it helps you correlate an IP address to a data link address, but it's different in terms of how the process works. To distinguish between the two, the Frame Relay version uses the word "inverse" in the name.

Chapter Summary

Routers typically route traffic between different subnets. To forward traffic between subnets that aren't in the same location, the router uses connectivity that a telco provides. Although routers can use WAN links, the more popular option today is to use Frame Relay. Frame Relay requires less hardware at the telco's customer site, and the telco charges less money for the same amount of bandwidth between sites. Beyond that, the routers typically can send more traffic than was paid for, and the telco will send it, as long as it doesn't impact other customers.

The Frame Relay service from a telco acts like a big Ethernet switch in concept. Routers connect to the Frame Relay network using a leased line from the router to a Frame Relay switch in the local CO. By sending Frame Relay frames over these access links to the nearby switch, the switch looks at the frame headers and forwards the frames based on the DLCI value in the header. The DLCI is essentially an address field that Frame Relay defines.

Chapter Review Questions

You can find the answers to the following questions in Appendix A, "Answers to Chapter Review Questions."

1. What layers of the OSI model does Frame Relay cover?

2. What is the name of the field in the Frame Relay header that identifies a PVC? Give the acronym and what the acronym stands for.

3. Imagine that a company has a router, router A, at its headquarters. The router will use point-to-point WAN links to send and receive traffic to and from five remote sites. How many 4-wire cables need to be run from router A to the telco CO near router A?

4. Imagine that a company has a router, router A, at its headquarters. The router will use Frame Relay to send and receive traffic to and from five remote sites. How many 4-wire cables need to be run from router A to the telco CO?

5. What term is used to describe the cable from a router to the CO when the router uses Frame Relay?

6. Define the term "PVC."

7. Does the access rate or the CIR define how many bits per second the telco commits to pass over a single PVC?

8. Does the access rate or the CIR define the clock rate of the physical link between a router and the local CO?

9. What does the acronym CIR stand for?

10. Define the meaning of the term "DLCI."

11. Explain why the term "virtual circuit" is used to describe how Frame Relay sends data to and from a pair of routers.

12. Explain the need for IP ARP on Frame Relay PVCs.

What You Will Learn

After reading this chapter, you should be able to

- ✔ Explain why connecting to the Internet provides a path for IP packets to be sent almost anywhere

- ✔ Describe how a modem can transmit data over an analog phone line

- ✔ Describe how telco creates DSL by using part of your local phone line

- ✔ Explain the basic concepts of sending data over your television cable

CHAPTER 16

Driving from Home onto the Globally Interconnected (Internet) Roadway

If you have a bunch of detailed road maps, you could probably find dozens of ways to drive to wherever you go on vacation. Some ways are faster or longer, use good roads, or use bad roads. But at least most places in the contiguous 48 states of the United States have a road nearby, which connects to the other roads. You can drive anywhere in the country, with lots of different options.

Similarly, there's already a large IP network that crisscrosses the globe—the Internet. The Internet is a combination of a ton of different individual IP internetworks, connected to each other, so that each device has at least one, if not many, routes over which it can send packets to other hosts. Just like you can take the road near your house and drive almost anywhere in the country in your car, an IP packet can get into the Internet and be routed to almost any IP host on the planet.

In this chapter, you'll read a little about why the Internet is useful for getting IP packets to and from an enterprise network. Then, you'll see the basics of three technologies that you can use to access the Internet from home—namely, modems, DSL, and cable modems. And like in Chapters 14, "Leasing a (Network) Roadway Between Two Points," and 15, "Leasing a (Network) Roadway Between Lots of Places," this chapter focuses on the OSI Layer 1 and 2 standards and protocols, with reminders of how routers can then forward packets to the right destinations.

Once on the Interstate (Internet), You Can Go Anywhere

Chapters 14 and 15 compared WANs to the interstate several times. The U.S. Department of Transportation (DOT) builds the interstates, and companies can transport goods using the roads; you can go visit grandma or do anything you want—as long as you obey the rules of the road. But the individual businesses that use the roads obviously don't build the roads.

The same general idea applies to WANs and the telephone company (telco). A company can't run a cable between two far-away buildings for legal and practical reasons. But the telco already has the ability to let you connect to its network physically, and then deliver the data over its network to the other office building. However, with WAN links, the telco allows two sites to communicate. With Frame Relay, many sites can communicate, but they all must use the same Frame Relay service from the same telco.

Now, take that same concept of having a provider of WAN service—the people I've been calling the telco—and apply it to the Internet. A company can connect to the Internet, typically with a WAN link or with Frame Relay. With that one physical connection, that company gains access to a huge number of people (literally billions of people) who also have access to the Internet. Figure 16-1 shows the basic idea.

Figure 16-1   Reaching the World Through One Connection to the Internet

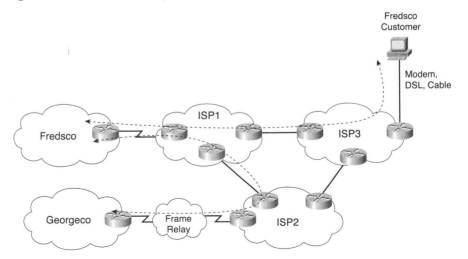

In the figure, ISP represents the term ***Internet service provider***. An ISP creates a network over which IP packets can be forwarded, similar to the way a telco creates a network over which bits (for WAN links) and Frame Relay frames (for Frame Relay) can be forwarded. In fact, some ISPs are also telcos.

The Internet consists of three major components:

- The IP networks that the ISPs create

- The enterprise IP networks that attach to one or more ISPs

- The individuals who connect their computers to ISPs

As you see in Figure 16-1, Fredsco's headquarters is now connected to the Internet. To connect to ISP1, Fredsco uses a point-to-point WAN link. In Chapter 14, the WAN links connect routers inside the Fredsco internal network. Now, a WAN link connects a FredsCo router to a router at ISP1.

IP routing is the key to appreciating what the Internet provides to Fredsco. Because Fredsco's router connects to a router in ISP1, it can forward packets to and from that router. And because the rest of the Internet is connected out there, somehow, someway, IP hosts in Fredsco's network can send and receive data to and from the rest of the IP hosts in the Internet. For instance, in Figure 16-1, Fredsco could exchange data with his supplier, GeorgeCo, who's connected to ISP2 over a Frame Relay permanent virtual circuit (PVC). Also, customers can connect to their local ISPs using the technologies you'll learn about in the rest of this chapter. Then, customers can order things from Fredsco from Fredsco's website, send e-mails to Fredsco's customer service department, and so on.

Notice that the actual connectivity between Fredsco and ISP1 and between GeorgeCo and ISP2 are familiar services from the telco (WAN link and Frame Relay, respectively). Because I've already covered those, the rest of this chapter focuses on some other WAN technologies, mainly ones that are used to access the

Internet from home. Table 16-1 summarizes the three options for WAN connectivity that you've learned about in this part of the book, with a few comments.

Table 16-1   Comparisons of WAN Links, Frame Relay, and the Internet

WAN Type	Generic Name of Provider	Physical Connectivity	Description of Service
WAN link (leased line)	Telco	4-wire cable from customer to telco CO at each site	Telco forwards bits between two sites
Frame Relay	Frame Relay service provider	4-wire cable from customer to telco CO at each site	Provider forwards frames, based on DLCI, to one of many possible sites
Internet	Internet service provider	Either WAN link or Frame Relay between customer and ISP	ISP routes IP packets to any IP host on the Internet

The rest of this chapter covers three popular technologies that are most often used today to connect to an ISP. Most of the time, people use these technologies at their homes. One of the main distinctions is that these three technologies take advantage of cabling that is typically already installed into a home, namely the phone line, or the cable TV cable. By using cabling that is already installed in the home, an ISP spends less money, making the service cheaper to the customer. Also, the time required getting the customer up and working can be reduced.

Using a Phone Line for Data

The telcos of the world were originally created to let you talk to someone else using a telephone. Almost every home in America has a local phone line installed in it. That phone line runs from your house, typically underground, to a local telco central office (CO). You can use your phone to make a call almost anywhere in the world, and the call goes over the phone line, called a *local loop*, to the telco CO, through its network, and on to the other phone.

When you make a call, the telco creates a new voice circuit on your behalf. A *voice circuit* is just telco lingo for the ability to send and receive voice between two phones. Another term you should know is ***Public Switched Telephone Network (PSTN)***, which refers to the combined telco networks in the world.

Although the local phone line was originally intended for supporting voice, it can also support the transmission of data. Next, you learn a little about how that works and then see how you can use a local phone line to send data to and from an ISP.

Making Data Sound Like Voice

First, let's cover a little bit about how voice works and how it works over a phone line. Then, I'll cover how to send data over that same phone line.

Sound waves travel through the air by vibrating the air. The human ear hears the sound because the ear vibrates as a result of the air inside the ear moving, which in turn causes the brain to process the sounds that the ear hears.

The telco, however, cannot forward vibrating air particles over its network. To send the voice over the phone line, something must convert the sound (the vibrating air) into an electrical signal, because the telco *local loop* (the phone line between your house and the CO) was designed to carry electrical signals. To convert the sounds into electricity, a telephone includes a ***microphone***. In case you've never stopped to think about it, a microphone simply converts sound waves into an analog electrical signal. The telco can send the electrical signal between one phone and another. On the receiving side, the phone converts the electrical signal back to sound waves using a ***speaker*** that is inside the part of the phone that you put next to your ear.

Enough talk about this voice stuff—our end goal is to be able to send data over the phone line. To understand how that happens, consider what occurs when a phone sends the electrical signal over a phone line, as shown in Figure 16-2.

Figure 16-2   Analog Electrical Signal: Frequency and Amplitude

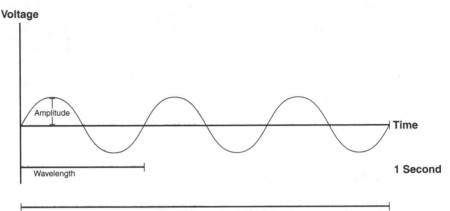

The graph shows that the voltage level on the wire changes continuously over time. Because the voltage changes continuously, the signal is considered to be an *analog electrical signal*. You might recall that Chapter 4, "How to Build a Local (Network) Roadway," covered how Ethernet uses a digital electrical signal to transmit data, with the digital signal having a discrete value for a time period, and then changing to another discrete value so that the graph shows a bunch of right angles. Digital transmission is convenient for transmitting data because when you transmit data, it's already in digits—0s and 1s—which are also discrete values.

The telcos created the local loop to support voice; that's why the loop uses analog electrical signals. The sounds that your voice makes happen to be a continuously changing sound wave, so analog electrical signals that continuously change work well for voice. In short, the word *analog* refers to a continuously changing signal, and the term *digital* refers to a signal that has discrete or exact states that imply a particular value, or digit.

The analog signal has a couple of characteristics that I'll define briefly, and then we'll talk about how to transmit data using such a signal:

- **Frequency**—Defined as how the number of times the signal repeats itself, from peak to peak, in one second (assuming that the sound the human makes doesn't change for a whole second). Figure 16-2 shows a frequency of 3 Hertz (Hz), or 3 per second. The greater the frequency of the electrical signal, the higher the pitch of the sound being represented.

- **Amplitude**—Represents how strong the signal is; a higher amplitude peak represents a louder sound.

The goal of the original telco was to create a circuit between any two phones. Each circuit consisted of an electrical path between two phones, which in turn supported the sending of an analog electrical signal in each direction, allowing the people on the circuit to have a conversation. Remember: The original telco predated the first vacuum tube computers, so the concept of support data communication between computers wasn't a consideration for the original telco. The original telco just wanted to get these analog electrical signals, which represented sounds, from one place to the other.

What Phones Do for Voice, Modems Do for Data

When you make a phone call and say something, the telco transmits the sounds you make to the telephone on the other end of the circuit. You and the other person, being humans, can speak to generate sound waves and listen to hear sound waves. The telephone converts what the human can do (sound waves) to what the telco network can do (analog electrical signals).

To use those same telephone lines to send data, you need a device that has some similarities to a phone. Like a phone, this device needs to know how to generate and receive the analog electrical signals. However, instead of converting sound waves to and from those analog electrical signals, the device needs to convert binary 0s and 1s on behalf of a computer. Figure 16-3 shows the general idea.

Figure 16-3 Comparing a Phone to a Modem

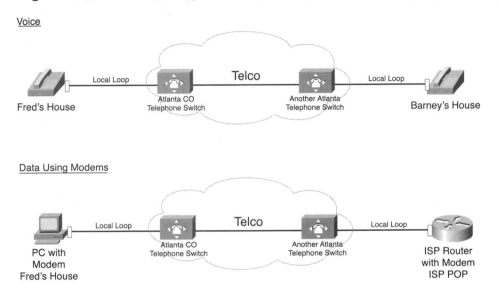

In the top half of the figure, the phones generate and receive analog electrical signals. The equipment in the telco CO is called a telephone switch because the device in the CO is built to support telephone traffic, and it thinks that there's a telephone on the other end of the local loop cable. To create a voice phone call, the telco causes the analog electrical signals to go from one side of the network to the other.

Modems allow two computers to send and receive a serial stream of bits over an analog phone circuit, with no physical changes required on the typical analog local loop between a residence and the telco CO. Because the telephone switch in the CO expects to send and receive analog voice signals over the local loop, modems simply send an analog signal to the PSTN and expect to receive an analog signal from the PSTN. However, instead of voice that a human speaker creates, the analog signal represents some bits that the computer needs to send to another computer. Similar in concept to a phone converting sound waves into a representative analog electrical signal, a modem converts a string of binary digits on a computer into a representative analog electrical signal. In fact, although most people simply use the term modem, you can also call these devices ***analog modems*** because they create and interpret analog electrical signals.

Modems encode a binary 0 or 1 onto the analog signal by varying the analog signal, for instance, by varying frequency or amplitude. Changing these characteristics of the analog signal is referred to as ***modulation***. For instance, one of the earliest modem standards used an analog signal of 2250 Hertz for a binary 1 and 2100 Hz for a binary 0. (Remember: Frequency is measured in Hertz.) A modem could *modulate*, or change, between the two frequency levels to imply a binary 1 or 0. Figure 16-4 outlines the basics of how a modem can transmit data.

Figure 16-4   Basic Operation of Modems over PSTN

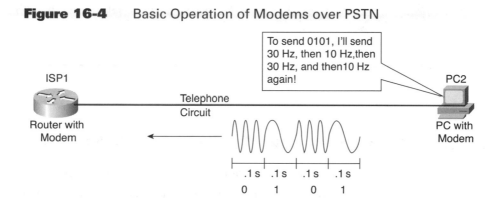

Modems agree to a particular encoding scheme to transmit and receive bits. In Figure 16-4, PC2 uses a higher frequency, shown as an analog waveform that moves up and down more quickly, to mean binary 0. PC2 uses a lower frequency (fewer movements up and down) to mean a binary 1. The receiver—in this case a router with a modem—uses those same rules to interpret the meaning of the signal. The telco passes the signal because the signal is just an analog electrical signal, and that's what the telco expects to happen on the local loop.

In the figure, the PC modulates (changes) between 30-Hz and 10-Hz signals to encode a binary 0 or 1, respectively. When the receiver interprets the analog signal, converting it back to binary digits using those same rules, the process is called *demodulation*. The term *modem* is a shortened version of the combination of the two words *modulation* and *demodulation*.

How Fast Can You Talk?

To achieve a particular transmission speed, the modems need to send and receive a signal that can change at that rate. For instance, Figure 16-4 implied that the frequency changed every .1 seconds, meaning that the PC could send 10 bits in every second, or for a rate of 10 bps. That's a ridiculously low speed, but showing faster speeds in the figure would have required a much larger piece of paper! Some early modems sent at 9600 bps, so the sending modem would change the signal (as necessary) every 1/9600 of a second. Similarly, the receiving modem would sample the incoming analog signal every 1/9600 of a second, interpreting the signal as a binary 1 or 0. Today, modems approach speeds around 56 Kbps.

Calling the Internet! Calling the Internet!

Let's face it: Practically everyone on the planet knows about the Internet. But we all probably have our own opinions about what the Internet is and is not. One definition of the Internet is that it is an IP packet forwarding service. The Internet is a bunch of networking devices, cables, and software, which collectively try to forward IP packets to their correct destination IP host.

As mentioned earlier, the Internet includes Enterprise networks, home users, ISPs and their networks, as well as all the connections between them. If you think of the Internet as an IP packet forwarding service, each Enterprise will want to have at least one router that can route packets to and from an ISP router. For instance, by using a point-to-point WAN link between a router in an Enterprise network and a router in an ISP network, the two routers can route IP packets back and forth.

Ultimately, the WAN link just lets the routers forward packets. And as long as each Enterprise network has some form of WAN link between itself and an ISP, the Enterprise can communicate with the Internet.

The rest of this chapter focuses on ways you can connect to the Internet from home. After you're connected, all your PC needs to do is send and receive IP packets so that your applications will work. Essentially, once your PC can send and receive IP packets with an ISP, it has become a part of the global Internet.

Now That I Know How to Talk, Whom Should I Call?

These days, you can pick up your home phone and call almost anywhere on the planet. Although the cost for long-distance calls has fallen a lot over the past 10 years or so, it still costs a little money to call someone far away. However, most local telcos let you make local phone calls—at least calls that they define as "local"—without charging extra cash for making the call.

Many ISPs allow you to connect to their networks using modems, but the trick is to keep the cost down. To keep the costs down, ISPs try to make sure that as many people as possible can make a local free phone call to one of their routers. ISPs strategically locate routers in various parts of the world so that you can make a local call from your house to a phone number of a phone line that runs into the building where the ISP puts its gear. That type of building, and the gear inside it, is called a *point of presence (POP)*, as shown in Figure 16-5.

Figure 16-5   Calling the ISP Local POP

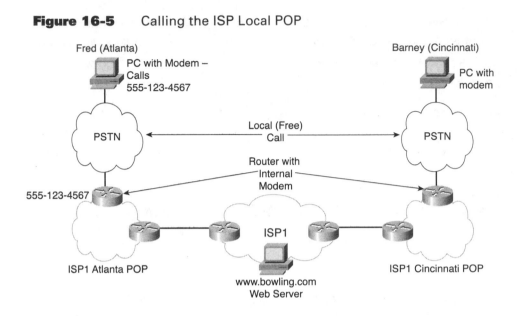

As you can see, Fred can make a local call to the POP in Atlanta, and Barney can make a local call to the POP in Cincinnati. Both calls are free because the ISP thought ahead and located a POP in the local calling areas near Fred and Barney. All Fred and Barney need to make the call is a local telephone line. The ISP also charges a small fee for the service, which in most markets in the United States today costs $10 to $20 per month.

Now That I Know Whom to Call, What Do I Say?

So far, you've learned a few of the concepts behind how two modems, on either end of a telephone circuit, can transmit and receive data. Those details mostly relate to OSI Layer 1, the physical layer.

Like all good networking devices, when a PC makes a phone call to an ISP, the PC typically needs to send and receive IP packets to and from the Internet. In most cases today, the PC and router use PPP as the data link protocol. (PPP was covered in Chapter 14.) PPP lets Fred send and receive packets over the dialed phone circuit.

For instance, in Figure 16-5, imagine that Fred hits the www.bowling.com website to check out the latest in bowling news. You know from Chapter 13 that Fred will need to send an IP packet to the DNS server to resolve the name www.bowling.com to an IP address. Then, he will need to send some IP packets to the web server, just to set up the TCP connection. After that, Fred can send a packet to the server asking for the home page of www.bowling.com. Routing takes place, just like it always did. Between the ISP router and Fred's PC, PPP is used to send and receive frames over the dialed circuit.

Using the Phone Line for Data— the DSL Way

Modems have a great purpose in the world of networking. Almost everywhere that you might put a PC, there's probably already a phone line nearby. Using a PC with a modem allows almost every computer the capability to connect to the Internet.

Modems do have some drawbacks, with one of the biggest having to do with talkative teenagers, roommates, or other family members. Modems use the phone line to make what the telco thinks is a voice call, so you can't make another call while you're surfing the Internet—or, in other words, you can't use the Internet with your modem while your teenager is using the phone! Another big negative is the speed. Although 56 Kbps for a single user might seem fairly fast, it's not fast enough for some people. Today, e-mails often have attached files with them; those e-mails might take a fairly long time to pull down onto a computer. Also, websites often have tons of graphics and animation today, all of which require a lot of bandwidth.

What the world needs now is a faster way to send and receive data using that same old ubiquitous phone line—while being able to make a simultaneous phone call. What the world got was exactly that, and it's called *digital subscriber line (DSL)*. DSL is an alternative technology for sending and receiving data to and from an ISP, using the same old phone line, but running at much faster speeds. Also, you can make phones calls and surf (send IP packets) at the same time. But, of course, it's a little more expensive.

Dr. Analog Voice and Mr. Hiding Digital

Dr. Jekyll and Mr. Hyde had a serious split personality issue in the classic book by Robert Louis Stevenson. Dr. Jekyll used advanced chemistry to create the split. DSL creates a split personality of sorts for the local phone line (local loop) using some advanced technology. DSL allows the same old analog voice signal to be sent over the line by a phone; at the same time, DSL allows a separate digital signal to go over the same phone line.

The telephone generates analog signals at frequency ranges between 0 and 4000 Hz. Most speech ranges from 300 Hz to 3300 Hz in frequency. The folks who created DSL defined the standards so that the digital DSL signal uses frequencies higher than 4000 Hz, which means they do not interfere with human speech or hearing. To appreciate what happens, take a look at Figure 16-6.

Figure 16-6   DSL Connection from the Home

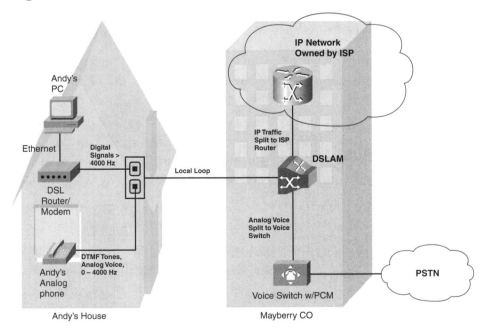

The figure shows an analog phone and a DSL modem connected to a single wall plate with two receptacles. (Most people's home phones plug into a wall plate with just one receptacle; to use DSL, you can buy a little plastic device that will create two receptacles for about $5 retail at most office supply stores.) Physically, you connect your DSL modem to a wall socket just like any of the phones in your house. You can pick up your same old phone and make a call, just like always. Simultaneously, the **DSL modem** can send data over the same phone line to the router in the ISP network, as shown in the figure.

DSL uses the same local loop wiring that's already run between the CO and your house, but now the CO connects the local loop wiring to a device called a **DSL access multiplexer (DSLAM)**. The **DSLAM** splits out the digital signal and analog signal from the local loop. The DSLAM gives the analog voice signal—the frequency range between 0–4000 Hz—to a telephone switch. The voice switch treats that signal just like any other analog voice line.

Conversely, the DSLAM does not pass the digital electrical signal to a telephone switch. The DSLAM forwards the data traffic to a router owned by the ISP that provides the service in this figure. Notice that the ISP's router is actually depicted as being resident in the local telco's CO—that is actually true in many cases. To support DSL, the ISP works with the local telco to install some of the ISP's gear in the CO—a process called **co-location**, or **co-lo** for short. The local telco DSLAM forwards and receives the IP packets to and from the ISP router, while the telco maintains control over the local voice traffic.

If you can get some binary digits from a PC, through a DSL modem, to the DSLAM, and finally to a router at an ISP, you can get IP packets to and from that router. Incidentally, DSL uses PPP as the Layer 2 protocol. Likewise, because DSL can get an analog electrical signal from the phone, over the local loop, to the DSLAM, and then to the telco switch, you can make voice calls.

Interestingly, with DSL, the ISP is often not the same company that provides local telephone service. Typically, the consumer requests DSL high-speed Internet access from an ISP, the ISP charges the customer for the service, and then the ISP pays the local telco some cut of the fee. You still need to pay for the local phone services as well. You end up with two services, basically—phone service and Internet—and you pay two bills, assuming that you get the Internet service from someone besides the local telco.

Faster Is Better

With all the types of physical networking standards covered in this book, there have been options for different speeds. Even Ethernet has several options. With WAN options, there are many more variations for speed, and DSL is no exception.

DSL standards come in many flavors to meet different needs. (Most of the standards come from the ITU, which also owns most of the modem standards.) For instance, DSL has limits on how long the local loop can be. (The length of the local loop is simply the length of the combined cables that stretch from a house to the CO.) Some DSL variants allow the local loop to be much longer than some other DSL variants, whereas others only allow for a shorter local loop. The distances tend to range from less than a mile to 4–5 miles. For the standards with a shorter local loop, the transmission rates tend to be much higher, which is a simple design tradeoff.

The speeds for DSL can go as high as 50 Mbps, but you must have a short local loop to the CO. The slower DSL speeds are approximately 384 Kbps, but that allows you to have a much longer local loop.

Interestingly, the speed at which data goes from the Internet to the home is faster than the other direction—a feature called ***asymmetric transmission rates***. As it turns out, a lot more data goes toward a PC at home than in the reverse direction for most TCP/IP applications. For instance, when you ask for a web page, the HTTP request might be a few hundred bytes, but the web page might be millions of bytes of data. So, rather than send at the same speed in both directions, it's better to have more bandwidth toward the home, where most of the bandwidth is needed.

Sending Data from Home Without Using a Phone Line

There is another popular alternative to analog modems and DSL about which you should at least know the basics. Many homes in the United States also have cable TV (CATV) service. Similar in topology to DSL, cable modems provide an always-on Internet access service, using the CATV cable to transmit the data. You can surf the Internet over the cable and make all the phone calls you want over your telephone line—and you can watch TV at the same time.

Cable modems use frequencies that would have otherwise been used for additional TV channels. It's a little like having an "Internet" channel to go along with CNN, TBS, ESPN, The Cartoon Network, and all your other favorite cable channels.

Although the details are much different, the general ideas are just like DSL:

- The cable can be split and connected to both the cable modem and the TVs in the house.

- The CATV company splits out the data from the TV signals at its local office.

- The CATV company gives the data to a router owned by an ISP.

- If the ISP is different from the cable company, you pay a monthly fee to the ISP for Internet service, and a monthly fee to the cable company for the basic TV service.

- Cable uses asymmetric speeds, typically maxing out at 40 Mbps toward the home, but the downstream bandwidth is shared among multiple subscribers.

Chapter Summary

Modems allow data to be sent over the PSTN. To do so, one modem calls the phone number of another modem. After the phone company has set up the call, it can send data by putting a particular analog signal on the circuit to mean binary 0, and another to mean binary 1.

Often, modems are used to send and receive data to and from a router that an ISP owns. By doing so, a PC at a house can connect to the Internet, thereby enabling it to send and receive IP packets from almost every IP host in the world. To keep the service inexpensive, ISPs try to locate a router in a POP in each local calling area.

DSL allows data to be sent using digital signals, over the same telephone line to the home. This allows you to use the Internet while also talking on the phone. To accommodate this service, the telco connects the local loop line to a DSLAM at the CO. The DSLAM splits the analog voice out to the telephone switch and the data over to a router that the ISP owns.

Cable modems use the same basic model as DSL, with a device at the CATV's office splitting out the data from the television traffic. Cable modems use the CATV cable for transmission of the data, using frequencies that would otherwise be used for more TV channels. Cable modems allow you to make phone calls, watch TV, and surf the Internet simultaneously.

Chapter Review Questions

You can find the answers to the following questions in Appendix A, "Answers to Chapter Review Questions."

1. According to this book, what are the three major components of the Internet?

2. Leased lines provide a service of forwarding bits, whereas Frame Relay provides a service of forwarding Frame Relay frames. With that same perspective, explain the service that the Internet supplies to hosts.

3. What is different about the type of electrical signal sent over the local loop by a phone, versus a modem?

4. What is different about the type of electrical signal sent over the local loop by a phone, versus a DSL modem?

5. What two features of analog electrical signals, mentioned in this book, can a modem vary or change to encode a binary 0 or 1?

6. Approximately what speed is the maximum transmission speed with modems?

7. Approximately what speed is the maximum transmission speed with DSL modems when the distance from the home to the CO is relatively long?

8. For DSL to work, the telco splits the data out from the voice using what kind of device?

9. What does DSL stand for?

10. What does modem stand for?

11. Which of the three Internet access technologies covered in this chapter does not allow you to talk on the phone while using the Internet?

12. What Layer 2 protocol is typically used when using a modem or DSL to connect to an ISP?

PART VI

Securing the Network

In Part VI, you learn about concepts and products that keep you safe by restricting users and packets from doing what they want and going where they want. Chapter 17 describes how to make sure end users are allowed to use a network and introduces you to the process of authentication, authorization, and accounting (AAA). Chapter 18 focuses on securing a company's connection to the Internet and preventing both curious and malicious people in the public Internet from doing harm to the devices inside a corporate enterprise network.

Chapter 17: Accepting the Right People and Rejecting the Wrong People

Chapter 18: Keeping a Watchful Eye Over Who Drives into Your (Network) Neighborhood

What You Will Learn

After reading this chapter, you should be able to

- ✔ List the three components of the AAA security model

- ✔ Describe the basic processes used for authentication, authorization, and accounting

- ✔ Explain the basic processing of customer usernames and passwords by an ISP

- ✔ Explain the benefits of using VPNs to connect to an enterprise network through the Internet

CHAPTER 17

Accepting the Right People and Rejecting the Wrong People

If you've been reading this book from the first page, congratulations! You've made it to the final part of the book. You've already learned the basics of how to build networks that forward IP packets everywhere they need to go. Next, you'll read about some security mechanisms that help protect your network. This chapter focuses on how to make sure that only specific end user devices are allowed to use your network. These devices typically are attached either to a LAN or to an ISP. After these devices are attached, end users will need to access applications on servers. In this chapter, you'll learn the basics of how servers use usernames and passwords to make sure they know the identity of the person who is using the server. Along the way, you'll learn about two types of security issues related to Internet use.

Safe Driving by Using AAA

In the United States, the Automobile Association of America (AAA) is one of the best-known companies that provides travel-related services. AAA originally helped people with things like emergency assistance when their vehicles broke down while traveling. When I was a kid, if you took a long car trip, you had better be a member of AAA to help in case things went bad, to get better deals from hotels near the interstate, to get discounts at various businesses, and a lot of other things that come in handy when traveling. It was just more secure to be part of AAA.

To keep a network more secure, most networks use some form of AAA as well, but in this case, *AAA* stands for authentication, authorization, and accounting. The acronym *AAA* (pronounced "triple A," just like the travel service) refers to three areas of security; there are more, but all three relate to issues regarding an individual device or user. Just like an individual might use the AAA road club when taking a road trip, you probably use the networking AAA when your PC takes a trip on the network by sending and receiving data.

Checking for Fake Drivers' (Users') Licenses

In most countries, the government builds the roads. Unsurprisingly, the government then regulates (that is what governments do, right?) who gets to drive on the road by requiring a driver's license.

Similarly, before you can use most servers, you need to have the license or right to use that server. Instead of a driver's license, you have a username and a password. The **username** essentially acts as your name on the network, and the **password** is a secret string of text that only you are supposed to know. The basic authentication process works something like Figure 17-1.

Figure 17-1   Basic Authentication Using a Username and Password

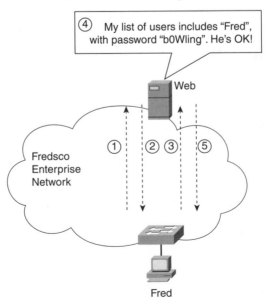

The figure shows a five-step process of how the server authenticates Fred. *Authentication*, the first "A" in AAA, is the process of determining if the user is who he says he is. The steps shown in the figure are as follows:

1. Fred requests a web page.

2. The web server replies, asking Fred's PC for a username and password.

3. Fred types in his username and password and sends it back to the web server.

4. The web server checks its list of usernames and verifies that the password is correct.

5. If the username and password are correct, the web page returns the contents of the web page.

Fred is happy so far because he still gets his web page. Later, Fred will want to send e-mail, and he'll have to plug in a username and password to use a POP3 server. He might want to transfer files using FTP and will need a username and password. But Fred's still good old Fred, and there's no need for him to have three sets of usernames and passwords, one for each application server.

To solve the problem, the usernames and passwords can be listed on a server called an *authentication server*, and the various application servers can then query the authentication server. Depending on the operating systems that run on the application servers and how they are configured, they can use different products and protocols between the application servers and the authentication server. For instance, with Microsoft, the authentication server might be called a domain controller, or an Active Directory server. With UNIX, a protocol called Kerberos might be used. Regardless of the details of the authentication server and the protocols used, the basic flow works as shown in Figure 17-2.

Figure 17-2   Basic Authentication Using a Username and Password

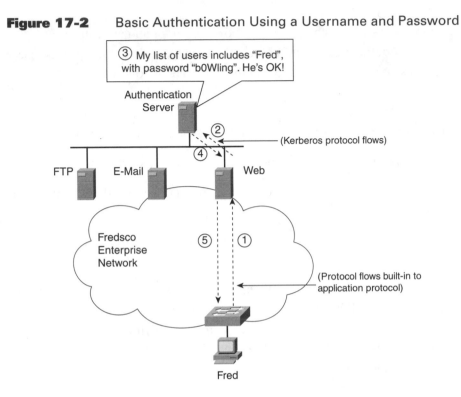

Each of the application servers asks for the username and password and then asks the authentication server for help. The steps shown in the figure are as follows:

1. After Fred is prompted for his username and password, he types in his username and password and sends it back to the web server.

2. The web server sends a query to the authentication server.

3. The authentication server checks the username and password.

4. The authentication server sends a message back to the web server as to whether the user passed the authentication check. (In this example, assume that the username and password are valid.)

5. The web server returns the web page to Fred.

Between Fred's PC and the application servers, each application protocol requests the username and password from the user. The individual application layer protocols handle the exchange of the username and password from the client. Between the application servers and the authentication server, several different protocols can be used to exchange the username and password information. *Kerberos*, a TCP/IP standard, is an example of one such protocol.

Hey! How Did You Get in Here?

In the figures so far in this chapter, the client (Fred) happens to be using a PC that's attached to a LAN inside the Fredsco corporate network. The applications prompt Fred for a password before he can use them, but Fred's PC can go ahead and use the network without verification of his identity. Many of us don't think about it, but in most places, the physical security of the LAN is assumed.

If a company has a LAN in an office building, and there is poor physical security, the network is exposed to people walking in to the building, connecting to the LAN, and trying to gain access to servers in the network. If physical security is good, it might be reasonable to allow anyone inside the building to just sit down, plug in his computer to an RJ-45 socket in the wall, and connect to the LAN. While most enterprise networks today allow any PC inside the corporate network to attempt to connect to servers, many enterprises are adding a security step to authenticate devices before they can even send a packet to a server.

Checking the License to Find Out if He Can Drive That Kind of Vehicle

A driver's license typically gives you the right to drive most popular passenger vehicles on the government roads that your hard-earned tax money pays for. However, to drive some vehicles, you need a special type of driver's license. For instance, to drive a big 18-wheel transfer truck, you need to have a special type of *commercial driver's license*. And before you're allowed to risk your life driving a motorcycle, you need a special type of driver's license as well.

A similar thing happens with security, and it relates to the second "A" in AAA—authorization. *Authorization* refers to the process of figuring out what a particular user is allowed to do. Figure 17-3 shows a network that uses a relatively straight-forward example of authorization.

Figure 17-3   Fred Can't See Others' Payroll Information

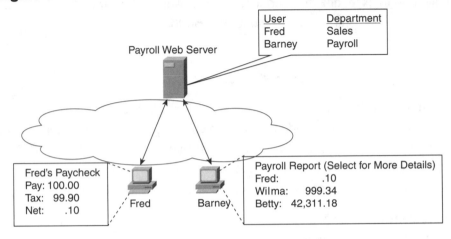

In the example, Fred can only see information about his own paycheck when he's browsing the payroll department's web server, but Barney can see everyone's paycheck information. As you see in the entry for Fred in the authentication server's configuration, Fred is in the sales department at the company, and Barney is in the payroll department. Because Fred is in sales and gets paid on commission, he has a legitimate need to look at a report that shows what his own paycheck will look like next week. Because Barney works in payroll, he needs to be able to fix problems with anyone's paycheck, so he needs full access.

In this case, the web server can check with the AAA server to find out the department in which each user resides. The web server can then decide which web pages each user is authorized to access.

Tracking Drivers' (Users') Violations

I personally can't recall a policeman looking at my driver's license in the past 10 years. I'm sure that's not because I have never sped on the way to work in

10 years; I just haven't gotten caught. Really. So some of this, I can only speculate about, but I hear that when the police do catch you doing something wrong on the road, they tend to write it down. These days, that information ends up in a database so that the police department can notice trends. For instance, the police might pull someone over for speeding. They write down the driver's license number and call it in to check whether that person has had any other violations. It can really help the law-enforcement guys: "Uhh, Mr. Jones, you've been caught speeding every Friday morning for the past month. I think we need to take your driver's license away!"

The last "A" in AAA is *accounting*. The same servers that perform authentication and authorization services can keep a record of each request to authenticate or authorize a user.

The most obvious, and probably most important, feature for accounting is to record and report when users type the wrong password. Although an occasional typo might be expected, seeing several consecutive attempts by Fred to connect to a server, but with an invalid password each time, might signal that someone is trying to guess Fred's password. Accounting features can record individual attempts, generate reports, and notify personnel if too many invalid attempts happen in a short timeframe.

Making Sure (Internet) Drivers Have Valid Drivers' Licenses

Before you can legally drive on public roads, you need a valid driver's license. The license identifies you by name, number, and photo.

Similarly, when using networks, you might be asked to verify your identity so that the network can confirm that you are allowed, or licensed, to use the network. For instance, if you've ever used a network before, you have probably been prompted for a username and password (authentication). Most people who have used web browsers figure that they can't look at some web pages that aren't appropriate for their jobs or check someone else's e-mail (authorization). And although users never see a report of foiled attempts to guess a password, you have to figure that a good security policy involves watching out for such mischief (accounting).

The examples in this chapter so far presume that the PC is attached to a LAN in a physically secure office building. But people who use modems or DSL to connect to the Internet from home have to go through an additional authentication step. ISPs want to know that a user who connects to them has paid her bill, and they want to make sure they know who the user is, just in case she breaks the rules of what's legally allowed to happen over the ISP's Internet connection. In the next two sections, you'll read about how ISPs authenticate users before they can even use the network, and how the protocols prevent someone from stealing the password.

No Appls Yet? Be a Good CHAP and Ask PAP

Earlier in this chapter, you read briefly that the servers ask the user for his username and password. The protocols that exchange the username and password are built in to most of the application layer protocols. For instance, back in Chapter 8, "Shipping Goods over a (Network) Roadway," you read about POP3 and the messages that a POP3 server uses to ask the POP3 client for the username and password.

ISPs want to authenticate the user, but it's better if they can authenticate before the user even tries to use an application. ISPs can't count on every one of their customers to have a web browser (some might just use e-mail), or they might have customers who just use a web browser but not e-mail. All the ISP wants to do is authenticate whether the user is allowed to connect, and more important, whether the user has paid the monthly service fee. As a result, the ISP has two issues regarding user authentication:

- The ISP wants to authenticate the user/customer.

- The ISP does not want to rely on the customer to authenticate using any particular application protocol.

To solve the problem, ISPs use part of Point-to-Point Protocol (PPP), which defines two options for the exchange of username and password information.

The names appear in the title to this section—PAP and CHAP. *Password Authentication Protocol (PAP)* and *Challenge Handshake Authentication Protocol (CHAP)* are both parts of PPP, and you know from the past several chapters that PPP is a data link protocol that's often used in WAN connections, particularly when using modems or DSL to connect to the Internet. Both PAP and CHAP provide a protocol for the exchange of the username and password. Figure 17-4 shows the basic process PAP uses for username and password exchange.

Figure 17-4   Basics of PAP

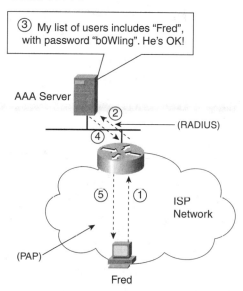

The process is indeed as simple as what's shown in the figure. The PAP protocol uses a two-way flow of messages, with other messages and events happening in the background:

1. Fred uses PAP to send a username (Fred) and password (b0Wling).

2. The router sends a request to an authentication server using RADIUS protocol messages.

3. The authentication server checks a list of usernames and passwords.

4. The authentication server confirms that Fred is authentic using RADIUS.

5. The router uses PAP to confirm that Fred is allowed to use the Internet.

In this example, when Fred dials the Internet with a modem, PAP is used between himself and the ISP router. However, a protocol called RADIUS (RFC 2865) is used between the router and the AAA server to authenticate Fred's username and password.

Although PAP and RADIUS are shown in Figure 17-4, other protocols can be used, too. TACACS+ is a popular proprietary protocol that Cisco developed before RADIUS existed and can be used in place of RADIUS. Also, CHAP can be used instead of PAP between the end user device and the ISP router. In the next section, you'll read about how the CHAP and PAP protocols are different.

Stopping Someone from Using Your License (Password)

Although most everyone reading this book probably has a valid driver's license, some people use fake, illegal driver's licenses. One way to make a fake driver's license work well, even when you are pulled over by a policeman, is to use a name and driver's license number of someone who has a real, valid driver's license.

Sending your passwords using PAP is similar to letting everyone know your driver's license number. It's not likely that someone will make a fake driver's license using your number right away, but you are exposed to the possibility. PAP sends the username and password in *clear-text*. That means anyone with the right tools can actually read your username and password, as clear as you can see the words on this page. Remember: The cable over which your packets flow is between your house and the central office (CO), so it's not too hard to imagine that someone could gain physical access to your phone line and figure out the data you are sending over the wire. All someone would have to do is walk up to the side of your house and use the right tools, and he would know what bits you are sending to and from the Internet.

People can use tools to see your frames that cross a LAN as well. You can attach a type of device called a ***network analysis tool***, often called a ***sniffer***, to a LAN to capture the frames crossing the LAN. If the protocols that transfer the usernames and passwords worked like PAP, and sent the passwords as clear-text, people could find your passwords using a sniffer. I have seen passwords dozens of times while using a sniffer (without trying)—it's that easy. (Sniffer is a trademark of the Network Associates Corp.; the word *sniffer* is somewhat synonymous with this type of analysis and packet capture tool.) You can download free analysis tools from Internet sites and make any PC work like a sniffer.

To protect against password theft, CHAP does not send the password as clear-text. Many application protocols also work similarly to CHAP, not sending the passwords in clear-text. So, whether your PC is offered a username and password prompt when you connect to the Internet, or whether you are providing a password to a web server, the protocols often don't send the password as clear text.

The process of using CHAP starts when the ISP customer first connects to the ISP. With modems, that occurs when the customer clicks something on the computer that causes the modem to call a phone number at the ISP. With DSL, that happens as soon as the DSL modem comes up again after being powered off. Outwardly, the user experiences the same thing: He is prompted for his username (Fred) and password (b0Wling). (Some users set up their software so that they type in the username and password once, and then it's saved, so you might not be prompted every time you connect to the Internet.) If the username and password are correct and the account is current/paid, the ISP approves the connection. If the username or password are wrong, the ISP typically hangs up if it's a modem connection; if it's a DSL connection, the ISP just doesn't allow the PPP data link protocol to keep working. Regardless of the detail, as with other authetication tasks, the user can continue working only if the username and password are correct.

CHAP has many useful features, including a way to prevent the password from being stolen by someone using a sniffer. Figure 17-5 shows several steps about what happens behind the scenes with CHAP, including how it keeps the password private.

Figure 17-5 Hashing Passwords to Create a Message Digest

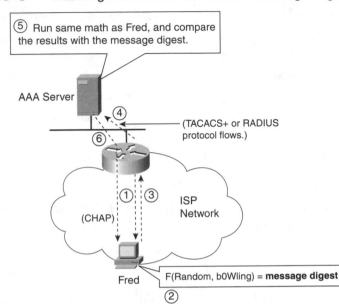

The figure shows six steps that are used in this case to authenticate the user, but the password never passes over the network; therefore, even if someone captures all the packets, it doesn't allow him to steal Fred's identity. The clear-text password is configured at the ISP, typically in a AAA server. The user knows the password and types it in. However, rather than sending the password, the PC sends in a *message digest*. A message digest is the result of running a mathematical function that has two inputs: the password and a random number. To see how it works, compare these points to the points in Figure 17-5:

1. The router generates a random number and sends it in a CHAP message to the PC.

2. The PC runs a math function, with the random number and the password typed by the user as input.

3. The PC sends the results of the function, called a *message digest*, back to the router.

4. The router sends the username, the random number, and the message digest to the AAA server.

5. The AAA server uses the same math that the client used at Step 2, with the same random number, plus the password associated with that username in the AAA user database. The result is another message digest. If the message digest calculated by the AAA server matches the one calculated by the PC, the password that the user typed must be the right one.

6. The AAA server tells the router that the user is authentic; the router tells the PC, and life goes on.

It seems laborious, but it works quickly, and it works well. Notice that the password never passed through a network connection.

This scheme works well because even if someone has a sniffer or another tool and captures the packets, it doesn't matter. The math function that's used to create the message digest is purposefully chosen so that it's hard to calculate the original password, even knowing both the mathematical function and the random number. And the next time the PC needs to authenticate, the router will send a new random number, causing a new message digest value to be calculated.

You're Wearing Your Credit Card Number on Your T-Shirt

There was a TV commercial in the recent past that showed people wearing T-shirts that had things like "My social security number is 123-45-6789" and "My credit card number is 1234-4321-5544-110" written on them. These days, you have to be careful with your credit card information and other vital personal information to prevent people from stealing your identity, taking your money, and driving up the cost of doing business.

When you connect to the Internet, connect to a server in the corporate network, and then view sensitive data, it really is just like wearing your credit card number on your T-shirt. The packets do pass through your ISP, and possibly several others.

The WAN cables do go outside where anyone can physically touch them, assuming they're willing to break the law. You are exposed, but thankfully, you can do something about it.

There are lots of movies with spies or bank robbers in which the bad guys have ended up stealing what they were after, only to find out it was worthless. In networking, you can send packets, knowing that other people can steal a copy, but you can make them worthless through encryption.

Encryption allows a computer to apply a mathematical formula to some data, sending the results of the mathematical function over the network. The computer receiving the data can then re-create the original data by *decrypting* the data. Anyone who looks at the data when it's encrypted can't read it. The data just looks like a bunch of random bits and bytes. The only way to tell what the data looks like is to decrypt the data, and to decrypt the data, you need a secret password called an *encryption key*. Of course, you don't let anyone know the encryption key, so the data stays private.

These days, it is somewhat common for users to encrypt data before sending it over the Internet. However, most people don't just call it encryption; instead, they call it a *virtual private network (VPN)*.

The enterprise network at Barney's company is a private network, with all the components inside privately controlled office space. The Internet is public. VPNs make the Internet act like a private network, in that there's no danger of others seeing the contents of the packets. Because the packets do go across the Internet, it's still a physical public network. VPNs create a private network, but they do so logically, or virtually, if you will. Figure 17-6 shows an example of a VPN.

Figure 17-6   Encrypting IP Packets for a VPN

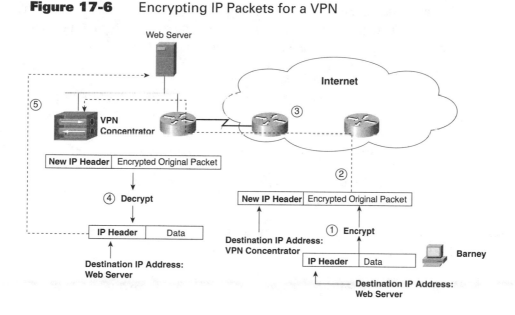

For Barney to use the VPN, he must encrypt the packet as he creates it. To do this, Barney needs to have VPN software installed on his computer. The **VPN client software** performs encryption before sending packets, and it performs decryption when receiving packets. Barney also needs to know what encryption key to use. Barney sends this packet to a VPN device inside the corporate network called a **VPN concentrator**, which decrypts packets received from Barney and others, as well as decrypting packets that need to be sent back to Barney.

The steps from Figure 17-6 are as follows:

1. Barney creates a new packet and then encrypts the packet. The original packet has a destination IP address of the web server, but the new IP header put around the encrypted packet has a destination IP address of the VPN concentrator.

2. Barney forwards the packet, destination IP address of the VPN concentrator, into the Internet.

3. The packet passes through the public Internet. However, the only thing in the packet that makes any sense is the IP header. The rest of the packet contents has been encrypted. If anyone were to capture the packet, he would see just a bunch of jumbled bits inside the IP packet.

4. The VPN concentrator receives the packet, extracts the encrypted original packet, and decrypts the packet. *Decryption* refers to the reverse of encryption, taking the encrypted data and converting it back to the original data—in this case, the same IP packet that Barney created in the first place.

5. The VPN concentrator forwards the packet to the original destination, which is the web server in this case.

The steps list the actions, as well as some of the implications, of using VPNs. In fact, this example shows just one type of VPN (called an IPSec VPN); there are many other types. However, in general, all VPNs make a public network, such as the Internet, work more like a private network, and often, VPNs include encryption to protect your data.

Chapter Summary

Security practices for end users tend to revolve around the authentication, authorization, and accounting functions. Although a device that is attached to a corporate LAN might be assumed to be secure, the users who use that device still need to be watched to make sure they are allowed to access services in the network.

Users who are connecting to an ISP also need to be authenticated before they are allowed to send packets into the Internet. The ISP wants to know whom the person is and if he has paid his bill to the ISP before allowing him to connect.

When an employee connects to the Internet from home, he runs the risk of exposing corporate secrets if he uses applications that run on servers in the corporate network. Curious or malicious people on the Internet can capture packets. To prevent someone from seeing sensative corporate data, corporate users can use VPNs to connect to the corporate network from home, which encrypts the data so that anyone who is capturing the packets can't read them.

Chapter Review Questions

You can find the answers to the following questions in Appendix A, "Answers to Chapter Review Questions."

1. What does the acronym AAA stand for—at least the networking version of it?

2. What information does a user typically supply to perform authorization?

3. What is the one major fact that was mentioned in this book regarding good information to report about using the accounting function of AAA?

4. What is the difference between authorization and authentication?

5. Comparing a LAN-based user inside a company to a corporate employee working via the Internet from home, what other security step does the home user typically have to go through?

6. Which two protocols that are part of PPP are used for authentication?

7. Of the two PPP protocols used for authentication, which passes the password in clear-text?

8. How does CHAP prevent someone from using a tool such as a sniffer to see the packets sent over a network and learn the password?

9. What feature of a VPN prevents packets that someone else has captured from being useful to him?

10. What are the two terms, one named for a particularly popular product, that refer to tools that can capture packets on a LAN?

What You Will Learn

After reading this chapter, you should be able to do the following:

- ✔ List some of the typical types of traffic that should and shouldn't be allowed between an enterprise network and the Internet

- ✔ Explain how a firewall can identify which host is trying to initiate a new TCP connection

- ✔ Explain how a firewall decides to allow some packets through, and not allow others

- ✔ Describe the general idea behind the use of a DMZ

- ✔ Explain the basic roles of IDS systems and anti-virus software

CHAPTER 18

Keeping a Watchful Eye Over Who Drives into Your (Network) Neighborhood

In many U.S. cities and towns, people in neighborhoods often take notice when they see someone driving or walking through the neighborhood who they don't know. Although it's good to be friendly to neighbors you haven't met, it also helps to figure out who doesn't really belong in the neighborhood, and possibly even who might be there to break into a house or cause other problems. In fact, some neighborhoods have a formal neighborhood watch program to watch for suspicious activity. Although you might be a little nosy when monitoring the traffic in your neighborhood, you might prevent a crime or two.

Similarly, when an enterprise network or a home PC connects to the Internet, you need to keep a watchful eye on network traffic. Although the Internet has some wonderful things, it also has many dangerous things—and dangerous people. So, to be safe, you have to be careful and watch for things coming into your network that look a little suspicious. In this chapter, I'll hit the highlights of a few of the kcy tools uscd to help secure a connection to the Internet and prevent, or at least reduce, the impact of dangerous things and dangerous people on a network.

Setting the Ground Rules

When you connect an enterprise network to the Internet, one of the first things you must think about is what you want to allow to pass to and from the Internet, and what you don't. Just like you already have an idea of who lives in your neighborhood, and maybc the cars that thosc neighbors drive, you need to have an idea about what type of traffic can be trusted in terms of your Internet connection. After you figure out what you want to use the Internet connection for, and what you don't want to use it for, you can take action to allow only the trusted types of traffic.

Although it might seem like a difficult task to figure out what should and shouldn't be allowed to pass back and forth from the Internet, some of the first steps are pretty easy to understand and appreciate. Figure 18-1 shows a sample network from which the basics can be explained.

Figure 18-1   An Enterprise Network Connecting to the Internet

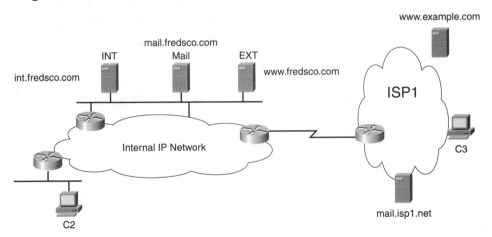

On the left is an enterprise network, labeled "Internal IP Network" in the figure. In the internal network, there are users at client PCs, like the one labeled C2. C2 uses the e-mail server and the internal web server, named mail.fredsco.com and int.fredsco.com, respectively. The internal web server has stuff that's only appropriate for employees who work for Fredsco. Finally, the web server called www.fredsco.com is meant for external users, but internal clients such as C2 will also want to browse that web server.

In the Internet side of the figure, you see a typical Internet-based web server (www.example.com) and a typical Internet-based e-mail server (mail.isp1.net). The client PC labeled as C3 represents a typical user on the Internet.

The first task to secure Fredsco's network is to define what is allowed and what shouldn't be allowed. You should keep two things in mind when considering this dilemma:

- Between which two hosts do packets need to flow?

- Which host begins that communication?

After you know which two hosts are involved and which one starts the process, you can determine what data is allowed to flow between the hosts. For example, Figure 18-2 shows the flows that I think should be allowed in the same network shown in Figure 18-1. To keep the figure a little less cluttered, I removed some of the icons so that you could focus on the flows between pairs of hosts. (The term *flow* refers to packets that are sent from a specific host to another host, and vice versa. For instance, when you browse a web page, packets go between your PC and that web server, and vice versa—that's a flow.)

Figure 18-2 Typical Types of Traffic Allowed Between an Enterprise and the Internet

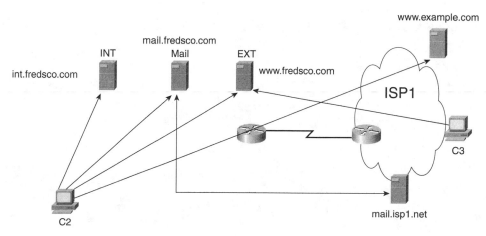

Look at C2 inside the internal Fredsco network. The figure shows lines from the client to almost every server. C2 needs to use POP3 to retrieve mail and SMTP to send mail—both to mail.fredsco.com. C2 needs to browse the internal and external Fredsco web servers, and you also want to allow C2 to get to all Internet websites.

Of course, the traffic flows from C2 don't go over the Internet. What about flows that pass through the Internet? A couple of types of flows are allowed in this case. C3, which is simply a user somewhere in the Internet, is allowed to get to the Fredsco website that's appropriate for external users (www.fredsco.com). Also, the two mail servers are sending packets to each other so that they can exchange mail.

The lines shown between hosts represent flows, but they also imply who initiates the flow. The lines mean that packets can go in either direction between the hosts; otherwise, no useful work could happen. However, the lines without an arrow on one end mean that that host initiated the flow. For instance, C2 only has lines *without* an arrow on the end near C2, meaning that C2 initiates all the flows shown. The line between the two mail servers shows arrows on both ends, which means that you want to allow either mail server to be able to initiate a flow.

Figure 18-2 shows what's allowed. Now let's consider what's not allowed, in Figure 18-3.

Figure 18-3   Traffic That's Typically Not Allowed

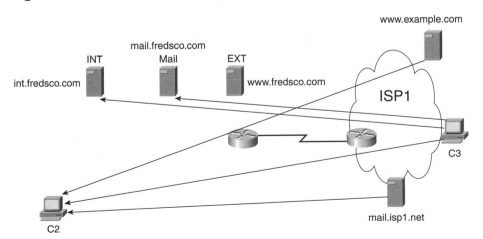

Notice which ends of the lines do not have arrows on them; in other words, focus on the IP host that initiates the flows. In this figure, all the IP hosts that initiate the flows are on the Internet. A lot of what Fred wants to prevent is stuff that's initiated by hosts on the Internet, which makes sense if you think of the bad guys on the Internet who are trying to get into your network. For instance, by definition, you do not want to let Internet users open a browser and browse your internal websites. Also, no one should try to initiate a TCP connection to C2. By definition, clients are hosts with users who typically need to initiate flows, not accept them.

Table 18-1 summarizes and characterizes what Fred wants to happen with security.

Table 18-1   Characterizations of What's Allowed and What's Not

Initiates Flow	Receives Flow	Protocol(s)	Allowed?
Internal client (such as C2)	Any internal server	POP3, SMTP, HTTP, FTP, and so on	Yes
Internal client (such as C2)	www.fredsco.com web server	HTTP	Yes
Internal client (such as C2)	Internet-based servers	HTTP and FTP	Yes
Internal mail server	External mail server	SMTP	Yes
External mail server	Internal mail server	SMTP	Yes
Any internal host	Any Internet host	Any protocols that are not otherwise specified	No
Internet clients	www.fredsco.com web server	HTTP	Yes
Internet clients	Any host inside Fredsco	Any protocols that are not otherwise specified	No

If you don't remember the protocols mentioned in the table, the details are covered in Chapter 8, "Shipping Goods over a (Network) Roadway." For the purposes of this chapter, just remember that e-mail clients use POP3 to retrieve mail, that e-mail servers use SMTP to transfer mail to other servers, that HTTP is used for web traffic, and that FTP is used to transfer files.

Enforcing the Ground Rules

Parents get to enforce ground rules all the time. Imagine that a kid wants to get permission from a parent to go somewhere or play with someone. "Can I go to Billy's house to play?" the kid asks. His parent replies, "No, Billy's dad leaves his R-rated video tapes lying around, and I don't want you and Billy to be tempted to watch them while his parents aren't home. But Billy can come over here to play." The parent knows what's safe and what isn't and enforces the rules.

Now that Fred knows what he does and doesn't want to happen in his network, he can enforce the rules with a *firewall*. The network engineer configures the firewall with a set of rules that tell it what's legal and what isn't. Then the firewall allows some packets to pass through it and discards others to enforce the rules.

To enforce the rules, the firewall needs to be in the path that is used for forwarding packets to and from the Internet. Figure 18-4 shows one typical topology.

Figure 18-4   Putting Up a Wall Between the Dangerous Folks and Your Network

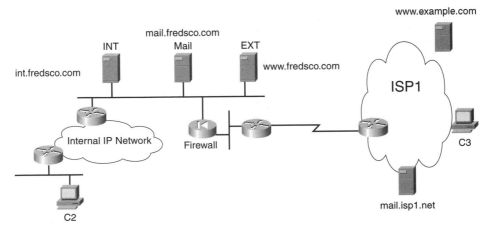

The only new icon in the figure is the icon that Cisco uses to represent its firewall product, called a *PIX Firewall*. Regardless of the model or brand of firewall, the firewall forwards the packets that enter and exit the Internet connection. The firewall behaves like a router in that it forwards IP packets. But because the firewall sees all the packets passing over the Internet connection, the firewall can decide whether each packet should or shouldn't be allowed, based on the rules set up for the network. A network engineer would have to configure the firewall to tell it the information included in Table 18-1. The firewall will simply pass what is allowed and discard what is not.

Ways to Watch Your (Network) Neighborhood

When watching out for strangers in the neighborhood, some parents—particularly moms—can get a reputation of knowing everything that the kids are up to. Children the world over often wonder how moms can somehow know what they are doing even when the parents aren't watching. It's like moms have another set of eyes in the backs of their heads. Of course, moms really just know human nature, so they can look for signs that somebody might be up to something, such as when a normally boisterous little boy is suddenly quiet for a few minutes.

A firewall acts a little like a mom who lives at the entrance of the neighborhood. Not only does the firewall watch the traffic entering the network, but it also knows the nature of the traffic that should be allowed to flow through it.

One of the more important things that a firewall must do is to recognize when a host is initiating a new flow. For instance, Fred allows clients in his network to initiate a new flow to an Internet-based web server, but Internet clients can't initiate a flow to Fred's internal servers or to other internal user hosts inside Fredsco's network. So it's pretty important that the firewall be able to figure out who's initiating the new flow.

A firewall knows what to expect with many network flows, particularly those that use TCP. With TCP, a firewall can easily identify who's initiating a flow. In TCP lingo, a flow is the equivalent of a *TCP connection*. The host that is initiating the TCP connection sends the first TCP segment, and there's something unique about that first segment. All the firewall has to do is look for TCP segments that have that unique characteristic to figure out when a new TCP connection, or flow, is being created. Figure 18-5 shows a view of the three TCP segments that are used to create a TCP connection.

Figure 18-5   TCP Connections and Well-Known Ports

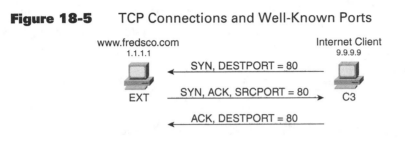

Before an application can use TCP to send data, TCP creates a TCP connection. The first TCP segment that is used to create a TCP connection sets the *SYN flag bit* (short for synchronize) to binary 1. TCP headers include a set of flag bits in the header, such as the SYN flag, and those flags are used for functions like this three-way connection establishment. For instance, the second segment has both the SYN and the ACK bits set, which is what TCP protocols define as the correct flags to be set in the second TCP segment in the three-segment TCP connection establishment flow.

Figure 18-5 shows an Internet-based client (C3) sending a segment with the SYN bit set to http://www.fredsco.com. The firewall, seeing that segment, knows that C3 is initiating the connection. How? Well, the only TCP segment that has the SYN bit set, and only the SYN bit, is the first segment sent between a pair of hosts. So, the first segment in the figure is indeed the first segment of a new TCP connection. To identify who sent the packet, all the firewall has to do is look at the source IP address of the packet. The firewall can also look at the destination IP address to know who's the receiver of the TCP connection—in this case, 1.1.1.1.

Firewalls also need to know what application protocol is in use. Back in Chapter 9, "Choosing Shipping Options When Transporting Goods over the (Network) Roadway," you read about how each server uses a well-known TCP or UDP port number. That way, when a client such as C3 wants to browse the http://www. fredsco.com website, the client can use a destination port number of 80—the well-known port number for HTTP.

Deciding When to Stop the Traffic

Based on the facts in this short section, a firewall can look at a packet, figure out who's the initiator (client) of the connection, and determine which protocol (well-known port) is being used. Knowing those facts, the firewall can apply the rules about what is and isn't allowed.

Figure 18-6 shows an example of how a firewall thinks when it sees the first packet in a new connection. In fact, it's the same TCP connection shown in Figure 18-5.

Figure 18-6   Allowing the TCP Connection from Figure 18-5

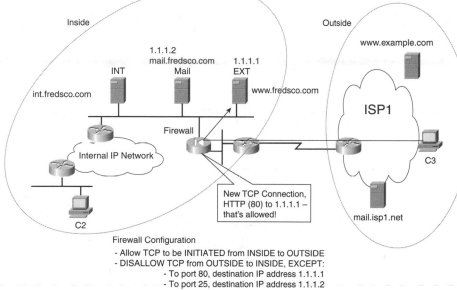

When C3 first sends the IP packet with the initial TCP segment, the firewall notices that the segment has the SYN bit set. The firewall then considers the interface in which the packet arrived—in this case, the interface connecting the firewall to the Internet. In firewall lingo, that's called the *outside interface* because it's outside the network that the firewall is trying to protect. The firewall also notices that the segment had destination port 80 in it, which is used for HTTP.

The firewall then looks at the rules that the network engineer configured for it. It appears that HTTP (port 80) traffic from the Internet (meaning from the "outside") to that web server (IP address 1.1.1.1, on the *inside interface*) is indeed allowed. In other words, clients on the Internet should be allowed to hit www.fredsco.com because that server is intended for customer use. So, the firewall passes this packet and all subsequent packets that are part of this single TCP connection.

The firewall uses similar logic to stop packets that should not be allowed. Imagine that C3 tries to open a browser to go to int.fredsco.com, one of Fredsco's internal web servers, whose IP address is 1.1.1.3. Figure 18-7 outlines the logic.

Figure 18-7   Disallowing a TCP Connection to an Inside Web Server

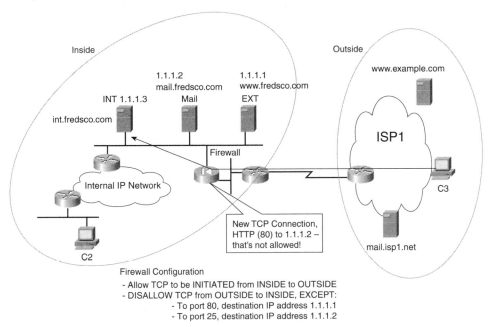

The firewall's rules, shown at the bottom of the figure, tell it two types of connections that can be initiated from the outside to the inside. This new connection does not match either of those rules. So, the firewall discards the IP packet, which

prevents the TCP connection from ever being completed. Because a TCP connection must be completed before any application data can be sent, there will never be HTTP application messages sent between the server and the client; in fact, not even this initial TCP segment reaches server 1.1.1.2. The server is completely unaware that C3 tried to reach it.

Safe Places Outside of Your Neighborhood (Network)

It could be that you live near a park, and most parents in the neighborhood let their kids hang out at the park. It's a public place, so it's not as safe as being at home, but it might be safe enough.

Likewise, many networks create the equivalent of a safe public park with their firewalls. Firewalls act like routers in that they forward packets based on the destination IP address. Like routers, a firewall typically has at least two physical interfaces, and like a router, a firewall can have more than two interfaces. Outside interfaces connect to the Internet, which is considered relatively unsafe. The inside interface connects to the internal network, which is relatively safe. In firewall lingo, a third interface might be connected to another LAN, called a ***demilitarized zone (DMZ)***, which is somewhere between the inside and outside interfaces in terms of safety. Figure 18-8 shows the general idea.

When using a DMZ, the flows that are allowed are the same as before, but the location of the servers that are accessible from the Internet has changed. The Internet-accessible servers have been placed on a different LAN. Because of that, a strong rule can be configured on the firewall: Absolutely no TCP connections can be initiated from the outside (Internet) to the inside (the internal network). The only flows that are allowed to be initiated into Fred's internal network are the ones to the servers in the DMZ. By using a DMZ, the firewall creates a stronger, more secure set of security rules.

Figure 18-8 A Safe but Potentially Risky Place: The DMZ

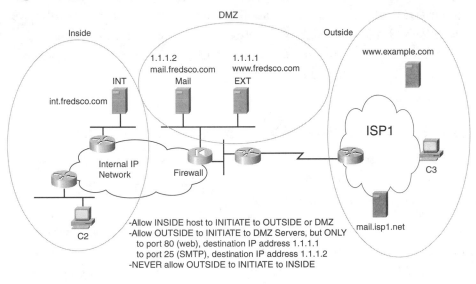

Using the Police to Watch for Bad Guys

Even with neighborhood watch programs, communities still have the police. Although the police can't stay in your neighborhood all day long, they can do a bunch of things to prevent crime, as well as to prevent crimes from recurring. They can arrest suspects and question them, look into their criminal records, and prosecute them as necessary. The police can go to great lengths to prevent future crimes, in part by looking at how past crimes were committed and stopping similar crimes in the future.

Firewalls prevent the types of flows that are known to be potentially harmful. However, firewalls do let packets into and out of an enterprise network. So, in addition to a firewall, networks need other security tools. These tools watch for known patterns of illegal network activity—activity that is intended to look like normal activity so that it can get past the firewall. In the next two sections, you'll read about a couple of tools that watch for trends, compare those to known illegal network activity, and do something to prevent problems as a result of the activity.

Watching for Wolves in Sheep's Clothing

In a spy movie, the spy might need to get in to look around a big office campus. He might cut the phone lines to the building complex and then show up in a telephone repair truck saying, "Hi, our monitoring center noticed that a telephone line was cut. Want to let me in to fix it?" The security guard waves him through because he knows that the telephones have been acting up. Whoops! The bad guy is now free to roam around and do his spying!

In networking, *intrusion detection systems (IDSs)* look out for the equivalent of spies who are impersonating a legitimate user. IDSs watch the packets that the firewall allows through, and they look for things in the packets that might mean someone is trying to trick the firewall, get their packets through the firewall, and do bad things to the servers and hosts in your network.

Whereas it's easy to think of a spy from the movie posing as a telephone repairman, it's hard to understand how a cracker might make his packets look like packets sent by a legitimate user, but still use those packets to do harm. (The term *cracker* refers to someone who purposefully tries to cause problems with devices on a network; the term *hacker* refers to someone who might be trying to break into a network but does not intend to cause problems.) In some cases, the cracker might do something that causes a server to fail; that's called a *denial of service attack*. In other cases, the cracker actually puts programs on a computer, hoping to harm the computer, or possibly steal information. In that case, the programs that the cracker puts on the servers are called *viruses*. Although most people have a hard time fully understanding how these tricks are done, it does happen. In fact, Microsoft has offered rewards into the hundreds of thousands of dollars for leads to help the police find and arrest crackers who create particularly harmful viruses.

Some IDS devices sit in the network, watching packets that pass over a LAN, whereas others are software that sits on the servers. The IDSs on the network are called *network-based IDSs*, and those on the host are called (you guessed it) *host-based IDSs*. Figure 18-9 shows the typical location of a network-based IDS.

Figure 18-9   Watching for Patterns with a Network-Based IDS

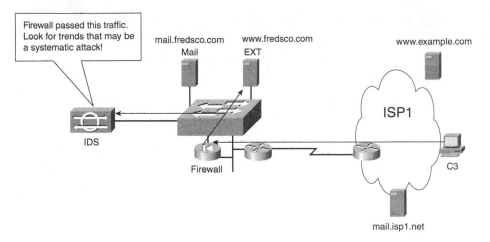

For a network-based IDS to work correctly, the LAN switch must be configured so that traffic to and from the firewall is copied and sent to the IDS. That way, the IDS can review the packets, searching for trends that might look like a cracker trying a cracker trick. It's like the difference between a security guard who just passed the phone repair truck through, versus one who passes the truck through but then sends someone to check up on the repairman and follow him around the building.

Avoiding Catching Cold

Computers can get viruses, just like people can. As mentioned earlier, a ***computer virus*** is a file, typically a program, which can cause problems after a copy of the virus gets on your computer. The file often gets on your computer via e-mail or web browsing. Just like real viruses, a computer virus can make your computer really sick, a little sick, or you might not even know that you have a virus. Often times, like real viruses, after your computer gets a virus, it can infect other computers.

To combat viruses, people install ***anti-virus software*** on end user computers as well as on servers. This software looks at the files copied to the computer to make sure there are no known viruses. For instance, some e-mails have files attached to them. The anti-virus software looks at the files, comparing the contents to a list of known viruses. If the file contains a virus, the anti-virus software either deletes the file or puts it somewhere safe.

Profiling What the Bad Guys Want to Do

When the police are patrolling around the neighborhood, they know what general things to look out for because that's what they were trained to do. For instance, if there's been a rash of bank robberies lately using a green van as the getaway car, you know the police will be looking for green vans in particular. In the real world, police usually call that *profiling*.

IDS systems and anti-virus software do a form of profiling, but in networking, the term *signature* is used. Whenever a new way to hack into the network is found, or whenever a new virus is discovered, the vendors that sell the IDS and anti-virus software create a signature for that problem. The signature tells the IDS or anti-virus software what to look for to identify the problem. As long as a network engineer updates the IDS to know about the latest signatures, the IDS will be well prepared for all known problems. Similarly, most PCs with proper security have their anti-virus software updated regularly with new virus signatures.

Chapter Summary

Practically every enterprise network connects to the Internet, but that connection creates some risks. Firewalls can watch the packets entering and exiting a network, comparing them to the security rules for that company, and allow only the types of traffic that the company believes should be allowed.

Firewalls take care of a lot of security problems; however, they must allow some traffic through if an Internet connection is to be used for its intended purposes. Crackers can make their packets look like packets that the firewall should allow through, but those packets might be part of an attempt to cause harm to the network. IDSs watch packets passed by the firewall, looking for signatures that identify the known ways for people to cause problems with packets that do pass the firewall.

Anti-virus software watches for files that are transferred to a host computer, usually when e-mail is downloaded or when the user uses a web browser. Like IDSs, anti-virus software uses signatures to help identify known viruses.

Chapter Review Questions

You can find the answers to the following questions in Appendix A, "Answers to Chapter Review Questions."

1. What restrictions are typically placed on clients inside a corporate network, in terms of what Internet-based servers they are allowed to use?

2. What restrictions are typically placed on clients on the Internet who want to connect to servers inside a corporate network, assuming that corporation uses a firewall?

3. How does a firewall figure out the IP address of a host that is trying to initiate a new TCP connection?

4. How does a firewall figure out what application protocol is being used?

5. What term does a firewall typically use to refer to the corporate network?

6. What term does a firewall typically use to refer to a small LAN that is less secure than the internal corporate network, but more secure than the Internet connection?

7. Consider the following statement: "Firewalls let packets go from the corporate network to the Internet, but they do not let packets go from the Internet back to the corporate network." State whether you agree or disagree, and explain why.

8. What docs IDS stand for?

9. Comparing network-based IDS devices and firewalls, which one is typically in the path through which packets are forwarded?

10. Define "signature" in terms of use with IDS and anti-virus software.

11. Which two TCP/IP applications most often allow the transfer of files to a computer, with those files possibly containing a computer virus?

PART VII

Appendixes

Appendix A: Answers to Chapter Review Questions

Appendix B: Converting IP Addresses Between Decimal and Binary

Answers to Chapter Review Questions

Chapter 1

1. In this chapter's definition of a network, what three components are used to create a network?

   Answer: Software, hardware, and cabling

2. What is the key function provided by a network?

   Answer: To allow multiple computers to communicate with each other

3. Related to the three components of a network, which component does a server support person work with most?

   Answer: Software—especially the software on servers

4. Which components of a network does a network engineer work with most?

   Answer: A network engineer works with hardware, software, and cabling, with most of the focus on the software running in networking devices.

5. What is an enterprise network?

   Answer: A network created for use by a single company or organization

6. Give a basic definition of the term "Internet."

   Answer: The global network to which almost every company and organization in the world is connected. The Internet allows communication among a large number of the computers on the planet.

7. Compare and contrast the terms "enterprise network" and "Internet" in general terms.

    Answer: An enterprise network is a network built for use by one enterprise—in other words, one company or organization. The Internet is a network that consists of a huge number of networks, connected together, allowing widespread communications across the entire planet.

8. Describe the concept of a network utility.

    Answer: A network utility treats the network like basic utilities—electricity, water, and so on. The user expects to be able to plug in to a wall socket with a cable and have the network be ready, working, and available—much like you plug in a power cable and expect it to work.

Chapter 2

1. List the five types of networking application services mentioned in this chapter.

    Answer: File services, print services, web services, e-mail services, and file transfer services

2. Which application services effectively hide the network from the end user?

    Answer: File and print services

3. Which application services make use of servers to hold and store data, waiting until another user is available in the network?

    Answer: E-mail clients send e-mail to e-mail servers, who hold the e-mail, waiting until the recipient checks his mail.

4. Which application service allows a server to present multiple text, graphics, video, audio images, and sounds to the client?

    Answer: Web services

5. In general terms, compare and contrast an enterprise network with the Internet.

Answer: An enterprise network is a network built for use by one enterprise—in other words, one company or organization. The Internet includes almost every enterprise network, as well as Internet service providers (ISPs).

6. Does the Internet include enterprise networks, home users who connect to the Internet, both, or neither? Explain your answer.

Answer: The Internet includes both enterprise networks and individual users because the Internet includes any and all computers that somehow have at least one path through which to reach the rest of the Internet.

7. Explain the basic difference between a web page and a website.

Answer: A web page typically refers to a single page—in other words, what you see inside a browser at one instant in time. A website refers to all the web pages that a company, organization, or individual creates. These web pages are typically interconnected, allowing the user to navigate to various pages by clicking something on each web page.

8. What's a network cloud?

Answer: A network cloud is a cloud-looking icon that represents parts of a network for which the details are not important in the figure. It simply means "There's a network here, but that's all you need to know."

9. Compare and contrast enterprise networks and Internet service provider networks in a few sentences.

Answer: Enterprise networks consist of hardware and software purchased by a single company or organization. An ISP network also consists of hardware and software purchased by that ISP. The main difference relates to their purposes: The enterprise network provides network services to the people inside the company, whereas ISP networks provide services to individual users to connect to the Internet. ISP networks also provide Internet connectivity to enterprise networks.

10. What three-word term refers to the text that you need to type into a web browser to reach a particular website? What popular jargon might be used instead of that term?

Answer: The formal term is Universal Resource Locator (URL). Many people refer to the URL as the *web address*.

11. Imagine that Fred connects to the Internet using ISP1, and Barney uses ISP2. When Fred sends Barney an e-mail, to what computer does Fred send the e-mail? If the e-mail is not sent directly to Barney's computer, explain why.

    Answer: Fred sends the e-mail to an e-mail server, typically a computer at his ISP—ISP1 in this case. That e-mail server forwards the e-mail to ISP2's e-mail server. Later, when Barney checks his e-mail, he retrieves the e-mail. This process allows Fred to send the e-mail, regardless of whether Fred has network connectivity to Barney at the time.

Chapter 3

1. Describe in general terms the benefits of using standards.

    Answer: Standards help makes things work well together, particularly when two things must work together. For instance, a lamp you buy at the store needs electrical power, so if the lamp maker follows the standards for how electrical sockets work, you should be able to plug in a lamp and have it work.

2. What were two of the early and popular proprietary networking models?

    Answer: IBM's Systems Network Architecture (SNA) and DEC DECnet

3. Define the term "networking model," and compare and contrast it with the term "networking standard."

    Answer: A networking standard defines a specific item. A networking model is a combination of many standards. By definition, if a network implements the multiple standards in the model, the network will work well and allow useful communications to occur.

4. List the two public networking models covered in this chapter, including the words represented by their acronyms.

    Answer: Transmission Control Protocol/Internet Protocol (TCP/IP) and Open Systems Interconnection (OSI)

5. List the names of the four layers in the TCP/IP networking model, in order, with the highest layer first.

Answer: Application, transport, internetwork, and network interface

6. List the names of the seven layers in the OSI networking model, in order, with the highest layer first.

Answer: Application, presentation, session, transport, network, data link, physical

7. List the two standards bodies that define LAN and WAN standards, as referenced by TCP/IP. Which one defines LAN standards?

Answer: The IEEE and the ITU. The IEEE defines LAN standards, and the ITU defines WAN standards.

8. What term refers to where a router stores the information that tells it how to forward packets?

Answer: Routing table

9. Networkers use OSI terminology to describe networking protocols in general. List two OSI terms that might describe the IP protocol.

Answer: "IP is a *Layer 3* protocol" and "IP is a *network* layer protocol."

10. Define the term "packet."

Answer: A group of bits that are combined for transmission in a network

11. This chapter uses the terms "standard" and "protocol," but it suggests one typical difference between a protocol and a standard. What is that difference?

Answer: A protocol typically defines a process, whereas a standard more often defines something static. For instance, the size and shape of a connector on the end of a cable is a standard, but the process through which a computer notices in-error packets and asks for replacement packets is defined as a protocol.

12. What term refers to bits that are added to end user data, for the purpose of allowing a protocol to have a place to keep information important to how the protocol does its function?

    Answer:　Header

Chapter 4

1. Give an example of how a computer might transmit binary 0s and 1s using variations in voltage on a wire.

   Answer:　The transmitting device could induce one voltage level on the wire to imply a binary 0 and a different voltage level to imply a binary 1.

2. Imagine that two computers are sending and receiving data over a wire. How often would the receiving device need to sample the electrical signal on the wire if the standard called for 20 bps transmission speed?

   Answer:　The receiving device would sample the signal 20 times in a single second, interpreting the signal as either a 0 or a 1. By doing so, it would receive 20 bits per second. The actual time interval would be 1/20 of a second, or .05 seconds.

3. As explained in the chapter, do computers usually transmit data over the same wires they use to receive data? Why or why not?

   Answer:　Computers use different wires for transmission and reception to avoid overlapping electrical signals. Overlapped electrical signals cause confusion, misinterpretation of the signals as meaning the wrong binary value, or the complete inability to interpret what binary value was meant by a particular electrical signal.

4. As explained in the chapter, do computers usually transmit data over a single wire, or do they use two wires?

   Answer:　Computers use a pair of wires, twisted together, for transmission. The twisted pair of wires reduces the impact of EMI.

5. How many wires can fit inside the end of an RJ-45 connector?

   Answer:　Eight

6. How many wires are needed for a PC to successfully send and receive data to another PC using an Ethernet LAN cable with RJ-45 connectors?

Answer: Four. Although the RJ-45 connector supports eight wires, the wires inserted in pin positions 1, 2, 3, and 6 are the ones Ethernet uses for data transmission and reception.

7. Explain why a straight-through LAN cable does not work when connecting two PCs directly, just using the cable.

Answer: Each PC's NIC sends data over the wires in pins 1 and 2. A straight-through cable terminates those wires in pins 1 and 2, respectively, on the other end of the cable. As a result, both NICs transmit data on wires 1 and 2, and neither NIC receives an electrical signal on pins 3 and 6.

8. Explain why a cross-over LAN cable *does* work when connecting two PCs directly, just using the cable.

Answer: Each PC's NIC sends data over the wires that use pins 1 and 2. A cross-over cable terminates those wires in pins 3 and 6, respectively, on the connector on the other end of the cable. When one device sends on pins 1 and 2, the other device receives that signal on pins 3 and 6, as expected. The same thing also occurs when the second device sends on pins 1 and 2.

9. Explain why a straight-through LAN cable works when connecting a PC to a hub.

Answer: The hub reverses its logic compared to a NIC, in terms of what pins are used for transmission and reception. The PC sends on pins 1 and 2, and the hub expects to receive data on pins 1 and 2, so the straight-through cable works. Similarly, the hub sends on pins 3 and 6, so that the NICs, which receive on pins 3 and 6, successfully receive the data.

10. What is the main difference between UTP and STP cabling? Which is more popular today?

Answer: Unshielded twisted-pair cabling does not add shielding against EM interference, whereas shielded twisted-pair cabling does. UTP is by far the more popular option today.

11. List some of the key benefits of a structured cabling plan.

    Answer: A structured cabling plan helps to minimize the need for running new cables because you can easily determine the distance from each wall plate to the wiring panel. This allows the electrician to run a cable between each wall plate and the wiring closet, while allowing other workers to connect a patch cable to complete the wiring.

12. Imagine a hub with ten physical ports, and cables connecting each port to ten different PCs. The hub receives an electrical signal from the PC on port 1. Where does the hub forward the electrical signal?

    Answer: The hub repeats the signal out ports 2–10. It does not repeat the signal out port 1 because that was the port in which it received the signal.

13. Define the term "pin" in relation to an RJ-45 connector.

    Answer: A pin is the physical position in the end of a connector, where the copper part of a wire sits.

Chapter 5

1. Complete this sentence: "Before sending end user data over an Ethernet LAN, the sender must _____ the data in an Ethernet _____."

    Answer: "Before sending end user data over an Ethernet LAN, the sender must encapsulate the data in an Ethernet frame."

2. Name the three general parts of an Ethernet frame.

    Answer: An Ethernet frame has an Ethernet header, an Ethernet trailer, and the end user data.

3. Imagine that PC1 has built an Ethernet frame, and it is ready to send the frame. What should PC1 do before sending the frame?

    Answer: PC1 should listen to find out if someone else is sending a frame at that time. If so, PC1 should wait until the LAN is silent.

4. What does the "CD" in CSMA/CD stand for?

Answer: CSMA/CD stands for carrier sense multiple access collision detect.

5. Imagine that PC1 and PC2 send a frame at the same time, and the frames collide. Which one sends the jamming signal?

Answer: Both PCs send the jamming signal.

6. Imagine that PC1 and PC2 send a frame at the same time, and the frames collide. How does the CSMA/CD algorithm minimize the chances that PC1 and PC2's frames might collide the next time they attempt to send the frames?

Answer: Both NICs generate a timer based on a random number. Often, one of their timers expires first, allowing that station to send its frame first.

7. How many bytes are in a source Ethernet address? A destination Ethernet address?

Answer: Both the source and destination Ethernet addresses are 6 bytes long.

8. Imagine that PC1 sends an Ethernet frame to PC2, but that PC3 and PC4 also get a copy, as a side effect of how a hub works. How does PC3 know to ignore the data in the frame?

Answer: All PCs, including PC3, look at the destination address. If that address does not match the PC3's NIC address, then PC3 discards the frame.

9. List the IEEE committee that standardized Ethernet-specific details of Ethernet. Use both the numeric name and the three-word text name.

Answer: The IEEE 802.3 committee, also known as Media Access Control (MAC), defines the Ethernet-specific parts of Ethernet.

10. List the IEEE committee that standardized Ethernet details that are in common with other types of LANS. Use both the numeric name and the three-word text name.

Answer: The IEEE 802.2 committee, also known as Logical Link Control (LLC), defines the parts of Ethernet that are shared with other types of LANs.

11. If you were using a networking device from Cisco Systems, and you saw the output of a command that displayed a MAC address, how would it be formatted? Give an example, assuming that all digits in the actual MAC address are 1.

    Answer: Cisco products show MAC addresses 4 hex digits at a time, with periods between them. For example, 1111.1111.1111 would be a sample Ethernet address.

12. What does the acronym FCS stand for?

    Answer: FCS stands for frame check sequence.

13. Imagine that PC1 sends a frame to PC2, and PC2 notices that the FCS sent with the frame is different from the value calculated by PC2. What should PC2 do?

    Answer: PC2 should discard the frame because the difference in values implies that bit errors occurred during the transmission of the frame.

14. Explain the difference between error detection and error recovery. Which does Ethernet perform?

    Answer: Error detection means that a device notices when frame errors occur, and when they do, the frame is discarded. Error recovery means that after the frame has been discarded, the receiver asks the sender to retransmit the data, and the sender obliges. Ethernet performs error detection.

Chapter 6

1. How many frames can pass through a 24-port hub at one instance in time, with no collisions occurring?

    Answer: One

2. How many frames can pass through a 24-port switch at one instance in time, with no collisions occurring, and with full duplex used on all ports?

    Answer: 24. Devices that are attached to all ports can send a frame at the same time because full duplex is used.

3. PC1, PC2, and PC3 are all attached to the same switch. Imagine that PC1 and PC2 each send a frame to PC3, at roughly the same instance in time. Will the switch forward both frames? Will a collision occur? Why or why not?

   Answer: The switch will forward both frames to PC3, one at a time, with no collisions. The switch simply buffers one of the frames while sending the other one.

4. PC1, PC2, and PC3 are all attached to the same switch. PC1 and PC2 use full duplex, and PC3 uses half duplex. Can PC1 send a frame to PC2 while PC2 sends a frame to PC3? Why or why not?

   Answer: Yes. PC3 can either send or receive, but not both, because it uses half duplex. In this case, PC3 only needs to receive a frame. Only PC2 needs to send and receive at the same time; using full duplex allows PC2 to do just that.

5. PC1, PC2, and PC3 are all attached to the same switch, but the switch is powered off. After the switch is powered up, PC1 sends a frame to PC2. How many MAC addresses are in the MAC address table of the switch? Why?

   Answer: There is one MAC address in the MAC address table of the switch. The switch learns MAC addresses by looking at the source MAC address of incoming frames. Because PC1 was the only PC that had sent a frame, only PC1's MAC address would show up in the address table.

6. Imagine that three PCs (PC1, PC2, and PC3) are connected to a switch. PC2 and PC3 have 10/100 NICs, and PC1 has a 10-Mbps only NIC. Could any PC use 802.3u?

   Answer: 802.3u is the IEEE standard for Fast Ethernet. With a 10/100 NIC, PC2 and PC3 could use Fast Ethernet.

7. Imagine that three PCs (PC1, PC2, and PC3) are connected to a switch. PC2 and PC3 have 10/100 NICs, and PC1 has a 10-Mbps only NIC. What would need to happen before PC2 could transmit at 100 Mbps?

   Answer: Autonegotiation would need to occur between PC2's NIC and the switch to determine the speed used on that segment.

8. If a frame with a destination MAC address of 0200.6666.6666 arrived at a switch, and the switch had the following two entries in its switching table, what would the switch do? Out which ports would the switch forward the frame? Out which ports would the switch not forward the frame?

   0200.5555.5555   E5

   0200.6666.6666   E6

   Answer: The switch would forward the frame out port E6, and it would not forward the frame out any other ports.

9. If a frame with a destination MAC address of 0200.7777.7777 arrived at a switch, and the switch had only the following two entries in its switching table, what would the switch do? Out which ports would it forward the frame? Out which ports would it not forward the frame?

   0200.5555.5555   E5

   0200.6666.6666   E6

   Answer: The switch would forward the frame out all ports except the port in which the frame arrived.

10. If a frame with a destination MAC address of FFFF.FFFF.FFFF arrived at a switch, and the switch had only the following two entries in its switching table, what would the switch do? Out which ports would it forward the frame? Out which ports would it not forward the frame?

    0200.5555.5555   E5

    0200.6666.6666   E6

    Answer: The switch would forward the frame out all ports except the port in which the frame arrived.

11. What does the word "flooding" mean in the context of LAN switch operation?

    Answer: The switch receives a frame and then forwards the frame out all ports except the port in which the frame arrived.

12. What is the most significant difference between Ethernet and Fast Ethernet?

Answer: Fast Ethernet is faster, with transmission rates at 100 Mbps versus 10 Mbps for Ethernet.

13. How many more bytes did the IEEE add to the address field in the Fast Ethernet header, as compared to Ethernet, when it created the Fast Ethernet standards?

Answer: Ethernet and Fast Ethernet use the same size of Ethernet address; the address size was not increased.

14. How many more bytes did the IEEE add to the address field in the Gigabit Ethernet header, as compared to Ethernet, when it created the Gigabit Ethernet standards?

Answer: Ethernet and Gigabit Ethernet use the same size of Ethernet address; the address size was not increased.

15. List the differences in the forwarding and learning logic used by a 10 Mbps Ethernet switch and a gigabit Ethernet switch.

Answer: The forwarding and learning processes are identical. The only difference comes in the actual transmission of data at the different speeds.

Chapter 7

1. Compare and contrast the terms "physical LAN" and "broadcast domain."

Answer: The devices in a physical LAN are in the same broadcast domain. The physical LAN includes the cabling switches and NICs.

2. Define the term "broadcast domain."

Answer: A set of devices for which a broadcast frame sent by one device is received by all other devices in the set

3. What happens to a broadcast frame when a hub or a switch receives it?

Answer: Both devices forward the frame out all ports except the one in which the frame was received.

4. Imagine a standalone switch with no VLANs configured, with 24 physical ports, each connected to a different PC. How many broadcast domains exist?

Answer: Because they each forward broadcasts out all ports, a broadcast sent by any of the 24 devices on the first switch is forwarded to the other 23, making a single broadcast domain.

5. Imagine that a 12-port switch has 11 PCs connected to it, with the twelfth port connected to a hub. The hub has 4 PCs connected to it as well. The switch does not have VLANs configured. How many broadcast domains exist?

Answer: Only one broadcast domain exists. Because both hubs and switches forward broadcasts out all ports, a broadcast sent by any device would be received by all other PCs.

6. Define the term "VLAN."

Answer: A virtual LAN (VLAN) is a broadcast domain that is created by a switch using a subset of the physical ports on the switch.

7. What is the key difference between a physical LAN and a VLAN, according to this chapter?

Answer: A physical LAN includes all the ports on a switch. A VLAN includes a subset of the ports on a switch, as configured on the switch.

8. Imagine that three VLANs were created on a single switch. The switch receives a broadcast into a port in VLAN1. Will devices in VLAN2 receive the broadcast?

Answer: No. The switch will not forward the broadcast into VLAN2 or VLAN3, treating VLAN1 as a separate LAN.

9. Imagine that three VLANs were created on a single switch. The switch receives a unicast frame, entering a port in VLAN1, with destination MAC address of 0200.5555.5555. The VLAN1 address table in the switch does not have an entry for that MAC address. What will the switch do with this frame?

Answer: The switch will do what it always does with unknown destination unicast frames: It will flood the frame out all ports. However, the switch will only flood the frames out all ports in VLAN1, because the frame was received in VLAN1; it will not forward the frame out ports in other VLANS.

10. Imagine that three VLANs were created on a single switch. The switch receives a unicast frame, entering port in VLAN1, with destination MAC address of 0.200.5555.5555. The VLAN2 MAC address table lists an entry for 0200.5555.5555, referencing port 18. What will the switch do with this frame?

Answer: Assuming that 0200.5555.5555 is not in the VLAN1 address table, which should be the case, the switch will do what it always does with unknown destination unicast frames: It will flood the frame out all ports. However, it will only flood the frame out all ports in VLAN1, because the frame was received in VLAN1.

11. List two reasons why a network engineer might want to use VLANs.

Answer: Four reasons were listed in this chapter:

— To reduce the size of an individual broadcast domain

— For business or political reasons, referred to as *Layer 8* issues

— Due to Layer 3 design issues, because all devices in the same VLAN will be in the same IP subnet

— For cost issues; no matter why you want more LANs, using VLANs can allow you to create the LANs, without buying more switches.

12. Imagine one LAN with 100 devices, and another with 1000 devices. Explain the similarities and differences of the impact of broadcasts in each LAN.

Answer: The end user devices in a LAN must process all received broadcasts to know if the broadcast is intended for that device. So, the broadcasts do affect the end user devices. The more devices in the LAN, the more broadcasts heard by each device in the LAN, having an adverse effect on wasteful CPU overhead on the devices. The devices in the larger LAN will spend more CPU cycles processing broadcasts, most of which are not intended for them.

13. Compare and contrast physical LANs and virtual LANs.

Answer: Both define a single broadcast domain. VLANs require that a switch not consider all physical ports to be in the same LAN, but instead, via switch configuration, treat some ports as if they are in one VLAN, and some as if they are in another. With physical LANs, the switch treats all physical ports as if they are in a single broadcast domain.

14. Imagine that two switches are connected with an Ethernet cable. Three VLANs—VLAN1, VLAN2, and VLAN3—are configured on each switch. Name the two trunking protocols that could be used on the segment between switches and explain their basic operation.

    Answer: VLAN trunking would be used between the two switches, using either ISL or IEEE 802.1Q. Each protocol calls for the switches to put a header in front of the Ethernet frames before sending so that the receiver can look at the header and decide in what VLAN the frame belongs.

15. Imagine that two switches are connected with an Ethernet cable. No VLANs are configured. Describe the meaning of the term "trunk," and tell whether a trunk is needed or used in this small network.

    Answer: Depending on who uses the term, "trunk" might simply refer to an Ethernet cable or segment between switches. With that use of the term, the cable between the switches is indeed a trunk. Others only use the word "trunk" specifically when VLANs are used, and a trunking header is placed in front of frames before they pass over the cable between the switches.

16. Identify the two VLAN trunking protocols and state which is Cisco proprietary.

    Answer: Inter-Switch Link (ISL) is Cisco proprietary, and IEEE 802.1Q, the alternative, is defined by the IEEE.

Chapter 8

1. Which two TCP/IP protocols transmit e-mails across a network? List the acronyms and what they stand for.

    Answer: Simple Mail Transfer Protocol (SMTP) and Post Office Protocol, Version 3 (POP3)

2. Fred and Barney each use a PC. They connect to the Internet using different ISPs. Describe the process by which Fred's e-mail to Barney traverses the Internet, in regard to which e-mail servers are used and how.

    Answer: Fred sends the email to his ISP's e-mail server. That e-mail server sends the e-mail to Barney's ISP's e-mail server. Finally, Barney retrieves his e-mail from his own ISP's e-mail server.

3. In a typical network, which e-mail protocol does a client use to retrieve messages from a server?

Answer: POP3

4. Describe the two parts of a typical e-mail address and tell what each part defines.

Answer: The format of an e-mail address is as follows.

username@servername

where the servername portion identifies the e-mail server for that user. The username portion identifies the individual user of that e-mail server.

5. Under which layer of the TCP/IP networking model do the e-mail protocols described in this chapter fall?

Answer: The TCP/IP application layer defines the protocols.

6. What does the acronym FTP stand for, and what is its main purpose?

Answer: The File Transfer Protocol (FTP) is an application layer TCP/IP protocol whose main purpose is to allow files to be transferred between a client and a server, and vice versa.

7. What are the names of the FTP operations to move a file to a server and move a file to a client?

Answer: FTP PUT refers to moving a file to the server, and FTP GET refers to moving a file from the server to a client.

8. Explain the usage of FTP servers for transferring a file from user1, which is connected to ISP1, to user2, which is connected to ISP2. In particular, point out to which servers each client moves the file.

Answer: Unlike e-mail servers, a single FTP server is required. Both user1 and user2 would need a working username and password on that server. So, user1 would move (put) the file to the FTP server, and later, user2 would connect to the server and get the file.

9. Considering the two main FTP commands to move files to and from an FTP server, which commands both move the file and delete the original file from the location it was copied? (For instance, if user1 moves file1.doc to an FTP server, does that delete file1.doc from user1's computer?)

Answer: Neither a GET nor a PUT deletes the original source file.

10. What term refers to the process of making sure a user is who he claims to be, before allowing him to use a server?

Answer: Authentication

11. What does the acronym HTTP stand for, and what is its main purpose?

Answer: The Hypertext Transfer Protocol (HTTP) is an application layer TCP/IP protocol whose main purpose is to allow files to be transferred between a web server and a web browser.

12. From what other standard did HTTP derive the first two letters in its name?

Answer: The Hypertext Markup Language (HTML) defines content of a website, formatting information, and other instructions. Because HTTP was originally defined to transfer HTML files, the first two letters behind the HTTP acronym are "Hypertext."

13. What HTTP operation does a browser use to request a particular file from a web server?

Answer: The HTTP GET command

14. What does the acronym URL stand for, and how is it used?

Answer: The Uniform Resource Locator identifies the protocol to be used, the name of the server, the name of a file at the server, and often the directory at the server in which the file resides.

Chapter 9

1. List three of the main features of TCP.

Answer: The three main features of TCP are segmentation, error recovery, and using port numbers to allow delivery to the correct application program. Also, TCP helps reduce complexity in applications by hiding the data delivery details from the application, as well as providing encapsulation to deliver the data across a network.

2. Imagine that you visit a website, and as a result, you download a graphics image called logo.gif. The logo is 4000 bytes. How many segment(s) will the server send back to your browser to send you the logo? Assume an mss of 1480 bytes. Explain your answer.

Answer: TCP will segment the data into pieces, typically no larger than 1460 bytes of data. (An mss of 1480 minus the 20 bytes of TCP header leaves 1460 bytes for the data in each segment.) To send 4000 bytes, 3 segments would be required.

3. Imagine that a web server sent 3 TCP segements to a browser on Keith's PC, each 1000 bytes long, with sequence numbers 4304, 5304, and 6304, respectively. Assuming no errors had occurred, explain how Keith's PC could acknowledge receipt of the data.

Answer: In the next TCP segment that Keith sends to the web server, his TCP software will set the acknowledgement field to 7304, the next byte that he expects to receive from the server.

4. Imagine that a web server sent 3 TCP segments to a browser on Keith's PC, each 1000 bytes long, with sequence numbers 4304, 5304, and 6304, respectively. Assuming that the third segment had errors in it, explain how the data would be recovered.

Answer: In the next TCP segment that Keith sends to the web server, his TCP software will set the acknowledgement field to 6304, the next byte that he expects to receive from the server. That tells the server that the third segment Keith had sent—the one with the sequence number field set to 6304—was not received. So, the server re-sends the third segment.

5. Define the word *encapsulation*, using TCP encapsulation as an example.

Answer: When TCP receives data from an application layer protocol on the same computer, TCP adds a TCP header to the data. That process is called encapsulation.

6. Imagine that Keith brings up a browser on his PC and browses a website. He then brings up another browser, browsing a second website. When Keith receives the next TCP segment, how does his PC know to which browser to give the data?

Answer: TCP on Keith's PC looks at the destination port number field in the received TCP segment's header. Each browser uses a different TCP port number, so Keith's PC can identify which browser should receive the data.

7. How many TCP segments flow between two computers to establish a TCP connection?

Answer: Three

8. What is the name of the other TCP/IP transport layer protocol?

Answer: User Datagram Protocol (UDP)

9. A TCP header, along with the application data, is called what?

Answer: A TCP segment

10. Define the term *forward acknowledgment*.

Answer: Forward acknowledgment refers to the process of acknowledging data by setting the acknowledgment field to the next byte of data that should be received, as opposed to setting the acknowledgment field to the last byte of data that was received.

11. Define the term *well-known port*.

Answer: A well-known port is a port number that a server purposefully uses for a particular application so that when client computers want to use that service, they know what destination port to put into the TCP destination port field.

Chapter 10

1. Imagine that a router receives a packet over an Ethernet. What does the router look at inside the IP packet to decide what to do with the packet?

   Answer: The destination IP address

2. PC1 sits on an Ethernet, with a web server on another Ethernet. A router, R1, is connected to both Ethernets. How does PC1 get its HTTP request to the web server?

   Answer: PC1 sends the packet to the router, which then forwards the packet to the web server.

3. PC1 sits on an Ethernet network, along with R1. R1 and R2 are connected to a second Ethernet. Finally, R2 is connected to a third Ethernet, along with a web server. PC1's IP address is 5.5.5.5, and the server's is 6.6.6.6. What IP address is in the destination IP address field of a packet sent from PC1 to the web server?

   Answer: 6.6.6.6

4. PC1 sits on an Ethernet network, along with router R1. Routers R1 and R2 are connected to a second Ethernet. Finally, R2 is connected to a third Ethernet, along with a web server. PC1's IP address is 5.5.5.5, and the server's is 6.6.6.6. When the web server sends a packet back to PC1, what IP address is in the source IP address field of the packet?

   Answer: 6.6.6.6

5. For Class B networks, what is the range of numbers allowed for the first octet?

   Answer: 128 through 191, inclusive

6. For Class C networks, what is the range of numbers allowed for the first octet?

   Answer: 192 through 223, inclusive

7. How many IP addresses exist in Class A network 7.0.0.0?

Answer: 2^{24}–2, or 16,777,214. (If you answered with something like "more than 16 million," that's close enough!)

8. How many IP addresses exist in Class B network 166.5.0.0?

Answer: 2^{16}–2, or 65,534. (If you answered with something like "more than 65 thousand," that's close enough!)

9. How many IP addresses exist in Class C network 192.55.0.0?

Answer: 254

10. Describe the structure of a Class A IP address.

Answer: Class A addresses have two parts: a network part and a host part. The network part is 1 octet long, and the host part is 3 octets long.

11. Describe the structure of a Class C IP address.

Answer: Class C addresses have two parts: a network part and a host part. The network part is 3 octets long, and the host part is 1 octet long.

12. What is an *octet*?

Answer: An octet is a string of 8 bits, typically referring to a portion of an IP address. IP addresses contain 4 octets, making them 32-bit numbers.

13. Define the term *IP network*. List a sample network, along with the first and last valid IP addresses.

Answer: An IP network is a set of IP addresses that have the same numeric value in the network part of the addresses. Class A network 1.0.0.0, for example, requires that all addresses begin with 1. 1.0.0.1 is the first valid IP address, and 1.255.255.254 is the last.

14. All hosts on a particular LAN segment use IP addresses that begin with 150.1.1. What network number describes the network in which these addresses reside?

Answer: Because 150 is in the range for Class B addresses, the network number is 150.1.0.0. It is formed by using the first two octets of the actual addresses, followed by 0s.

15. All hosts on a particular LAN segment use IP addresses that begin with 150.1.1. Subnetting was used, treating the first 3 octets as the subnet. What subnet number is used to represent the subnet?

Answer: 150.1.1.0. With subnetting, the subnet number includes the same value as the individual IP addresses, for the network and subnet parts of the addresses, and all 0s in the host part.

16. What is the main motivation for using IP subnetting?

Answer: Without subnetting, each physical network requires a separate Class A, B, or C network. Class A and B networks have far too many IP addresses compared to the actual need for addresses. Subnetting reduces the waste of the IP address space.

17. Describe how subnetting is accomplished, particularly how it changes or relaxes some rules about how IP addresses are structured.

Answer: Without subnetting, Class A, B, and C rules define what must be true about addresses for them to be considered part of the same group. With subnetting, a longer portion of the addresses must be in common for the addresses to be considered part of the same group. Using the longer portion of the addresses to identify the group allows you to define more groups, while making each group smaller.

18. Imagine that Class B network 128.1.0.0 is subnetted by treating the first 3 octets as if they were the network number. A network diagram requires four subnets. Describe how you might go about deciding what the addresses should look like in each subnet.

Answer: In this case, the first 3 octets of addresses in each subnet must be the same number. So, in one subnet, all addresses could start with 128.1.1; in another, 128.1.2; in another, 128.1.3; and in the fourth subnet, 128.1.4.

19. What two main functions does the IP protocol define?

Answer: Logical IP addressing and end-to-end routing of packets

Chapter 11

1. PC1 sits on an Ethernet and uses IP address 130.1.1.1. PC1 needs to send a packet to an FTP server whose IP address is 19.1.1.1. To what IP address should PC1 forward the IP packet next?

Answer: PC1 should send the packet to its default gateway IP address.

2. Imagine that PC1, with IP address 130.1.1.1, needs to send a packet. PC1 decides to send the packet to its default router, at IP address 130.1.1.2. PC1 has never sent a packet to that router. Two messages must flow over the network before PC1 can forward the packet. Identify the acronym for the protocol that defines those two messages, and state what the letters in the acronym stand for.

Answer: ARP, which stands for Address Resolution Protocol, defines a means for a LAN device to discover the LAN MAC address of another IP host on the same LAN.

3. Imagine that PC1, with IP address 130.1.1.1, needs to send a packet to its default router at IP address 130.1.1.2. Both PC1 and the router are attached to the same Ethernet switch, along with PCs Larry, Moe, and Curly. PC1 doesn't know the router's Ethernet MAC address. Name the message that PC1 sends to try to find out the router's MAC address, and identify which of the devices on the LAN will receive the message.

Answer: PC1 sends an ARP broadcast asking for 130.1.1.2 to reply with its MAC address. The ARP broadcast has a broadcast destination LAN MAC address. So, the switch forwards the ARP broadcast to the router, as well as to Larry, Moe, and Curly.

4. PC1, with IP address 130.1.1.1, needs to send a packet to Curly, at IP address 130.1.1.3. PC1's default router is the router whose IP address is 130.1.1.2. Both PCs and the router are attached to a single Ethernet switch and are in the same subnet. Describe the role of the default router for routing this packet from PC1 to Curly.

Answer: PC1 first notices that the destination, 130.1.1.3, is in the same subnet as its own IP address (130.1.1.1). As a result, PC1 knows that it can send the packet directly to Curly. PC1 sends the packet directly to Curly, ignoring its default router.

5. PC1 (130.1.1.1) is attached to an Ethernet switch. It needs to send a packet to a web server (19.1.1.1). The IP packet is sitting in memory in PC1. Describe the process of encapsulation that is required before PC1 can transmit the bits.

   Answer: Only an Ethernet frame can be transmitted onto an Ethernet LAN. Because the data link TCP/IP layer sits just below the internetwork layer, a host can reasonably expect that the Internetwork layer IP packet can be encapsulated inside a data link layer frame—in this case, an Ethernet frame. PC1 adds an Ethernet header and trailer to the IP packet, creating an Ethernet frame. The frame can then be transmitted over the Ethernet.

6. Refer to Figure 11-15 for this question. In the sample network, PC1 is sending a packet to PC2. Describe whose IP and MAC addresses would be contained in the Ethernet frame that passes between PC1 and R1.

   Answer: It would contain a source IP address of 150.1.1.1, a destination IP address of 150.1.3.3, a source MAC address of PC1's MAC address, and a destination MAC address of R1's E1 MAC address.

Figure 11-15   Internetwork Referenced in Some of the Questions in Chapter 11

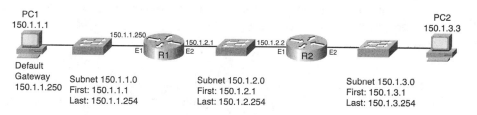

7. Refer to Figure 11-15 for this question. In the sample network, PC1 is sending a packet to PC2. Describe whose IP and MAC addresses would be contained in the Ethernet frame that passes between R2 and PC2.

   Answer: It would contain a source IP address of 150.1.1.1, a destination IP address of 150.1.3.3, a source MAC address of R2's E2 MAC address, and a destination MAC address of PC2's MAC address.

8. Refer to Figure 11-15 for this question. In the sample network, PC1 is sending a packet to PC2. Describe the contents of the routing table entry on R1
   that would be needed for R1 to forward the packet correctly.

   Answer: The routing table would have to list the destination subnet—in
   this case, 150.1.3.0. In that same routing table entry, the forwarding instructions would refer to the outgoing interface—E2 in this case—as well as the
   next-hop router, which is 150.1.2.2 in this case.

9. Refer to Figure 11-15 for this question. In the sample network, PC1 is sending a packet to PC2. Describe the contents of the routing table entry on R2
   that would be needed for R2 to forward the packet correctly.

   Answer: The routing table would have to list the destination subnet—in
   this case, 150.1.3.0. In that same routing table entry, the forwarding instructions would refer to the outgoing interface—Ethernet2 in this case—but no
   next-hop router because R2 would not need to forward the packet to another
   router.

10. Define the term "routing."

    Answer: Routing is the process of receiving a packet and comparing the IP
    destination address to a list called a routing table, which contains possible
    destinations. The matched entry defines where to forward the packet next so
    that it eventually reaches the destination.

11. Define the term "default gateway."

    Answer: For a host computer, the default gateway is the IP address to
    which that host can forward packets, relying on that router (gateway) to
    know how to forward the packet to the destination.

12. Describe the differences between routing when you are not using subnetting and when you are using subnetting.

    Answer: The routing process is no different whether you use subnetting or not. The routing table lists the groups of IP addresses that can be reached, whether they are IP networks or IP subnets.

13. Describe the logic that a host computer uses when deciding whether it needs to send a packet to its default gateway or directly to the destination host.

    Answer: The sending host looks at the destination IP address of the packet and compares it to the network or subnet to which the sending host is connected. If the destination of the IP packet is on the same network/subnet as the sender, the sender sends the packet directly to that host; otherwise, it sends the packet to the default gateway.

14. Referring to Figure 11-15, between the time that PC1 sends the packet and PC2 receives it, many things might have changed. Explain what is the same and what is different about the transmitted data. Compare what PC1 sends versus what PC2 receives.

    Answer: PC1 creates an Ethernet header and trailer to put around the IP packet, but R1 strips off the Ethernet header and trailer. R1 creates a new Ethernet header and trailer, but R2 strips those off. The only thing that is delivered across the whole internetwork from PC1 to PC2 is the IP packet.

15. This chapter suggests that you will find three items in a single routing table entry. What are they, and which one(s) are useful for knowing where to send the packet next?

    Answer: Although there might be more information in a single routing table entry in real life, this chapter focused on the destination network or subnet, the outgoing interface, and the next-hop router. The last two of these tell the router how to forward a packet.

16. Of the three parts of a routing table entry from the previous question, which one of these parts might not always be needed? Using R2 from Figure 11-15 as a reference, describe one routing table entry where that field would not be needed in the routing table entry.

    Answer: The next-hop router field is not always needed. For instance, R2 does not need to send the packets to another router to forward packets to subnet 150.1.3.0 because it is directly connected to that subnet. R2's routing table entry for subnet 150.1.3.0 would not have a next-hop router field.

Chapter 12

1. Router R4 has two working Ethernet interfaces, and each interface has been configured with an IP address. What is the least number of routes that R4 should have in its routing table, and why?

    Answer: R4 should have two routes, one for each directly connected subnet.

2. Router R4 has a working Ethernet1 interface whose IP address is 10.10.10.10. The subnet number of the subnet attached to that interface is 10.10.10.0, with all hosts that share the first 3 octets of 10.10.10 in the same subnet. List the routing table entry that R4 will place in its routing table for this route, including the destination, outgoing interface, and next-hop router fields.

    Answer: The route will list 10.10.10.0 as the subnet, Ethernet1 as the outgoing interface, and nothing as the next-hop router. For directly connected routes, no other router is needed to reach that subnet, so a next-hop router is unnecessary.

3. Referring to Figure 12-8, list the three parts of the IP route that could be statically added to R1's configuration so that it could forward packets to the web
server. Include the destination, outgoing interface, and next-hop router as
appropriate.

Answer: The route will list 173.18.13.0 as the destination subnct,
Ethernet2 as the outgoing interface, and 173.18.12.43 (R2) as the next-hop
router.

Figure 12-8   Figure Referenced in Chapter 12 Review Questions

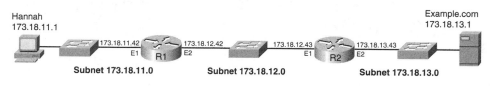

4. Referring to Figure 12-8, list the three parts of the IP route that R1 would
learn from R2 using a routing protocol. Include the destination, outgoing
interface, and next-hop router as appropriate.

Answer: This route would be identical to the route that was statically
defined in answer to question 3. The route will list 173.18.13.0 as the destination subnet, Ethernet2 as the outgoing interface, and 173.18.12.43 (R2) as
the next-hop router.

5. Referring to Figure 12-8, list the three parts of the IP route that R2 would
learn from R1 in the figure. Include the destination, outgoing interface, and
next-hop router as appropriate.

Answer: The route will list 173.18.11.0 as the destination subnet,
Ethernet1 as the outgoing interface, and 173.18.12.42 (R1) as the next-hop
router.

6. What is the primary purpose for using a routing protocol?

Answer: Routing protocols enable routers to learn the routes to all the
networks and subnets in an internetwork.

7. What is a routing update?

Answer: A routing update is a message, as defined by a routing protocol, that another router sends to advertise routes.

8. What two routing protocols are the most popular ones used today inside a single company?

Answer: EIGRP and OSPF

9. What routing protocol is most often used to exchange routing information between an ISP and its customers (exterior routing protocol)?

Answer: BGP

Chapter 13

1. What is the one alternative for name resolution that doesn't use DNS?

Answer: You can put a local host file on each TCP/IP host.

2. What does DNS stand for?

Answer: Domain Name System

3. Imagine that Lenny uses a PC inside the fredsco.com domain. Lenny opens a browser and tries to browse www.fredsco.com. His PC is configured to use DNS. How many DNS requests will Lenny's PC likely send before he gets a response to a request for host name www.fredsco.com?

Answer: Lenny's PC will send one request to the DNS server that he has configured.

4. Imagine that Lenny uses a PC inside the fredsco.com domain. Lenny opens a browser and tries to browse www.example.com. His PC is configured to use DNS. How many DNS requests will Lenny's PC likely send before he gets a response to a request for host name www.example.com?

Answer: Lenny's PC will send one request to the DNS server that he has configured and expect a response from that DNS server. Lenny's PC will not send a request to the DNS server for domain example.com; instead, Lenny's

DNS server will handle the rest of the work.

5. Imagine that Lenny uses a PC inside the fredsco.com domain. Lenny opens a browser and tries to browse www.example.com. Imagine that his PC gets a DNS response that www.example.com's IP address is 192.0.33.166. When Lenny's PC sends a packet to that web server, does the PC include the destination IP address of 192.0.33.166 in the IP packet header, or the destination name of www.example.com in the IP packet header, or both?

Answer: The IP packet header does not include a place for a host name. Lenny does put the destination IP address into the header, so that this host, along with any intermediate routers, will forward the packet correctly to that web server.

6. State whether you agree with the following statement and why: "Each TCP/IP host refers to its DNS server using a well-known IP address 0.4.1.1."

Answer: Disagree. Each TCP/IP host does need to know the IP address of its respective DNS servers, but it must know the actual IP address of the server. 0.4.1.1 is not a legal IP address, and the DNS server for each domain will have a different IP address. There is no standard IP address for a DNS server.

7. Given a name like www.example.com, identify the likely domain name, and using that example, define the term "domain name."

Answer: The domain name would be "example.com." It is likely that all names that end in "example.com" are resolved by an authoritative DNS server controlled by the same company that registered to use "example.com" as a domain name. A domain name simply identifies the authority, organization, or company that controls all names that end in that suffix.

8. When a client inside one company tries to browse a web server in another company, using a name, describe in general terms how the authoritative name server for the web server name is found.

Answer: The user's host asks its DNS server to resolve the name. The local DNS doesn't know the name because the name is in another domain. The local DNS asks a root name server for help. The root refers the local DNS to another DNS server, which might be the authoritative DNS for that name. The local DNS now asks this newly discovered DNS server for help.

That DNS server would return the correct IP address to the original IP host.

9. State whether you agree with the following statement and why: "When a user who is configured to use DNS opens a web browser and types in www.example.com, the next IP packet that he sends is to the web server."

Answer: Disagree. The first packet would be the DNS resolution request to the DNS server. After the host learns the IP address of that web server, it will send packets to the server.

Chapter 14

1. How many twisted pairs of wires are typically used in a leased line between two routers?

   Answer: Two pairs are used, one for transmission in each direction.

2. Imagine that you wanted to create a WAN link between two routers (Router A and Router B) in cities that are 1000 miles apart. How long are the cables that the telco needs to run?

   Answer: The telco would probably just need to run a cable from its local CO in each city to the office building in that city where each router resides. Those cables might be several miles long. The telco would not need to run a cable between cities because it already has those cables installed.

3. What is a WAN link?

   Answer: A WAN link is a physical transmission medium between two end points, as created by a telco. WAN links typically connect devices that are not in the same building or office campus.

4. What are some of the other names for a WAN link?

   Answer: Leased line, leased circuit, point-to-point link, and serial link 4-wire circuit

5. Explain whether point-to-point WAN links need something like the Ethernet CSMA/CD algorithm.

   Answer: There is no need for an algorithm like CSMA/CD for WAN links. A router that is connected to a WAN link can send anytime it wants to send.

6. What kind of physical interface does a router use to connect to a WAN link?

   Answer: A serial interface

7. Imagine that a WAN link has been installed between routers A and B. The physical cable from the telco was plugged directly into the serial interfaces on the routers. What feature must be included in the serial interface cards on these routers to allow the cable to be connected directly to the routers?

   Answer: An internal CSU/DSU must be installed on the card. The engineer who orders the router would make that choice when ordering.

8. What is the main function of the CSU/DSU, as covered in this chapter?

   Answer: To control the transmission speed on the link

9. What is the base transmission speed typically used for WAN links that run at relatively lower speeds (up to 1.5 Mbps)?

   Answer: WAN links typically use a transmission speed of 64 Kbps, or a multiple of that number, up through 24 times 64 Kbps, or about 1.5 Mbps.

10. What are the two most popular data link protocols used on WAN links?

    Answer: HDLC and PPP

11. What does HDLC do to alert a router that is receiving a frame that an error has occurred?

    Answer: HDLC, as well as PPP, includes an FCS field in the trailer.

12. Of the two more popular WAN link data link protocols, which was developed later and has more features?

    Answer: PPP

13. Explain whether IP ARP is needed on WAN links. Why or why not?

Answer: There is no need for IP ARP on a WAN link. The PPP and HDLC address fields do not carry a meaningful number because anything sent out a point-to-point WAN link always goes to the same place. There is no need to identify the recipient of the frame anyway.

Chapter 15

1. What layers of the OSI model does Frame Relay cover?

Answer: Just Layer 2. Frame Relay uses the same Layer 1 specifications that point-to-point WAN links use.

2. What is the name of the field in the Frame Relay header that identifies a PVC? Give the acronym and what the acronym stands for.

Answer: DLCI—data-link connection identifier

3. Imagine that a company has a router, router A, at its headquarters. The router will use point-to-point WAN links to send and receive traffic to and from five remote sites. How many 4-wire cables need to be run from router A to the telco CO near router A?

Answer: You would need one 4-wire cable for each WAN link, or a total of five.

4. Imagine that a company has a router, router A, at its headquarters. The router will use Frame Relay to send and receive traffic to and from five remote sites. How many 4-wire cables need to be run from router A to the telco CO?

Answer: Only one 4-wire cable would be needed.

5. What term is used to describe the cable from a router to the CO when the router uses Frame Relay?

Answer: Access link

6. Define the term "PVC."

   Answer: PVC refers to the ability to transfer Frame Relay frames between two devices that are attached to the same Frame Relay network when the provider has preconfigured that ability. "PVC" stands for permanent virtual circuit.

7. Does the access rate or the CIR define how many bits per second the telco commits to pass over a single PVC?

   Answer: CIR

8. Does the access rate or the CIR define the clock rate of the physical link between a router and the local CO?

   Answer: Access rate

9. What does the acronym CIR stand for?

   Answer: Committed information rate

10. Define the meaning of the term "DLCI."

   Answer: The data-link connection identifier (DLCI) is a 10-bit number, usually written in decimal (range 0–1023), which identifies an individual Frame Relay PVC.

11. Explain why the term "virtual circuit" is used to describe how Frame Relay sends data to and from a pair of routers.

   Answer: One term for a WAN link between two routers is "leased circuit," or simply "circuit." Frame Relay allows a pair of routers to send and receive data. However, there is no real physical cable or line associated with each VC, so the term "virtual" refers to the fact that it's not physical, and the term "circuit" refers to the fact that it acts like a leased circuit in some ways.

12. Explain the need for IP ARP on Frame Relay PVCs.

   Answer: There is a need for something like ARP so that after a router knows the IP address to which it should forward the packet, it can then find the right data link address to put in the data link header of the frame. With Frame Relay, ARP is not used; instead, Inverse ARP is used.

Chapter 16

1. According to this book, what are the three major components of the Internet?

   Answer: Networks built by ISPs, enterprise networks built by individual organizations, and the individual users who connect to an ISP

2. Leased lines provide a service of forwarding bits, whereas Frame Relay provides a service of forwarding Frame Relay frames. With that same perspective, explain the service that the Internet supplies to hosts.

   Answer: The Internet provides a service of forwarding IP packets.

3. What is different about the type of electrical signal sent over the local loop by a phone, versus a modem?

   Answer: There is no difference. Both phones and modems send an analog electrical signal.

4. What is different about the type of electrical signal sent over the local loop by a phone, versus a DSL modem?

   Answer: The DSL modem sends a digital electrical signal, whereas the phone sends an analog electrical signal.

5. What two features of analog electrical signals, mentioned in this book, can a modem vary or change to encode a binary 0 or 1?

   Answer: Modems can vary, or modulate, the frequency and amplitude.

6. Approximately what speed is the maximum transmission speed with modems?

   Answer: 56 Kbps

7. Approximately what speed is the maximum transmission speed with DSL modems when the distance from the home to the CO is relatively long?

   Answer: 384 Kbps

8. For DSL to work, the telco splits the data out from the voice using what kind of device?

   Answer: A DSL access multiplexer (DSLAM)

9. What does DSL stand for?

Answer: Digital subscriber line

10. What does modem stand for?

Answer: Modem is not an acronym, but the term is formed by shortening and combining *modulate* and *demodulate*.

11. Which of the three Internet access technologies covered in this chapter does not allow you to talk on the phone while using the Internet?

Answer: Modems

12. What Layer 2 protocol is typically used when using a modem or DSL to connect to an ISP?

Answer: PPP

Chapter 17

1. What does the acronym AAA stand for—at least the networking version of it?

Answer: Authentication, authorization, accounting

2. What information does a user typically supply to perform authorization?

Answer: Username and password

3. What is the one major fact that was mentioned in this book regarding good information to report about using the accounting function of AAA?

Answer: To report repeated invalid authentication attempts for the same username

4. What is the difference between authorization and authentication?

Answer: Authorization defines what you're allowed to access, but authentication confirms that you are who you say you are.

5. Comparing a LAN-based user inside a company to a corporate employee working via the Internet from home, what other security step does the home user typically have to go through?

   Answer: Internet users need to authenticate to the ISP when they connect before they can access the ISP's network. For LAN-based users inside a corporate location, there is the presumption that they have the right to access the LAN, so there is no authentication for the right to access the LAN. Interestingly, more corporations in the coming years will likely require authentication before allowing a user to use a LAN.

6. Which two protocols that are part of PPP are used for authentication?

   Answer: PAP and CHAP

7. Of the two PPP protocols used for authentication, which passes the password in clear-text?

   Answer: PAP

8. How does CHAP prevent someone from using a tool such as a sniffer to see the packets sent over a network and learn the password?

   Answer: CHAP passes a message digest, which is a mathematical function based on a random number and the password. Message digests use mathematical functions that are designed specifically to prevent the re-creation of the password.

9. What feature of a VPN prevents packets that someone else has captured from being useful to him?

   Answer: The packets that are sent over a VPN connection have been encrypted.

10. What are the two terms, one named for a particularly popular product, that refer to tools that can capture packets on a LAN?

   Answer: Network analysis tool and Sniffer

Chapter 18

1. What restrictions are typically placed on clients inside a corporate network, in terms of what Internet-based servers they are allowed to use?

   Answer: Although the answer is somewhat subjective, most of the time, clients inside a company can connect to any Internet servers that they want to connect to.

2. What restrictions are typically placed on clients on the Internet who want to connect to servers inside a corporate network, assuming that corporation uses a firewall?

   Answer: The corporate firewall typically prevents Internet-based clients from connecting to servers inside the corporate network, except for those servers that are intended specifically for use by the general public.

3. How does a firewall figure out the IP address of a host that is trying to initiate a new TCP connection?

   Answer: The firewall looks at TCP segments that have the TCP SYN flag set, and only that flag. That segment is the first segment in a new TCP connection. The firewall then simply looks at the source IP address of the packet.

4. How does a firewall figure out what application protocol is being used?

   Answer: The firewall looks at TCP segments that have the TCP SYN flag set, and only that flag. That segment is the first segment in a new TCP connection. The firewall looks at the destination TCP port number, which is the well-known port that particular application protocol uses.

5. What term does a firewall typically use to refer to the corporate network?

   Answer: The inside network

6. What term does a firewall typically use to refer to a small LAN that is less secure than the internal corporate network, but more secure than the Internet connection?

   Answer: The DMZ

7. Consider the following statement: "Firewalls let packets go from the corporate network to the Internet, but they do not let packets go from the Internet back to the corporate network." State whether you agree or disagree, and explain why.

    Answer: Disagree. Firewalls let packets through in both directions because packets must flow in both directions for an application to be useful. Firewalls allow packets in both directions, but only for packets that meet the rules configured on the firewall.

8. What does IDS stand for?

    Answer: Intrusion detection system

9. Comparing network-based IDS devices and firewalls, which one is typically in the path through which packets are forwarded?

    Answer: Firewall

10. Define "signature" in terms of use with IDS and anti-virus software.

    Answer: The word "signature" refers to the description of which packets and files look like attempts by a cracker to deny service or to put a virus on a computer.

11. Which two TCP/IP applications most often allow the transfer of files to a computer, with those files possibly containing a computer virus?

    Answer: Web (HTTP) and e-mail (POP3)

Converting IP Addresses Between Decimal and Binary

As mentioned in Chapter 10, "Delivering the Goods to the Right Street (IP) Address," IP addresses are 32-bit binary numbers, but they are also frequently written and seen as decimal numbers. Although you could read Chapter 10 without thinking about IP addresses in their binary format, if you decide to read further to gain more knowledge about IP and IP addressing, you need to understand binary decimal, and how to convert numbers between each format.

Many of the books that tell you more about IP addressing and subnetting don't really tell you how to do the math to convert the numbers. Often, they suggest that you use a calculator or use a conversion chart like the one shown later in this appendix. Both of those options are reasonable. However, to prepare you for the future, if you decide to learn even more about IP, this appendix gives you the basics of decimal and binary conversion, including how to convert IP addresses between the two types of numbers.

This appendix includes three main sections. The first section explains decimal and binary numbering. The second section describes how to convert numbers from decimal to binary, and vice versa. Finally, the third section closes with some details of how to convert decimal and binary IP addresses to the other numbering system.

Decimal and Binary Numbering Systems

This section starts with a description of the familiar decimal numbering system, followed by the binary numbering system.

Decimal Numbering System

The decimal numbering system should be familiar to everyone reading this book, because it's what you've been taught since early childhood. However, unless you love math, there are a few details that you might have forgotten about decimals that will help you better appreciate binary numbering; those details will be covered in this section.

Consider, for example, the number 235. The number is made up of three numerals—2, 3, and 5. *Numerals* are simply symbols that represent a number; the word *digit*, short for *decimal digit*, is often used instead of *numeral*. For instance, 3 is the second digit of the number 235.

What does the number 235 really mean? Well, if you say the equivalent in English, you say something like "two-hundred thirty-five." To better appreciate how other numbering systems—such as binary—work, consider a contrived and unusual expansion of the English language version of 235, as follows:

Two 100s, three 10s, and five 1s

It's a lot easier to say "two-hundred thirty-five" than "two 100s, three 10s, and five 1s." However, they both basically mean the same thing. You could even think of it in mathematical terms:

(2*100) + (3*10) + (5*1) = 235

Both the contrived English phrasing and the mathematical formula describe the core meaning of a multidigit decimal number. Each decimal digit represents its own value multiplied by a value associated with that digit's position in the number. It's more obvious with a table, such as Table B-1.

Table B-1   Decimal Numbering: 1s, 10s, and 100s Digits

Value Associated with That Digit or Column	100	10	1
The digits	2	3	5

With decimal numbering, the right-most digit in a number represents a value of that digit times 1; the second from the right represents the value of the digit times 10; and the third from the right represents a value of that digit times 100. This same logic continues for larger numbers, with each successive digit to the left having a value 10 times the digit to its right. In this example, the 5 means 5 times 1 because it's in the 1s column. Similarly, the single digit in the 10s column represents 3 times 10. Finally, the 2 in the 100s digit column means 2 times 100.

With decimal, each digit, going right-to-left, represents a multiple of an increasing power of 10. The rightmost digit of a decimal number lists the number of 1s, if you will, because $10^0 = 1$. That digit is called the *1s digit*. The second digit from the right is the number of 10s, called the *10s digit*, because $10^1 = 10$; the third from the right is the *100s digit*, because $10^2 = 100$; and so on.

Because you've used it all your life, the math is probably so intuitive that you really don't need to think about it to this depth. However, thinking about decimal in this way will help you appreciate binary. For instance, decimal numbering works with the 1s, 10s, and 100s digits because you only have 10 numerals to work with—0, 1, 2, 3, 4, 5, 6, 7, 8, and 9. If you count starting at 0, after you reach 9, you're out of numerals; there is no single symbol or numeral that represents the idea behind the number 10. So, to write down a number bigger than 9, you need at least two digits—one that represents a multiple of 10 and another that represents a multiple of 1.

Next, you'll see how binary numbering works on the same basic premise, but with just two numerals or digits.

Binary Numbering System

Binary numbering is just a different way to represent numbers than decimal numbering. Both decimal numbering and binary numbering use numerals or digits to represent the idea of a particular number. However, binary uses just two digits—0 and 1.

Binary numbering works on the same general principles as decimal numbering, but with differences in the details. The best way to understand the similarities and differences is to look at a sample binary number. Binary is simply another way to write a number. For each decimal number, you can write the same number in binary. For instance, the following binary number is the equivalent of the decimal number 235:

11101011

If you worked with numbers a lot, it would probably be more convenient to use a three-digit decimal number, instead of this eight-digit binary number. However, sometimes it's better to work with the binary number. In particular, computers tend to process things using binary, so many computing topics require you to be able to examine and understand binary numbers. Also, when you work with networks and plan and implement IP subnetting, you need to be able to work with binary numbers.

Like with decimal, a multidigit binary number has assigned values for each digit in the number. For instance, Table B-2 shows 11101011, with values assigned to each digit.

Table B-2   Binary Numbering: 1s, 2s, 4s, 8s (and so on) Digits

Value Associated with That Digit or Column	128	64	32	16	8	4	2	1
The number itself	1	1	1	0	1	0	1	1

With decimal, the digits in a multidigit decimal number represent various powers of 10. The same kind of thing happens in binary, with the rightmost binary digit meaning the number of 1s (2^0), the second from the right representing the number of 2s (2^1), the third from the right representing the number of 4s (2^2), and so on.

Table B-2 shows the value associated with each digit (or column), with each being a consecutive power of 2, increasing from left to right. So, what does this really mean? Well, just like the decimal number 235 means (2*100) + (3*10) + (5*1) = 235, the binary number 11101011 means the following:

(1*128) + (1*64) + (1*32) + (0*16) + (1*8) + (0*4) + (1*2) + (1*1) = 235 decimal

If you add up the numbers, you actually get the number 235 in decimal. The numbers 235 (decimal) and 11101011 (binary) both represent the same number; they're just written in different formats.

Converting Between Binary and Decimal Numbers

You read earlier in this appendix that binary was simply a different way to write numbers as compared to decimal. In some cases, it's easier to work with one format or the other. However, you might only see the decimal version of the number, and you need to work with the binary version. Or the opposite could be true. That's why it's useful to be able to convert between the two formats.

note
The remainder of this appendix only uses examples with binary numbers that require eight or fewer digits.

Converting from Binary to Decimal

Converting from binary to decimal is actually pretty straightforward, at least compared to converting from decimal to binary. In fact, you've already seen the math in the text after Table B-2. To convert a binary number to decimal, you have to think about the binary number in a table, such as Table B-3, and apply what the table's numbers mean.

Table B-3   Example of Binary-to-Decimal Conversion: 10101101

Value Associated with That Digit or Column	128	64	32	16	8	4	2	1
The number itself	1	0	1	0	1	1	0	1

Table B-3 looks just like Table B-2, except the binary number is slightly different. To convert to decimal, you simply multiply each pair of numbers that are in the same column in the table and then add them together. Table B-4 repeats the same information, but now with the products shown.

Table B-4   Converting 10101101 to Decimal: Multiplying Each Column and Then Adding Them Together

Value associated with that digit or column	128	64	32	16	8	4	2	1
The number itself	1	0	1	0	1	1	0	1
Product of two numbers in the same column	128	0	32	0	8	4	0	1
Sum of all numbers in third row	173							

The process is indeed simple, as long as you remember all the powers of 2! When you're working with IP addressing, you'll need to memorize all the powers of 2 up through 2^8, or 256. (The lowest powers of 2 are listed in Table B-5 later in this appendix.) The basic algorithm to convert binary to decimal can be summarized as follows:

Step 1 Write down the powers of 2, in decimal, in the top row of a table, similar to Table B-4.

Step 2 On the second line, write down the binary number that is to be converted, lining up each binary digit under the powers of 2.

Step 3 Multiply each pair of numbers (the numbers in the same column) together and then total those products.

Converting from Decimal to Binary

Converting from decimal to binary doesn't take any difficult math, but the algorithm is a little longer. In this section, you'll read about a general algorithm for converting from decimal to binary, followed by a couple of examples.

The general algorithm is as follows:

Step 1 Find the decimal power of 2 that is closest to, but not larger than, the decimal number being converted.

Step 2 Write down a binary 1 as the left-most binary digit of the new binary number.

Step 3 Subtract that power of 2 from the original decimal number. (The resulting number will be called the *remainder* in this algorithm.)

Step 4 Repeat the following steps until the steps have been completed for the case in which the power of 2 is 1 (2^0). As a result of passing through these steps repeatedly, another binary digit—either 0 or 1—will be added to the right side of the binary number for each pass through this step:

    a. If the next lower power of 2 (compared to the previous step) is larger than the remainder, write down a binary 0 as the next binary digit.

    b. Otherwise, write down a binary 1 as the next digit. Also, subtract the current power of 2 from the remainder, with the resulting remainder being used as the remainder in the next pass through Step 4.

To appreciate how to use this algorithm, you need to either know the powers of 2 or have them listed somewhere handy. Table B-5 lists the powers of 2 that will be used in this appendix.

Table B-5   Decimal Powers of 2

Power of 2	Decimal Value
2^0	1
2^1	2
2^2	4
2^3	8
2^4	16
2^5	32
2^6	64
2^7	128
2^8	256

The first example will be the conversion of decimal 235 into binary 11101011. To make the conversion happen, the following describes the first 3 steps of the algorithm:

1. The closest power of 2 not bigger than 235 is 128.

2. The first binary digit will be 1.

3. The remainder is calculated as $235 - 128 = 107$. The first pass through Step 4 of the algorithm will use this remainder value.

Although describing these first three steps might be helpful, putting the same information into a table can help as well. Because the eventual binary number will be an eight-digit binary number in this example, the table will have places for eight digits. (When you use this algorithm, you might not know how many digits the new binary number will have, so leave plenty of space on the right side of your paper.) Table B-6 shows the details of the first three steps.

Table B-6   First Three Steps of Converting Decimal 235 to Binary

Decimal Number to Be Converted	235
2^x closest to number, not bigger than the number	128
Binary number	1
Remainder	107

You do Step 4 repetitively for each successive lower power of 2, until you complete Step 4 for 2^0, or 1. Because the first 3 steps used 2^7 (128), the first pass through Step 4 uses 2^6 (64) as the power of 2, as shown in Table B-7.

Table B-7   First Pass Through Step 4 of the Conversion Algorithm, with 2^6 (64) as the Power of 2

Decimal Number to Be Converted	235	
Remainder (from previous step/column)	—	**107**
Next lower 2^x value as compared to previous step	—	**64**
Binary number	1	**1**
Remainder	107	**43**

This first pass through Step 4 adds another digit to the converted binary number— in this case, a binary 1. The next lower power of 2 is 64 in this case. The remainder from the previous step was 107, so from the generic algorithm, Step 4A is not used because 64 is not bigger than 107. Step 4B is used, so the next digit's value is a binary 1, and a new remainder (107 – 64 = 43) is calculated.

Next, Step 4 is repeated with the next lower power of 2, 2^5 (32), as shown in Table B-8.

Table B-8   Second Pass Through Step 4, for 2^5 (32)

Decimal Number to Be Converted	235		
Remainder (from previous step/column)	—	107	**43**
Next lower 2^x value as compared to previous step	—	64	**32**
Binary number	1	1	**1**
Remainder	107	43	**11**

As in Table B-7, the pass through Step 4 shown in Table B-8 adds another binary 1 to the binary number, with the remainder being recalculated. In the next step, for 2^4 (16), the power of 2 is bigger than the remainder, yielding a binary 0 for the next digit. Table B-9 shows the values.

Table B-9   Third Pass Through Step 4, for 2^4 (16)

Decimal Number to Be Converted	235			
Remainder (from previous step/column)	—	107	43	**11**
Next lower 2^x value as compared to previous step	—	64	32	**16**
Binary number	1	1	1	**0**
Remainder	107	43	11	**11**

You're halfway through the example now, but hopefully, the general idea of how Step 4 works is becoming more obvious. Table B-10 summarizes the next three passes through Step 4.

Table B-10   Fourth, Fifth, and Sixth Passes Through Step 4

Decimal Number to Be Converted	235						
Remainder (from previous step/column)	—	107	43	11	**11**	**3**	**3**
Next lower 2^x value as compared to previous step	—	64	32	16	**8**	**4**	**2**
Binary number	1	1	1	0	**1**	**0**	**1**
Remainder	107	43	11	11	**3**	**3**	**1**

With a power of 2 of 2^3, another binary 1 was added to the binary number. For 2^2 (4), 4 is larger than the remainder of 3, so a binary digit of 0 was added to the number. Finally, in the third of the 3 bold columns, for 2^1 (2), 2 is less than the remainder of 3, causing a binary digit of 1 to be added, with the remainder being recalculated as 1.

The final pass through Step 4 is shown in Table B-11. The logic is not any different from the other passes through Step 4, other than the fact that you should know that this is the last time to use Step 4 because the next lower power of 2, 2^0 (1), is the last possible digit in a binary number.

Table B-11   Last Pass Through Step 4, for 2^0 (1)

Decimal Number to Be Converted	235							
Remainder (from previous step/column)		107	43	11	11	3	3	1
Next lower 2^x value as compared to previous step		64	32	16	8	4	2	**1**
Binary number	1	1	1	0	1	0	1	**1**
Remainder	107	43	11	11	3	3	1	**0**

With the completion of this step, the whole binary conversion process is complete. Binary number 11101011 is the binary equivalent of decimal 235.

The next example shows how to convert decimal 100 to binary. Table B-12 shows Steps 1 through 3. Table B-13 shows the passes through Step 4 except for the final pass. Table B-14 shows the final pass through Step 4.

Table B-12   First Three Steps of Converting Decimal 100 to Binary

Decimal Number to Be Converted	100
2^x closest to number, not bigger than	64
Binary number	1
Remainder	36

Table B-13   Passes Through Step 4 for 2^x Values of 32, 16, 8, 4, and 2 of Decimal-to-Binary Conversion of Decimal 100

Decimal Number to Be Converted	100					
Remainder (from previous step/column)	—	36	4	4	4	0
Next lower 2^x value as compared to previous step	—	32	16	8	4	2
Binary number	1	1	0	0	1	0
Remainder	36	4	4	4	0	0

Table B-14   Final Pass Through Step 4 of Decimal-to-Binary Conversion of Decimal 100

Decimal Number to Be Converted	100						
Remainder (from previous step/column)	—	36	4	4	4	0	0
Next lower 2^x value as compared to previous step	—	32	16	8	4	2	1
Binary number	1	1	0	0	1	0	0
Remainder	36	4	4	4	0	0	0

As you see from the final result in Table B-14, decimal 100 has a binary equivalent of the 7-digit number 1100100.

Now that you have seen how to convert from decimal to binary, and vice versa, this appendix will close with an examination of how to convert decimal IP addresses to their binary version, and vice versa.

Converting IP Addresses

IP addresses are 32-bit binary numbers, but because humans would find it inconvenient to write down 32-bit numbers, the addresses are written in decimal. The format of decimal IP addresses is often called *canonical* format, and sometimes called *dotted decimal* format. For example, the next two lines show the binary version of an IP address, followed by the same IP address written as a dotted decimal number. It's obvious from comparing the two that, given a choice, it's typically much easier to work with the decimal version:

00001000 00000100 00000010 00000001

8.4.2.1

The next two sections cover the conversion process for IP addresses, first from decimal to binary, and then vice versa.

Converting Decimal IP Addresses to Binary IP Addresses

You have already read about the math behind the conversion process between decimal and binary. To convert IP addresses, you simply need to follow a few additional rules:

1. When converting from a decimal IP address to binary, each of the 4 decimal numbers in the decimal IP address converts to an 8-bit number, giving you a total of 32 bits.

2. If a decimal number converts to a binary number that has less than 8 digits, put binary 0s in front of the number to create an 8-digit binary number.

3. The 32-bit binary IP address is formed by simply writing down each of the 4 sets of 8 bits in order.

In other words, to convert a decimal IP address to its 32-bit binary equivalent, you would convert each of the 4 decimal numbers in a decimal IP address to a binary number. You might recall from Chapter 10 that each of the 4 numbers in a decimal IP address, separated by periods, is called an octet. Essentially, you convert each of the 4 decimal octets to 8-bit binary numbers. For any of these binary numbers that converted to less than 8 digits, you would put binary 0s to the left to make them 8 digits long. Finally, just think of the 4 octets as one long 32-bit number, and you're done!

Table B-15 shows a sample conversion of the IP address 100.235.2.2.

Table B-15   Conversion of Decimal IP Address 100.235.2.2 to Binary

	First Octet	**Second Octet**	**Third Octet**	**Fourth Octet**
Decimal octet	100	235	2	2
Each octet converted to binary (Step 1)	1100100	11101011	10	10
Binary octets, after putting 0s in front (Step 2)	0**1**100100	11101011	**00000010**	**00000010**
Resulting 32-bit number (Step 3)	0110010011101011000000010000000010			

Table B-15 begins with the decimal IP address in the first row, and the results of each of the three conversion steps in the next three rows. The actual math for converting the decimal numbers (Step 1) is not shown, but you can refer to the previous section for examples using decimal 100 and 235. For the first, third, and fourth octets, the converted binary numbers are less than 8 bits long, so at Step 2, binary 0s were added to the left to make them all 8 bits long. Step 3 just lists all

32 bits in succession. In real life, there's no need to actually write down Step 3; you can just see the 4 sets of 8 bits all in a row and think of it as a 32-bit number.

Converting Binary IP Addresses to Decimal IP Addresses

To convert from a binary IP address to its decimal equivalent, you already know the 32-bit IP address. The process is rather simple compared to converting from decimal to binary:

Step 1   Separate the 32 bits into 4 groups of 8 bits (4 octets).

Step 2   Convert each binary octet to decimal.

Step 3   Put a period between the four decimal numbers.

The algorithm can be shown with a sample binary value— 01100100111010110000000100000001. Table B-16 organizes the bits into octets with 8 bits each.

Table B-16   Conversion of Binary IP Address to Decimal

	First Octet	Second Octet	Third Octet	Fourth Octet
Binary value, separated into 4 octets (Step 1)	01100100	11101011	00000001	00000001
Each octet converted to decimal (Step 2)	100	235	1	1
Decimal IP address in dotted decimal format (Step 3)				100.235.1.1

The resulting IP address, with the periods added, would be 100.235.1.1. The math used for the conversion was covered in the section titled "Converting from Binary to Decimal" earlier in this appendix. But the conversion process is not the tricky part. When you start with a 32-bit number, as long as you organize it into 4 sets of

8 bits (4 binary octets), you can go through the math to convert each 8-bit binary to decimal. However, if you misstep and convert a 9-bit binary to decimal and then a 7-bit binary number to decimal, you'll be converting the number incorrectly.

Using a Conversion Chart

Now you understand the basics of how decimal and binary work and how to convert between the two. You also know a few rules you must follow when converting IP addresses between the two formats.

You can always use a calculator to do the math of converting a decimal number to binary, or vice versa. Because IP addresses only use decimal numbers between 0 and 255, you can also use a binary/decimal conversion chart. A binary/decimal conversion chart simply lists decimal numbers along with their binary equivalents. That way, you can look in the chart and find the numbers without using all the math covered earlier in this appendix.

For instance, to convert 100.235.1.1 to binary, you could look in the chart and find the decimal number 100. Beside it, you would find the 8-bit binary number 01100100. You would simply write those digits down as the first 8 binary digits. Next, you would find 235 in the chart, find the binary value beside it—namely 11101011—and write that down.

You can also use the chart to convert from binary IP addresses to decimal. You follow the same algorithm, but instead of doing the math, you find the 8-bit binary number in the chart and record the decimal number beside it as the value of the IP address in that octet.

Table B-17 lists a binary/decimal conversion chart for your reference. Note that all the binary numbers are shown as 8-digit numbers, because when they're used for converting IP addresses, you will want a full 8 bits for each octet.

Table B-17 Binary/Decimal Conversion Chart

Decimal Value	Binary Value	Decimal Value	Binary Value
0	0000 0000	23	0001 0111
1	0000 0001	24	0001 1000
2	0000 0010	25	0001 1001
3	0000 0011	26	0001 1010
4	0000 0100	27	0001 1011
5	0000 0101	28	0001 1100
6	0000 0110	29	0001 1101
7	0000 0111	30	0001 1110
8	0000 1000	31	0001 1111
9	0000 1001	32	0010 0000
10	0000 1010	33	0010 0001
11	0000 1011	34	0010 0010
12	0000 1100	35	0010 0011
13	0000 1101	36	0010 0100
14	0000 1110	37	0010 0101
15	0000 1111	38	0010 0110
16	0001 0000	39	0010 0111
17	0001 0001	40	0010 1000
18	0001 0010	41	0010 1001
19	0001 0011	42	0010 1010
20	0001 0100	43	0010 1011
21	0001 0101	44	0010 1100
22	0001 0110	45	0010 1101

continues

Table B-17   Binary/Decimal Conversion Chart (continued)

Decimal Value	Binary Value	Decimal Value	Binary Value
46	0010 1110	70	0100 0110
47	0010 1111	71	0100 0111
48	0011 0000	72	0100 1000
49	0011 0001	73	0100 1001
50	0011 0010	74	0100 1010
51	0011 0011	75	0100 1011
52	0011 0100	76	0100 1100
53	0011 0101	77	0100 1101
54	0011 0110	78	0100 1110
55	0011 0111	79	0100 1111
56	0011 1000	80	0101 0000
57	0011 1001	81	0101 0001
58	0011 1010	82	0101 0010
59	0011 1011	83	0101 0011
60	0011 1100	84	0101 0100
61	0011 1101	85	0101 0101
62	0011 1110	86	0101 0110
63	0011 1111	87	0101 0111
64	0100 0000	88	0101 1000
65	0100 0001	89	0101 1001
66	0100 0010	90	0101 1010
67	0100 0011	91	0101 1011
68	0100 0100	92	0101 1100
69	0100 0101	93	0101 1101

Table B-17   Binary/Decimal Conversion Chart (continued)

Decimal Value	Binary Value	Decimal Value	Binary Value
94	0101 1110	118	0111 0110
95	0101 1111	119	0111 0111
96	0110 0000	120	0111 1000
97	0110 0001	121	0111 1001
98	0110 0010	122	0111 1010
99	0110 0011	123	0111 1011
100	0110 0100	124	0111 1100
101	0110 0101	125	0111 1101
102	0110 0110	126	0111 1110
103	0110 0111	127	0111 1111
104	0110 1000	128	1000 0000
105	0110 1001	129	1000 0001
106	0110 1010	130	1000 0010
107	0110 1011	131	1000 0011
108	0110 1100	132	1000 0100
109	0110 1101	133	1000 0101
110	0110 1110	134	1000 0110
111	0110 1111	135	1000 0111
112	0111 0000	136	1000 1000
113	0111 0001	137	1000 1001
114	0111 0010	138	1000 1010
115	0111 0011	139	1000 1011
116	0111 0100	140	1000 1100
117	0111 0101	141	1000 1101

continues

Table B-17   Binary/Decimal Conversion Chart (continued)

Decimal Value	Binary Value	Decimal Value	Binary Value
142	1000 1110	166	1010 0110
143	1000 1111	167	1010 0111
144	1001 0000	168	1010 1000
145	1001 0001	169	1010 1001
146	1001 0010	170	1010 1010
147	1001 0011	171	1010 1011
148	1001 0100	172	1010 1100
149	1001 0101	173	1010 1101
150	1001 0110	174	1010 1110
151	1001 0111	175	1010 1111
152	1001 1000	176	1011 0000
153	1001 1001	177	1011 0001
154	1001 1010	178	1011 0010
155	1001 1011	179	1011 0011
156	1001 1100	180	1011 0100
157	1001 1101	181	1011 0101
158	1001 1110	182	1011 0110
159	1001 1111	183	1011 0111
160	1010 0000	184	1011 1000
161	1010 0001	185	1011 1001
162	1010 0010	186	1011 1010
163	1010 0011	187	1011 1011
164	1010 0100	188	1011 1100
165	1010 0101	189	1011 1101

Table B-17 Binary/Decimal Conversion Chart (continued)

Decimal Value	Binary Value	Decimal Value	Binary Value
190	1011 1110	214	1101 0110
191	1011 1111	215	1101 0111
192	1100 0000	216	1101 1000
193	1100 0001	217	1101 1001
194	1100 0010	218	1101 1010
195	1100 0011	219	1101 1011
196	1100 0100	220	1101 1100
197	1100 0101	221	1101 1101
198	1100 0110	222	1101 1110
199	1100 0111	223	1101 1111
200	1100 1000	224	1110 0000
201	1100 1001	225	1110 0001
202	1100 1010	226	1110 0010
203	1100 1011	227	1110 0011
204	1100 1100	228	1110 0100
205	1100 1101	229	1110 0101
206	1100 1110	230	1110 0110
207	1100 1111	231	1110 0111
208	1101 0000	232	1110 1000
209	1101 0001	233	1110 1001
210	1101 0010	234	1110 1010
211	1101 0011	235	1110 1011
212	1101 0100	236	1110 1100
213	1101 0101	237	1110 1101

continues

Table B-17 Binary/Decimal Conversion Chart (continued)

Decimal Value	Binary Value	Decimal Value	Binary Value
238	1110 1110	247	1111 0111
239	1110 1111	248	1111 1000
240	1111 0000	249	1111 1001
241	1111 0001	250	1111 1010
242	1111 0010	251	1111 1011
243	1111 0011	252	1111 1100
244	1111 0100	253	1111 1101
245	1111 0101	254	1111 1110
246	1111 0110	255	1111 1111

Chapter Summary

For reading this book, you can mainly ignore the binary version of IP addresses. However, if you intend to learn more about IP, you will certainly want to know how to work with IP addresses in their binary format. This appendix explained the basics of binary numbering, how to convert back and forth between binary and decimal, as well as how to convert back and forth between the decimal and binary formats of IP addresses.

If you would like more practice, or you would like to learn more about numbering systems, feel free to check out some of the following websites:

- For basic information on base 10, base 2 (binary), and conversion practice, visit http://www.ibilce.unesp.br/courseware/datas/numbers.htm#mark2.

- For a description of the conversion process, try http://www.doit.ort.org/course/inforep/135.htm.

- For another description of the conversion process, try http://www.goshen.edu/compsci/mis200/decbinary.htm.

Glossary

1s digit   In mathematics, in a number with multiple digits or numerals, this is the digit on the far-right end of the multidigit number. This digit represents the value of the digit timcs 1.

4-wire circuit   A reference to the fact that a leased line typically uses two pairs of wires.

10 GigE   An abbreviation of the term *10 Gigabit Ethernet*.

10 Gigabit Ethernet   An Ethernet standard that transmits data at 10 billion bits per second, or 10 Gigabits per second.

10/100 NIC   An Ethernet NIC that can run at either 10 Mbps or 100 Mbps, including autonegotiation of the speed and duplex setting.

10BaseT   A name for 10 Mbps Ethernet when using twisted-pair cabling.

10s digit   In mathematics, in a decimal number with multiple digits or numerals, this is the digit second from the right end of the multidigit number. This digit represents the value of the digit times 10.

100s digit   In mathematics, in a decimal number with multiple digits or numerals, this is the digit third from the right end of the multidigit number. This digit represents the value of the digit times 100.

100BaseT   A name for 100 Mbps Ethernet when using twisted-pair cabling.

802.2   The IEEE committee that defined common features for several types of LANs, including Ethernet. Also known as Logical Link Control (LLC).

802.3   The IEEE committee that defined Ethernet-specific details of Ethernet. Also known as Media Access Control (MAC).

AAA   The process of authentication, authorization, and accounting. Pronounced "triple A."

AAA server An authentication, authorization, and accounting server. This term is typically used when the AAA functions are being performed as users access an ISP.

access link The leased line between the customer site and a local CO that connects to a router to a Frame Relay service.

access rate The speed at which the access link is clocked. This choice affects the price of the Frame Relay connection.

accounting In the context of network security, the process of recording and reporting events that occur as part of the authorization and authentication processes.

acknowledgment number A field in the TCP header that identifies the number of the next byte of data that the computer sending the TCP segment expects to receive next. It is used as part of the error recovery process.

Address Resolution Protocol *See* ARP.

addressing The process of putting a number in a header, with that number defining where to send the data in the packet.

amplitude The distance in a graph between the X-axis and the highest point on the graphed curve.

analog electrical signal An electrical signal whose voltage level changes continuously. When graphed over time, the curve gently changes between the maximum and minimum voltage levels, creating a continuous curve, which works well for transmitting voice traffic.

analog modem *See* modem.

anti-virus software Software that typically resides on the end user computer; it examines all files that are copied to the computer, typically by e-mail or web browsers, and removes files that contain computer viruses.

ARP (Address Resolution Protocol) The protocol by which any IP host can, given an IP address on the same LAN subnet, discover the LAN address used by that other IP host.

ARP broadcast   A LAN broadcast frame that holds an ARP request. The request has an IP address listed; if the host who uses that IP address gets the request, it should reply, stating its LAN MAC address in an ARP reply message.

ARP cache   A table on each IP host, including routers, which holds the IP address and MAC address mappings learned using the ARP protocol. (Note that "cache" is pronounced just like the word "cash.")

ARP reply   A LAN unicast frame that holds an ARP reply. The reply has an IP address listed and the MAC address used on the same LAN interface. It is sent in reply to an ARP broadcast.

asymmetric transmission rates   The use of different transmission speeds depending on the direction that traffic is sent.

authentication   The process of verifying the identity of a user, typically by exchanging usernames and passwords.

authentication server   A server that holds a list of usernames and passwords for the purpose of allowing other servers to query the authentication server as to whether a particular username/password combination is valid.

authoritative DNS server   The DNS server that knows the names and IP addresses that are related to a particular domain.

authorization   The process of deciding what resources a particular user can access.

autonegotiation   A process by which a NIC and a switch port can choose the Ethernet speed to use, as well as whether to use full duplex.

bandwidth   Jargon that generally refers to the speed at which bits can be sent across a physical link.

BGP (Border Gateway Protocol)   An IP routing protocol, defined in RFCs, making it a public protocol. BGP is used mainly to exchange routing information between different companies, including between ISPs and their customers.

binary digit   In mathematics, a digit or numeral that is part of a number based on the binary numbering system.

binary numbering system   In mathematics, a convention for numbering things in which 2 separate numerals are used, namely 0 and 1.

bit (binary digit)   A single binary number, either 0 or 1, as stored by a computer in memory.

bits per second (bps)   *See* bps.

Border Gateway Protocol (BGP)   *See* BGP.

bps (bits per second)   Units used to describe the speed at which data is sent over some communication media, as measured by the number of bits sent during a single second.

broadcast address   An Ethernet MAC address that represents all devices on a LAN. Switches flood frames that are sent to the broadcast address.

broadcast domain   A set of devices for which a broadcast frame sent by one device will be received by all devices in the same broadcast domain.

buffer   (Noun) Storage location inside a switch in which frames can be stored when the switch is waiting for the output port to become available. (Verb) The switch process of storing frames in memory.

bunch of bits   Jargon used in this book to describe some information, in binary form, that sits in a computer.

byte   8 consecutive bits as stored on a computer.

cable   A long, somewhat cylindrical piece of plastic, often used to enclose some wires.

canonical   A shortened version of the term *canonical format*.

canonical format   A term referring to the format of TCP/IP addresses when written in decimal.

carrier sense multiple access collision detect (CSMA/CD)   *See* CSMA/CD.

Challenge Handshake Authentication Protocol (CHAP)   *See* CHAP.

channel service unit/data service unit (CSU/DSU)   *See* CSU/DSU.

CHAP (Challenge Handshake Authentication Protocol)   A component protocol of PPP that is used to pass username and password information, sending the password as a message digest instead of clear text.

CIR (committed information rate)   The rate at which the router can send data for an individual Frame Relay PVC, for which the provider commits to deliver that amount of data. The provider sends any data in excess of this rate for this PVC if its network has capacity at the time. This choice typically affects the price of each PVC.

class of network   In IP addressing, this term refers to whether a particular IP network is a Class A, Class B, or Class C type of network.

clear text   Information that is in its original form, with no attempt to encode, encrypt, or change the information before transmission.

client   A generic term used to refer to software on an end user's computer, or to the computer itself. The term refers to the fact that the end user typically wants to use one or more network services, so the end user is a client or customer of those services.

clock rate   A term that refers to the speed at which bits are sent over a physical link. Often used to describe the speed setting on a CSU/DSU.

clocking   The act of making a WAN link operate at the speed agreed upon with the telephone company.

CO (central office)   An office or building in which the telephone company installs its equipment.

collision   In Ethernet, a condition in which two (or more) frames are transmitted over the same pair of wires simultaneously.

co-lo (co-location)   A practice in which a telco cooperates with an ISP, allowing the ISP to locate its equipment inside the telco's CO.

co-location (co-lo)   *See* co-lo.

commercial driver's license   A license to drive on public roads that also allows the driver to drive certain types of commercial vehicles.

committed information rate (CIR)   *See* CIR.

computer virus   *See* virus.

configuring a router   A process by which someone types in commands that tell a router what to do. For instance, an engineer would configure a router to tell the router which IP addresses to use on each interface.

content (web content)   A term referring to the text, graphics, images, video, and audio that comprise a web page.

cracker   A person who attempts to cause problems with networks and computers.

cross-over cable   An Ethernet LAN cable for which the wire in pin 1 of the connector on one end of the cable connects to pin 3 on the other end of the cable. The wire in pin 2 on one connector is connected to pin 6, pin 3 connects to pin 1, and pin 6 connects to pin 2. By doing so, the twisted pair on pins 1 and 2 connect to pins 3 and 6 on the other end of the cable, and the twisted pair at pins 3 and 6 connect to pair 1 and 2 at the other end.

CSMA/CD (carrier sense multiple access collision detect)   Algorithm that defines how Ethernet-attached computers should behave in order to reduce collisions and to recover from collisions when they do occur.

CSU/DSU (channel service unit/data service unit)   A device or a component of a router serial interface that performs many functions, including clocking a serial link at the appropriate transmission speed.

data-link connection identifier (DLCI)   *See* DLCI.

decimal digit   In mathematics, a digit or numeral that is part of a number based on the decimal numbering system—namely 0, 1, 2, 3, 4, 5, 6, 7, 8, and 9.

decimal numbering system   In mathematics, a convention for numbering things in which ten separate numerals are used.

DECnet   DECnet was Digital Equipment Corporation's proprietary networking model.

decrypting   The process of re-creating the original data that was transmitted over a network after being encrypted by the sender of the data.

default gateway   *See* default router.

default router   A setting on a TCP/IP host that refers to the IP address of a router. The host sends packets to this default router, expecting the router to then be able to forward the packet to the destination.

default web page   *See* home page.

demodulation   The act of interpreting a received analog electrical signal to decode a binary 0 or 1.

denial of service attack   An action that a cracker takes to cause a service or server to have problems, or possibly fail, which then denies legitimate users the opportunity to use the service.

Destination Address field   The 6-byte long portion of an Ethernet header in which a NIC places the intended recipient's Ethernet address before sending a frame.

destination IP address   A field in the IP header that lists the IP address of the intended recipient of the packet.

digit   In mathematics, a single symbol that can be used to represent part of a number; for instance, the digit "1" is part of the number "321." Another word for *numeral*.

digital subscriber line (DSL)   *See* DSL.

directly connected route   A route that refers to a network or subnet that is connected to an interface on that router.

directly connected subnet   A subnet for which a router has a working physical interface connected to the physical network where the subnet resides.

directory assistance   A service from a phone company by which you call a well-known phone number and get help in finding someone's phone number.

disk drive   A component of a computer that can permanently hold the contents of computer files.

DIX Ethernet   A term referring to the original Ethernet standard, as developed by people at Digital Equipment Corporation, Intel, and Xerox.

DLCI (data-link connection identifier)   A Frame Relay address used in Frame Relay headers to identify the PVC.

DMZ   A LAN where servers are installed in an enterprise network, with those servers available to users on the Internet. This allows separation of servers intended for internal use only (on the inside) from the servers that are available to the general public (on the DMZ).

DMZ interface   An interface on a firewall that is connected to the DMZ LAN. It is considered to be more secure than the outside but less secure than the inside.

DNS (Domain Name System)   The protocols and conventions that define a worldwide, distributed TCP/IP host name database, which allows a client computer to use host names, request name resolution, and get a correct response that identifies the IP address that corresponds to the name.

DNS resolution request   A DNS protocol message, sent by an end user host to a DNS server, that supplies a TCP/IP host name and requests the corresponding IP address.

DNS resolver   A TCP/IP host that makes a DNS resolution request, asking for resolution between a host name and the corresponding IP address.

DNS server   A computer running DNS server software, providing name resolution services.

domain   The set of computers whose names all end with the same domain name.

domain name   A term referring to a suffix of a host name that identifies the authority, organization, or company that controls all names that end in that suffix.

Domain Name System (DNS)   *See* DNS.

Dot 1 Q   Jargon referring to the IEEE 802.1Q standard of VLAN trunking.

dot-com   Jargon that refers to businesses that are primarily Internet based. The term refers to the top-level domain (.com) of their respective domain names.

dotted decimal format   A term referring to the format of TCP/IP addresses when written in decimal.

download   A file transfer in which the computer receives or gets a file that it did not previously have a copy of.

DSL (digital subscriber line)   Public network technology that delivers high bandwidth over conventional copper wiring at limited distances. The most common types of DSL are ADSL, HDSL, SDSL, and VDSL. Because most DSL technologies do not use the complete bandwidth of the twisted pair, there is room remaining for a voice channel.

DSL access multiplexer (DSLAM)   *See* DSLAM.

DSL modem   A device that generates and receives data over a local phone line.

DSLAM (DSL access multiplexer)   A device, typically found at a telco CO, that splits the digital signals sent by DSL modems to a router and splits the voice signals out to a telephone switch.

dynamically assigned port   A port number that is chosen at the TCP client computer. The computer simply chooses a currently unused port number.

EIGRP (Enhanced Interior Gateway Routing Protocol)   An IP routing protocol, defined by Cisco, making it proprietary. It is an enhanced version of IGRP.

electrical cabling   Cabling that includes copper wires inside the cable so that electricity can be sent over the wires.

electromagnetic interference (EMI)   *See* EMI.

electronic mail (e-mail)   *See* e-mail.

e-mail (electronic mail)   The process of creating, sending, and receiving messages electronically.

e-mail address   A text string that identifies an individual e-mail user. The address has two parts—a username and a computer name—separated by an @ sign, such as user1@isp1.net.

e-mail client   Software, running on an end user computer, that provides a user interface to the end user to create and read e-mail. It also implements the protocols required to transmit and receive the e-mail.

e-mail server   Software, running on some server computer hardware, that receives and forwards e-mail in a network. It's much like what the postal service does for paper snail mail.

EMI (electromagnetic interference)   The effect by which an electrical current running over a wire induces a magnetic field, outside the wire, which in turn can induce an electrical current in another nearby wire. In layman's terms, this phenomenon interferes with the electricity in nearby wires, and when transmitting data, this effect might cause errors in the data transmitted over that nearby wire.

encapsulation   The process of taking data from a higher-layer protocol and adding a header and possibly a trailer.

encode   The process of varying the characteristics of an electrical signal to transmit binary values across a cable.

encoding standard   A particular standard that defines what electrical characteristics mean binary 0 or binary 1.

encryption   The process of performing a mathematical formula against some data for the purpose of hiding the original data.

encryption key   A secret set of characters used to encrypt and decrypt data.

Enhanced Interior Gateway Routing Protocol (EIGRP)   *See* EIGRP.

enterprise network   A network created for use by a single company or organization.

enterprise WAN   A WAN used by a single company or enterprise to connect LANs at different sites.

ephemeral port   *See* dynamically assigned port.

error detection   The process of realizing that a received frame had some bits changed in it as a result of traveling across the network.

error recovery   The process of causing the retransmission of lost or in-error data.

Ethernet   A widely popular standard for LAN communications.

Ethernet address   A 6-byte long hexadecimal number used to identify a NIC that is attached to an Ethernet.

Ethernet hub   A networking device that allows multiple devices to be cabled to it. The hub repeats incoming electrical signals out all other physical ports, thereby requiring only a single cable to each device, while allowing all devices to communicate with all other devices.

Ethernet version 2   Another name for DIX Ethernet.

Exterior Routing Protocol   A routing protocol that is designed for use between different companies and organizations.

external CSU/DSU   A CSU/DSU that sits outside a router, with a cable between the router serial interface and the CSU/DSU.

Fast Ethernet (FE)   *See* FE.

FCS (frame check sequence)   A field in an data link protocol trailer that allows the receiver of a frame to determine whether the frame had errors during transmission.

FE (Fast Ethernet)   Defined by IEEE 802.3u, FE specifies Ethernet with a transmission speed of 100 Mbps.

field   A particular part of a header or trailer in which a specific piece of information is carried. For instance, the Ethernet destination address field in an Ethernet header is a field inside the header.

file read   A process that a computer uses to look for a file, find it, and give the data inside the file to an application program.

file server   A computer that performs *file services*.

file services   The process by which one computer, typically called a *file server*, keeps files on its disk drive and allows other computers to read and write the files by using the network.

file transfer   A network application that allows a user to copy files from one computer to another. Whereas *download* usually means copying into a computer, file transfer typically means the file can be copied in either direction between two computers.

File Transfer Protocol (FTP)   *See* FTP.

file write   A process that a computer uses to replace an existing file's content.

firewall   A networking device that sits in the path through which packets are forwarded, examining the packets, and allowing only the packets that are determined to be acceptable based on the security policy of a network.

flooding   The process whereby a switch forwards a frame out all ports except the port in which the frame arrived at the switch.

flow   A series of IP packets that go from one IP host to another, and vice versa. Sometimes used as a generic term to refer to a TCP connection.

forward acknowledgment   The process of acknowledging data by setting the acknowledgement field to the next byte of data that should be received, as opposed to setting the acknowledgement field to the last byte of data that was received.

forward versus filter   A term referring to a switch's decision to forward a frame on one port, and not to forward—in other words, to filter—the frame on other ports.

forwarding   When this term is used in the context of IP routing, it is another term for *routing*. *See also* routing.

forwarding decision   When this term is used in the context of IP routing, it refers to the process of matching a router's routing table and making a decision of where to forward the packet.

frame   A bunch of bits that includes some data in the middle, with a header in front of the data, and a trailer after the data. This term specifically refers to headers and trailers as defined by OSI data link layer protocols.

frame check sequence (FCS)   *See* FCS.

Frame Relay   A data link layer protocol defined in part by the Frame Relay Forum, ANSI, and the ITU. These protocols define how routers and service providers together create Frame Relay networks.

Frame Relay Forum   A vendor consortium that defined the earliest Frame Relay protocols, before ANSI and ITU created Frame Relay standards.

Frame Relay network   The cabling and equipment that together create the capability to forward Frame Relay frames between two devices.

Frame Relay service   A telco-provided service that creates PVCs between pairs of customer sites.

Frame Relay service provider   A business, typically a telco, that provides Frame Relay services.

Frame Relay switch   A generic term referring to a type of equipment, found in the COs of Frame Relay service providers, that can be configured to forward Frame Relay frames.

frequency   The number of times per second for which a repetitive electrical signal repeats itself.

FTP (File Transfer Protocol)   A TCP/IP protocol specification used to allow file sharing by copying files to and from a server.

FTP client   Software, running on an end user computer, that provides a user interface to the end user to get files to and from an FTP server. It also implements the FTP application layer protocols required to transmit and receive the e-mail.

FTP Control Connection   A connection between an FTP client and server over which the client sends all control information, such as changing the directory, naming the file, and requesting a GET or a PUT operation.

FTP data connection   A connection between an FTP client and server over which the actual data is transferred.

FTP GET   *See* GET.

FTP PUT   *See* PUT.

FTP server   Software, running on some server computer hardware, that allows FTP clients to connect to it for the purpose of getting files from the server and putting files on the server so that others can come and get them.

full duplex   The process of both sending and receiving data on a physical interface at the same point in time.

full mesh   In Frame Relay, a network in which all pairs of Frame Relay-connected devices have a PVC between them.

gateway   A term for a myriad of networking devices that generally convert from one standard to another.

Gbps   Acronym for gigabit per second.

GE (Gigabit Ethernet)   Defined by IEEE 802.3z and IEEE 802.3ab, it specifies Ethernet with a transmission speed of 1000 Mbps, or 1 Gbps.

GET   FTP term meaning that the FTP client is moving a file from the server to itself—in other words, it's getting the file from the server.

Gigabit Ethernet (GigE)   *See* GigE/GE.

gigabit per second (Gbps)   *See* Gbps.

GigE (Gigabit Ethernet)   Defined by IEEE 802.3z and IEEE 802.3ab, it specifies Ethernet with a transmission speed of 1000 Mbps, or 1 Gbps.

hacker   A person who attempts to access networks and computer systems, but without malicious intent.

half duplex   Logic used by a device on a LAN, for which it chooses to either send or receive a frame at a point in time, but not both at the same time. CSMA/CD logic imposes half duplex logic on a NIC.

HDLC (high-level data link control)   A data link layer protocol that is used on WAN links.

header   A bunch of bits placed in front of data prior to transmission. The bits allow some protocol to have a place to include information along with the user data to accomplish the function of the protocol.

high-level data link control (HDLC)   *See* HDLC.

home page   When a web browser requests a web page from a web server, if the URL does not include text after the name of the server, the server returns the default web page. That default web page is called a home page.

host name   A name that represents a TCP/IP host computer.

host part   The portion of an IP address that has a unique value as compared to all other hosts inside the network. Class A, B, and C networks have 3, 2, and 1 octet long host parts, respectively.

host-based IDS   IDS software that is installed on a computer, typically a server.

HTML (Hypertext Markup Language)   A standard, which is not part of the TCP/IP model, that defines the format and meaning of one type of object used to build a web page.

HTTP (Hypertext Transfer Protocol)   A TCP/IP protocol, defined in RFC 2616, that defines the protocols through which a web browser identifies the web pages and web objects it wants to download, as well as the processes by which the browser downloads the pages and objects.

Hypertext Markup Language (HTML)   *See* HTML.

Hypertext Transfer Protocol (HTTP)   *See* HTTP.

IDS (intrusion detection system)   A device or software that examines packets that are allowed by a firewall, looking for things that a cracker might use to deny service or to place a virus on a computer.

IDS signature   A set of characterizations of the types of packets that crackers have used in the past to cause viruses or to deny service.

IEEE (Institute of Electrical and Electronics Engineers)   A standards organization that defines standards for a large variety of topics, including computer networking (http://www.ieee.org).

IEEE 802.1Q   The IEEE-defined standard VLAN trunking protocol.

IEEE 802.3ab   A name for an IEEE committee, as well as a set of standards, relating to Gigabit Ethernet. Defines Gigabit Ethernet over copper cabling.

IEEE 802.3ae   A name for an IEEE committee, as well as a set of standards, relating to 10 Gigabit Ethernet. Defines 10 Gigabit Ethernet over optical cabling.

IEEE 802.3z   A name for an IEEE committee, as well as a set of standards, relating to Gigabit Ethernet. Defines Gigabit Ethernet over optical cabling.

IEEE Ethernet   Jargon referring to Ethernet standards as defined by the IEEE.

IETF (Internet Engineering Task Force)   The standards body that creates and manages TCP/IP standards. The IETF, to quote their website (http://www.ietf.org), is "a large, open international community of network designers, operators, vendors, and researchers concerned with the evolution of the Internet architecture and the smooth operation of the Internet. It is open to any interested individual."

IGRP (Interior Gateway Routing Protocol)   An IP routing protocol, defined by Cisco, making it proprietary.

information   In the context of services provided by a telephone company, this is the same thing as directory assistance. *See also* directory assistance.

inside interface   An interface on a firewall connected to the LAN that is considered to be the most secure of all the LANs connected to the firewall.

Institute of Electrical and Electronics Engineers (IEEE)   *See* IEEE.

interconnected networks   *See* internetwork.

Interior Gateway Routing Protocol (IGRP)   *See* IGRP.

Interior Routing Protocol   A routing protocol designed for use inside a single company or organization.

internal CSU/DSU   A CSU/DSU integrated onto a router serial interface card, which is then installed in a router.

International Organization for Standardization (ISO)   *See* ISO.

International Telecommunication Union (ITU) *See* ITU.

Internet The global TCP/IP network to which almost every company and organization in the world is connected. The Internet allows communication between a multitude of computers on the planet.

Internet draft A document that describes a protocol or standard that is under development but not yet approved.

Internet Engineering Task Force (IETF) *See* IETF.

Internet Explorer The name of a popular web browser software product written by Microsoft Corporation.

Internet Message Format RFC A TCP/IP protocol, defined in RFC 2282, that defines the headers placed around e-mail messages when they are being sent through a network.

Internet Protocol (IP) *See* IP.

Internet service provider (ISP) *See* ISP.

internetwork (interconnected networks) Multiple networks that are connected using routers.

Inter-Switch Link (ISL) *See* ISL.

intrusion detection system (IDS) *See* IDS.

Inverse ARP A process and protocol that allows a router to announce its IP address with a message sent over a Frame Relay PVC.

IP (Internet Protocol) A TCP/IP protocol, defined in RFC 791, that defines logical IP addressing and routing.

IP address A 32-bit number, usually written in dotted decimal format. It identifies a network interface on a computer to the IP protocol, and it transmits and receives IP packets.

IP header   Information that the IP protocol adds to the front of a transport layer segment to create an IP packet. The header is typically 20 bytes long and includes the source and destination IP addresses.

IP host   Any computer that has at least one IP address.

IP network   A grouping of IP addresses for which some initial portion of their IP address values are in common.

IP network number   A dotted-decimal number that represents a single network. The number has the same value as the IP addresses inside the network part of the number, and all decimal 0s in the host part of the number.

IP packet   An IP header, along with any encapsulated data after the IP header.

IP routing table   *See* routing table.

ISL (Inter-Switch Link)   The Cisco-proprietary VLAN trunking protocol.

ISO (International Organization for Standardization)   Organization that developed the OSI model and that continues to work with standards today. To quote the website (http://www.iso.ch), the ISO is "a network of national standards institutes from 147 countries working in partnership with international organizations, governments, industry, business, and consumer representatives. A bridge between public and private sectors."

ISP (Internet service provider)   A company that provides a service of network connection to the Internet. ISPs support individual users as well as corporations.

ITU (International Telecommunication Union)   A standards organization composed of telecommunications companies from around the world. The ITU defines standards for a large variety of topics, including telephony and wide-area networks (http://www.itu.org).

jamming signal   An electrical signal specified by Ethernet standards that is sent when a collision occurs to ensure that all devices realize a collision took place.

Kbps (kilobits per second)   Units that describe the speed at which data is sent over some communication media. Kbps represents 1000 bits in 1 second; for example, 2 kbps is 2000 bits per second.

Kerberos   A TCP/IP standard protocol used to exchange AAA information between application servers and authentication servers.

key   *See* encryption key.

kilobits per second (kbps)   *See* Kbps.

LAN (local-area network)   A network that by definition includes components that are relatively near to each other, typically in the same building.

LAN legal   A term created just for this book to make an analogy to having a car be "street legal."

LAN switch   A networking device that forwards frames based on their destination address.

layer   A subset of protocols of a single networking model. The protocols in the same layer have the same general or related goals.

Layer 8   A sarcastic term referring to business, political, or other nontechnical issues that might affect network design choices. It refers to a nonexistent OSI layer, just above the highest OSI layer.

learning   With LAN switches, "learning" refers to the process of examining the source MAC address of frames that the switch received, and adding new entries to the MAC address table. The switch adds an entry listing the source MAC address of the frame, along with the port in which the frame was received.

leased circuit   *See* WAN link.

leased line   A service from telephone companies that provides a communication path between a pair of sites.

lightning bolt   A style of drawing a line so that it looks like a bolt of lightning. WAN links are often drawn with a lightning bolt line style in network diagrams.

LLC (Logical Link Control)   Another name for 802.2.

local-area network (LAN)   *See* LAN.

local host file   A file on an individual computer that holds a list of host names and their corresponding IP addresses. A host computer can look at this local host file to perform name resolution.

local loop   A cable from the premises of a telephone subscriber to the telephone company CO.

Logical Link Control (LLC)   *See* LLC.

loopback circuit   On an Ethernet NIC, hardware that causes the electrical signal sent by the NIC to also be received on the NIC, without passing over the cable.

MAC (Media Access Control)   Another name for 802.3.

MAC address   Another name for Ethernet Address.

MAC address table   A table containing a list of MAC addresses and the physical switch ports out which a switch should forward frames that are destined to each MAC address. LAN switches use a MAC address table to make good forwarding and filtering decisions.

maximum segment size (mss)   *See* mss.

Mbps (megabits per second)   Units that describe the speed at which data is sent over some communication media. Mbps represents 1,000,000 bits in 1 second; for example, 2 mbps is 2000 kbps, or 2,0000,000 bits per second.

Media Access Control (MAC)   *See* MAC.

megabits per second (Mbps)   *See* Mbps.

message digest   The result of a mathematical formula that is used to hide a password during transmission.

metric   A number that represents how good a particular route to a particular destination is. Lower metric routes are better than routes with larger metrics.

microphone   A device that converts sounds into analog electrical signals.

modem (modulator-demodulator)   A device that converts digital and analog signals for the purpose of communicating over analog telephone lines.

modulation   The act of changing an analog electrical signal to encode a binary 0 or 1.

modulator-demodulator (modem)   *See* modem.

mss (maximum segment size)   The largest TCP segment that a computer is allowed to send.

name resolution   The process of finding an IP address that corresponds to a known name.

Netscape   The name of a popular web browser software product, more fully named Netscape Navigator. The product was originally written by a company called Netscape and is now owned by AOL, Inc.

network analysis tool   A device that connects to a network, collects copies of frames passing over the network, and allows the user to analyze and read the contents of the frames.

network-based IDS   An IDS that sits in the network, monitoring the packets that pass over a LAN.

network cloud   A style of drawing diagrams, with a cloud representing all or part of a network.

network interface   The lowest layer of the TCP/IP architectural model, matching both Layer 1 and Layer 2 of the OSI model.

network interface card (NIC)   *See* NIC.

network part   The portion of an IP address that has the same value as all the other addresses in the same network. Class A, B, and C networks have 1, 2, and 3 octet long network parts, respectively.

network utility   The idea of treating the basic ability to communicate between two computers just like you think of the telephone, electrical power, water, and so on.

networking protocol   A well-defined set of rules regarding the behavior of a networking device, networking cable, or networking software. Often synonymous with *networking standard*, this term typically refers to a process.

networking rulebook   This term is actually just used in this book to make a point. In concept, the rulebook lists a set of standards and protocols so that if all the devices conform to these standards, the network will work.

networking standard   A well-defined set of rules regarding the characteristics of a networking device, networking cable, or networking software.

next-hop router   A field in the IP routing table that identifies the IP address of the next router that needs to receive a packet to ensure delivery to the correct destination.

NIC (network interface card)   A computer card that gives a computer the ability to send and receive data across a physical network. The term comes from the idea that the card is the PC's interface to the network.

numeral   In mathematics, a single symbol that can represent part of a number; for instance, the digit "1" is part of the number "321." Another word for *digit*.

object   In the context of WWW, an object is a single file that can be transferred using HTTP. Web pages consist of one or more objects, with more complex single web pages containing hundreds of objects.

octet   A different generic term that can be used instead of the word *byte*. Often used to describe each byte of IP addresses.

Open Shortest Path First (OSPF)   *See* OSPF.

Open Systems Interconnection (OSI)   *See* OSI.

operating system (OS)   *See* OS.

optical cabling   Cabling that uses glass fibers instead of copper wires, with light being sent over the glass fiber, rather than electricity, to encode bits for transmission.

OS (operating system)   Software whose purpose is to control the general operation of a computer. For PCs, Microsoft Windows variants are the most popular operating systems.

OSI (Open Systems Interconnection)   A public networking model. Few computers use OSI today. The International Organization for Standardization (ISO) manages OSI protocols.

OSPF (Open Shortest Path First)   An IP routing protocol, defined in RFCs, making it a public protocol.

outgoing interface   A field in the IP routing table that identifies this router's interface out which a packet should be sent for it to be delivered to the correct destination.

outside interface   An interface on a firewall that is connected to a LAN. It is considered to be the least secure of all the LANs that are connected to the firewall.

packet   A group of bits that are combined for transmission in a network. This term specifically refers to the header and data defined by OSI layer 3 (network) layer protocols.

PAP (Password Authentication Protocol)   A component protocol of PPP, used to send usernames and passwords as clear text.

partial mesh   In Frame Relay, a network in which not all pairs of Frame Relay-connected devices have a PVC between them.

password   A string of characters, kept private from other people, that is used to prove that a user is who he claims to be.

Password Authentication Protocol (PAP)   *See* PAP.

patch cable   A short LAN cable used as one of several cables in a structured wiring system. For example, the cable from a PC to a wall plate is a patch cable.

patch panel   A convenient place for an electrician to connect the wires in cables that terminate in a wiring closet. The wires are connected to one side of the panel. The panel provides an electrical pathway to other plugs, or receptacles, much like the ones in the wall plate in a cubicle. The patch panel allows an electrician, or network engineer, to use a short patch cable to connect those pairs of wires to other devices.

PC (personal computer)   A computer that a singer user typically uses. It usually has one keyboard, one display, and one mouse.

permanent virtual circuit (PVC)   *See* PVC.

personal computer (PC)   *See* PC.

phone switch   *See* telco switch.

physical connectivity   Generic term referring to the combination of cabling, networking devices, and network interface cards (NICs) in the computers, which together provide the physical capability to transmit and receive data across a network.

physical LAN   A broadcast domain created by a combination of computers, cables, and networking devices.

physical medium   A cable with either copper wires or optical fibers over which electrical (copper) or light (fiber) energy can be passed. Binary data can be transmitted over such media through encoding conventions that define what particular electrical or light energy implies a binary 0 or 1.

pin   The physical position at the end of a connector where the copper part of the wire sits.

PIX Firewall   The name Cisco uses to brand its firewall product line.

point of presence (POP)   *See* POP.

point-to-point link   *See* WAN link.

Point-to-Point Protocol (PPP)   *See* PPP.

POP (point of presence)   A building that houses equipment that an ISP owns.

POP3 (Post Office Protocol, Version 3)   A TCP/IP protocol, defined in RFC 1939, that defines the messages that control the transfer of e-mail. POP3 is typically used only by clients, and only when retrieving e-mail from a POP3 server.

POP3 Server   Another term for *POP3 Server Software*.

POP3 Server Software   Software that implements the POP3 server features.

Post Office Protocol, Version 3 (POP3)   *See* POP3.

postal code   Generic term for what is called a zip code in the U.S. *See also* zip code.

PPP (Point-to-Point Protocol)   A data link layer protocol that is used on WAN links.

preamble   In Ethernet, a series of alternating binary 1s and 0s at the beginning of a new frame.

print server   A computer that performs *print services*.

print services   The process by which one computer, typically called a *print server*, allows other computers to send it files that are then printed on a printer that is physically attached to the print server.

profiling   In law enforcement, a characterization of how criminals typically operate, so that law enforcement personnel can more easily catch the criminals.

PSTN (Public Switched Telephone Network)   A general term referring to the variety of telephone networks and services in place worldwide. Sometimes called plain old telephone service (POTS).

public networking model   A networking model for which no one vendor dictates the standards and protocols, with individuals from many companies and organizations participating in the standards definition process.

Public Switched Telephone Network (PSTN)   *See* PSTN.

PUT   FTP term meaning that the FTP client is moving a file from itself to the server   in other words, it's putting the file on the server.

PVC (permanent virtual circuit)   A predefined Frame Relay VC. A PVC can be equated to a leased line in concept.

RADIUS   A TCP/IP standard protocol that routers and AAA servers use to exchange AAA information.

remainder   In an algorithm in Appendix B, "Converting IP Addresses Between Decimal and Binary," this term represents the result of subtracting one number from another.

Request for Comments (RFC)   *See* RFC.

resolver   A term that refers to a TCP/IP host that is asking for help in resolving a host name to its IP address.

RFC (Request for Comments)   Each RFC defines some protocol or standard that is important to the TCP/IP model. An RFC has been through several reviews by the IETF. The term RFC comes from the fact that anyone can comment on the protocol while it is being reviewed. In fact, the document is posted on the Internet so that anyone can look at it and comment before it becomes an RFC.

right-of-way   Legal term that refers to the right to disrupt normal access to some physical location to do some work. For example, the telephone company can dig up the street to put in new cables because it has the right-of-way.

RIP (Routing Information Protocol)   An IP routing protocol, defined in RFCs.

root DNS server   A DNS server that lists domain names and their corresponding DNS server IP addresses. They are used to refer DNS requests to the authoritative DNS server for a domain.

router   A networking device with multiple network interfaces, whose purpose is to forward IP packets from one physical network to another. Routers provide an important packet-forwarding function for the TCP/IP internetworking layer to perform end-to-end delivery of IP packets.

routing   The process of receiving IP packets, making a decision of where to send the packet next, and forwarding the packet.

Routing Information Protocol (RIP)   *See* RIP.

routing protocol   A type of networking protocol designed to allow routers to exchange routing information with each other, with the end goal of having all the routers eventually learn routes to all IP subnets and networks in an internetwork.

routing table   A table that routers use so that they know where to forward packets.

routing update   A message defined by a routing protocol that contains the routing information that a router wants to share with other routers.

sales engineer (SE)   *See* SE.

SE (sales engineer)   A person who sells a company's products or services, with focus on the engineering or technical aspects of the sale.

segment   *See* TCP segment.

segmentation   The process by which an application gives TCP some data, with TCP breaking the data into smaller pieces, called segments, for transmission into a network.

sequence number   A value in the TCP header that is used to number the packets, for the purpose of noticing lost or in-error packets so that bad packets can be resent.

serial interface   A type of physical interface that a router uses to connect to a WAN link.

serial link   *See* WAN link.

shielded twisted-pair (STP)   *See* STP.

signature   See *IDS signature*.

Simple Mail Transfer Protocol (SMTP)   *See* SMTP.

SMTP (Simple Mail Transfer Protocol)   A TCP/IP protocol, defined in RFC 2821, that defines the messages used to control the transfer of e-mail.

SMTP Server   Another term for *SMTP Server Software*.

SMTP Server Software   Software that implements the SMTP server features.

SNA (Systems Network Architecture)   IBM's proprietary networking model.

snail mail   Jargon referring to the postal service, which delivers paper letters in a matter of days, as compared to e-mail, which delivers e-mails in a matter of seconds.

Sneakernet   A somewhat sarcastic term used to refer to the process of not using a computer network, but instead walking back and forth between computers with disks or CDs, moving files manually and requiring comfortable sneakers!

Sniffer   The trade name of a particular vendor's network analysis tool. (Sniffer is a trademark of the Network Associates Corporation.)

Source Address field   The 6-byte-long portion of an Ethernet header in which a NIC places its own Ethernet address before sending a frame.

source IP address   A field in the IP header that lists the IP address of the sender of the packet.

speaker   A device that converts analog electrical signals into sounds.

static IP route   A routing table entry that was created by having a network engineer configure a router with the routing information.

STP (shielded twisted-pair)   A type of cabling that holds twisted pairs of wires and for which extra shielding is added to the wires to reduce EM interference.

straight-through cable   An Ethernet LAN cable for which the wire in pin 1 of the connector on one end of the cable connects to pin 1 on the other end of the cable; the wire in pin 2 on one connector is connected to pin 2; and so on.

structured wiring   An approach to running cables in a building that results in less clutter, fewer times to install a cable under the floor or inside the ceiling, and added convenience when installing new devices.

subnet   A subdivision of a Class A, B, or C network.

subnet number   A dotted-decimal number that represents a single subnet. The subnet number has the same value as the subnet's individual hosts in the network and subnet parts of the number, and all binary 0s in the host part of the number.

subnetting   The process of subdividing an IP network into multiple subnets.

switch   Networking hardware and software that forwards the network traffic back and forth between the various devices on the network.

switch port   A physical socket on the side of a switch into which an Ethernet cable can be inserted.

switching table   *See* MAC address table.

SYN bit   *See* TCP SYN flag.

SYN flag   *See* TCP SYN flag.

Systems Network Architecture (SNA)   *See* SNA.

T1 circuit   *See* T/1 line.

T1 line   A 4-wire circuit that runs at 1.544 Mbps and is composed of 24 channels at 64 Kbps each, plus 8 Kbps of management overhead.

TACACS+   Cisco proprietary protocol used between routers and AAA servers to exchange AAA information.

TCP ACK flag   A single bit inside the TCP header that signals whether a segment is anything except the first segment in a new TCP connection.

TCP connection   An agreement between application processes on two computers to use TCP to send data. The connection is created by sending three overhead messages between the two computers, which initialize the values of the fields in the TCP header.

TCP connection establishment   A process by which two computers exchange three TCP segments to initialize TCP header fields, thereby allowing an application program on each computer to communicate with an application program on the other computer, using TCP.

TCP destination port   A field inside the TCP header that identifies the specific application program on the receiving computer that should ultimately receive the data in the segment.

TCP port   A number that identifies an application process on a computer. TCP uses a source port and a destination port so that the receiver of a TCP segment can look at the destination port number and know to which application to give the data.

TCP segment   A TCP header, along with encapsulated data, created by TCP on behalf of an application.

TCP source port   A field inside the TCP header that identifies the specific application program on the sending computer that created the data in the segment.

TCP SYN flag   A single bit inside the TCP header that signals whether a segment is either the first or second segment in a new TCP connection. The first segment in a new connection has the SYN flag set to binary 1, and no other TCP flags set.

TCP/IP (Transmission Control Protocol/Internet Protocol)   A public networking model that has widespread acceptance. The creation and management of the standards included in TCP/IP are performed by the Internet Engineering Task Force (IETF).

TCP/IP host name   *See* host name.

telco   Jargon for telephone company.

telco switch   Equipment owned by the telephone company and installed in a CO.

telephone company (telco)   *See* telco.

top-level domain   The last suffix in any TCP/IP host name, which either identifies the purpose of that domain (such as .com for commercial enterprises), or the country of origin for the organization.

trailer   A bunch of bits placed after data prior to transmission. The bits allow a protocol to have a place to include information along with the user data to accomplish the function of the protocol.

Transmission Control Protocol/Internet Protocol (TCP/IP)   *See* TCP/IP.

transmission speed   The rate at which bits are transmitted over a WAN link, either in bits per second, kilobits per second, megabits per second, or gigabits per second.

trunk   Either refers to a VLAN trunk or to an Ethernet segment between two switches.

twisted pair   A pair of wires that are twisted together to significantly reduce electromagnetic interference.

UDP (User Datagram Protocol)   A TCP/IP transport layer protocol that provides basic transport services but does not provide error recovery.

unicast address   An Ethernet MAC address that represents a single NIC.

uniform resource locator (URL)   *See* URL.

unshielded twisted-pair (UTP)   *See* UTP.

upload   A file transfer in which the computer gives a file that it has to another computer.

URL (uniform resource locator)   A string of characters that can be used to uniquely identify a particular web page. Also known as a *web address*.

User Datagram Protocol (UDP)   *See* UDP.

username   A string of characters that represents a user of the network.

UTP (unshielded twisted-pair)   A type of cabling that holds twisted pairs of wires, but for which no specific shielding is added to the cable. UTP cables are the most popular type in today's LANs.

VC (virtual circuit)   A logical concept that represents the path that frames travel between Frame Relay DTEs. VCs are particularly useful when comparing Frame Relay to leased physical circuits.

vendor consortium   An organization of vendors who have similar goals and who cooperate to make their products work together, typically while waiting on standards organizations to finish finalizing a standard. The Frame Relay Forum is one such consortium.

virtual circuit (VC)   *See* VC.

virtual LAN   A broadcast domain created by configuring a switch and telling it which ports should be considered to be in the same broadcast domain.

virtual private network (VPN)   *See* VPN.

virus   A file, typically a program, that is placed onto a computer system using methods that circumvent security devices, with the intent to cause problems.

VLAN trunk   An Ethernet segment between two switches, over which the switches add a VLAN header to frames before sending the frames. The VLAN trunking header identifies in which VLAN the frame resides.

VLAN trunking   The process of adding and removing VLAN trunking headers when using a VLAN trunk.

VLAN trunking header   The header added to an Ethernet frame before it is sent over a VLAN trunk.

voice circuit   The physical path that the telco creates to carry the analog voice signal to support a voice phone call.

volt   The unit of measurement of voltage.

voltage   A term referring to electrical potential or electromotive force. In general terms, it is the energy and power that flow in electricity.

VPN (virtual private network)   VPNs allow users of a public network, such as the Internet, to protect their data through encryption, making their network connection virtually private.

VPN client software   Software installed on an end user's PC that performs the encryption and decryption required to create a VPN.

VPN concentrator   A device and software installed at a corporate site, inside the corporate network, that performs the encryption and decryption required to create a VPN.

wall plate   A rectangular plastic mold that is used to cover a hole in a wall. The wall plate has a plug in it, into which a networking cable can be connected. The hidden side of the wall plate also has a cable, which in turn connects to the rest of the network.

WAN (wide-area network)   A network that by definition includes components that are relatively far apart, typically in different buildings, and almost always requiring connectivity through a telephone company.

WAN link   Term referring to a service that the phone company provides, through which a pair of devices can send and receive data to each other, with the data passing through the telco's network.

WAN switch   *See* telco switch.

waveform   Refers to the graph of the electrical signal on a wire, over time. A square waveform is used for the transmission of digital information.

web address   A string of characters that can be used to uniquely identify a particular web page. Also known as a *uniform resource locator (URL)*.

web browser   Software that resides on the computer that the end user uses. The browser requests a web page from a web server, and after the server responds, the web browser displays the information that a web server sends.

web client   Software, running on an end user computer, that provides a user interface to the end user to display the web pages that are stored on web servers.

web content   *See* content.

web object   *See* object.

web page   Term that describes the actual content transferred from the web server to a web browser. This typically refers to what is seen at one point in time in the web browser.

web server   Software, running on some server computer hardware, that allows web browsers to connect to it for the purpose of retrieving web pages.

website   Jargon that refers to the web pages and web server that compose the web content for a particular organization or individual. This term typically includes all the web pages built by the company or person who owns the website.

well-known port   A port number that a server purposefully uses for a particular application, so when client computers want to use that service, they know what destination port to put into the TCP destination port field.

wide-area network (WAN)   *See* WAN.

wiring   A thin, long, somewhat cylindrical piece of metal that is used to transmit data. The wire typically has a plastic coating to provide strength to the brittle wire.

wiring closet   Typically a small room (hence the word *closet*) where all cables from all the computers run.

wiring panel   *See* patch panel.

World Wide Web (WWW)   *See* WWW.

WWW (World Wide Web)   The combined set of all websites in the universe. Often, the term WWW is used to generally refer to the Internet, specifically in the context of all the websites available through the Internet.

zip code   Stands for zone improvement plan. It's a five- or nine-digit decimal number that the U.S. Postal Service uses for fast, easy, high-speed sorting of mail.

INDEX

Numerics

4-wire circuits, 298, 300–301

10 Gigabit Ethernet, 124

10/100 cards, 127

10BaseT, 122

100BaseT, 122

802.1Q trunking, 146

802.3 committee, 101

802.3ae working group, 10 Gigabit Ethernet, 124

802.3u working group, Fast Ethernet, 122

A

AAA

　accounting, 360–361

　authentication, with username and password, 356–359

　authorization, 359–360

access links, 317, 460

access rates, 325

accounting, 360–361

acknowledgment number field, TCP header, 189

acknowledgment numbers, 51

addressing

　Ethernet, 94–96

　on WAN links, 309

amplitude, 339

analog modems, 341

analog signals, properties, 338–339

anti-virus software, 386–387

application layer protocols, 181, 184

applications

　e-mail, 28–31

　file read, 18

　file transfer, 32–33, 38

　file write, 18

　web browsers, 25–26

　word processing, 18

ARP (Address Resolution Protocol), 240

　broadcasts, 244

　replies, 245

ARP cache, 246

assigning IP addresses to interfaces, 264–265

asymmetric transmission rates, 348

M

N

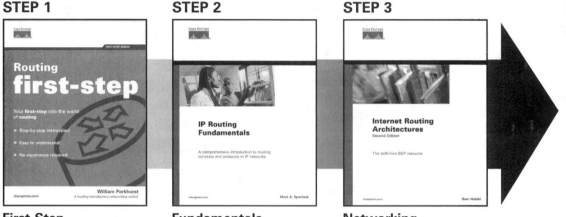

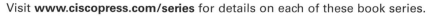

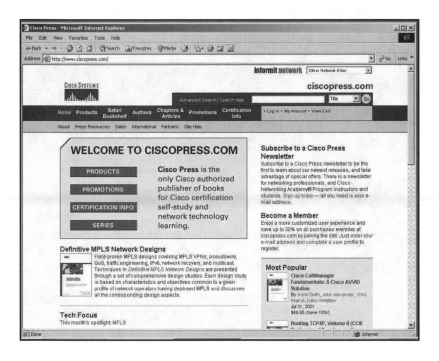

SEARCH THOUSANDS OF BOOKS FROM LEADING PUBLISHERS

Safari® Bookshelf is a searchable electronic reference library for IT professionals that features thousands of titles from technical publishers, including Cisco Press.

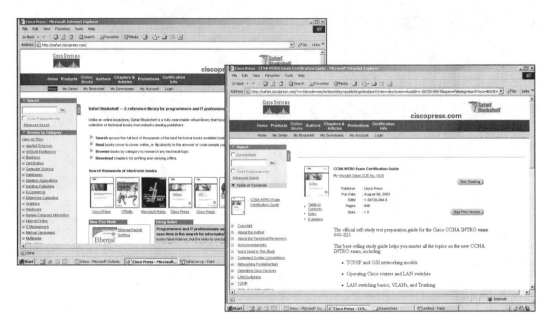

With Safari Bookshelf you can

- **Search** the full text of thousands of technical books, including more than 130 Cisco Press titles from authors such as Wendell Odom, Jeff Doyle, Bill Parkhurst, Sam Halabi, and Dave Hucaby.

- **Read** the books on My Bookshelf from cover to cover, or just flip to the information you need.

- **Browse** books by category to research any technical topic.

- **Download** chapters for printing and viewing offline.

With a customized library, you'll have access to your books when and where you need them—and all you need is a user name and password.

TRY SAFARI BOOKSHELF FREE FOR 14 DAYS!

You can sign up to get a 10-slot Bookshelf free for the first 14 days. Visit **http://safari.ciscopress.com** to register.